Skill and Mastery

East Asian Comparative Ethics, Politics and Philosophy of Law

Series Editors: Sungmoon Kim, Associate Professor of Political Theory at City University of Hong Kong; Eirik Lang Harris, Assistant Professor of Philosophy at City University of Hong Kong

This series consists of path-breaking and field-defining works in East Asian comparative philosophy with a special interest in works of normative and applied ethics, political theory and philosophy of law.

Titles in the Series

Confucianism, Law, and Democracy in Contemporary Korea, edited by Sugmoon Kim

Traditional Korean Philosophy: Problems and Debates, edited by Youngsun Back and Philip J. Ivanhoe

Contemporary Korean Political Thought and Park Chung-hee, Jung In Kang

Korean Confucianism: The Philosophy and Politics of Toegye and Yulgok, Hyoungchan Kim

Skill and Mastery: Philosophical Stories from the Zhuangzi, edited by Karyn Lai and Wai Wai Chiu

Skill and Mastery

Philosophical Stories from the Zhuangzi

Edited by Karyn Lai and Wai Wai Chiu

ROWMAN & LITTLEFIELD
INTERNATIONAL
London • New York

Published by Rowman & Littlefield International, Ltd.
6 Tinworth Street, London SE11 5AL
www.rowmaninternational.com

Rowman & Littlefield International, Ltd. is an affiliate of
Rowman & Littlefield
4501 Forbes Boulevard, Suite 200, Lanham, Maryland 20706, USA
With additional offices in Boulder, New York, Toronto (Canada), and London (UK)
www.rowman.com

British Library Cataloguing in Publication Information
A catalogue record for this book is available from the British Library

ISBN: HB 978-1-78660-912-0
ISBN: PB 978-1-78660-913-7

Library of Congress Cataloging-in-Publication Data Available

ISBN 978-1-78660-912-0 (cloth : alk. paper)
ISBN 978-1-78660-913-7 (pbk. : alk. paper)
ISBN 978-1-78660-914-4 (electronic)

∞™ The paper used in this publication meets the minimum requirements of American
National Standard for Information Sciences Permanence of Paper for Printed Library
Materials, ANSI/NISO Z39.48-1992.

Contents

Introduction

Karyn Lai and Wai Wai Chiu

The *Zhuangzi* occupies an important place in Chinese intellectual history not least because it interrogates a model of life lived in conformity with conventional pursuits and practices. It offers stories that depict the elegant and even daemonic performances of skill masters who undertake ordinary activities such as swimming, woodcarving, and cicada-catching. These wonderful displays of skill communicate the masters' absorption in their respective activities, their mental acuity and physical agility, and the brilliance of their performances.

The chapters in this volume delve into the *Zhuangzi*'s intriguing views on skill, including especially those expressed in its fascinating stories of craftsmanship. These wonderfully imaginative stories operate at a range of levels and are often referred to as the "skill stories". The craftsmen include a butcher, a wheel maker, a cicada catcher, a ferryman, a trainer of fighting cocks, a swimmer, a bell stand maker, a scribe, and a forger of buckles. The text presents enthralling accounts of their practice, often executed with spellbinding fluency, and sometimes with awe-inspiring outcomes such as swimming in treacherous cascades and butchering without hacking, or in producing beautiful items such as bell stands. Distinctively, the *Zhuangzi* highlights the responsiveness of these craftsmen to the world within which they live and act. And yet, at other times, such as in the story of the fighting cocks and the scribe, it seems that the moral of the stories is to not respond or, at least, not in conventional ways.

What messages are these stories attempting to convey? The aim of this volume is to explore these multifaceted stories and accounts of skill in the text and to unpack them sensitively, in consideration of the text's intellectual context and its intended effect on readers. This text dates from the fourth century BCE. It is named after its putative author, Zhuangzi,[1] and has been

Csikszentmihalyi, FLOW ; Tellegen Absorption Scale

aligned with the Daoist tradition. In its vivacious and jocund way—in its stories, allegories, and spoofs of conventional pursuits—it considers weighty and profound questions about the conditions of life and the roles of the courts and its officials in facilitating human well-being. The *Zhuangzi* dwells on issues including the human condition and life and death; the elements of an ideal life; human relationality and personhood; the nature and place of knowledge in society; regulations, norms, and conduct; leadership and the nature of government; the place of humanity within cosmological processes; and, of course, *dao*.

As the chapters in this volume demonstrate, the stories, and the *Zhuangzi* more generally, address the topic of skill at a range of levels. First, we may interpret the text as directing readers to the importance of being attuned to natural and cosmological processes. Skill is required to rethink and perhaps undo our years of acculturation, primarily to human needs and interests, so that we may develop sensitivity to the events and processes beyond the merely human. Nurturing one's life—our emotional states, awareness, vital energies, and physical conditions—is critical to our alignment with Heaven (*tian* 天). On one reading of the *Zhuangzi*, we could say that such openness to our world is so fundamental to humanity that it is effectively a prerequisite to skill cultivation and mastery! [2]

Secondly, questions about skill also seem to scrutinise widely held assumptions about official life and its aims. The *Zhuangzi* is not only wary about the perceived roles of those in official positions but also sceptical about the aims of regulation and government. The text comes across as subversive at many points, quite detached from entrenched practices and norms and the constraints they place on the lives of ordinary people. Its stories of masterly or daemonic (*shen* 神) performances, by ordinary men who undertake everyday tasks, express the enviable composure, elegance, and virtuosity of these craftsmen. Their performances inspire their audiences' and readers' awe and aesthetic appreciation, often exceeding the levels of respect nobility might command. On the one hand, the *Zhuangzi* seems to advocate detachment from official life when it upholds the marvellous skills of ordinary folk. On the other, it seems to offer the skill masters' *daos* as exemplary ways to tread the fine line between engagement and detachment.

Third, at the level of the individual, the *Zhuangzi* offers many perspectives on well-being. For example, its approach to knowledge and learning extends beyond the normative and the quantifiable, turning readers' attention to the fluency and responsiveness that are so distinctive in some of the skill masters' performances. Some of the skill masters concentrate deeply on the task at hand, sometimes by controlling their emotions and attention so as not to be distracted. This allows them to evade performance anxiety or, to put it positively, to undertake their task with remarkable composure. Could some

2. Compare to The Jedi.

of these cases be described in terms of "flow"[3] experiences, which are marked by both the absorbed attentiveness of a person to an activity and the effectiveness of the activity's execution? Could some of these reflections on deep engagement in an activity inform our thoughts on skill in everyday life? In the *Zhuangzi*, skill and mastery are concerned with practical knowledge and a performance orientation, but more importantly they also offer insights into a process of transformation and personal satisfaction.

To allow for in-depth analyses of the *Zhuangzi*'s views on skill, this anthology is divided into two sections. The first has a more pronounced conceptual focus, with each of seven chapters identifying a particular theme in the *Zhuangzi* that is enlightened by the text's views on skill. Chapters in the second section are story-specific so as to showcase the irreducible plurality of skills associated with the different stories. We have selected a set of the more prominent stories, nine in total, in which a master turns, or is about to turn, some ordinary practice into an extraordinary performance, elegantly and efficaciously. We hope readers will encounter this suite of discussions on performance as if they are viewing a set of curated works at an exhibition. Across the sections, this interplay of general and particular approaches to the study of skill generates previously unexplored insights for *Zhuangzi* scholarship. In what follows, we present the arguments of each of the chapters.

THE CHAPTERS

There are but a few philosophical texts that put skill at the centre of their investigation and reflection, and the *Zhuangzi* is one of them. Sketching an overview of Zhuangzi's philosophy of skill, Wai Wai Chiu proposes that skilful performance consists of fluency and adaptation, and liberation from rigid preferences. In "Skilful Performances and the *Zhuangzi*'s Lessons on Orientation", Chiu proposes that, by focusing on these features, readers may come to see that the *Zhuangzi* does not evaluate skill through measuring its outcomes. The *Zhuangzi*'s skill masters are neither profit oriented, nor do they seek to standardise their methods or promote their products. While their skills might be useful—as, for example, in the construction of wheels—usefulness is not their ultimate goal. Rather, by concentrating on but not indulging in their activities, the skill masters' performances are spontaneous and flexible. Chiu points out that spontaneity and flexibility are prerequisites for an ideal life. While this way of life is not bound by conventional values, it nevertheless does not simply turn its back on ordinary human pursuits. Those who tread this path can reduce tensions and friction between a person and his or her environment, allowing their spontaneous skilful performances to become a source of intrinsic fulfilment and aesthetic pleasure. In the final

3. Again, Csikszentmihalyi

analysis, skill learning is an indispensable part of self-cultivation, a process in which a person becomes increasingly adept at navigating the world.

In "Skill and Nourishing Life", Franklin Perkins presents a novel account of nourishing life (*yangsheng* 養生). Through the lens of skill in the *Zhuangzi*, Perkins takes the theme of nourishing life beyond the widely accepted, individually focused notion of life and how it is enriched. In his original argument that focuses on the "*Da sheng*" ("Fathoming Life") chapter of the *Zhuangzi* and the skill stories therein, Perkins proposes that nourishing life has many important dimensions, including looking after one's own material needs; cultivating one's relational interests; and engaging with the human, cosmic, and natural worlds. In this final and most significant strand of his argument, Perkins expands the vision of the self, and of its well-being, in the *Zhuangzi*. He concludes that *yangsheng* should not be conceived as a self-seeking or self-preserving project but rather as one that sets out to align oneself with the world, in participation with the life forms therein.

Is the Daoist sage unaffected by emotions, or is he passionately engrossed in his activities? What do the stories of the skill masters tell us about emotions? Are they hindrance or help? These are some of the questions David Machek sets out to investigate in "Skill and Emotions in the *Zhuangzi*". Machek's multifaceted analysis of emotions brings out different shades of their place and function in the lives of sages, skills masters, and ordinary people. Emotions can be distracting and draining, negatively affecting a person's handling of a task. On the other hand, a person's passionate execution of a task, and enjoyment of its processes, can facilitate his engagement with the natural, Heavenly patterns. Some of the skill masters are elegant performers precisely because they have successfully harnessed their emotions, allowing them to concentrate fully on their task. Yet, Machek cautions, the mastery stories tell us about human excellence only in relation to particular activities; these surely do not capture all of life's richness. Importantly, the discussion here draws our attention to passages in the *Zhuangzi* that emphasise how we are invariably touched by emotions, which may be productive or distracting. Machek's analysis is illuminating not least because it refuses to simplify the complex view of emotions expressed in the text.

Tim Connolly's discussion of "Zhuangzi's Politics from the Perspective of Skill" dwells on a fundamental tension in the Zhuangzi's discussion of political life. While the text expresses scepticism about participation in official life, it also hints at deeper, engrossed attentiveness characteristic of many of the skill masters handling their respective tasks. How do we reconcile these two strands that seem to pull in opposite directions? While some scholars believe that Zhuangzi's endorsement of ironic detachment undermines a life of political engagement, Connolly thinks that figures in the text such as Cook Ding point the way towards a "politics from the perspective of skill." Drawing on the commentator Wang Fuzhi, he argues that Cook Ding provides a model of how to navigate difficulties that arise in political life. Informed by a sceptical perspectivism that reinforces values such as humility, patience, and respect for particularity, Zhuangzi's political craftsperson is able to find a "frictionless point" from which to resolve the dilemmas of statecraft.

What is the *Zhuangzi* attempting to impart to its readers? Romain Graziani's investigation of sages, teachers, masters, and followers reveals deep perceptiveness on both the content and methods of Zhuangzi's teaching. In "Elusive Masters, Powerless Teachers, and Dumb Sages: Exploring Pedagogic Skills in the *Zhuangzi*", Graziani's analysis deftly reveals the complicated nature of pedagogic relationships in the text: teachers do not set out to teach virtue, but teaching happens, as it were, in passing, by encouraging the viewers of a performance or the readers of the text to reflect on the narration and scenarios of teaching. The *Zhuangzi*'s sages and masters do not seek to be revered and are therefore not flouting their skills. In contrast to how, in the text, some eager disciples seek actively to be instructed, Graziani invites us as readers to focus on the sages' silences. More tensions are also revealed in the "pedagogic nastiness" of some of the masters, who sometimes engage in shock tactics to derail the pursuits and paths of their followers. In the midst of this fascinating exploration, Graziani also highlights features of the (pedagogic) text with profound philosophical implications: its open-ended narratives cast light on not only the master-disciple, but also the author-reader relationship. There is much to learn from dumb and even failed teachers!

Steven Coutinho attempts to construct an overview of Daoist philosophy of skill in the *Zhuangzi* and the *Liezi*. As the *Liezi* is related to the *Zhuangzi*, with some stories containing overlapping details, Coutinho uses these details to help illuminate the nature of skill learning and mastery in the *Zhuangzi*. In "Skill and Embodied Engagement", he considers two pertinent questions: first, whether all skilful action should be understood as embodying sagely wisdom in the *Zhuangzi*, or whether we can distinguish wise from unwise skilful action. Secondly, does the text propose and uphold ethical boundaries? Are there unethical tasks that the skill masters will not undertake? Coutinho suggests that the Daoist strand of thought represented in the skill stories of the *Zhuangzi* is at best ambivalent about both questions. Nevertheless, there are important features of skill revealed in comparing these two texts. Coutinho demonstrates the whole-person engagement of the masters in their respective activities in the following ways: discipline in order to acquire, develop, and transfer psychophysical expertise; the development of epistemological fluency exemplified in "seeing" without the eyes; and the cultivation of perceptive sensitivity within specific contexts of action. Some important tensions are explored in this chapter, including the interplay between concentration and forgetting, and that between sensitivity and responsive-

ness, where the master is simultaneously "getting" (*de* 得) from the environment within which he acts, as well as responding to it.

A volume on the *Zhuangzi* would not be complete without dissenting
voices. In the final chapter in section 1—giving the subversive voice the final
say—Eric Schwitzgebel challenges a view shared widely by *Zhuangzi* scholars, that the text upholds and actively promotes skill and mastery of the kind
embodied in the performances and manifested in the products of artisans and
craftsmen. In "The Unskilled Zhuangzi: Big and Useless and Not So Good at
Catching Rats", he unsettles this dominant assumption in scholarly debates,
including views expressed in this volume. Schwitzgebel focuses on the pictures of skill expressed in the Inner Chapters section of the text. In chronological order as they appear, he argues that the discussions on skill are at best
ambivalent about its and value. (He acknowledges that other skill stories
in the *Zhuangzi* present positive accounts of skill, but these are in the text's
Outer Chapters [*Waipian*]). In the Inner Chapters, only one story, that of
Butcher Ding, seems to give a positive place to skill. However, Schwitzgebel
suggests that this one story needs to be placed in context, in light of all other
negative representations of skill. What, then, are we to make of this story? In
the playful style of the *Zhuangzi*, Schwitzgebel proposes that it is an outlier
and, possibly, its main focus is not so much on the butcher but on his knife!

In the first chapter of section 2, which examines the skill stories, we ask,
what does the Butcher Ding story hold for readers? James Sellmann proposes
that the story of the butcher, as with the other skill stories in the *Zhuangzi*,
does not intend to impart lessons that are primarily content based. Rather,
these stories are metaphors for the kind of life the text upholds. Sellmann
suggests in "Butcher Ding: A Meditation in Flow" that sagely life in the
Zhuangzi can be captured quite effectively by the terms of reference provided
in recent scholarly debates on the flow experience, where a person's entire
being is fully engaged in an activity. Sellmann does not suggest that the
Zhuangzi holds a theory of flow, but rather that it has elements that can be
accommodated into, or explained by, contemporary discussions on flow.
From this angle, he also explains the various sceptical questions and allu-
sions to seemingly mystical ideas in the text, proposing that they are elements of being in the flow. In this state, one is no longer hampered by
conventional discourse and its expectations but is responding spontaneously
to the world and engaging fully in life.

The story of Wheelwright Bian, discussed in "Wheelwright Bian: A Difficult *Dao*", presents many fascinating angles on skill. Lisa Raphals's investigation of this story begins with the question, "Why cannot Bian teach the
skill to his son?" This opens up a rich array of possibilities from which we
can understand this story. Raphals systematically presents the passage's view
on skill, beginning with the term *dao* in its intellectual context. This helps
embed the Wheelwright's position in light of what it rejects. In her novel

proposal, Raphals highlights the fact that the Wheelwright does *not* use the compass and square. Why is this so? The compass and square represent tools of measurement for standardised, mechanical tasks. In the *Zhuangzi*, both the tools and what they measure are rejected. This is so that the Wheelwright—and we, the readers—may be *enabled* through not using standardised tools, to arrive at a different kind of knowledge. Such knowledge cannot be articulated in words and therefore cannot be transmitted in words. A freehand approach to life is what this story suggests!

The cicada catcher seems an unusual Daoist, in the way he eloquently speaks about his training program and experiences. Karyn Lai considers the story's emphasis on learning and the significant place of physical fitness to undertake this activity. In "The Cicada Catcher: Learning for Life", Lai covers some debates in recent discussions in embodied cognition theory (ECT), focusing especially on its destabilisation of the mind as the centre of cognition. ECT, Lai contends, is more suited than traditional accounts of mind in western philosophical debates to highlighting the pertinent details of performance in this story. ECT helps us understand how a person's navigation of the environment, and manipulation of the things therein, are part of her epistemic and cognitive processes. These discussions are then used to help frame how learning occurs in this story: it is a process of attunement to contexts so as to understand typical and atypical versions of the activity; it is also the development of perceptive sensibilities to deal with these situations, masterfully. Finally, Lai proposes how this approach to learning is instructive for us, not simplistically to act like the cicada catcher, but to learn from the way he prepares himself for cicada-catching.

Performance anxiety is a theme that runs across a number of the skill stories, and Chris Fraser investigates it as a particularly prominent feature in the Ferryman story. The Ferryman adeptly navigates his boat in treacherous waters, and his advice is to "Forget the Deeps". What does "forgetting" entail? In "The Ferryman: Forget the Deeps and Row!", Fraser proposes a sophisticated account of the elements that work together to reduce performance anxiety. One important aspect of forgetting is to turn our attention away from concerns that are external to the task at hand. This will in turn enable performances of an activity in a spirit-like manner. Fraser demystifies the notion of spirit-like action, arguing that we may understand the idea in the *Zhuangzi* without holding deeper metaphysical commitments. He argues that spirit-like action is characterised by the ability to pull together different considerations—ones that are not external to the activity—in one action. Although Fraser's analysis dwells primarily on the psychological elements of performance anxiety, the discussion is also mindful that the physicality of performances is an irreducible aspect of skill. To onlookers, the performance manifests fluency and ease, even if it is clear that the task is no easy feat.

While the story is about piloting a ferry, its thoughts on performance anxiety could well be instructive for life more generally.

There is more to mastery in the *Zhuangzi* than skilled action, Wim De Reu proposes in "The Unresponsive Fighting Cocks: Mastery and Human Interaction in the *Zhuangzi*". In this story of the fighting cocks, the *Zhuangzi*'s message focuses on the capacity not to be impacted by external conditions. In particular scenarios, this could well be more relevant than having skill. De Reu examines many elements of the story in relation to other passages in the *Zhuangzi*. This distinctive account of the (non-)fighting cocks emphasises the unresponsiveness of the cocks, in praise of their impact reduction and non-combative ring presence. The account accentuates how the *Zhuangzi*, in its typically playful style, draws readers' attention to the reduction of violence, on the non-fighting cocks' own terms! They have enviable abilities not to be impacted by the threatening violence of a cockfighting scenario and, indeed, to avert it. De Reu reminds us that, in this story, the *Zhuangzi* has a clear message, that is, that conflict and harm should be avoided where possible. Importantly, we should also be mindful of the cock trainer's acumen and abilities in training cocks with such amazing ring presence.

Confucius is spellbound by the swimmer in the dangerous cascades, who impresses not only by his agility in the water but also in his subsequent recount of how he has come to acquire such ability. This popular rendition of the swimmer's story is challenged by Albert Galvany in "The Swimmer: Panic, Parody, and Pedagogy at the Waterfall; Morality as a Misleading Principle for Moral Actions". Through detailed study of relevant themes in texts contemporaneous with the *Zhuangzi*, he shows that this dominant interpretation of the story fails to capture its subtler message. That subtler message, Galvany contends, is one of a life of virtue and moral failure. The swimmer espouses virtue, rightly learned and aptly embodied. The discussion in this chapter highlights the tragicomic picture of Confucius, the ardent and well-trained "virtuous" person who in fact does the right thing by his training. (Galvany presents a fascinating argument that the cascades represent Confucian ritual and morality, with Confucius as an accomplished person and keen observer of the waters.) In contrast to such accomplishment, the swimmer, with his hair down—typical of a Barbarian or a ghost—seems oblivious to the anxiety of Confucius and his followers. Galvany reminds us of the parody on virtue and moral failure in this story by drawing on some contemporary discussions on virtue. Confucius is both a success in light of his training, and a failure in his overenthusiasm to display his virtue. By contrast, the swimmer has learned to swim non-intentionally, without intending to conquer the waters, and now swims successfully in the dangerous cascades by following the water's *dao*. Thoughts on the practice of true virtue, Galvany suggests, are what the swimmer story has to offer.

destiny

The woodworker's bell stands are so marvellously crafted that they seem like the work of spirits. Kim-chong Chong examines this story in "Woodworker Qing: Matching Heaven with Heaven". He argues that the story's reference to spirit-like activity is an attempt to refute shamanism. In other words, the story's aim is to assert that such awe-inspiring work is possible without shamanic activity. The story focuses on the woodworker's cultivation, in developing both his biological-physiological being and his vitality. The complete integration of the human person is achieved in the woodworker's application of *qi* (氣, vital energies) and in stilling his heart-mind in order that he may observe and respond to Heavenly patterns. Chong's analysis focuses on an intriguing question: why does the woodworker attempt to "match Heaven with Heaven"? Chong takes a non-mystical interpretation of this statement, and of the story. He demonstrates that the process of matching Heaven with Heaven involves engagement with the natural world, insomuch as humans are already part of it, through observing and aligning with its patterns. Such engagement is of course only possible when a person has "mastered life"—the title of the chapter this story appears in.

The story of the naked scribe is set against a ceremonial backdrop. However, the scribe's actions make light of this serious occasion. Hans-Georg Moeller argues that this story on scribes does not tell us about scribely skill, for there is no description of scribing activity, but only of the preparation for the event. In "The Naked Scribe: The Skill of Dissociation in Society", Moeller proposes that the aim of the story is to bring out the naked scribe's skill to deal in a stress-free way with the requirements of official life. In some ways, the story comes across as a rude and deliberate rejection of the requirements of Confucian official life. However, the focus is actually on the scribe's acceptance of his lot in life. Moeller argues that, as a scribe who would have been born into his current position, there is no choice for the naked scribe but to assume the role. This story is about the acceptance of his allotment in life (*ming* 命, destiny), yet, in the face of it, he has the skills to detach himself from these cumbersome requirements of official life. Although this story is set in the context of courtly ritual, Moeller suggests that its implications are relevant beyond the courtly domain and also for contemporary life.

The belt buckle forger's story is the only one that relates skill to the uses of things. In "The Forger: The Use of Things", Wai Wai Chiu proposes that the forger's insights into things and their potential uses expresses one way to attain detachment from social norms. That his perfectly forged buckles meet the official standard should be regarded not as a conscious goal of his cultivation, but a natural result of it. The forger's words bring home the point that, in conventional life, we often only focus on the things that are directly involved in our production goals, for example, the metal used for forging belt buckles. Chiu draws on this story to demonstrate that, conceptually, for us to deem a particular thing "useful" to the particular goals or outcomes we seek, implies that we also think of some others as "useless" to these pursuits. Further, he suggests that all things be placed in the perspective of a web of relations in which they maintain their distinctiveness but are yet interdependent with other things. A person who appreciates this view will come to see things independently of their perceived or putative functionality. This allows her flexibly to grasp that the qualities of particular things vary across contexts. By placing things on an equal footing as far as functionality is concerned, a person may, in the first instance, possess a neutrality to properly assess each thing's potential in light of a particular activity in its context. Finally, Chiu also points out that the forger's words may have sociopolitical implications, referring to a model of governing by non-interference so as to facilitate a nurturing and restful environment.

The reflections in this volume are informed by scholarly views on the literary texts, historical circumstances, and intellectual and philosophical traditions in early China. Yet all of its chapters consider how the *Zhuangzi*'s portrayals of skill can contribute to contemporary debates. Together, the contributors to this volume affirm the contemporary significance of the *Zhuangzi*'s insights. Summarily, we believe the text, and the discussions in the volume, draw our attention to three important areas of enquiry. First, in being performance oriented, they open up avenues for exploring ideas such as spontaneity, attentiveness, habit, and practice. These aspects of performance—and the idea of *performance* itself—necessitate interdisciplinary scholarly enquiry that cuts across the human and social sciences. We speak not only of investigations that traverse discussions in politics, ethics, and epistemology, but also of those that involve psychology and the cognitive sciences, philosophy, and anthropology. Secondly, skilled action in the *Zhuangzi* involves the engagement of the entire person. The integration of physical discipline, mental awareness, and emotional composure is a prerequisite for skilled performance. This conception of skill prompts us to rethink the often-assumed independence of cognitive and sensorimotor processes. Additionally, the *Zhuangzi*'s focus on skill cultivation heightens our awareness of the aims and approaches used in education, of what it is that we seek to teach, and how we propose to teach it. In this light, we should also consider the impact of acculturation within our sociopolitical contexts, which instils in us conventional values as well as expectations about how we should respond to things. Third, in reflecting on the place of skill in human life, we are urged to consider questions of use and functionality and the role of humanity in driving these values. The *Zhuangzi*'s reflections are embedded in a broader cosmological context that rejects mechanistic and instrumentalist accounts of individuals and entities. The skill masters' sensitivity to place, and their alignment with entities and beings in contexts, highlight their composure in potentially stressful situations. These scenarios help us appreciate how thinking beyond the self can contribute to human well-being.

We are particularly fortunate to have had the opportunity to curate this volume. We appreciate the gracious encouragement and help of Philip J. Ivanhoe, Sungmoon Kim, and Eirik Lang Harris, editors of RLI's East Asian Comparative Ethics, Politics and Philosophy of Law series, to which this volume belongs. It is our privilege to have worked closely with the contributors, a group of distinguished *Zhuangzi* scholars.

K. L. Lai and W. W. Chiu
University of New South Wales, Sydney, Australia
Lingnan University, Hong Kong

NOTE

1. We assume the majority view that the thirty-three-chapter extant text, the *Zhuangzi*, was authored by different hands, while the seven Inner Chapters (*Neipian*) contain the most philosophically interesting materials. This is by no means a view held unanimously by scholars. Some hold that these first seven chapters of the text (not necessarily the earliest chapters) are more likely to have been written by Zhuangzi himself. See, for example, Eric Schwitzgebel's discussion of the status of the Inner Chapters, and their message on skill, in chapter 7 of this volume.

Here, the term "Zhuangzi" is used for ease of expression rather than to identify the historical Zhuang Zhou (莊周) as the author of the text. For studies of the *Zhuangzi*'s authorship, see Klein, "Were the 'Inner Chapters' in the Warring States?", and Knaul, "Kuo Hsiang and the *Chuang Tzu*".

REFERENCES

Klein, Esther. "Were there 'Inner Chapters' in the Warring States? A New Examination of Evidence about the *Zhuangzi*." *T'oung Pao* 96, no. 4 (2010): 299–369.
Knaul, Livia. "Kuo Hsiang and the *Chuang Tzu*." *Journal of Chinese Philosophy* 12, no. 4 (1985): 429–47.

Part I

Reflections on Skill

Chapter One

Skilful Performances and the *Zhuangzi*'s Lessons on Orientation

Wai Wai Chiu

1. INTRODUCTION

Among all extant texts that bear a pre-Qin master's name, the *Zhuangzi* is best known for expressing its philosophical vision through a variety of skill stories. Although in the Warring States period (403–221 BCE)[1] it was common to make a living by mastering a skill, the phenomenology, physiological, and psychological mechanism of skill performance had received relatively little attention from the then contemporary mainstream thinkers such as the Confucians and the Mohists. Zhuangzi,[2] however, gives us paradigms for understanding human psychology and action through his meticulous observation and reflection on a range of skills. Even the very focus on skill masters from lower social classes can be read as an implicit response to the social and political setting at that time. Regardless of whether they are working, their performances are elegant and extraordinary. While their elegance does not come at a cost to effectiveness, Zhuangzi does not measure their performance by productivity or conformity to social roles. Rather, he ponders the features that drive and underlie their outer elegance and inner peace.

In this chapter, I highlight the perlocutionary force of the skill stories, which involve the transformation and reorientation of readers through a number of stages. The stories refocus readers' attention, from habit to skill, from outcomes to performance, and eventually to life. In what follows, I work through each of these stages, hoping also to demonstrate how and why skill mastery occupies an irreducible place in Zhuangzi's philosophy.

2. DEVELOPING SKILFUL PERFORMANCES

One approach to examining skill (*ji* 技) is to see it as a mark of personal growth, and sometimes also to see how its excellence constitutes a person's identity. Skills are in some ways like habits: they are developed as responses to the world, and development usually begins with effort and discipline until it gradually becomes effortless and can be exercised without step-by-step, rule-following deliberation.[3] It is likely that the training of skill requires one first to have some appropriate habitual modes, or to develop them during training. For example, to become a skilful swimmer, one must first get used to breathing and moving in water, allowing these movements to become habitual rather than having to consciously call to mind every movement involved. Indeed, much of our learning is made possible by basic habits developed in the early stages of learning, typically when young (in the case of many activities). As the *Kongzi Jiayu* states, "if one accomplishes it when one is young, that becomes like one's nature (*xing* 性); [this is to say that] one's habit becomes like one's self-so (*ziran* 自然)" (38/69/23).[4]

In both classical and modern Chinese, the character 習 (*xi*) can refer to learning, practising, modelling, and habit forming. It highlights a feature of the ancient Chinese view on knowledge and self-cultivation: acquiring new knowledge is hardly like collating pieces of information, but rather like shaping one's patterns of thought and action, or orienting oneself in an environment. As we are constantly reminded by the *Zhuangzi*, learning a skill is not easily expressible or directly transmittable in words.[5] Etymological studies show that one of 習's old meanings is a special type of divination, in which a person uses the same set of shells or bones to read an event many times consecutively (*Gu Wen Zi Gu Lin*, vol. 4, 51–56). The character is sometimes interchangeable with its homophone 襲, which originally means wearing multiple layers of clothing. We can see that their common feature is the repetitiveness of the task at hand. In the case of 習, this is extended to cover activities in training and exercise. For example, in the first passage of the *Analects* (a fifth- to second-century BCE text), we see that learning (*xue* 學), an idea emphasised so much by Confucius, can lead to a paradigmatic person's (*junzi* 君子) profound pleasure through his repeated practice (*xi* 習). Forming habits is a basic method for humans to respond to the world. It serves as a basis for learning, which in turn gives us improvement and pleasure.

Of course, not every habit is a skill. Many people have learned, and manifest, the typical habitual moves of swimming, such as breathing correctly, making timely and fitting arm and leg movements, and so on. However, only some swimmers are skilful at swimming. That classical Chinese pairs skill with ingenuity or cleverness (*qiao* 巧) (*Gu Wen Zi Gu Lin*, vol. 9, 698), originally meaning good craftsmanship, shows that skill surpasses the level of the mechanical and becomes intelligent[6] and fluent. How do we articulate the differences between the habitual and the skilled in light of the *Zhuangzi*'s views? There are several elements that draw our attention.

The first element is the fluency of performance, enabled by the integration of body and mind in a person's engagement with the task at hand. In becoming skilful, not only does a person's bodily movements change, but his or her perception and intellection do as well. As Zhuangzi says, skill is that which lends art to ability (29/12/4). In fact, the association between skill and self-cultivation can be established precisely because the refinements one undertakes in the practice of skill help one go beyond mechanical repetition and context-based limitations. Billeter suggests that, when we start to learn a skill, we see objects as resistance: they thwart our forces and block our ways (Billeter, *Zhuang Zi Si Jiang*, 8). We "get lost" when facing them. In contrast, when we have mastered that skill, the resistance of objects greatly diminishes, and we can interact with them smoothly. We come to understand how things work, and in understanding this we also improve our ability to coordinate our attention and our movements to each new context in which the skill is to be articulated. This emphasis on practical understanding is shared by Zhuangzi and other pre-Qin thinkers, although other texts have not dealt with the fluency and mastery in such precision.

When one considers how skill is realised fluently across various contexts, one comes to realise that skilful performance includes altering and adapting what one typically does in an activity in order to do what is fitting in that context. This is the second element of the difference between habit and skill. Those who merely act habitually do not necessarily have the dispositions to fine-tune their movements to fit different contexts or to improve their skills in the longer run. Skill is developed only because of a person's vigilance and ability to adapt the skill to be optimally realised in different settings (Ryle, *The Concept of Mind*, 42). The *Zhuangzi* presents detailed observations of skill refinement. The cicada catcher who uses his pole as swiftly as using his hands undergoes a training program of balancing balls on poles (48/19/18–19). Confucius comments on the ferryman, pointing out that some of them can see the depths as dry land and their exercise of skill is free from distractions (49/19/24–25). The famous Cook Ding can spot and explain differences among cooks of different skill levels (7/3/7–8).

In order to attain such fluency in performance, a skilled person must overcome tendencies to act only in the ways that they have been trained to act. Sometimes a skilful person needs to be cautious about the inertia of habits. Habitual actions may not involve much self-aware thinking about the activity, as pointed out previously, and therefore do not allow a person to detect potentially weak manoeuvres or to adapt the execution to context. For the *Zhuangzi*, it is the attainment of *dao* that "advances skill", as said by Cook Ding (7/3/5). *Dao* is that which pervades all things (4/2/35–36) and enables one to respond to things from infinitely many perspectives (4/2/ 30–31). Having a *dao* means one can better develop awareness of potential difficulties, and fine-tune one's movements and expectations to liberated performance. One comes to realise the shortcomings of sticking to habits so as to become open-minded and flexible. As mentioned previously, habits are developed as responses to the world. Nevertheless, once one acquires a habit it can, paradoxically, repress responsiveness. This is because in the learning phase, a person has to focus on coordinating different aspects of the activity in order to build a pattern for dealing with the task at hand. The success of building the pattern brings satisfaction and a feeling of control, which may induce one to reproduce the same pattern in the future even when it does not fit the new context. The mediocre cook and the good cook in the Cook Ding story apply the same method every time without realising that they are trapped in their own habits. Their responsiveness is therefore limited. By contrast, the Woodworker Qing says that, before working, he frees himself from any thoughts about his capabilities or clumsiness, and only after that can his capacities become concentrated on the task at hand (50/19/57–58). This reflects that he does not take past achievements for granted and does not judge the trees he encounters by assessing them according to a fixed standard in his heart-mind. To become a skilful woodworker like Qing, one needs always to pay attention to the very context one is in, through not being subdued by habitual thinking or movements.

There is more to the importance of shedding formerly acquired habits and patterns as those are often instilled in individuals, undergirding rigid preferences for a particular way of doing things. To reduce this rigidity is the third element of skilful performance in the *Zhuangzi*. I have already mentioned that successes in constructing patterns of activity can bring satisfaction and a feeling of control. This of course leads a person to prefer their own patterns to those of others, sometimes to the extent that they can only feel pleasure in their own ways, disliking those outside their routines and comfort zones. In this way, a person's bodily movements, perceptions, attitudes and thoughts, and preferences may be rigidly entrenched in the familiar. A common example is a student's identification with a teacher's standards, acquired through modelling his or her teachers' ways at an earlier point in time. Such identification can turn into a deep preference for the ways—the *daos*—of one's group or social organisation. Unfortunately, if one's preferences become obsessive, they will generate intense and monotonous emotions, causing distraction and distress. Also, the obsession becomes one's master, blocking a person's awareness of the situation or possibilities proposed by other people. This further confines a person's responsiveness to the world, as an instance of "becoming so weary as though being sealed up" described by Zhuangzi (3/ 2/12). For him, turning fixed ways into skills lies in distancing oneself from conventions, even self-imposed ones, and their associated likes and dislikes.

This does not mean that one should try to suppress one's feelings when acting.[7] It is not inappropriate to delight in one's swimming or dancing, and these may very well be transformed into skilful action through refinement. Appropriate detachment from one's own habits not only allows one to be less stubborn and more creative, but also reduces psychological disturbance brought about by intense emotions and pressure to conform to the standard imposed by one's superiors.

So far, I have discussed three elements of skilful performance in the *Zhuangzi*: fluency, adaptation and fine-tuning, and liberation from previously instilled preferences. In the following section, I continue to explore the dynamics of performance in the *Zhuangzi*, focusing especially on its relation to the production of outcomes, before I return to the issue of emotional engagement in section 4, in light of how readers of the text can reorient themselves to a life of skilful performance.

3. OUTCOMES, PERFORMANCE, AND WANDERING

Zhuangzi's emphasis on spontaneity reveals that he is not keen to apply an outcome-based approach to life's pursuits. This approach may seem a modern preoccupation, but in the Warring States period, a commodity economy was already developing,[8] and the competition for dominance between individuals, and among states, was fierce. As a result, the emphasis on efficiency was not uncommon. This can be seen from a story in the *Zhuangzi*, where Zi Gong, a renowned disciple of Confucius, recommends a shadoof (*gou* 槔) to a vegetable gardener for irrigation because it "uses very little effort but produces great results" (31/12/54). However, the gardener rejects his recommendation because it makes one's spirit (*shen* 神) unstable, causing it to deviate from *dao* (31/12/57). There is perhaps a reason why Zhuangzi gives Zi Gong the role of introducing the machine: Zi Gong is famous for his talents in business and diplomatic negotiations. In these negotiations, people are especially eager to see tangible and quantifiable results. So it seems Zhuangzi could be mocking those who boast about their efficiency and profit-generation capacities and who assess all human achievements according to those criteria. The *Zhuangzi* knowingly represents Zi Gong as one who sees sagely *dao* in terms of efficiency and profit (31/12/63). The gardener points out that Zi Gong will be unable to govern his own person, much less the whole world, because it induces the heart-mind of scheming (*ji xin* 機心). Apart from having the meaning of "scheming", the character 機 can also mean "machine" and "opportunity". I suggest that, in this context, it probably includes all three meanings: (a) overemphasis on efficiency that (b) drives one to see every occasion as an opportunity for profit, and which in turn causes (c) a person to operate like a machine that computes according to preset formulas and targets.

The heart-mind of scheming may suppress a person's spontaneous faculty, that is, the spirit, not because of calculativeness per se, but because his or her attention is wholly bent to the outcomes of their action—or more precisely, the quantifiable social value of the product. In the process, one becomes a mere producer rather than a performer. His or her identity is therefore subsumed under the products they are able to create or produce. Through the comparison of their products with those of others, they will be in strife and will come into conflict with things (4/2/18), bringing psychological instability to oneself.

Contrary to Zi Gong in the shadoof story, Zhuangzi's skill masters are not profit-oriented, nor do they conduct their work according to economic principles.[9] Cook Ding's skill is surely impressive, but from an economic perspective many of its features are redundant. For example, his cutting movements form a rhythm that matches the music of ancient sage kings, but this is not relevant if one simply wants to use minimal resources to cut an ox (Xu, *Zhong Guo Yi Shu Jing Shen*, 52). His cutting technique surpasses those of mediocre cooks and good cooks, but it takes him at least nineteen years to attain this level. Although we are not told how many years it takes to train a mediocre cook and a good one, presumably Lord Wen Hui and people in the court would not expect to wait for nineteen years for a new cook. We are not even told that the meat prepared by Cook Ding is better tasting than that of others. In short, Cook Ding's skill cultivation is not primarily product focused, despite the fact that the product is an outcome of the skilled action. Here, one might think that the story of the Woodworker Qing is different from that of Ding and other masters, for we are explicitly told about the feature of his product apart from Qing's preparation and performance: his bell stands are like the work of ghosts and spirits! This may raise readers' expectations that high-level skill in the *Zhuangzi* must produce high-quality products. Still, when Qing talks about how his bell stands are created, he recalls that he will start carving only when he finds a tree that has a "perfectly fitting shape". His heart-fasting can let him perceive clearly whether a tree fits, but it does not give him a fixed idea of perfect shape and does not guarantee that he can find it (50/19/59). So from an economic perspective his method is not as predictable as one that simply carves bell stands from less-than-perfect wood and maintains an average standard. This is why the *Hanfeizi* says:

> And even if, without the application of such tools [of straightening and being woods], there were an arrow shaft that made itself straight or piece of wood that made itself round, a good craftsman would not prize it. Why? Because it is

not only one man who wants to ride, and not just one shot that the archer wants to make. (Watson, *Han Fei Tzu*, 126)

For Hanfei, a good craftsman is someone who can apply a standard (*fa* 法) consistently and produce results every time. With this standard, there should be no expectation that the object produced is naturally in perfect shape. Nonetheless, Qing does not produce bell stands according to a predetermined rule and is not interested in standardisation. He seeks the cooperation of nature and does not insist on getting the job done. Eventually his skill cultivation is like that of Ding and free from the heart-mind of scheming.

Many skill masters in the Zhuangzi perform with calm and ease. In many cases, the sense of ease is expressed in their accounts of their learning or their actions. For example, the Woodworker Qing mentions that he "fasts" his heart-mind (*xin* 心) and does not waste his *qi* (氣, energy) before working (50/19/56). This preparation for skilled activity allows him to forget even his own body so as to be free from anxiety, excitement, and bias. Ji Shengzi, who raises fighting cocks for a king, points out that the best cock does not display fierce vigour but stands like a piece of wood (50/19/46–49). Presumably, the story tells us to pay attention to the danger of being emotionally aroused so that one's performance is driven, and hindered, by the emotion or desire.[10]

The three skill masters Zhao Wen, Shi Kuang, and Hui Shi are criticised as they are too eager to make other people "understand" their achievement (5/2/45). Their performance may be fluent and impressive, but they focus too much on the display of their skills and do not realise that their conceit prevents mutual understanding in the first place. Their vanity leads to what Zhuangzi regards as "putting weight on the external", which results in one getting "clumsy with the internal" (49/19/26). Indeed, from the emphasis on "internal" we can see that Zhuangzi does not measure the performance of skill masters by productivity or conformity to social roles. While their performance can be regarded as an achievement in the realm of use (*yong* 用), this achievement is not their ultimate goal. Nowhere in the text is it stated that skills are secondary to the pursuit of predetermined objectives or in the production of specific objects. Rather, skilful performance emerges spontaneously (*ziran* 自然), after much disciplined practice. The first step of understanding spontaneity is to see it as a dissolution of a calculated mind which, I suggest, is also the text's intention for its readers.

Through the stories of skill masters, Zhuangzi reorients readers from outcomes to performance. However, the focus on performance is just half the story. As mentioned in section 2, skill cultivation is indispensable from self-cultivation, and one who possesses skills is not driven by vanity. Skill masters do not feel lost when their performances do not go as expected. As Qing says, sometimes no appropriate tree is found, or as Ding says, sometimes there is a complicated joint through which he cannot move as fluently as usual. Also, they are not excited when they succeed. At most, they feel a mild degree of satisfaction when their intention is fulfilled (8/3/11).[11] Contrary to ordinary people who find joy when and only when they indulge in their professions or produce outcomes valued in conventional terms (66/24/33–38), skill masters seem to keep the distinction between concentration and indulgence intact. They immerse in their performances deeper than ordinary people do, and if they also understand that every skill is useful only when the time comes (43/17/35–37),[12] then they also know better than ordinary people about how *not* to give too much credit to their skill. This paradoxical combination of immersion and detachment constitutes Zhuangzi's conception of *you* (遊, wandering). *You* is the word used by Ding to describe the motion of his knife, and elsewhere in the *Zhuangzi* it reflects an ideal way of living one's life.[13] However, this way is special: while the skills of carving oxen, making bell stands, and swimming, for example, would have been originally developed for particular goals (preparing meat, making music, and surviving in water), the way of *you* is not fixed and has no determined goal. It can mean travelling or playing, and in the text it refers to the skill masters' flexible attitude towards skill cultivation and performance. For a skill master to have an attitude of *you* does not mean that he trivialises what he does or regards it as mere entertainment. Rather, *you* captures the skilful utilisation of things at hand which, at the same time, remains open to the form of "use", in such a way that the master "leaves nothing unused", as mentioned in the story of the forger (60/22/70). For one to *you*, therefore, is for him or her to wander on a path, or metaphorically, to have a way that is not simply following on a path that had previously been walked upon (*bu dao zhi dao* 不道之道) (5/2/61). Zhuangzi reorients readers from outcomes to performance, only to reorient them again to the interplay between performance and non-performance.

4. LIFE AFTER REORIENTATION

From the above sections, we have a glimpse of Zhuangzi's idea of skill and its relation to self-cultivation. The process of transforming habits to skills and eventually to acquiring the ability to *you* is accompanied by a reduction of rigid practices and obsessions. One who is reoriented from product to performance also loses the scheming and calculative heart-mind. We can begin to sketch an overview picture of the lifestyle of the skill masters. In one sense, they share certain characteristics with recluses (*yin shi* 隱士), people who are intellectuals but who shun the political arena and live a simple life in remote areas.[14] Of course, recluses do not need to possess marvellous skills like skill masters in the *Zhuangzi*, and those masters do not necessarily reside in remote areas or totally distance themselves from government. Many skill masters work under feudal lords,[15] and we are told that Zhuangzi himself once filled a minor post (Mair, *Wandering on the Way*, xxxi–xxxii). Nevertheless, being a recluse represents a lifestyle, and being a skill master, for Zhuangzi, represents a similar lifestyle. This similarity should be understood in terms of their non-attachment to conventional values. Although some skill masters do not live in solitude and still need to interact with other people, they do not seek to be recognised. They are not interested in profit, fame, or power, not even the moral influence emphasised by Confucians and Mohists.[16] Keeping a low profile, they do not even actively talk about their skills and give explanations only when pressed. Their skills seem to be their only source of fulfilment, but they have no desire to promote their skills or quantify their productivity, as mentioned in section 3. We may say that their recluse-like attitude plus their high-level skills have an effect of "nourishing life" (*yangsheng* 養生) or "fathoming life" (*da sheng* 達生).[17] This can be appreciated from two aspects, one negative and one positive.

The negative aspect of nourishing life is the reduction of friction between oneself and one's environment. According to Chen Guying, the story of Cook Ding tells us a way to live one's life. The complicated structure of oxen's tendons and bones is a metaphor for the complications in life, and Ding's marvellous practice symbolises a way that helps us deal with hardship in life. Useful strategies include understanding the situation; having a cautious, modest, and focused attitude; and not taking forcible and aggressive actions (Chen, *Lao Zhuang Xin Lun*, 170). This should be understood in conjunction with Zhuangzi's idea that, in certain times, living one's life is like walking through thistles and thorns (12/4/89). On the one hand, being obsessed with conventional values or being too eager to meet their demands often results in exhaustion. Therefore, a person is advised to shun these. On the other hand, in engaging with others in the world it is sometimes necessary to undertake conventional activities. In such cases, one is advised to focus on the task at hand while remaining open to new possibilities. This can help prevent both physical and psychological damage in life. Arguably, the freshness of the knife in Cook Ding's story is an analogy for those who can maintain an intact life.

The positive aspect of nourishing life is that spontaneous performance is intrinsically fulfilling and aesthetically pleasing. Cook Ding says that, after working, he looks around with satisfaction before he puts the knife away (8/3/11).[18] The swimmer of Lüliang sings after swimming in turbulence, expressing a carefree attitude (50/19/51). Both of them enjoy what they do. To the extent that their exercise of skill is free from obsession, their feeling of joy, if any, should arise spontaneously and not derive from their conscious evaluation of their performance. Some scholars suggest that this spontaneous joy has an aesthetic dimension. Billeter notes that, in the context of skill cultivation, the idea of Heaven refers to a spontaneous way of activities

(Billeter, *Zhuang Zi Si Jiang*, 31–36), by which we express our vitality beautifully like an artist (ibid., 41). Xu notes that Cook Ding's (and presumably other skill masters') satisfaction is derived from his "artistic" spontaneous performance, in the sense that his skill is liberated not only from the resistance presented by objectives but also from goal-directed consciousness (Xu, *Zhong Guo Yi Shu Jing Shen*, 53). Since Zhuangzi says that skill is that which lends art to ability (29/12/4), this entails that spontaneity lies at the core of art. When a person exercises their skills spontaneously, it results in artistic performance;[19] when one retains spontaneity not only in a particular skill but also in one's life more generally, one turns life itself into art and experiences spontaneous joy (Xu, *Zhong Guo Yi Shu Jing Shen*, 56–59). Of course, it should be remembered that the fulfilment and joy of skill masters are possible only when their concentration does not slip into indulgence, as mentioned in section 3. In other words, their joy must accompany their exercise of *you* and is usually gentle and calm. Since *you* reflects Zhuangzi's ideal way of living one's life, we can conclude that the ideal way of life is artistic, spontaneous, and free.

5. CONCLUSION

The *Zhuangzi* is not the only pre-Qin text that discusses the relationship between skill, art, and self-cultivation. Nevertheless, the text gives the relationship utmost attention. Many, if not all, of our movements and practices can be developed into skills, but not so many philosophers put skill at the centre of their thought and writings. Through a series of stories, Zhuangzi not only helps us to see the significance of skill in our lives, but also prompts us to reflect on our assumptions about knowledge, action, and the value of life. Although their performance may be efficient, skill masters show only a secondary interest in participating in economic or political processes during their time. Instead, they are spontaneous and free from rigid preferences, navigating their lives in the world like a knife that stays fresh even when put to use frequently. On one hand, their spontaneity resembles Heaven, while on the other, they live an ordinary life and still respond to society to a certain extent. Not totally discarding human conventions and not totally determined by them, skill masters may be on the way to the state in which "neither Heaven nor humanity is victorious over the other" (16/6/20).

NOTES

1. The dates here are in accordance with the *Comprehensive Mirror to Aid in Government* (*Zi Zhi Tong Jian* 資治通鑑) written by Sima Guang (1019–1086), who took the split of Jin into three states, Han, Wei, and Zhao, as the beginning of the Warring States period.

2. I shall not judge the authorship issue of the *Zhuangzi* text here. I assume that the content of the text emerged as a reflection of the social environment of the Warring States period, as well as the discourse made by early Confucians and Mohists. The term "Zhuangzi" refers not to any specific historical figure but is only used as a label for the author(s) of the text. All references to the Chinese text of the *Zhuangzi* are from Hong, *Zhuangzi Yinde*.

3. When emphasising the physical basis of habits, William James notes that "habit diminishes the conscious attention with which our acts are performed", so that when one performs a habitual action, "the results follow not only with the very minimum of muscular action requisite to bring them forth, but they follow from a single instantaneous 'cue'" (James, *Psychology*, 139). This idea is developed by recent psychologists. For example, Wood and Rünger point out that habits are learned automatic responses, which are activated by recurrent context cues and not dependent on goal-directed thoughts (Wood and Rünger, "Psychology of Habit", 292).

4. My translation. References to the Chinese text of the *Kongzi Jiayu* are from Lau and Chen, *A Concordance to the Kongzi Jiayu*.

5. This is a lesson from the story of Wheelwright Bian.

6. Ryle distinguishes knowing-how from mere mechanical actions by noting that only the former is "intelligent". See Ryle, *The Concept of Mind*, 29.

7. For a detailed discussion of the relationship between emotion and feelings on one hand, and skill development on the other, please refer to David Machek's discussion in chapter 3 of this volume.

8. Mencius, who was a contemporary of Zhuangzi, mentions that it is common to practise division of labour among craftsmen, with merchants buying and selling products according to their worth. See Lau, *Mencius*, 110–21.

9. Some of their works may still be economic. For example, if the king rewards Ding for his marvellous work, then it is an ipso facto economic activity. This of course does not imply that Ding himself sees it as solely economic or that his work should be purely judged on an economic basis.

10. Also, Zhuangzi's skill masters do not emphasise their social status or that of their teachers. Unlike Confucians and Mohists, Zhuangzi does not promote skill cultivation as a means of socialisation.

11. More about the relationship between skill and fulfilment will be discussed in section 4.

12. This generates doubt on the status of skill masters in Zhuangzi's thought. For a critique of taking skill as a core theme in the Inner Chapters, please refer to Eric Schwitzgebel's discussion in chapter 7 of this volume.

13. The basic meaning of *you* is "wandering" or "playing". Metaphorically, it refers to one's not attaching to a particular path, hence being flexible, playful, and free. See, for example, 10/4/52–53, 14/5/52, 20/7/10–11, 52/20/24, 55/21/30.

14. In book 18 of the *Analects*, we are told that Confucius and his disciples met several recluses who criticised Confucius's practice. These people stated that it was pointless to seek political influence in a time in which virtue was not respected. See Lau, *Analects*, 182–89. In the *Zhuangzi* we find more recluses. Some of them even represent ideal personhood. See, for example, Xu You, who refuses to rule the world even when he has the opportunity (2/1/23–26) and Jie Yu who sings a satirical song to Confucius (12/4/86–89).

15. Examples are Cook Ding, Wheelwright Bian, Ji Shengzi, the anonymous forger, the Woodworker Qing, and the naked scribe.

16. For Zhuangzi, Confucians and Mohists emphasise moral ideals such as benevolence (*ren* 仁) and rightness (*yi* 義). Adherence to benevolence and rightness constitutes their *dao*. Generally, and especially in the Inner Chapters, Zhuangzi's attitude towards these ideals is sceptical or even critical (see, for example, 6/2/70, 8/4/7, 17/6/83–84). These ideals do not appear in skill stories, nor do they form the background of the skill masters' stories.

17. The term "fathoming life" is the title of *Zhuangzi* chapter 19, which contains most skill stories in the Outer Chapters.

18. As mentioned in section 3, skill masters are not excited when they succeed, and they at most feel a mild degree of satisfaction when their intention is fulfilled. Here, I want to suggest that this feeling of satisfaction does not last long and will be "put away" shortly like Ding's

knife. Otherwise, it may develop into rigid preferences that hamper skill cultivation, as mentioned in section 2.

19. As mentioned in section 4, there is a sense in which an open-minded skill master can maintain a balance between performance and non-performance. Therefore, it is possible that one remains spontaneous even if no skill is being exercised. For a discussion about how a skill master shows his ability before performing, please refer to Hans-Georg Moeller's discussion in chapter 15 of this volume.

REFERENCES

Billeter, Jean-François. *Zhuang Zi Si Jiang* 莊子四講 [*Leçons sur Tchouang-tseu*]. Translated by Gang Song 宋剛. Taipei: Linking Publishing, 2011.

Chen, Guying 陳鼓應. *Lao Zhuang Xin Lun* 老莊新論 [New Discussion on the *Laozi* and *Zhuangzi*]. Taipei: Wunan Book Incorporation, 2007.

Gu Wen Zi Gu Lin Bian Zuan Wei Yuan Hui 古文字詁林編纂委員會, ed. *Gu Wen Zi Gu Lin* 古文字詁林 [The Explanatory Dictionary of Ancient Chinese Characters]. Vol. 4. Shanghai: Shanghai Jiao Yu Chu Ban She, 2001.

———. *Gu Wen Zi Gu Lin* 古文字詁林 [The Explanatory Dictionary of Ancient Chinese Characters]. Vol. 9. Shanghai: Shanghai Jiao Yu Chu Ban She, 2004.

Hong, Ye 洪業, ed. *Zhuangzi Yinde* 莊子引得 [A Concordance to the *Zhuangzi*]. Shanghai: Shanghai Classics Publishing House, 1986.

James, William. *Psychology: The Briefer Course*. New York: Henry Holt, 1920.

Lau, D. C. *Confucius: The Analects*. Hong Kong: The Chinese University Press, 1992.

———. *Mencius*. Hong Kong: The Chinese University Press, 2003.

Lau, D. C., and Fong Ching Chen, ed. *A Concordance to the Kongzi Jiayu*. Hong Kong: Commercial Press, 1992.

Mair, Victor H. *Wandering on the Way: Early Taoist Tales and Parables of Chuang Tzu*. New York: Bantam, 1994.

Ryle, Gilbert. *The Concept of Mind*. Abingdon: Routledge, 2009.

Watson, Burton. *Han Fei Tzu: Basic Writings*. New York: Columbia University Press, 1964.

Wood, Wendy, and Dennis Rünger. "Psychology of Habit." *Annual Review of Psychology* 67, no. 1 (2016): 289–314.

Xu, Fuguan 徐復觀. *Zhong Guo Yi Shu Jing Shen* 中國藝術精神 [The Spirit of Chinese Art]. Taipei: Student Book, 1979.

Chapter Two

Skill and Nourishing Life

Franklin Perkins

In themselves, the various "skill stories" in the *Zhuangzi* are perfectly clear. There is a person who can swim in rapids without worry or risk. There is a bell carver whose products seem magical. There is a skilled boatman, a great butcher, and an expert catcher of cicadas. The problem comes, as it so often does in the *Zhuangzi*, when we try to determine what the stories mean. We assume that the text is doing more than just telling us how to become a great artisan or cicada catcher, but what is that greater point? The stories themselves contain few hints of their significance, or how they fit with other aspects of the philosophies of the *Zhuangzi*. The one exception to this rhetorical practice appears in the most famous of all skill stories—the story of Cook Ding butchering an ox. At the conclusion of that story, Lord Wen Hui reports, "I have heard the words of Cook Ding and from them have attained the way to nourish life [*yangsheng* 養生]" (Guo, *Zhuangzi jishi*, 124).[1] Might this interpretation provide a key for understanding the skill stories in general? Someone involved with the formation of the *Zhuangzi* must have thought so. The majority of the skill stories are collected in chapter 19, which mixes discussions of life with exemplars of great skill and is given the title "Fathoming Life" (*Da sheng* 達生). This chapter will follow these interpretive gestures by considering the skill stories in relation to the theme of nourishing life. The first section will discuss the story of Cook Ding. The second section analyzes the passages addressing life in the "Fathoming Life" chapter. The third section applies these accounts of life to the skill stories in the rest of that chapter.

1. NURTURING LIFE AND BUTCHERING AN OX

The story of Cook Ding begins with a description of his movements, which are precise and rhythmic like a dance. His sovereign, Lord Wen Hui, sees him as he is passing by and asks if technique (*ji* 技) can really reach such a high level. Cook Ding pauses and replies:

> What your servant loves is the way [*dao* 道], which advances beyond technique. At the time when your servant began to cut up oxen, what I saw was nothing but whole oxen. After three years, I no longer saw whole oxen. Now, your servant does not use the eyes to look but meets it with spirit; perception from the senses stops and spirit acts as it wants. I rely on the heavenly contours, strike into the large gaps, let myself be guided by [*dao* 導] the large hollows, and adapt to what is firmly so. (Guo, *Zhuangzi jishi*, 119)[2]

He explains that by inserting his knife into the spaces and hollows of the carcass, the blade never dulls. He concludes:

> Even so, each time I reach a tangle, I see the difficulty of the action (*wei* 為). Alert and cautious, looking comes to a stop and action (*xing* 行) slows down. I move the knife subtly and with a whoosh! it is already cut, like clumps of soil scattered on the ground. I raise my knife and stand, looking around admiringly, pleased and content. I wipe the knife and store it. (Guo, *Zhuangzi jishi*, 117–24)[3]

At this point, Lord Wen Hui gives his judgement, that in hearing the words of Cook Ding, he has learned how to nourish life.

The story of Cook Ding appears in chapter 3 of the *Zhuangzi*, and the title of the chapter, "The Primacy of Nourishing Life" (*Yangsheng zhu* 養生主), reflects the importance of Lord Wen Hui's comment. The problem is that neither Cook Ding's actions nor his explanation have any apparent connection to nurturing life. On the contrary, Ding seems to be on the side of death—he is, after all, carving up a once living being. Whether deliberate or not, the passage calls to mind Mengzi's claim that the noble (*junzi* 君子) keep away from the kitchen, because they cannot bear the cries of the animals to be killed (*Mengzi* 2A6).[4] Ding does not stay away from the kitchen. Insofar as Ding earns a living wage from his skill, we could say that he thereby nourishes his own life and that of his family. If he is providing meat for others to eat, then he might be nourishing them as well. Surely, though, his lord is not recommending him as a model for earning a living or providing food for others, neither of which would be done by a lord, who, for that very reason, can dine on meat while keeping distant from the kitchen. Thus, the connection to nourishing life is unlikely to be in the specifics of butchering.

We might instead focus on Ding as an exemplar of skill in general. If nurturing life is a skill and Ding teaches us about skill, then one might learn how to nurture life from him. On this reading, though, the passage is no more about nurturing life than any other activity. Lord Wen Hui could just as well have concluded, "I have heard the words of Cook Ding and from them have attained the way to play ukulele." Rohan Sikri provides an alternative, by arguing that Cook Ding's butchering does not exemplify skill in general but is a metaphor for philosophical practice. Through this story,

> [Zhuangzi] calls for a reinvigorated method in the skill of *wuwei* 無為, which requires a limited "division" of the world using categories that are both contextually bound and flexible in their usage. Moreover, Zhuangzi imparts an explicitly therapeutic resonance to this model by associating the practitioner of *wuwei* 無為 with the goal of "nourishing life/*yangsheng* 養生." (Sikri, *The Cut that Cures*, 93)

On this reading, the story of Cook Ding illustrates the positive alternative to the scepticism found in parts of the Inner Chapters, while also showing that the goal of philosophical practice is ultimately therapeutic.[5] Sikri gives one of the few discussions of the Cook Ding story that takes seriously the connection to nourishing life.[6]

Sikri's interpretation is plausible, but the description of Cook Ding may be more than just a metaphor for the proper way of dividing the world. In any case, the meaning of "nourishing life" requires clarification. The phrase is used in only two other places in the *Zhuangzi*. One appears in chapter 28, "Yielding Kingship" (*Rangwang* 讓王):

> The genuine of the way is in managing one's self. What is leftover can be used for the state and district. The dregs can be used to manage the realm. Looking at it from this point of view, the accomplishments of emperors and kings are just the leftover work of the sage, not that by which one preserves the body and nourishes life. Many of the noble of these times make their bodies abandon life in order to pursue mere things. How sad is that! (Guo, *Zhuangzi jishi*, 971)[7]

Our highest priority should be self-preservation, explained as nourishing life and keeping the body whole (*wanshen* 完身). The opposite of nourishing life is to take risks for the sake of external things. The second appearance of the phrase also refers to preserving one's own life, by avoiding internal illness and external threats. That passage appears in the "Fathoming Life" chapter, which will be discussed below. In both uses, *yangsheng* means self-preservation. That focus is supported by the passage that precedes the story of Cook Ding and opens the "Primacy of Nourishing Life" chapter:

> My living has a boundary but knowing has no boundary. To use what has a boundary to follow what has no boundary—that is dangerous! It being so and to still seek knowledge—that is nothing but dangerous! For goodness do not get near a reputation; for badness do not get near punishment. Follow the central meridian as a guide and you can thereby protect your body, keep life intact, nourish your parents, and reach the end of your years. (Guo, *Zhuangzi jishi*, 115)[8]

This passage uses protecting the body (*baoshen* 保身) and keeping life whole or intact (*quansheng* 全生) rather than nourishing life (*yangsheng*), but the point is the same. The goal is to live out one's natural lifespan.

The phrase *yangsheng*, though, does not refer exclusively to maintaining one's own life. Even the above *Zhuangzi* passage also mentions nourishing one's parents or those who are close (*qin* 親).[9] In a Ru context, the phrase *yangsheng* is most often used in caring for other people, usually paired with providing an adequate funeral. Thus, Mengzi says that with proper government, there will be enough goods for the people to nourish the living and mourn the dead. He concludes: "Nourishing the living [*yangsheng*] and mourning the dead without regret—that is the start of the way of the true king" (養生喪死無憾，王道之始也) (*Mengzi* 1A3; Jiao, *Mengzi zhengyi*, 55). It is possible that the phrase "nourishing life" extends even further. The term *sheng* 生 has a broad meaning, including growing, generating, and giving birth. The term often refers to the life and growth of individuals, as we have seen, but it can refer to the generative forces of nature. Thus the "Xici" (繫辭) commentary takes the foundation of the *Changes* as *shengsheng* (生生) (Gao, *Zhouyi*, 388), which could be translated as "generating and generating," "living and growing," "generating life," and so on. Given that life and growth are a fundamental characteristic of reality, *sheng* has an ontological dimension. Thus, the phrase *yangsheng* may hint at assisting the broader generative forces of the world, fostering life, growth, and creativity. There are traces of such a view in the Inner Chapters, as in descriptions of a sagely figure whose mere presence inspires chickens to copulate, or another whose presence protects the local crops.

In many cases, the focus of nourishing life is on concrete material goods like adequate food, shelter, and clothing, sometimes called the "tools for nourishing life" (養生之具).[10] This focus on material goods, though, was also criticised. Another passage from the *Mengzi* says: "Nourishing life is not enough for the great duty; only sending off the dead can suit the great duty" (養生者不足以當大事，惟送死可以當大事) (4B13; Jiao, *Mengzi zhengyi*, 558). The great duty (*dashi* 大事) refers to care for parents, and the point is that merely providing them with what they need to survive is not enough to count as filial. Another line of critique in relation to *yangsheng* is in a shift towards an internal basis for cultivating life. We see this in a line from the *Huainanzi*:

Having spirit clear, intentions at ease, and the hundred joints all at rest—that is the root of nourishing one's natural dispositions. Fattening the muscles and skin, stuffing the bowels and belly, satisfying cravings and desires—these are merely the branches of nourishing life. (He, *Huainanzi jiaoshi*, 1401)[11]

One would normally think of eating and drinking as the basis for nourishing life, but the real foundation is stillness and emptiness. The same view appears in the passage quoted earlier from the "Yielding Kingship" chapter, which says the danger to nourishing life is the pursuit of external things. Achieving such inner stillness is a central theme throughout the *Zhuangzi*.

With this context, we can see a suitably complex tangle of meanings to Lord Wen Hui's comment. On one level, Cook Ding demonstrates a skilful way to earn a living and to provide the food that people need for nourishment. On another level, Ding's real skill is in achieving the kind of calm, mirror-like state of mind that is the true foundation for nourishing life. Based on the use of the term in related contexts, nourishing life here probably means nourishing one's own life, but it could mean nourishing the lives of other people or even supporting the generative processes of nature itself. This interpretation comes from taking the story of Cook Ding seriously, and it will be supported by the analysis of the "Fathoming Life" chapter below. Should we take the story seriously, though? The explanation in terms of nourishing life is not given in an authorial voice. It is not put into the mouth of Zhuangzi himself, or Laozi, or some sagely character with a mysterious name. It comes from Lord Wen Hui. He is obviously marked as part of the political elite, and they rarely come off well in the *Zhuangzi*. The anti-elitist choice of a butcher as exemplar is immediately undermined by presenting his sovereign, his *jun* 君, as his interpreter and spokesperson. Should we listen to him?

The concrete associations around the phrase *yangsheng* provide another reason not to take the story of Cook Ding at face value. Donald Harper, drawing on the medical materials found at Mawangdui, connects *yangsheng* to a broad approach to health that included diet, structured breathing, physical exercise, and sexual practices (Harper, *Early Chinese Medical Literature*, 115).[12] Thomas Michael associates *yangsheng* with a form of early Daoism that integrated meditation, structured breathing and vital energy (*qi* 氣) flow, physical exercises modelled on the movements of animals, and a tradition of mountaintop recluses (Michael, "Hermits, Mountains, and *Yangsheng*").[13] It is uncertain that the term *yangsheng* would have brought to mind such practices at the time the Inner Chapters were written, but the *Zhuangzi* does mention and reject those who seek a long life through exercises based on animal movements ("Keyi" 刻意; Guo, *Zhuangzi jishi*, 535). If the story of Cook Ding is placed in that context, it appears most of all as a form of mockery.[14] Instead of a famous sage or specialist, one has a common butcher. Instead of highly technical and secretive physical exercises and forms of meditation, one has the common act of cutting up an ox. Instead of reclusion one has the most menial of jobs. In that context, the story of Cook Ding should be seen as parody. Even so, there is a question of how far that goes. At one extreme, it might reject the whole idea of an internal basis for nourishing life. If you want to nourish life, get a job and eat meat. That seems unlikely in the broader context of the *Zhuangzi*, and the story of Cook Ding deliberately emphasises a particular kind of mental state. The most likely point is that this inner condition does not depend on specific practices, forms of meditation, withdrawal from society, or finding a sage.

2. FATHOMING LIFE

We can now turn to the chapter called "Fathoming Life." The term translated by Graham and Ziporyn as "fathom" is *da* 達.[15] *Da* means to reach, pass through successfully, or progress. *Da* is sometimes interchangeable with *tong* 通, which means to pass along smoothly, penetrate, master, or commune with. Both terms are often contrasted with *qiong* 窮, which means extreme poverty or destitution but also has a sense of reaching a limit or being blocked. To *da sheng* is to align with, participate in, penetrate through, or grasp the life forces of nature itself. We cannot place too much weight on a chapter title, since we do not know when the titles were created, but the chapter contains several discussions of life mixed in with the skill stories.

To present this full context, it is best to begin with an outline of the chapter, which seems to contain thirteen distinct passages:

1. A short essay on fathoming life.
2. A dialogue between Liezi and Guanyin on avoiding harm.
3. The skilful cicada catcher.
4. The skilful ferry driver.
5. Advice for nourishing life (*yangsheng*), with anecdotes of two people who failed in opposite ways.
6. A comparison of the perspective of a pig and a human being on the value of life.
7. An anecdote in which Duke Huan is troubled about a ghost.
8. Training a fighting rooster.
9. The skilful swimmer.
10. The skilful bell carver.
11. A charioteer who pushes his horses too hard, and a minister who predicts it.
12. A description of the skill of Chui the artisan.
13. An encounter between a consistent loser, Sun Xiu, and Master Bian Qingzi.

Passages 3, 4, 8, 9, 10, and 12 are classic skill stories. Passages 11 and 13 can be grouped with them as illustrations of the opposite of skilfulness. The passages at the centre of the chapter (passages 5–7) give practical advice on achieving a long life. They occupy a middle ground between the skill stories and the theoretical accounts of life that introduce the chapter. I will begin with these three passages, then turn to the broader theoretical context presented in the initial two passages. The subsequent section will consider how these frame the skill stories.

We can begin with passage 6, which argues for the value of preserving one's own life. It begins with the Invocator of the Ancestors speaking to the pigs he is about to sacrifice. He lists the ways they are being pampered and honoured, as if that compensates for their impending death. The passage then switches to the pigs' point of view, saying that they would prefer to stay alive and give up the honours and fine grains. The gap between one's own perspective and the perspective of other animals is pointed out in passages across the *Zhuangzi*, but with different purposes. The point here is not to equalise perspectives in order to make a sceptical point, as seems to be the case, for example, in the dialogue between Nie Que and Wang Ni in the "Equalising Assessments of Things" chapter (Guo, *Zhuangzi jishi*, 91–96). In this passage, the pig's point of view is used to criticise the ritualist, who values honours over his own life. Thus, the passage concludes: "In planning for a pig one would reject these, but in planning for himself he selects them, yet what difference is there from the pig!" (為彘謀則去之，自為謀則取之，所異彘者何也) (Guo, *Zhuangzi jishi*, 648). The ritualist and pigs are all living things and in that sense are not so different. The implication is that the pig, in valuing life, has more sense than the person, who, as Cheng Xuanying comments, does not fathom life (Guo, *Zhuangzi jishi*, 649). This story resembles Zhuangzi's response when he is asked to take political office. He describes a turtle who is dead but whose shell is honoured in the courts, asking if the turtle would not prefer to be still alive living in the mud ("Autumn Floods" [Qiushui 秋水], Guo, *Zhuangzi jishi*, 603–4). When the messengers say the turtle would prefer to be alive in the mud, Zhuangzi replies that he will make the same choice, refusing office. As we have seen, our highest goal should be staying alive, not serving the state.

The passages around this story give practical advice for staying alive. Passage 5 is a dialogue between Duke Wei of Zhou and Tian Kai. The duke asks Tian Kai what he learned in his time wandering with Zhu Shen, a person famous for studying life (*xuesheng* 學生). After some coaxing, Tian Kai gives this principle: "Being good at nourishing life (*yangsheng*) is like shepherding a flock of sheep: watch which ones fall behind and then spur them on" (善養生者，若牧羊然，視其後者而鞭之) (Guo, *Zhuangzi jishi*, 644). He gives two examples of one-sided cultivation. Shan Bao left society and lived simply in the wilds, cultivating his health so that he looked young even at the age of seventy. Zhang Yi did the opposite, spending his life gathering power by developing political connections. Bao was killed by a hungry tiger; Yi died of illness. Tian Kai concludes: "Bao nourished the internal but a tiger eating him was external; Yi nourished the external but a sickness attacking him was internal. Neither of these two masters spurred on what fell behind" (豹養其內而虎食其外，毅養其外而病攻其內。此二子者，皆不鞭其後者也) (Guo, *Zhuangzi jishi*, 645). This claim is followed by a quotation attributed to Kongzi (referred to as Zhong Ni), saying that one should occupy the centre rather than going inside to hide or going outside to be on display. The ideal combines the internal and the external, but Kongzi notes that most people fall behind on the internal side, so that is usually the side that must be spurred on.

The threat of internal disruptions to nurturing life is illustrated in passage 7. While out on a hunt in the marshlands, Duke Huan sees a ghost and falls ill. His minister, Huangzi Gao'ao, explains to him the cause of his illness:

> The duke is harming himself—how could a ghost harm the duke! Now, if the vital energy is aroused and aggressive, it disperses without return and then is insufficient. If it goes up but not down, then it makes people good at being angry. If it goes down but not up, then it makes people good at forgetting. If it goes neither up nor down, centring in the body and at the heart, then it becomes illness. (Guo, *Zhuangzi jishi*, 650)[16]

Gao'ao gives a naturalising account of the effects of ghosts—it is not ghosts but fear of ghosts that causes harm. Vital energy, *qi* 氣, is used to explain the close link between emotions and health, showing why internal disruptions shorten life. The duke, though, is unconvinced and asks if ghosts really exist. The minister says they do and then lists their types, including one common to marshlands like where the duke was hunting. When the duke asks for a description, the minister describes it and explains that such ghosts are only seen by those who would become leaders of all the states. The duke joyfully says that is what he saw, and his illness disappears the same day. It is likely that the minister manipulates the duke: since he cannot calm the duke by claiming that ghosts have no power, he instead tells him that the ghost he saw was an auspicious sign. The original anecdote may have arisen with the purpose of debunking the power of ghosts, but in the context of "Fathoming Life," it shows how imbalanced emotions harm life and how such emotions arise not from pure experience but from the perspective we bring to that experience.

Neither of these stories demonstrate skill (except the skill of Huangzi Gao'ao in persuading his sovereign), but they give practical advice on how to nourish one's life well. The first two passages give a more philosophical account. I will quote and discuss the passages in full, since they are complex and have previously drawn little attention. The first begins by emphasising the limits of our ability to maintain life:

> Those who fathom the real condition (*qing* 情) of life do not work on that which life has no way to enact.
>
> Those who fathom the real condition of fate do not work on that which knowing can do nothing about.
>
> Nourishing the form first requires using other things, but there are cases in which there are more than enough things and yet the form is not nourished.
>
> Having life first requires that the form is undivided, but there are cases in which the form is undivided and yet life is lost.
>
> The coming of life cannot be refused and its going cannot be stopped. It's sad! (Guo, *Zhuangzi jishi*, 630)[17]

Nourishing the bodily form (*yangxing* 養形) is equivalent to nourishing our own individual life. That requires basic resources. People thus think that having plenty of supplies and avoiding danger will guarantee a long life, and yet sometimes people die anyway. The coming and going of life cannot be stopped. One who truly grasps, penetrates, or fathoms life and fate does not put effort into what cannot be controlled. The next lines make the same point but raise a general problem:

> Common people of the times consider that nourishing the form suffices to preserve life but really nourishing form does not suffice to preserve life. Then what action in this age is sufficient for it? Although action is not sufficient, one cannot but act. How can action be avoided? (Guo, *Zhuangzi jishi*, 630)[18]

If our actions cannot guarantee a long life, then why bother? The answer is that action also is unavoidable, even if it does not guarantee success.

The passage then moves on to what one should—or should not—do:

> If one wishes to avoid acting for the bodily form, nothing is better than abandoning the age. By abandoning the age there will be no exhaustion and without exhaustion then they will be right and balanced; being right and balanced, they can be revitalised in their interactions with others; being revitalised, they will be almost there! Why is it worth abandoning the age and forgetting life? If one abandons duties then the form will not be labored; if one lets go of life then the refined essence will not be lost. (Guo, *Zhuangzi jishi*, 632)[19]

Driven by obsessive concern with their own lives, people wear themselves out in their involvement with the world, bringing an early death. If one can abandon these concerns, then the body will not be labored, and the refined or vital essence (*jing* 精) will not be damaged. We see here the turn towards cultivating certain internal states as the best way to nourish life, as well as an irony familiar from the *Laozi*: only by giving up seeking a long life can one attain a long life (e.g., *Laozi* 7).[20] The passage again links nourishing life to avoiding politics. The phrase describing the culmination of this progression is difficult to interpret. It literally says "with [*yu* 與] others [*bi* 彼] to again [*geng* 更] live/be born [*sheng* 生]." The phrase could refer to being born into a new identity, either at death or in our day-to-day interactions with things. Ziporyn translates it as "reborn along with each presence that confronts you," and Watson as "born again with others." The term *sheng*, though, is not necessarily individuated into distinct lives. A more plausible interpretation in context is that one will be revitalised by encounters with others, rather than being exhausted by them. Both Guo Xiang and Cheng Xuanying explain it as being renewed every day (*rixin* 日新), borrowing a phrase from the "Great Learning" (*Daxue* 大學).

The passage concludes by expanding beyond its individualistic focus on caring for one's own life:

> Now if the form is kept intact and refined essence returns, then you become one with heaven. Heaven and earth are the father and mother of the myriad things. When they combine then the body forms and when they disperse a beginning forms. If form and refined essence are not lost, this is called being able to change. Refined and again refined (*jing er you jing* 精而又精), it returns to assist heaven. (Guo, *Zhuangzi jishi*, 632)[21]

Life comes and goes with the transformations arising from heaven and earth. By not being excessively attached, one can go along with these changes. Penetrating or fathoming life, then, is not just a matter of one's own life but rather of becoming one with the processes of nature, going along with the broader flow of life. When the form is whole and vital essence is restored, one is united with heaven. There is an even higher level of attainment, though. If this refined essence is further refined, we can assist in the generative process of nature itself. Guo Xiang links this claim to *Laozi* 64, which says that sagely people "assist the self-so spontaneity [*ziran* 自然] of the ten thousand things."

This short essay is followed by a dialogue between Liezi and Guanyin. Liezi starts by asking how to become immune to harm:

> Liezi asked Guanyin: "The utmost people walk underwater without suffocating, tread through fire without getting burnt, walk high above the myriad things without trembling. May I ask how one reaches this?" (Guo, *Zhuangzi jishi*, 633)[22]

Similar descriptions of sagely figures who are immune to harm appear in the Inner Chapters (e.g., Guo, *Zhuangzi jishi*, 226) and in the *Laozi* (e.g., *Laozi* 50). Liezi seems to take such descriptions literally.[23] Guanyin replies:

This is a matter of protecting pure vital energy. It is not from such things as knowledge, craft, resolve, or daring. Stay, let me tell you. Anything that has appearance, shape, sound, and color is a thing [*wu* 物]. How far apart can one thing be from another? How can one suffice to have priority? They are just colors and that is all. Thus, things are made from formlessness and stop in what has no transformations. If you take this and go with it thoroughly, how could things be able to stop you? (Guo, *Zhuangzi jishi*, 634)[24]

In saying that immunity to harm cannot come from any form of active seeking, Guanyin picks up themes from the previous passage on giving up work. Protecting vital energy (*qi* 氣) in the right balance and quality was commonly associated with practices for nourishing life, and the refined essence (*jing* 精) central to the previous passage was often explained as a form of vital energy. Disrupted vital energy causes illness, as in the example of Duke Huan and the ghost. The concrete method Guanyin gives is through a phenomenological account of the equality of all things. In themselves, things are just momentary configurations of colours, sounds, and shapes. They come from the formless and return to the changeless. Given this status, how could one thing be superior to any other? This focus on equalising things echoes themes in the "Equalising Assessments of Things" (*Qiwulun* 齊物論) chapter, as well as the dream dialogue between Carpenter Shi and the useless tree in the "In the Human World" (*Renjianshi* 人間世) chapter, in which the tree says "you and I are both things—how can one thing rank another thing?" (Guo, *Zhuangzi jishi*, 172). All of this can be seen as an argument against attachment and for going along with changes.

Guanyin then describes the internal state this detachment generates and the broader connection to the world that follows:

They reside in the measure that has no excess, hide in the basis that has no limits, and wander in that which begins and ends the myriad things. They unify the dispositions, nurture the vital energy, and merge virtuosities in order to commune with that which creates things. Now, when one is like this, the heavenly in them is protected and kept intact, and the spirit in them is without blockage. How can things enter and exit! (Guo, *Zhuangzi jishi*, 634)[25]

The passage starts by juxtaposing the external and the internal. Those who achieve the highest state relate to the external world not through its divisions but by residing or wandering in that which generates those divisions. The internal has three dimensions: dispositions (*xing* 性), vital energy (*qi* 氣), and virtuosity (*de* 德). The appeal to heaven and spirit (*shen* 神) brings the internal and external together. Heaven and spirit are features of the external world, but here they are modified by the possessive *qi* 其, so that it is literally "their heavenly" and "their spirit." The final result integrates internal and external again, as we simultaneously are undisturbed by things but in communion or alignment (*tong* 通) with that which generates things. This communing with that which generates things leads to preserving life. Guanyin continues with an illustration:

> Now if a drunk person falls from a chariot, even if it is going fast he will not be killed. His bones and joints are the same as those of other people but the harm and injury is different, because the spirit in him is intact. He does not know riding in the chariot and does not know falling either. Life and death, surprise and fear do not enter into the centre of his chest. Therefore, he meets things without flinching. (Guo, *Zhuangzi jishi*, 636)[26]

Guanyin's example is a mocking response to Liezi's original question about magical powers. Avoiding harm requires no magic, just being drunk. It is also a kind of ironic skill story. The drunk falling from the chariot is not so different from the expert ferryman or the swimmer in rapids. What they have in common is a disregard for external things.

Drunkenness is not the ideal. The passage continues:

> Now if one who attains being intact through alcohol is like this, how much more one attains being intact through the heavenly? Sagely people hide in the heavenly and thus nothing can harm them. Even one seeking revenge on enemies does not go so far as to break up their swords and shields. Even one with a bad temper will not get angry with a tile blown down by the wind. By this, the world can be peaceful and even. Eliminating the disruptions of war and invasion and the penalties of death and mutilation thus come from following this way. Do not open up the heavenly of the human but open up the heavenly of heaven. Opening the heavenly empowers life. Opening the human plunders life. Do not tire of the heavenly but do not neglect the human. The people will soon come to use the genuine. (Guo, *Zhuangzi jishi*, 636–38)[27]

The focus of the passage has been on preserving one's own life, but the result is good for everyone. This method of calming emotions makes the world peaceful and without war or penalties. The phrase translated as "the heavenly empowers life" uses *de* 德 (virtue/virtuosity) as a verb with *sheng* as its object. While *de* has a sense of power, it has connotations of goodness, generosity, and a transformative influence on other people. The conclusion of the passage is not about keeping oneself alive but rather having other people return to the genuine.

3. SKILL AND "FATHOMING LIFE"

In conclusion, we might take the core of the chapter as the argument in passage 6 that life should be valued over honour and external things. The other passages move from giving concrete practical advice for maintaining our lives to a more precise philosophical account. On that level, disengagement from individuated things goes along with engaging the world through what all things have common, enabled by an internal calm and stillness. [28] At the same time, the goal of preserving one's own life is extended to participation in the generative processes of nature. The question is, how do these discussions of life relate to the skill stories that fill the rest of the chapter? The theme that most consistently links the various passages in "Fathoming Life" is the connection between successful action and being free of disturbances caused by the world around us. As Kongzi says, "Anyone who puts weight on the external will be clumsy with the internal" (凡外重者內拙) (Guo, *Zhuangzi jishi*, 642). That comment follows an empirical observation about archery, that the higher the stakes, the worse one shoots, which follows the skilled ferry driver's claim that all it takes to steer across the river safely is to have no fear of water. The swimmer explains his skill as a result of his calm and ease (*an* 安). He grew up in the water, and this shaped his genuine dispositions (*xing* 性). The drunk person falls from a chariot without harm because he does not know the danger he is in. In these examples, the fear of failure makes us ineffective. The skilful bell carver broadens the point by listing the various concerns he sets aside:

> When I will make a bell, I do not dare let it consume my vital energy, and so I must fast to quiet my heart. After fasting for three days, I dare not care about praise, reward, position, or salary. After fasting for five days, I dare not care about criticism or fame, skill or clumsiness. After fasting for seven days, I forget that I have four limbs or a bodily form. At that time, there is no duke or court. The skill is concentrated and the external slips away. I enter the forest and see natural dispositions (*tianxing* 天性). (Guo, *Zhuangzi jishi*, 658–59) [29]

The term *wang* 忘 has the same ambiguity as the term "forget" in English, in that it can refer to not remembering but also not attending to, as we might tell a performer to forget about the audience watching. It is a central term in the skill stories. The ferry driver says that the key to success is to forget the water. Master Bian tells Sun Xiu the loser that the utmost people forget their liver and gallbladder and give up their eyes and ears. The ideal of forgetting is developed in the story of Chui the artisan, which says:

> When shoes are comfortable, the feet are forgotten. When a belt is comfortable, the waist is forgotten. When the heart is comfortable, right and wrong are forgotten. When affairs are comfortable, one does not change on the inside or labor on the outside. When one begins in comfort and is never not comfortable, that is the comfort of forgetting comfort. (Guo, *Zhuangzi jishi*, 662) [30]

In these cases, the external is present but of no concern. This forgetting frees us from emotional disturbances brought about by external things.

Freedom from negative responses to the external world is a common theme throughout the *Zhuangzi*, but the discussions of nourishing life and the skill stories use this state of mind as a means towards skilful engagement with the external world. Cook Ding becomes aware of the natural contours (*tian li* 天理) of the ox he is cutting up (Guo, *Zhuangzi jishi*, 119). The bell carver is able to see the natural dispositions, *tianxing* 天性, of the trees. Having stripped himself of all artificial disruptions, he is then able to match his naturalness to that of the tree, literally matching heaven to heaven (*yi tian he tian* 以天合天) (Guo, *Zhuangzi jishi*, 659). Chui the artisan transforms along with things (*yu wu hua* 與物化) because he imposes nothing (Guo, *Zhuangzi jishi*, 765). The swimmer has no *dao* of his own but rather follows the *dao* of the water, without any private concerns (*si* 私). Having no private concerns is precisely what allows him to succeed and stay safe (Guo, *Zhuangzi jishi*, 657). This linkage of internal calm with worldly efficacy should be distinguished from several other views that appear in the *Zhuangzi*. It differs from free and easy wandering (*xiaoyaoyou* 逍遙遊), which is a matter of enjoying and going along with whatever happens. In the skill stories and the discussions of life, one has a goal to achieve. The skill stories also contrast more esoteric images of sagely activity. They involve forgetting, but not a specific practice of "sitting and forgetting" (*zuowang* 坐忘) (Guo, *Zhuangzi jishi*, 284) or such sagely things as leaning on a desk and appearing like dead ashes or dried wood (Guo, *Zhuangzi jishi*, 43). They present an image of engagement with the world quite different from images of sages who utter bizarre phrases when encountered in the wilderness. In fact, the "Fathoming Life" chapter, like the story of Cook Ding, may be a criticism of such images of sageliness.

If we take the "Fathoming Life" chapter as a whole, the skill stories are subordinated to a broader concern for nourishing life. In particular, they illustrate a certain kind of cultivation that achieves success in the world through an inner calm grounded in not worrying about success. While the skills are not directly aimed at nurturing life, their connection goes beyond just illustrating skilfulness. Having skill itself tends towards supporting life. Some of the skills involve avoiding danger, as with the ferry driver, the swimmer, the drunk, and the fighting rooster. Their calm responsiveness to the world allows them to avoid harm, as well as to do their other tasks. Similarly, those who are unskilled, like the assertive charioteer or Sun Xiu the loser, risk death. Almost all of the skills are simultaneously ways of making a living. In a way, they contrast advice in other parts of the *Zhuangzi* that say safety comes from being useless. These skilful actors are employed because of their usefulness. Given the warnings about the risks of politics in the same chapter, though, these skilful actors may be examples of ways to make a living while avoiding excessive risk. If you have to get a job, the safest thing is to be a butcher, a woodcarver, or ferry driver. On a higher level, emotional disturbances directly harm our health. Insofar as any of the skilful actors achieve a sense of emotional calm, they would tend to be healthier. We might say that all of the skilful actors are making progress in nourishing life, but their focus on a specific skill brings limitations. If the cicada catcher only sees cicada wings, he will be in trouble when a hungry tiger comes along. Cultivating skill is not the same as nourishing or fathoming life, but it illustrates what is needed and is a step in the right direction.

Even if this account of the "Fathoming Life" chapter is correct, that does not mean we have found the true meaning of the skill stories. Four of the skill stories from "Fathoming Life" (the cicada catcher, the ferry driver, the rooster, the swimmer) are gathered in the "Yellow Emperor" (Huangdi 黃帝) chapter of the *Liezi* 列子, but the focus there is on power and efficacy, with no reference to nourishing life. Cook Ding is mentioned as an example of skill in the *Lüshi chunqiu* 呂氏春秋 and the *Huainanzi* 淮南子, but the *Lüshi chunqiu* uses it to illustrate the power of sincerity of purpose (*cheng* 誠) ("Jingtong 精通," Chen, *Lüshi Chunqiu Xinshi*, 514), while the *Huainanzi* makes a more general point about needing both the right tools and the right skill ("Qisu lun," He, *Huainanzi jiaoshi*, 801). It is unlikely that these stories were originally written as part of the *Zhuangzi*. If the "Fathoming Life" chapter were composed as a whole, one would expect the chapter to contain a more explicit bridge between skill and life. Similarly, if the skill stories were written by a single author, we would expect a consistent vocabulary across them, but different key terms are used in different stories.[31] What we have in the "Fathoming Life" chapter, then, is an interpretation of the skill stories performed by setting them in a context of discussions of life. The comment added by Lord Wen Hui does the same thing to the story of Cook Ding. This focus on life would likely be the earliest interpretation of the skill stories that we have, and there are good reasons to think that the skill stories appear in the *Zhuangzi* because of their relationship to nourishing and fathoming life. If we consider the context of the *Zhuangzi* as a whole, though, one lesson we learn is that nothing can be reduced to a single meaning. Just as the *Zhuangzi* itself gives us reasons to doubt the authority of Lord Wen Hui as an interpreter of Cook Ding, it gives us reasons to doubt the interpretations of its own editors.

NOTES

1. References to the *Zhuangzi* are based on the Chinese text in Guo, *Zhuangzi jishi*. All translations are my own, but I have regularly consulted and sometimes borrowed from Ziporyn, *Zhuangzi: The Essential Writings*, as well as Graham, *Chuang-Tzu: The Inner Chapters*; Mair, *Wandering on the Way*; and Watson, *The Complete Works of Chuang Tzu*. For ease of reference, I have used Ziporyn's translations of chapter titles.

2. 臣之所好者，道也，進乎技矣。始臣之解牛之時，所見無非全牛者。三年之後，未嘗見全牛也。方今之時，臣以神遇，而不以目視，官知止而神欲行。依乎天理，批大郤，導大窾，因其固然。

3. 雖然，每至於族，吾見其難為，怵然為戒，視為止，行為遲。動刀甚微，謋然已解，[牛不知其死也，]如土委地。提刀而立，為之四顧，為之躊躇滿志，善刀而藏之。」

4. References to the *Mengzi* are based on the Chinese text in Jiao, *Mengzi zhengyi*, cited by passage number.

5. Ivanhoe also takes the skill stories as clear evidence for a positive alternative to scepticism in the *Zhuangzi* (Ivanhoe, "Skepticism, Skill, and the Ineffable Tao").

6. The most influential discussions of the skill stories give no significance to the phrase nourishing life. See, for example, Graham, *Disputers of the Tao*, 186–94; Ivanhoe, "Skepticism, Skill, and the Ineffable Tao"; Eno, "Cook Ding's Dao"; and Yearley, "Zhuangzi's Understanding of Skillfulness." Conversely, one of the few papers to focus on the theme of nourishing life in the *Zhuangzi*, Michael, "Hermits, Mountains, and *Yangsheng*," ignores the story of Cook Ding.

7. 故曰：道之真以治身，其緒餘以為國家，其土苴以治天下。由此觀之，帝王之功，聖人之餘事也，非所以完身養生也。今世俗之君子，多為身棄生以殉物，豈不悲哉！

8. 吾生也有涯，而知也无涯。以有涯隨无涯，殆已；已而為知者，殆而已矣。為善无近名，為惡无近刑。緣督以為經，可以保身，可以全生，可以養親，可以盡年。

9. A reference to nourishing parents or loved ones seems out of place, in this line, in the passage, and even in the *Zhuangzi* as a whole. Chen Guying argues that *qin* is an error, most likely for *shen* 身, the body or self (*Zhuangzi jinzhu jinyi*, 115). Victor Mair also emends the line, translating this phrase as "Nourish your inmost viscera" (26). Given that the line makes sense as is, I do not think the emendation is justified. Another possibility is to read *qin* very broadly to mean something like "what is cherished." That is possible but would be very unusual for the phrase *yangqin*, which consistently refers to nourishing parents. Ziporyn translates the phrase as "nourish those near and dear to us" (*Zhuangzi: The Essential Writings*, 22), and Watson has "look after your parents" (*Complete Works of Chuang Tzu*, 50).

10. See, for example, *Huainanzi*, "Integrating Customs" (Qisu lun 齊俗論) (He, *Huainanzi jiaoshi*, 822).

11. 神清志平，百節皆寧，養性之本也；肥肌膚，充腸腹，供嗜欲，養生之末也。

12. For a broader discussion of these medical practices in relation to the *Zhuangzi*, see Sikri, *The Cut that Cures*, 59–91.

13. For precedents of this view, see Roth, "The Laozi," and Robinet, *Taoism*, 91–92.

14. On the importance of attending to elements of humour and parody in the *Zhuangzi*, see Moeller and D'Ambrosio, *Genuine Pretending*.

15. Watson translates the title as "Mastering Life." Mair translates it as "Understanding Life."

16. 公則自傷，鬼惡能傷公！夫忿滀之氣，散而不反，則為不足；上而不下，則使人善怒；下而不上，則使人善忘；不上不下，中身當心，則為病。

17. 達生之情者，不務生之所無以為；達命之情者，不務知之所無奈何。
養形必先之以物，物有餘而形不養者有之矣；
有生必先無離形，形不離而生亡者有之矣。
生之來不能卻，其去不能止。悲夫！

18. 世之人以為養形足以存生；而養形果不足以存生，則世奚足為哉！雖不足為而不可不為者，其為不免矣！

19. 夫欲免為形者，莫如棄世。棄世則無累，無累則正平，正平則與彼更生，更生則幾矣！事奚足棄而生奚足遺？棄事則形不勞，遺生則精不虧。

20. References to the *Laozi* are by traditional chapter number, based on the Mawangdui B manuscript as reconstructed in Gao, *Boshu Laozi*.

21. 夫形全精復，與天為一。天地者，萬物之父母也。合則成體，散則成始。形精不虧，是謂能移。精而又精，反以相天。

22. 子列子問關尹曰：「至人潛行不窒，蹈火不熱，行乎萬物之上而不慄。請問何以至於此？」

23. Liezi may have a particular association with magical powers in the *Zhuangzi*, as he is said to have had the ability to fly (Guo, *Zhuangzi jishi*, 17) and is described as particularly impressed with a master of physiognomy (Guo, *Zhuangzi jishi*, 297–306).

24. 關尹曰：「是純氣之守也，非知巧果敢之列。居，予語女！凡有貌象聲色者，皆物也，物與物何以相遠？夫奚足以至乎先？是色而已。則物之造乎不形，而止乎無所化。夫得是而窮之者，物焉得而止焉！

25. 彼將處乎不淫之度，而藏乎無端之紀，游乎萬物之所終始。壹其性，養其氣，合其德，以通乎物之所造。夫若是者，其天守全，其神無郤，物奚自入焉！

26. 夫醉者之墜車，雖疾不死。骨節與人同而犯害與人異，其神全也。乘亦不知也，墜亦不知也，死生驚懼不入乎其胸中，是故遻物而不慴。

27. 彼得全於酒而猶若是，而況全於天乎？聖人藏於天，故莫之能傷也。復讎者，不折鏌干；雖有忮心者，不怨飄瓦，是以天下平均。故無攻戰之亂，無殺戮之刑者，由此道也。不開人之天，而開天之天。開天者德生，開人者賊生。不厭其天，不忽於人，民幾乎以其真。

28. On these two sides, Sikri writes: "This dialectical quality involves both a negative and positive stage, wherein a divestment of a rigid apparatus of knowledge prepares the ground for a subsequent organisation of categories that accord with the 'natural patterns (*li* 理)' of the *dao*" (Sikri, *The Cut that Cures*, 161).

29. 臣將為鐻，未嘗敢以耗氣也，必齊以靜心。齊三日，而不敢懷慶賞爵祿；齊五日，不敢懷非譽巧拙；齊七日，輒然忘吾有四枝形體也。當是時也，無公朝。其巧專而外骨消，然後入山林，觀天性。

30. 忘足，履之適也；忘要，帶之適也；知忘是非，心之適也；不內變，不外從，事會之適也；始乎適而未嘗不適者，忘適之適也。

31. The framework of *gu* 故, *xing* 性, and *ming* 命 in the story of the swimmer is used nowhere else. *Xing* also appears in the story of the bell carver, but in the phrase *tianxing* 天性. *De* 德, virtuosity or efficacy, is used only in the description of the rooster and in Master Bian's response to Sun Xiu the loser. The cicada catcher and Chui the artisan both mention internal unification, but the first refers to using the heart in an undivided way while the latter refers to the numinous platform (*lingtai* 靈臺). The heart (*xin* 心) is mentioned only in the stories of the bell carver and of Chui the artisan. The stories of the rooster and bell carver both suggest the cultivation of *qi* 氣, vital energy, and the story of Duke Huan seeing a ghost discusses internal harms in terms of the movement of *qi*, but *qi* is not mentioned in the other stories. The swimmer says that he has no *dao*, while the cicada catcher does have a *dao* (and Cook Ding says that what he loves is *dao*). It is possible that the dialogue between Liezi and Guanyin was written to draw this vocabulary together, as it uses almost all of these terms, particularly in the summary line: "Unify the dispositions, nurture the vital energy, and merge virtuosities in order to commune with that which creates things" (壹其性，養其氣，合其德，以通乎物之所造) (Guo, *Zhuangzi jishi*, 634).

REFERENCES

Chen Guying 陳鼓應. *Zhuangzi: Contemporary Notes and Explanations* [*Zhuangzi jinzhu jinyi* 莊子今注今譯]. Beijing: Zhongguo Shuju, 1983.

Chen Qiyou 陳奇猷. *New Explanations of the Lüshi Chunqiu* [*Lüshi Chunqiu Xinshi* 呂氏春秋新釋]. Shanghai: Shanghai Guji, 1984.

Eno, Robert. "Cook Ding's Dao and the Limits of Philosophy." In *Essays on Skepticism, Relativism, and Ethics in the* Zhuangzi, edited by Paul Kjellberg and Philip J. Ivanhoe, 127–51. Albany, NY: SUNY Press, 1996.

Gao, Ming 高明. *Annotated Silk Manuscript Laozi* [*Boshu Laozi jiaozhu* 帛書老子校註]. Beijing: Zhonghua shuju, 1996.

Gao Heng 高亨. *New Notes on the Zhouyi and Great Commentaries* [*Zhouyi dachuan jinzhu* 周易大傳今注]. Jinan: Qilu Shushe, 1998.

Graham, A[ngus]. C. *Chuang-Tzu: The Inner Chapters*. Indianapolis: Hackett, 2001.

Graham, Angus C. *Disputers of the Tao: Philosophical Argument in Ancient China*. Indianapolis: Open Court, 1989.

Guo, Qingfan 郭慶藩. *Zhuangzi: Collected Explanations* [*Zhuangzi jishi* 莊子集釋]. Beijing: Zhonghua Shuju, 1978.

Harper, Donald. *Early Chinese Medical Literature: The Mawangdui Manuscripts*. London: Kegan Paul, 1997.

He Ning 何寧. *Huainanzi: Collected Explanations* [*Huainanzi jiaoshi* 淮南子集釋]. Beijing: Zhonghua Shuju, 1998.

Ivanhoe, Philip J. 1993. "Skepticism, Skill, and the Ineffable Tao." *Journal of the American Academy of Religions* 19 (1993): 13–25.

Jiao, Xun 焦循. *Mengzi: Corrected Meanings* [*Mengzi zhengyi* 孟子正義]. Beijing: Zhonghua Shuju, 1987.

Mair, Victor. *Wandering on the Way: Early Taoist Tales and Parables of Chuang Tzu*. Honolulu: University of Hawai'i Press, 1994.

Michael, Thomas. "Hermits, Mountains, and *Yangsheng* in Early Daoism: Perspectives from the *Zhuangzi*." In *New Visions of the* Zhuangzi, edited by Livia Kohn, 145–60. St. Petersburg, FL: Three Pines, 2015.

Moeller, Hans-Georg, and Paul D'Ambrosio. *Genuine Pretending: On the Philosophy of the* Zhuangzi. New York: Columbia University Press, 2017.

Robinet, Isabelle. *Taoism: Growth of a Religion*. Translated by Phyllis Brooks. Stanford, CA: Stanford University Press, 1997.

Roth, Harold. "The Laozi in the Context of Early Daoist Mystical Praxis." In *Lao-tzu and the Tao-te-ching*, edited by Livia Kohn and Michael LaFargue, 59–96. Albany, NY: SUNY Press, 1998.

Roth, Harold D. "Bimodal Mystical Experience in the 'Qiwulun' Chapter of *Zhuangzi*." *Journal of Chinese Religion* 28 (2000): 31–50.

Sikri, Rohan. "The Cut That Cures: Therapeutic Methods in the Platonic Dialogues and the *Zhuangzi Neipian*." PhD diss., DePaul University, 2015.

Watson, Burton. *The Complete Works of Chuang Tzu*. New York: Columbia University Press, 1968.

Yearley, Lee H. "Zhuangzi's Understanding of Skillfulness and the Ultimate Spiritual State." In *Essays on Skepticism, Relativism, and Ethics in the* Zhuangzi, edited by Paul Kjellberg and Philip J. Ivanhoe, 152–82. Albany, NY: SUNY Press, 1996.

Ziporyn, Brook. *Zhuangzi: The Essential Writings, with Selections from Traditional Commentaries*. Indianapolis: Hackett, 2009.

Chapter Three

Skill and Emotions in the *Zhuangzi*

David Machek

The skill stories of the *Zhuangzi* on several occasions refer to emotional states of master practitioners. In so doing, they imply two rather different evaluative perspectives on emotions. On the one hand, emotions are disruptive forces that waste the psychophysical energy needed for an excellent execution of the task at hand; for this reason, master practitioners are typically free from emotions. On the other hand, there is an aspect of emotional experience that seems to play a positive, in fact indispensable, role in the acquisition and exercise of their virtuosity, namely the enjoyment of the very exercise of this skill. If the skill stories exemplify some characteristic attributes of perfect human agency in general, such as responsiveness, effortlessness, and efficacy, then we may assume, by default, that this double evaluative perspective on the role of emotions in the context of skill stories reflects a double evaluative perspective on the role of emotions in the human life in general. If indeed the master practitioners exemplify sages, and their performances exemplify the perfect human agency of "wandering" (*you* 遊), it would follow that the sages are free from ordinary, disruptive emotions aroused by things that are external to their activity of wandering and are only passionate about this very wandering itself. In fact, it is this passion for wandering that makes them immune to those disruptive emotions.

The Zhuangzian view about the role of emotions in the human life, both what it amounts to and its coherence, has been the subject of much debate in recent scholarship. Scholars have grappled with the fact that the *Zhuangzi* argues that sages are free from disruptive emotions, and at the same time it seems to make them susceptible to these emotions. This chapter does not aspire to settle these debates. Its objective is more modest, namely to show that approaching the problem of emotions from the narrow perspective of skill stories can access new interpretive perspectives and bring the available

33

evidence about emotions in the *Zhuangzi* into sharper relief, but also make us sensitive to some important limitations of the skill stories as explanatory tools. The role of emotions in the skill stories suggests an attractive possibility to explain coherently how the sage can be both passionate and dispassionate. At the same time, there is an important portion of the evidence about the Zhuangzian view about emotions that cannot be readily accommodated in the framework of the analogy between skills and human life.

This chapter is divided into two parts. In the first, I focus on the references to emotions in the skill stories and, in particular, in the bell stand maker story. In the second part, I turn to the Zhuangzian account of emotions more broadly considered and ask how the specific perspective of skill stories contributes to our understanding of emotions in the *Zhuangzi*.

1. EMOTIONS WITHIN SKILL STORIES

1.1. The Virtuosity of Master Practitioners

Ideal human agency as espoused by the *Zhuangzi* seems to have three main characteristic attributes. It is *responsive*, since it "responds to" (*ying* 應) or "follows" (*cong* 從) things as they are.[1] This responsiveness makes action seemingly *effortless*, since the responsive attitude enables one to achieve the goal with the least possible resistance. This effortlessness also typically happens to make the performance *efficient*. It has been widely noted that all these closely connected attributes are exemplified by analogies with virtuoso performance of a craft or skill. Somewhat less attention has been paid to the psychological attitudes of single-mindedness and concentration that underlie, at least on the level of skill analogies, these attributes. Generally, the master practitioners themselves emphasise that the area of their specialty is narrow and that they owe their success to a single-mindedness with which they have been dedicated to learning and exercising their skill.[2] This single-mindedness is closely connected with their ability to fully concentrate on their task. Not only is their field very narrow, but they excel in the ability to channel the entirety of their mental and physical energy into this narrow field and the specific task at hand. This is most clearly brought out by the story of the bell stand maker, that underlines the importance of avoiding "wasting energy" (*hao qi* 耗氣):

> When I am going to make a bell stand, I never let it wear out my energy. I always fast in order to still my mind. When I have fasted for three days, I no longer have any thought of congratulations or rewards, of titles or stipends. When I have fasted for five days, I no longer have any thought of praise or blame, of skill or clumsiness. And when I have fasted for seven days, I am so still that I forget I have four limbs and a form and body. By that time, the ruler

and his court no longer exist for me. My skill is concentrated and all outside distractions fade away. After that, I go into the mountain forest and examine the Heavenly nature of the trees. If I find one of superlative form, and I can see a bell stand there, I put my hand to the job of carving; if not, I let it go. (*Zhuangzi* 19.3)

The waste is avoided by undergoing a regimen of "fasting" (*zhai* 齋) that helps him to "still his heart" (*jing xin* 靜心) and to "forget" (*wang* 忘) all about things and affairs that are external to his current task. All his energy has to be directed into the task, like a quantity of light is channelled into a laser ray (cf. *Zhuangzi* 19.11). In the description of the cicada catcher, we learn that, similar to the bell stand maker, he "does not divide his attention" (*yong zhi bu fen* 用志不分) and that "his spirit concentrates", or literally "congeals" (*ning yu shen* 凝於神) (*Zhuangzi* 19.3). The idea of psychological concentration, or of directing one's attention on a single focal point, is here understood also in physical terms as concentration of "energy" (*qi* 氣).

The reason why this concentration is a prerequisite for master performance is, presumably, that it puts the agent in a position to epistemologically access those deep structures in the material that enable him to proceed at once effortlessly and efficiently. As indicated by the note in the butcher story that the cognition emerging from one's "spirit" (*shen* 神) directly "encounters" (*yu* 遇) things, this access is warranted by a physical alignment between the agent's heart and the relevant "natural patterns" (*tian li* 天理) or action-guiding structures in the material. Once one's energy achieves the requisite tension or degree of concentration that matches the energetic tension of the material—that is, once one's mind gets to operate cognitively in the mode of "spirit"—one's mind becomes virtually at one with the natural patterns in the material.[3] An assumption of this sort about the physical basis of epistemological processes seems also to be at work in an important passage about "fasting of the heart" (*xinzhai* 心齋) (*Zhuangzi* 4.1). This passage is a part of what is also, in a sense, a story about a skill virtuosity, namely virtuosity in the arena of political life. How can one accomplish one's mission of reforming a depraved ruler without jeopardising one's dignity or one's life? The answer is this: fast your mind so that you can "listen by energy" (*ting yi qi* 聽以氣) which is "empty" (*xu* 虛) and "waits for things" (*dai wu* 待物). If your energy is something you should "listen by", then you must make sure that this energy is not wasted but is plentiful (*yang qi* 養氣) so that you can "penetrate into the making of things" (*yi tong hu wu zhi suo zao* 以通乎物之所造).[4]

1.2. Disruptive Emotions

It is against this background that we can understand the disruptive effect of at least some kind of emotions on virtuoso performance. While it does not exhaust the entire spectrum of the Zhuangzian views about emotions, there is a pervasive strand of thinking about the emotions as epistemologically misguided and psychophysically disruptive forces that should be avoided.[5] This view is most succinctly summarised in a passage from chapter 5, in which Zhuangzi argues against Hui Shi that a human being can be without *qing* 情, "characteristically human inclinations" or "emotions":

> What I call emotions (*qing* 情) are positive and negative affirmative evaluations of things (*shi fei wu suo wei qing ye* 是非吾所謂情也). What I call having no emotions is not to harm the inside of one's body by likings and dislikings (*bu yi haowu nei shang qi shen* 不以好惡內傷其身), to constantly follow what-is-so-of-itself (*chang yin ziran* 常因自然) and not to add anything to life (*bu yi sheng* 不益生). (*Zhuangzi* 5.12)

The problematic aspect of emotions is that they are implicated in, or lead to, evaluative judgements about what is "right" and "wrong" that give rise to corresponding inclinations of "liking" and "disliking".[6] These judgements and attitudes have no foothold in how things are by themselves, but are imposed on them by the human heart. But it is exactly in clinging to our likings and dislikings of how things are or should turn out to be that we become their slaves. The reason that the sage is free from these disruptive emotions is, ultimately, that he "sees everything as one" (*shi qi suo yi* 視其所一) (*Zhuangzi* 5.1), including his own death and life, and therefore does not attribute any particular value or disvalue to getting or avoiding anything. But discriminating judgements and corresponding inclinations "tie" (*jie* 結) people to things so that their satisfaction depends on how those things turn out. This is, presumably, why emotions are typically described as forces that "invade" (*ru* 入) our innermost self and "harm our body" (*Zhuangzi* 3.5, 7.5, 21.40). To understand the kind of harm the emotions inflict, we have to take into account that both one's bodily well-being and the emotions that harm it are understood in terms of "energy" (*qi* 氣).[7] The emotions disrupt the balance of *yin* and *yang* energy in our bodies and allow the "evil energy" (*xieqi* 邪氣) to "attack" (*xi* 襲) (*Zhuangzi* 15.2). Along with disarranging and infecting our energy, emotions "diminish" (*kui* 虧) it and thus virtually "exhaust" (*lei* 累) us (*Zhuangzi* 15.2, 11.6, 23.16). They are thus counterproductive to the ideal of "nourishing one's energy".

Since the concentration of one's energy is the prerequisite for the virtuoso exercise of a skill, it is clear why emotions are an impediment to it. They are a particularly powerful kind of distraction that not only disperses our energy into several different directions but also decreases its overall level. Rather than helping us accumulate energy and direct it to the task at hand, they function like channels by which our energy bleeds into the pursuit of what is external to the task at hand. The reason that the bell stand maker needs to forget all about all sorts of considerations, and particularly those that typically elicit strong emotional responses, such as the ruler's court, is that he cannot afford to waste his energy on pursuits motivated by these considerations: it is when he is "fully concentrated on his skill" (*qi qiao zhuan* 其巧專) that "all external distractions subside" (*wai gu xiao* 外骨消). The absence of emotions ensures that he has the abundance of energy that enables him to grasp cognitively the "Heavenly nature" (*tianxing* 天性) of the wood and to choose the right piece of material for his work.

The disruptive role of emotions on one's concentration is most clearly brought out in the following passage about archery:

> When you're betting for tiles in an archery contest, you shoot with skill. When you're betting for fancy belt buckles, you worry about your aim. And when you're betting for real gold, you're a nervous wreck. Your skill is the same in all three cases—but because one prize means more to you than another, you let outside considerations weigh on your mind (*zhong wai* 重外). He who looks too hard at the outside gets clumsy on the inside (*wai zhong zhe nei zhuo* 外重者内拙). (*Zhuangzi* 19.4)

It is because we like the idea of winning, and dislike the idea of losing, that we worry. Both desire and fear interfere with our concentration on the performance. Not only does the fear of losing split our energy between concentration on shooting and worries about the outcome, thus weakening our concentration, but it also turns us into a leaky jar that does not have enough energy, and not enough concentrated energy, to hit the target.

The emotions of course may, and typically do, also diminish the responsiveness, effortlessness, and efficacy of the performance: the archer fails to hit the target, and the bell stand maker, had he not calmed his mind, would have failed to respond properly to the "Heavenly nature" of the wood. But this impact seems to be the consequence of the fact that emotions interfere with our concentration and drain our internal resources of energy.

1.3. Supportive Emotions

And yet master practitioners are not emotionless. They are subject to one important kind of emotion that is not only compatible with their excellence but also contributes to it, namely the enjoyment in exercising their skill. This is most clearly attested by the forger of swords, who, similar to other virtuosos, explains his excellence by his perseverance and single-mindedness. Asked for an explanation of how he has preserved his dexterity up to such a high age, he responds: "I have always kept to my work (*chen you shou* 臣有守). From the time I was twenty I have loved (*hao* 好) to forge swords. I never look at other things—if it's not a sword, I don't bother to examine it" (*Zhuangzi* 22.9). We find exactly the same word, *hao* 好, in the story of a butcher, who explains his excellence as follows: "What I love is the *dao* which goes beyond skill" (*chen zhi suo hao zhe dao ye, jin hu ji yi* 臣之所好者道也，進乎技矣) (*Zhuangzi* 3.1). Strictly speaking, the butcher's love is a love of *dao*, rather than of the skill, but clearly it is through exercising his skill that he grasps the Dao, and in that sense he also enjoys his skill. Moreover, being at one with the natural patterns of the cow, and being animated by the "desire of the spirit" (*shen yu* 神欲), it would seem that the exercise of his skill really becomes a part of the Dao itself, and hence there is no difference between loving the skill and loving the Dao.

This love is clearly a different kind of love than the one that, coupled with aversion, harms our psychophysical integrity. Rather than disrupting our concentration and responsiveness, this emotion seems to be an important ingredient, if not a prerequisite, of the virtuoso performance. The reason for its positive value is the same as the reason for the disruptive emotions' negative value: just as the disruptive emotions are channels by which we bleed our energy into the world, because they are aimed at external things, so is the love of activity a channel by which all our energy flows into and remains dammed in the activity, because it is aimed at this very activity. One could debate whether it is the concentration and single-mindedness that give rise to the love of activity, or whether it is rather the love of activity that promotes single-mindedness and concentration; but it seems to be the case that the causality could well go both ways, so that the single-mindedness and love mutually reinforce each other.

1.4. The Relationship between Disruptive and Supportive Emotions

The above analysis implies that the emotions that disrupt and that support excellent skill performance belong to two very different kinds of emotional experience: to misguided evaluative judgements about external things, on the one hand, and to appropriate enjoyment of one's present activity, on the other. The former are "additions" to life, whereas the latter belong, we could say, to the life itself. It is presumably the self-contained character of the craftsmen's pleasure in their own activity that is a part of what made the skill stories attractive for the authors of the *Zhuangzi*. In enjoying what they are actually doing in the moment, rather than worrying about what could, should, or shouldn't happen, they exemplify the emotional stance of the sages who, instead of worrying about their wealth, success, or death, enjoy their free "wandering" (*you* 遊), in which they are able to find satisfaction without injuring either themselves or others.

Despite having different objects and values, these two kinds of emotions use the same mechanism to disrupt or to support the excellent performance: they channel energy either towards or away from activity. Since there is a single resource of energy, it follows that the disruptive and supportive emotions are antithetical to each other: if your energy is channelled into desires or fears about external things, there will be no energy left for doing and enjoying the activity; but if your energy is channelled into your engagement with the activity, then you will do it single-mindedly, regardless of external distractions. Therefore, in order to liberate themselves from desires or fears that are bound to interfere with their performance, it was sufficient for the master practitioners to become passionate about this performance. On this view, then, the freedom from disruptive emotions is just a consequence of the intensity of one's love for the activity, and, in turn, the presence of disruptive emotions follows from a lack of positive engagement in one's present activity. Let us now turn to Zhuangzian views about emotions in general to see if the validity of this account goes beyond the ambit of the skill stories.

2. IMPLICATIONS FOR THE ROLE OF EMOTIONS IN THE HUMAN LIFE

2.1. The Doubleness in the Zhuangzian View of Emotions

Commentators have widely noted that the *Zhuangzi* contains two different assessments of the role of emotions in the fully accomplished human life. On the one hand, as we have seen, emotions are seen as man-made, disruptive forces based on erroneous evaluative judgements about things as they are. They unduly attach us to things, and thus conflict with the ideal of "wandering". For this reason and in this sense, the Zhuangzian sage is free from emotions. On the other hand, the text implies that even the sage is subject to emotions, and hence emotions must also be, in some sense, a part of the natural order of things. The evidence pointing in this direction is that even the sage is susceptible to "joy" (*le* 樂) and "delight" (*xi* 喜), and that all emotions are sometimes described as inevitable forces that are an inescapable part of the human condition and therefore need to be enjoyed and accepted as such and are not necessarily a sign of misalignment with the way things are.[8]

Given this double evaluative perspective on emotions, it is not surprising that there has been a plurality of views in the scholarship about how, and whether at all, this duality can be articulated in terms of a single, coherent view about the role of emotions in ideal human agency. How can the sage be both dispassionate and passionate, or in what sense is he passionate and in what sense is he dispassionate? Broadly, existing views can be divided into two factions. One faction consists of those who hold that the sage is never susceptible to the disruptive, *shi-fei* emotions but only to some special kind of emotional responses that differ from the disruptive emotions in terms of feeling,[9] epistemological status,[10] or the object they are directed at. One particular suggestion within this strand that is worth paying closer attention to, in the context of this chapter, has been proposed by Chris Fraser. On his view, the distinctive sagely emotion is a positive emotional response to the very activity of "wandering":

> We focus on the higher-order, ongoing process of wandering, rather than on the outcome of any particular first-order activity. Having identified with this "constant" (常), higher-order project, we experience affective equanimity, for we "bind" ourselves to no particular external things and our aims can be neither wholly completed (as wandering continues indefinitely) nor defeated (as we can wander with virtuosity regardless of external circumstances). As some *Zhuangzi* passages indicate, wandering itself can produce emotions of ease, happiness, or fulfilment, much as a virtuoso performer is likely to experience satisfaction or fulfilment during a performance. (Fraser, "Emotion and Agency", 112)

Belonging to the other faction are those who argue that the *Zhuangzi* grants that the sages are, with some qualifications, sometimes also subject to the disruptive *shifei* emotions. The most often cited piece of evidence for this view is the story about Zhuangzi grieving for his wife, where the text seems to acknowledge that the emotions are an inescapable part of the human predicament (*Zhuangzi* 18.2). In some situations of the human life, even the sage is overwhelmed by responses to the things he values. At the same time—and this is what marks the difference between the sage and the non-sage—the sage's emotional responses are tempered by his habitually disengaged stance. As to how exactly this happens, interpreters have proposed different accounts. It may be that the sages are able to detach themselves from their emotions *while* they feel it;[11] or it may be that they do lose their detachment altogether, but only for a short time, and then resiliently resume their detached perspective.[12]

2.2. The Role of Emotions from the Perspective of the Skill Stories

Taking into account the role of emotions within the narrow perspective of the skill stories, which of these interpretations should we defend? We have seen that the master practitioners are generally free from all disruptive emotions; the only kind of emotion they have is the satisfaction or joy at exercising their skill in the best possible manner. This speaks in favour of the above view that the sages are emotionally detached from things external to their activity of "wandering", but they do take pleasure in this very activity. This is corroborated by the fact that the exercise of masterly skill is closely associated with the notion of wandering, since the butcher's knife is said to "wander" (*you* 遊) through the joints of the cow without encountering any resistance, and this is, after all, why the activity is enjoyed. A closer look at the relationship between craftsmen's enjoyment of their activity and their freedom from disruptive emotions can supplement this view: not only is one's enjoyment of wandering typically associated with freedom from disruptive emotions; it is *because* all one's energy is channeled into the activity of wandering and its enjoyment *that* there is no energy left for other emotional responses, and least of all for the kind of responses that would interfere with the activity that one so much enjoys.

Should we conclude, therefore, that the relevant evidence from the skill stories supports strongly, if not conclusively, the above version of the view that the sage is free from the disruptive emotions of ordinary people? This would follow, perhaps, in the case that the question of what the fully accomplished human life amounts to could be exhaustively answered by the analogy with master practitioners of skills. But that is not necessarily the case. On the one hand, the skill stories do of course do an important service in exemplifying the central attributes of the fully realised human agency. On the other hand, some constitutive elements of the craft paradigm are in tension with the vision of human life they are supposed to exemplify, and some aspects of human life cannot be readily accommodated by these stories at all.

The parallel between master practitioners and sages holds only to the extent to which we think it is appropriate to think about human life as a series of craft-like challenges, or episodes in which we, like craftsmen, are to achieve the desired goal with greatest efficacy and least possible effort. The interpreters often characterise the ideal of "wandering" as aimless, or not slavishly tied to particular objectives. In some respects, perhaps, such an aimlessness can be integrated in the framework of skill stories; but, at base, the ideal exercise of skills or crafts is certainly not aimless, as the skill stories in the *Zhuangzi* clearly bring out, but narrowly focused on the attainment of a given goal. In order to preserve the plausibility of the parallel, we would have to opt for an alternative interpretation of *you* that would de-emphasise the aimlessness and instead accentuate adaptability and willingness to take whichever road is the most convenient at the moment. This is an interpretive question that we cannot settle now.

Besides worrying that the skill paradigm might be at odds with one important attribute of the ideal agency that it is supposed to exemplify, one may also worry that certain aspects of the human life are not satisfactorily covered by the skill paradigm at all. Perhaps the most obvious cases are exactly the situations of dealing with grief and bereavement. Unlike, say, the challenge of embarking on a political mission, the challenge posed by a painful bereavement cannot be as conveniently exemplified by the challenge faced by a butcher or a bell stand maker. For we do not find ourselves in the situations of those who are proactive towards the world (who impose their own objectives on things), but rather those who suffer things, who are being acted upon. It is exactly in this kind of situation that we are bound to be subject to emotional disturbances; but this is the kind of situation that is not easily encompassed by the skill stories. [13]

To conclude, therefore, we could say that the skill stories powerfully exemplify and reinforce one important, and perhaps prevalent, strand in the Zhuangzian account of the place of emotion in the fully realised human life. On this view, the sage is entirely dispassionate, with the salient exception of being passionate about the "wandering" as the exercise of his own craft of living. In fact, it is this passion in wandering that makes the sage dispassionate to everything that is external to this activity. At the same time, given their structural explanatory limitations, the skill stories do not carry sufficient weight so as to undermine or even rule out the alternative, and I would say competing, strand in Zhuangzian thinking about emotions that makes even the sage, at least in some sense, subject to disruptive emotions.[14]

ACKNOWLEDGEMENT

I would like to thank Wim De Reu and the editors for helpful comments on earlier versions of this draft.

NOTES

1. E.g., *Zhuangzi* 2.5, 7.6, 19.10, 22.5. Throughout, my references are from the ctext.org database (https://ctext.org). The translation used is by Burton Watson, with frequent modifications by me.

2. In particular the forger of swords, Engraver Qing, the cicada catcher, and Butcher Ding.

3. I acknowledge that the text never explicitly describes the epistemological process exactly in these terms. But this is the view we arrive at by considering collectively several relevant indications: the importance of an abundance of energy for knowing (19.11), the spirit-based account of ideal cognition (3.1, 19.3), and, perhaps most importantly, the energy-based notion of spirit as the capacity, or the state of mind, that is able to penetrate the patterns of things. In early Chinese Daoist texts, *shen* typically "represents a force, a cosmic energy underlying all existence" (Sterckx, "Searching for Spirit", 27). For the evidence of a close connection, indeed a synonymous use, between *shen* and *qi* in the *Zhuangzi*, see 12.11, 21.9.

4. *Zhuangzi* 19.2. In the same passage, we learn that the perfect man can walk underwater, tread on fire, etc., because he "preserves his pure energy" (*chun qi zhi shou* 純氣之守).

5. *Qing* 情 is the most proximate collective word for different kinds of emotions, but in its basic and more often used meaning it refers to something like the "true condition" of things, or, in ethical contexts, to "characteristically human inclinations" (this is the rendering used in Virág, *The Emotions*, 4). On the other hand, the text often refers to individual emotions, typically "delight, anger, sorrow, joy" (*xinuaile* 喜怒哀樂) without mentioning *qing* 情 at all.

6. For what is perhaps the most comprehensive set of references to the relevant Zhuangzian passages about emotions, see Fraser, "Emotion and Agency". I have relied on much from Fraser's piece in the following brief account of the disruptive emotions.

7. The idea that the emotions are a particular form of *qi* 氣 was widespread in early Chinese thought. The clearest evidence comes from *Xing Zi Ming Chu* (strips 2–3), where emotions (joy, anger, etc.) are referred to as kinds of *qi*. In the *Zhuangzi* itself, it is implicit in some passages, such as *Zhuangzi* 19.8 and 23.19, where emotional disturbances are described in terms of different conditions of *qi*.

8. The most important evidence includes *Zhuangzi* 2.2, 6.1, 22.11.

9. Moeller expresses this as "a feeling one no longer feels" (Moeller, *Daoism Explained*, 65).

10. Møllgaard sees this as a distinction between the appropriate "objective" and inappropriate "subjective" emotions (Møllgaard, *An Introduction to Daoist Thought*, 72).

11. Yearley, "The Perfected Person", 133; Lundberg, "A Meditation on Friendship", 216.

12. Wong, "The Meaning of Detachment"; Olberding, "Sorrow and the Sage".

13. It has been suggested to me by Wim De Reu that there is a level at which a virtuosity in skill can be explanatorily useful even in these situations: just as the virtuosos respect the constraints inherent in their materials and adjust themselves to it, rather than fight against it, so does the sage accept the death of those close to him, as that is not only inevitable but should be accepted as a part of the universal order. I agree, but it still does not quite help us with the difference between activity and passivity. This comes clearly to light when we consider the role of supportive emotions as higher-order responses to one's own activity. What the virtuoso craftsmen enjoy is their doing something; it is much more strained to argue that the sages do, in a similar manner, enjoy the fact that they suffer something.

14. Overall, I would suggest that we should give more consideration to the possibility that the role of emotions in the life of the sage is neither just "ambivalent", as it brings out the inherent ambivalence in the human condition (Fraser, "Emotion and Agency"), nor "multivalent", since emotions can be of different kinds (Virág, *The Emotions*), but incoherent, simply because the *Zhuangzi* was written by different authors that did not necessarily espouse their views with an objective of making their position compatible with different strands in the text.

REFERENCES

Chinese Text Project: https://ctext.org.

Fraser, Chris. "Emotion and Agency in Zhuangzi". *Asian Philosophy* 21, no. 1 (February 2011): 97–121.

Lundberg, Brian. "A Meditation on Friendship". In *Wandering at Ease in the* Zhuangzi, edited by Roger Ames, 211–18. Albany, NY: SUNY Press, 1998.

Moeller, Hans-Georg. *Daoism Explained: From the Dream of the Butterfly to the Fishnet Allegory*. Chicago: Open Court, 2004.

Møllgaard, Eske. *An Introduction to Daoist Thought: Action, Language and Ethics in Zhuangzi*. London: Routledge, 2007.

Olberding, Amy. "Sorrow and the Sage: Grief in the Zhuangzi". *Dao: A Journal of Comparative Philosophy* 6, no. 4 (December 2007): 339–59.

Sterckx, Roel. "Searching for Spirit: Shen and Sacrifice in Warring States and Han Philosophy and Ritual". *Extrême-Orient, Extrême-Occident* 29 (2007): 23–54.

Virág, Curie. *The Emotions in Early Chinese Philosophy*. New York: Oxford, 2017.

Wong, David. "The Meaning of Detachment in Daoism, Buddhism, and Stoicism". *Dao: A Journal of Comparative Philosophy* 5, no. 2 (June 2006): 207–19.

Yearley, Lee. "The Perfected Person in the Radical Zhuangzi". In *Experimental Essays on Zhuangzi*, edited by Victor Mair, 126–36. Honolulu: University of Hawai'i Press, 1983.

Chapter Four

Zhuangzi's Politics from the Perspective of Skill

Tim Connolly

A number of stories in the *Zhuangzi* suggest that politics can benefit from the contributions of the craftsperson. A cook teaches a king "how to nourish life." A duke learns from a wheelwright how to understand the teachings of the sages. Tiger training gives the secret to advising a dangerous and unpredictable ruler. Whereas for Plato and Aristotle philosophers and political scientists guide the craftspeople via their knowledge of the ultimate good, in the *Zhuangzi* insights gleaned from particular crafts are used to enlighten the ruling class.

At the same time, efforts to enlist Zhuangzi's craftspeople as political thinkers are complicated by the scepticism and perspectivism we find elsewhere in the text. The latter aspects of the text's philosophy appear to support a life of detachment rather than one of political engagement. Since the perspective of skill is subject to the same sceptical arguments as any other point of view, why think the craftsperson has a privileged vantage point?

In the first section of this chapter, I examine recent attempts by Bryan W. Van Norden and David Wong to enlist Zhuangzi in the service of politics. While both of their accounts make use of the skill stories we find in the text, ultimately they argue that these stories do not offer a "final vocabulary" of guiding values. In the chapter's second half, I offer a different account of the relationship between the skill stories and the text's sceptical perspectivism, using it as the basis for a new understanding of Zhuangzi's politics from the perspective of skill.

1. TWO RECENT ACCOUNTS OF ZHUANGZI'S POLITICS

Perhaps many scholars will agree with Roger Ames that the *Zhuangzi* is "for the most part addressed to the project of personal realisation, and only derivatively concerned about social and political order" (Ames, "Introduction," 1). However, both of the accounts just mentioned try to enlist Zhuangzi in the service of contemporary politics. In this section we will begin with Wong's use of Zhuangzi for thinking through the challenges facing liberal societies, then turn to Van Norden's discussion of the thinker in the context of contemporary China. Both accounts incorporate the skill stories—focusing on Cook Ding in particular—and attempt to fit these stories into the text's sceptical and perspectival concerns.

1.1. Wong on Zhuangzi and Liberalism

Wong begins from Joseph Raz's discussion of a tension between liberalism and multiculturalism in contemporary societies. According to Raz, enmity is a universal feature of relations between members of different cultural groups; even when relations between these groups are friendly, members of one group will have disapproval for the way of life practised by the other. He sees such conflict as "endemic to value pluralism in all its forms" (Raz, "Multiculturalism," 73). If we pursue one way of life successfully, we will necessarily miss out on the values that are embodied in other ways. While we can approve these other ways in the abstract, a commitment to our own way will mean rejecting them in practice. For this reason, our appreciation for diversity will always be in tension with our allegiance to a particular mode of living.

Wong argues that Zhuangzi also faces this tension between detached appreciation and engaged rejection. A number of stories in the Inner Chapters convey the usefulness of objects that most people will think to be useless. If we can imagine many different uses for an awkwardly large gourd or a gnarled old tree, then all the more so for something like a human life. Yet Wong notes that this appreciation for diversity "is a moral stance at the same time that it constitutes a distancing from one's own original moral commitments" (Wong, *Natural Moralities*, 235). The recognition of a multitude of acceptable values will undermine a person's commitment to the particular ones around which his or her own life is structured. Many scholars have recognised the difficulty of reconciling Zhuangzi's emphasis on viewing things from an overall perspective, withdrawn from any particular way of life, with the kind of sustained engagement that we find in stories like that of Cook Ding.[1]

Wong thinks a solution to the problem facing Zhuangzian and other forms of value pluralism can be derived from within the text itself. This solution consists in seeing how the detached perspective contributes to the engaged one. As he contends, the detached point of view from which we recognise a multiplicity of values "is also an engaged perspective from which our original moral commitments become broader and more inclusive" (ibid., 236). Because we cannot dedicate ourselves to many ways of life at once, we will always end up pursuing some values at the expense of others. Nonetheless, because even those values that we presently reject could turn out to be useful to us in future circumstances, our commitments at any given moment "must remain open-ended and flexible, to a certain degree indeterminate" (ibid., 237).

In another essay, Wong sets this project of open-ended commitment in the context of Zhuangzi's *interrogative scepticism*. This variety of scepticism is not a doctrine but more like an attitude that is reflected in our practice, involving "a continuous willingness to be surprised, and openness to being jolted, even an enjoyment in being jolted" (Wong, "Obsession," 99). Cultivating such an attitude will help us to learn from people we have previously judged to be defective. Applied to the challenge of multiculturalism, Zhuangzi can help us see diversity as something that should be celebrated rather than merely tolerated.[2]

1.2. Van Norden on Zhuangzi and China

Whereas Wong focuses on liberalism and multiculturalism, Van Norden sets Zhuangzi within a debate about contemporary values in China. Recent discussions have focused on Chinese leaders' search for "a usable past," that is, a way of understanding its history that can help to guide its future in an age of materialism (Gewirtz, "Usable Past"). As Van Norden frames the problem, China lacks what Richard Rorty refers to as a "final vocabulary." Without such a vocabulary, there is nothing to give our individual choices significance, to prevent wrongdoing among the citizens or abuse of authority by those in power. What in the Chinese philosophical tradition might provide such a final vocabulary? Confucianism is one option, though in addition to the weakening of familial structures that once bound Chinese society together, Van Norden also thinks it suffers from problems of traditionalism, nepotism, and disregard for the rule of law. Legalism is another resource, but Van Norden contends that it is an amoral system that cannot serve as a source of value.

When we turn to the *Zhuangzi*, however, we notice that the latter thinker promises "a pluralistic acceptance of others that encompasses lifestyle, social class, gender, and physical deformity" (Van Norden, "Ironic Detachment," 6). In the opening story of the text, a fish named Kun transforms into the gigantic Peng Bird and flies high above the earth. When Peng is criticised by the quail, cicada, and dove for flying so high, Zhuangzi says that the problem is that these creatures lack understanding. In another story, the emperors of the North and South Sea decide to drill seven holes into their friend Chaos in order to make him like a human. Each day they drill a hole, until on the seventh day Chaos dies. Van Norden suggests we understand these stories as "political parables," with the underlying message that it is "wrong . . . to coerce others to live according to our own lifestyles in matters of gender roles, sexual preference, religious practices, taste in art, music, popular entertainment, and so on" (ibid., 7). While starting from different contemporary political problems, both Wong and Van Norden draw messages from the text about open-mindedness and diversity.

Van Norden, however, maintains that Zhuangzi is also what Rorty calls an "ironist." He quotes a passage from chapter 2:

> Suppose you and I get into a debate. If you win and I lose, does that really mean that you are right and I am wrong? If I win and you lose, does that really mean that I'm right and you're wrong? Must one of us be right and the other wrong? Or could both of us be right, or both of us wrong? If neither you nor I can know, a third person would be even more benighted. (Ziporyn, *Zhuangzi*, 19)[3]

This and other sceptical passages in the text appear to satisfy Rorty's three criteria for irony: (1) persistent doubts about the final vocabulary we use, (2) a realisation that no arguments drawn from within this vocabulary are sufficient to overcome these doubts, and (3) the belief that our final vocabulary is no "closer to reality" than any of the others (Rorty, *Contingency*, 73).

Van Norden sees Zhuangzi's irony as problematic. Ethically speaking, he writes, "irony is 'the night in which all cows are black': since it regards all positions as equally undermined, an ironic stance cannot be enlisted in support of tolerance or humanitarianism or in opposition to absolutism or cruelty" (Van Norden, "Ironic Detachment," 15). For those of us living in the contemporary world, the absence of ethical purpose will leave us with no limitation on our pursuit of material desires. Ultimately Van Norden opts for the Confucian life of commitment: "A life of unironic commitment is a vulnerable one, but also one that is filled with great meaning and value" (ibid.).

1.3. The Skill Stories and Contemporary Politics

Both Wong and Van Norden rely on a Zhuangzian discourse of pluralism and scepticism to draw conclusions about contemporary political life. Whereas Wong argues that Zhuangzian detachment-in-engagement can enrich our liberal democracy, Van Norden claims the thinker's detachment goes too far and that his philosophy cannot generate values to guide contemporary China. Here I want to focus on the role the skill stories play in each account.

We discover in Zhuangzi, according to Van Norden, "a refreshing valor-ization of the lives of those who tend to be marginalised not just from a Confucian perspective but from many other traditional viewpoints" (Van Norden, "Ironic Detachment," 9). He draws out the political implications of the Cook Ding story by contrasting it with Mengzi's dialogue with King Xuan of Qi (1A7). Noting that the king finds it difficult to witness the suffering of an ox, Mengzi says that cultivated people are also reluctant to view the suffering of animals—that is why they "keep their distance from the kitchen" (trans. Van Norden, *Mengzi*, 9). In the case of Cook Ding, however, it is the kitchen worker who teaches the king the secret of caring for life. While Mengzi's discussion with the king reveals a condescension towards ordinary laborers, the Cook Ding story suggests that "an ordinary butcher, covered in blood and gore, manifests the Way to a greater extent than any so-called gentleman" (Van Norden, "Ironic Detachment," 7). The skill stories teach us that wisdom can come from unexpected places.

In an earlier work, Van Norden also wonders how to reconcile the skill stories with Zhuangzi's scepticism. If Cook Ding is able to "follow Heaven's unwrought perforations [*tian li* 天理] . . . go[ing] by how they already are, playing them as they lay," then this assumes that there is some way that things are in reality, which the skilled craftsperson is able to understand and utilise in his work. But how do we know this is so? As Van Norden asks: "How do we know that it is better to be skillful than clumsy? . . . How do I know that loving skillfulness is not a mistake?" (Van Norden, *Introduction*, 153).[4] Though the text of the *Zhuangzi* does not subject skill to the same level of sceptical scrutiny as it does other aspects of our knowledge, we may wonder what happens when we try to put these two elements of the Inner Chapters together.

Van Norden interprets Zhuangzi's scepticism as "therapeutic" in nature. Zhuangzi does not want us to give up the beliefs we currently hold in favour of other more sensible ones, but rather to change our attitude and behaviour. His sceptical arguments are intended to free us from the power of words, and the beliefs and doctrines they express. In the end, Zhuangzi is a mystic who thinks there is "a kind of knowledge important to human life that cannot be expressed in words" (ibid., 154). Cook Ding provides a "small illustration" of what it means to follow the Way in the sort of tasks we might face from day to day (ibid., 151). In this regard, Van Norden's understanding is similar to other commentators who think that Zhuangzi criticises propositional knowledge (knowing-that) but not practical knowledge (knowing-how).[5]

A strength of Van Norden's discussion of Zhuangzi and contemporary politics is that it draws out an important political implication of the skill stories, making the thinker an interesting competitor to early Confucian ideas about political wisdom. Nonetheless, Van Norden does not say how Zhuang-zi's view of skill fits into his interpretation of Zhuangzi as an ironist who

aims at undermining all philosophical doctrines. What are the political implications of Cook Ding's ability to follow the Way in the course of everyday
life? Could this idea serve as the basis of a Zhuangzian final vocabulary? Or
is it subject to the same fate as other doctrines?

Wong also addresses the problem of reconciling Zhuangzi's scepticism
with the sort of engagement in the world that we find in the skill stories.
Several points distinguish him from Van Norden. First, he thinks that the
scepticism of the Inner Chapters extends further than language and concepts,
implying a "relativity of perception" that imperils even our non-linguistic
access to the way things are (Wong, "Obsession," 95).[6] But at the same time
Zhuangzi often gives prescriptive statements, suggesting that there is at least
something about the Way that can be put into words. Wong therefore rejects
a therapeutic interpretation of Zhuangzi's scepticism because it seems to
miss both the target of his arguments and the depth of his worries about what
we are able to know.

Whereas the therapeutic interpretation suggests that scepticism is a kind
of ladder that we can kick away once we have rid ourselves of our troubled
habits of thinking and talking, Wong wants to look at ways in which scepticism and the engaged life can mutually support one another. While Zhuangzi's scepticism is aimed at undermining certain narrow perspectives that limit
our experience, he thinks its ultimate goal is to *broaden* our perspective so
that we can get more out of life. Experience is an "inexhaustible resource for
new perspectives," some of them revealing genuinely useful features of
things that were invisible to us beforehand.[7] In endowing us with an "openness to being jolted," Zhuangzi's interrogative scepticism allows us to enjoy
the richness of the world we inhabit.[8]

Wong believes that interrogative scepticism has something in common
with the skill stories we find in the text. Both aspects of Zhuangzi's philosophy teach "the need to pay attention to one's present experience"—scepticism through its attitude of questioning, and stories such as that of Cook
Ding through immersion in skill. Paying attention, Wong writes, "yields new
discoveries that undermine one's current beliefs, but also supremely satisfying experiences of activity in response to the matter at hand."[9] However, he
wants to resist two different temptations in reading the skill stories. The first
temptation is to say that these stories suggest "some direct line to the *dao*
unmediated by words or concepts." While experiences of flow may be satisfying, we do not know if they offer us privileged access to the world. The
second is to believe that the values we find in the skill stories are *enduring*
ones. The goal of Zhuangzi's scepticism is precisely to help us avoid the
tendency to "put forward a final thesis" about which values are meaningful.

The view of the perspective of skill that I will lay out in this chapter is
largely in line with Wong's account of Zhuangzi's sceptical perspectivism.
Here, however, I would like to point out two issues with his conclusion

regarding the skill stories. First, his denial that the skill stories can be a source of ultimate values is difficult to reconcile with the king's conviction that Cook Ding has taught him "how to nourish life." Second, while Wong's account suggests that some perspectives may be broader or narrower than other ones, he does not tell us where the skill stories fit within this continuum of possibilities. Even if Zhuangzi wants to undermine any "final thesis" about values, in what sense can the perspective of skill contribute to the broadening of the values at our disposal? In the rest of this chapter, I want to argue that the skill stories do have a special place in Zhuangzi's political thinking and that this "perspective of skill" is compatible with the thinker's scepticism.

2. POLITICS FROM THE PERSPECTIVE OF SKILL

As we have seen, both Van Norden and Wong make use of the Cook Ding story. However, they do not discuss what is perhaps the most important political implication of this passage. Focusing on this aspect will help us better understand the perspective of skill in Zhuangzi's politics.

2.1. Cook Ding and Politics

Cook Ding is able to cut through the ox without any strain to his knife. He compares himself to both an ordinary cook, who has to sharpen his knife once a month, and a good one, who does it once a year. By contrast, he has had the same knife for 19 years, and it is still as sharp as ever. His skill at carving the ox is connected with his practice of following *tian li*. To return once more to the passage mentioned in the last section, he says, "I depend on Heaven's unwrought perforations and strike the larger gaps, following along with the broader hollows. I go by how they already are, playing them as they lay. So my knife has never had to cut through the knotted nodes where the warp hits the weave, much less the gnarled joints of bone." A key part of his craft is his ability to avoid the obstructions mentioned in the last line of this quote.

Even a skilled craftsperson like Cook Ding will come to a point where it appears that there is no way out. When he arrives at a "clustered tangle," he will have to pause before he can go any further. As some scholars have noted, there is a kind of deliberation involved in Cook Ding's work, in that sometimes he has to stop and think about how to navigate a particular difficulty.[10] At these points, the Cook says, "I . . . restrain myself as if terrified, until my seeing comes to a complete halt. My activity slows, and the blade moves ever so slightly" (trans. Ziporyn, *Zhuangzi*, 23). Before he realises it, the ox appears butchered at his feet.

The commentator Wang Fuzhi takes the Cook Ding passage to be relevant to cutting through more substantial things:

> Wherever great fame is at stake, wherever great punishment threatens, wherever great good and great evil are battling, there is great danger and great obstruction there. These are the "gnarled joints." But the dangers and obstructions are not really unavoidable: there is always some hollow within them. The problem is just that we inflate our own feelings, talents, and understanding consciousness into a "thickness" and then try to force our way in with them. (trans. Ziporyn, *Zhuangzi*, 168)

This reading implies that in the political realm as well, there is a skill of navigating through difficult obstructions. Just as an unskilled butcher will both damage the ox and wear out his knife in the process, an unskilled ruler may ruin things by trying to be too forceful. As Wang Fuzhi suggests, such a ruler will do so through overestimating his ability to work through the particular obstruction. The King who is listening to Cook Ding says that he has learned an important secret from the latter's technique.

We can understand the political analogue of Cook Ding's technique by looking more closely at the meaning of *tian li*. While this is the term's only use in the Inner Chapters, passages in the Outer Chapters use other terms translated variously as "the reasonableness of Heaven" (*tian zhi li* 天之理), "principle of Heaven and earth" (*tian di zhi li* 天地之理), "the Great Principle" (*da li* 大理), or "principles of the ten thousand things" (*wan wu zhi li* 萬物之理) (trans. Watson, *Complete Works*). From these passages we can piece together several aspects. The "Autumn Floods" chapter tells us that if one understands the Way (*dao* 道), then one will understand *li*; and if one understands *li*, then one will know "what is appropriate to each situation" (*quan* 權) and thus will be able to avoid being harmed. Or as the "Constrained in Will" chapter says, the sage "follows along with the reasonableness of Heaven" (*tian zhi li*). Therefore he incurs no disaster from Heaven, no entanglement from things, no opposition from man, no blame from the spirits" (trans. Watson, *Complete Works*, 168). Understanding *tian li* is, in other words, of the utmost necessity for avoiding calamity.

While *tian li* is present in all things, it is constantly changing. To return once more to the "Autumn Floods" chapter:

> The Way is without beginning or end, but things have their life and death—you cannot rely on their fulfillment. One moment empty, the next moment full—you cannot depend on their form. The years cannot be held off; time cannot be stopped. Decay, growth, fullness, and emptiness end and then begin again. It is thus that we must describe the plan of the Great Meaning [*da yi zhi fang* 大義之方] and discuss the principles of the ten thousand things [*wan wu zhi li*]. The life of things is a gallop, a headlong dash—with every moment

they alter, with every moment they shift. (trans. Watson, *Complete Works*, 182)

Since things are always shifting, *tian li* is dependent on the particular circumstances of the given moment. Therefore, the same chapter says, it is impossible to approach them with fixed considerations of what is noble (*gui* 貴) or mean (*jian* 賤), or right (*shi* 是) or wrong (*fei* 非).

Since *tian li* is dependent on the particular situation, being able to follow it would seem to involve a special sort of skill. Rather than involving principles or some kind of formula, as Kim-Chong Chong writes, *tian li* means "the spontaneous, dance-like performance of Cook Ding that cannot be emulated by someone who follows a set of rules" (Chong, *Zhuangzi's Critique*, 59). A person at a similar level of skill as Cook Ding could carve the ox in a different way. Here we can begin to see why Zhuangzi privileges craftspeople such as Cook Ding, whose livelihood depends on detailed knowledge of a specific domain. We now turn to the question of how this knowledge fits in with Zhuangzi's perspectivism.

2.2. The Craftsperson and Greater Knowledge

My own understanding of Zhuangzi's scepticism is more like Wong's than Van Norden's. The reason Zhuangzi wants to undermine final vocabularies is not because he wants us to go beyond conventional knowledge until we arrive at a "way without words," but rather because such vocabularies prevent the accumulation of the kind of knowledge of particulars that we need to thrive in a dangerous and ever-shifting world. Zhuangzi's scepticism about final values does not mean we are unable to gather a great deal of knowledge about the world.

When the cicada and the dove mock the high-flying Peng bird, Zhuangzi asks, "What do these two little creatures know? Small knowledge (*xiao zhi* 小知) cannot keep up with great knowledge (*da zhi* 大知); short duration cannot keep up with long duration" (trans. Ziporyn, *Zhuangzi*, 4, with slight revision). However, his point is not that creatures of short duration should admire and try to emulate those of long duration. Since regardless of how long something has lived, there is always something else that has lived longer, it doesn't make sense to try to match the creature that seems to be longest lived. Rather, recognising that these terms are relative, we should refrain from fixed judgements about their application. Similarly for knowledge: no matter how much we know, there is always more to be known.

In an earlier essay, I argue that Zhuangzi's perspectivism is similar to the one sometimes associated with Nietzsche (Connolly, "Perspectivism"). While there is no view that is completely detached from perspective, some ways of looking at the world are broader or more encompassing than others.

By looking at things from multiple perspectives, we gain a more accurate picture of reality. As Nietzsche puts it, "the more eyes, different eyes, we can use to observe one thing, the more complete will our 'concept' of this thing, our 'objectivity,' be" (Nietzsche, *Genealogy*, 3.12). While Zhuangzi does not share Nietzsche's goal of disinterested knowledge of the world, he does believe that having many different perspectives on a particular thing's value can help us flourish in the world.

Zhuangzi's sceptical perspectivism is thus not a means for undermining knowledge but for accumulating it. His technique of perspective shifting is intended to counteract our tendency to become too attached to one point of view, encouraging us to look at things with more and different lenses. The first time we float above our previous perspective and see it from a broader point of view, we realise that all perspectives—including the one we now inhabit—are subject to this kind of shift. What Zhuangzi means by *da zhi* or "greater knowledge" encompasses not just a state in which we have a broader perspective than others, but also an attitude in which we are open to increasing our knowledge further.

According to the "Autumn Floods" chapter, it is only after a person has had the attitudinal shift that comes with greater knowledge that one is prepared to hear about the Heavenly principle. During the flood season, when the Yellow River swells to enormous proportions, the River God believes that he is the most magnificent thing imaginable. But then he travels east, until he arrives at the never-ending vastness of the Northern Sea. In a passage that echoes the opening story of the *Zhuangzi*, Ruo of the Northern Sea tells the River God that the ocean can't be discussed with a well turtle, nor ice with a summer insect, nor the Way with a "nook-and-corner scholar," because each of these creatures is limited: the frog by its habitat, the insect by its season, and the scholar by his doctrines. The River God, on other hand, is now prepared for this discussion: "Now that you have emerged from your dusty banks and had a look at the great ocean, you finally realise how hideous you are! Only now can you understand anything about the Great Guideline [*da li*]" (trans. Ziporyn, *Zhuangzi*, 69). Even the ocean, Ruo goes on to explain, is small compared to the space between Heaven and earth. A person who possesses greater knowledge thus "does not find what is small to be too little nor what is great to be too much, for he knows that comparative measurings are endless. Witnessing the totality of ancient and modern times . . . he knows that the temporal changes of things are endless" (trans. Ziporyn, *Zhuangzi*, 70). Once we have undergone the type of perspective shift associated with greater knowledge, we are prepared to see that the guideline (*li*) we must rely on to navigate through the world is always shifting and changing.

Zhuangzi's craftspeople are privileged not just because they understand one small portion of the natural makeup of things, but because they have the kind of attitude that comes with "greater knowledge." Being immersed in particulars, they recognise the uniqueness of each situation. Cook Ding knows that it takes years to master the specifics of carving an ox, and even so, he will arrive at unforeseen obstructions that will require patience and humility in order to be resolved. He thus embodies the sort of adaptability to particular circumstances, along with its associated virtues, that Zhuangzi thinks is necessary to thrive in the world.

Aware that his own perspective is limited, a person of greater knowledge will look around for the appropriate point of view, the right "eye" through which to view the situation in question. In the case of Cook Ding, his ability to cut through these difficult places involves a re-envisioning of the dimensions at hand: "For the joints have spaces between them and the very edge of the blade has no thickness at all. When what has no thickness enters into an empty space, it is vast and open, with more than enough room for the blade" (trans. Ziporyn, *Zhuangzi*, 22). As with the "Autumn Floods" passage, the capacity to shift between perspectives is indispensable for following *tian li*.

2.3. Applying Skill to the Political Realm

The model of craft in the political realm suggests a distinctive mode of power. The political philosopher and diplomat Joseph Nye famously distinguished between "hard" and "soft" varieties of power. In his book *The Craftsman*, Richard Sennett notes the similarities between craft and soft power:

> In hand coordination the issue turns on inequalities of strength; the unequal hands working together rectify weakness. Restrained power of the craftsman's sort, coupled with release, takes a further step. The combination provides the craftsman's body self-control and enables accuracy of action; blind, brute force is counterproductive in handiwork. All these ingredients—cooperation with the weak, restrained force, release after attack—are present in "soft power": this doctrine, too, seeks to transcend counterproductive blind force. Here is the craft contained in "state-craft." (Sennett, *Craftsman*, 171)

The restrained mode of power described in this passage calls to mind Cook Ding's ability to find the frictionless point. The difficulty is with translating this conception of the craftsperson's power into the world of politics. How to get from "craft" to "state-craft"?

For Zhuangzi, the political realm is a dangerous and ever-shifting place. Since getting involved in politics is a good way to get oneself killed, perhaps the best solution is not to be involved at all. But since one may inevitably find oneself entangled in such affairs, one must develop the right sort of survival skills. Knowledge of different perspectives can enlarge our imagination for thinking about dilemmas of power. The analogy between Cook Ding's skill at carving the ox and the political craft of navigating difficult obstructions suggests that for any political dilemma, there is a perspective from which it can be resolved without counterproductive blind force. The ability to shift between perspectives until we have found the appropriate one will be indispensable for making our way in the political realm.

In one story from the "In the Human World" chapter, Yan He is the tutor to the crown prince of Wei. The trouble is that the crown prince is not a good person. If Yan He leaves him unrestrained, he will bring ruin to the state; but if he tries to restrain him, the crown prince will have him killed. So Yan He goes to Qu Boyu, asking him how to navigate this dilemma.

The first part of Qu Boyu's answer is that he must be "compromising in appearance" and "harmonious in mind." Yet, he says, even this may not be enough, because the compromising aspect can corrupt him internally, and the inner harmony can lead to an external reputation that could eventually destroy him. As we know from the discussion of *tian li* above, focusing on the right principles will not allow us to survive in a constantly shifting world. There is no formula that we can use to navigate the dangers that await us in the political realm.

However, we do need to approach these dangers with the right attitude. Qu Boyu next appeals to the perspective of the praying mantis: "Don't you know the story of the praying mantis? It flailed its pincers around to stop an oncoming chariot wheel, not realising the task was beyond its powers. This is how it is for those with 'great talents.' Be careful, be cautious" (trans. Ziporyn, *Zhuangzi*, 29). The message is that we must approach such tasks with the appropriate caution and humility. The reference to "great talents" again shows the logic of greater and smaller knowledge. If one has not had the awakening that comes with greater knowledge, then one will not realise that there is always something larger than oneself.

In a passage in the Miscellaneous Chapters, Qu Boyu is described in terms of his flexibility: "Qu Boyu has been going along for sixty years and has changed sixty times. There was not a single instance in which what he called right in the beginning he did not in the end reject and call wrong" (trans. Watson, *Complete Works*, 288, with slight revision). However, this scepticism about final values does not mean that he is unable to make any contribution to the human world. Rather, it endows him with precisely the kind of flexibility that enables him to move back and forth fluidly between different domains. The passage from the Miscellaneous Chapters goes on to suggest that being aware of the limits of what we know is a necessary precondition for advancing beyond them: "Men all pay homage to what understanding understands, but no one understands enough to rely upon what understanding does not understand and thereby come to understand. Can we call this anything but great perplexity?" (trans. Watson, *Complete Works*, 288). Because Qu Boyu is aware of these limitations, he is as prepared as any of the characters who populate the *Zhuangzi* to give meaningful advice about how to survive in the world.

Qu Boyu's ultimate answer to Yan He appeals to the method of tiger training:

> Don't you know how the tiger trainer handles it? He doesn't feed the beast live animals for fear of arousing its lust for killing. He doesn't feed it uncut sides of meat for fear of arousing its lust for dismemberment. He carefully times out the feedings and comprehends the creature's propensity for rage. The tiger is a different species from man but can be tamed through affection for its feeder. The ones it kills are the ones who cross it. (trans. Ziporyn, *Zhuangzi*, 29)

The skilled trainer understands the specific nature of the kind of creature he is dealing with and uses this knowledge to ensure not only his own survival, but also to manage the creature in question. The skill of the tiger trainer is clearly relevant to Yan He's role as minister: the two domains share enough of their particular features that knowledge can be transferred from the one to the other. Yet the very end of Qu Boyu's advice also supports a particularism about the use of one's skills. Even a horse, he says, could kill someone who goes about caring for it the wrong way. So it is not just that we must understand the art of tiger training in order to be successful ministers, but that we must grasp the particular difficulties that abound in every situation we may encounter.

Qu Boyu's approach consists not in fixed principles but in finding the appropriate lens through which to view Yan He's situation. Finding such a perspective is a matter of knowledge and skill. The *Zhuangzi*, as I understand it, can be understood not just as a collection of arguments meant to ensure that we recognise the limitations of our own knowledge, but also as a collection of different perspectives that are meant to ensure our survival in a dangerous world.

3. CONCLUSION

At the end of his article, Van Norden sides with Confucian commitment rather than Zhuangzian scepticism about a final vocabulary. He contends that none of the moral revolutionaries of the modern age—Abraham Lincoln, Mohandas Gandhi, Martin Luther King Jr.—were ironists in a Zhuangzian sense. "Indeed," he continues, "I cannot myself think of anyone who played a significant role in any major progressive social movement who was an ironist." He argues that, in contrast with Rorty, "one of Zhuangzi's deep insights" is that there is a "deep connection" between irony about values and doing everything in one's power to avoid a life of politics (Van Norden, "Ironic Detachment," 13).

As I have argued, Zhuangzi's doubts about our ordinary moral and political values are compatible with political engagement. The focus on greater knowledge allows us to see the values—humility, patience, respect for particularity—that might form the basis of a Zhuangzian final vocabulary. Whereas our ordinary values may be undermined by a shift in perspective in which we come to see their limitedness, these latter values are only deepened by this kind of experience.

Because the skilled craftsperson embodies such values, he or she is able to find the "frictionless point" from which any dilemma can be resolved. The skilled craftsman is not just one useful source among many for thinking about Zhuangzi's politics. Rather, the ability to find the "frictionless point" that is displayed by a skilled person is the key to understanding Zhuangzi's political views as a whole. Of course, there are important differences between the politician and the craftsperson. Perhaps the most significant is that the latter has a well-defined aim—to carve an ox, train a tiger, etc.—that we can use to evaluate his or her skill.[11] For Zhuangzi, however, the analogy between the two realms arises from a shared method for dealing with obstructions. If, as Wang Fuzhi suggests, larger affairs also have their gnarled joints, as well as the spaces in between through which safe passage can be navigated, then a successful politics should also be able to find these spaces and navigate them as effortlessly as Cook Ding carving the ox. If those engaged in politics were to imitate the skilled craftsperson, society would be changed for the better.[12]

NOTES

1. Wong cites Nivison, "Hsün Tzu." For further discussion, see Lai and Chiu, "Enlightened Engagement," and Connolly, "Perspectivism."
2. Ivanhoe derives a similar view from the *Zhuangzi*, which he names "ethical promiscuity." Emphasising how we can learn from those whose lives instantiate different sorts of goods, he uses this view to argue that we should celebrate (rather than merely tolerate) diversity, seeing it as a feature of the good life. See Ivanhoe, "Relativist?," and Ivanhoe, "Pluralism." Karyn Lai similarly highlights the significance of Zhuangzi's view for "an increasingly globalised world that is characterised by a plurality of ethical and value commitments" ("Philosophical Reasoning," 373).
3. All translations of passages from the *Zhuangzi* are taken from Ziporyn.
4. For further discussion of Zhuangzi's scepticism about skill, see Eric Schwitzgebel's chapter 7 in this volume. While I disagree with Schwitzgebel's position there, engagement with his arguments has led me to a more careful formulation of the view defended below.
5. Some prominent examples of this view include Ivanhoe, "Zhuangzi on Skepticism," and Eno, "Cook Ding's Dao." For a recent discussion and critique, see Chiu, "Zhuangzi's Knowing-How."
6. For a discussion of this point, see Huang, "Ethics of Difference," 84, n. 20.
7. Ibid.
8. Ibid.
9. Ibid.
10. Ibid.
11. I thank Karyn Lai for this point.

12. I am grateful to Karyn Lai, Wai Wai Chiu, and Eric Schwitzgebel for their helpful feedback on this chapter. I presented a much earlier version of this chapter at the SUNY New Paltz Department of Philosophy in 2015; I thank David Elstein and several others there for providing me with direction.

REFERENCES

Ames, Roger T. Introduction to *Wandering at Ease in the* Zhuangzi: *A Postmodern Critique*, edited by Roger T. Ames, 1–14. Albany, NY: SUNY Press, 1998.

Chiu, Wai Wai. "Zhuangzi's Knowing-How and Skepticism." *Philosophy East and West* 68, no. 4 (October 2018): 1062–1084.

Chong, Kim-Chong. *Zhuangzi's Critique of the Confucians: Blinded by the Human*. Albany, NY: SUNY Press, 2016.

Connolly, Tim. "Perspectivism as a Way of Knowing in the *Zhuangzi*." *Dao: A Journal of Comparative Philosophy* 10, no. 4 (2011): 487–505.

Eno, Robert. "Cook Ding's Dao and the Limits of Philosophy." In *Essays on Skepticism, Relativism, and Ethics in the* Zhuangzi, edited by Paul Kjellberg and Philip J. Ivanhoe, 127–51. Albany, NY: SUNY Press, 1996.

Gewirtz, Paul. "Xi, Mao, and China's Search for a Usable Past." *ChinaFile*, January 14, 2014. https://www.chinafile.com/xi-mao-and-chinas-search-usable-past.

Huang, Yong. "The Ethics of Difference in the *Zhuangzi*." *Journal of the American Academy of Religion* 78, no. 1 (March 2010): 65–99.

Ivanhoe, Philip J. "Pluralism, Toleration, and Ethical Promiscuity." *Journal of Religious Ethics* 37, no. 2 (2009): 311–29.

———. "Was Zhuangzi a Relativist?" In *Essays on Skepticism, Relativism, and Ethics in the* Zhuangzi, edited by Paul Kjellberg and Philip J. Ivanhoe, 196–214. Albany, NY: SUNY Press, 1996.

———. "Zhuangzi on Skepticism, Skill, and the Ineffable Dao." *Journal of the American Academy of Religion* 61, no. 4 (1993): 639–54.

Lai, Karyn L. "Philosophy and Philosophical Reasoning in the *Zhuangzi*: Dealing with Plurality." *Journal of Chinese Philosophy* 33, no. 3 (2006): 365–74.

Lai, Karyn L., and Wai Wai Chiu. "*Ming* in the *Zhuangzi Neipian*: Enlightened Engagement." *Journal of Chinese Philosophy* 40, nos. 3–4 (2013): 527–43.

Nietzsche, Friedrich. *On the Genealogy of Morals* and *Ecce Homo*. Translated by Walter Kaufmann and R. J. Hollingdale. New York: Vintage, 1989.

Nivison, David. "Hsün Tzu and Chuang Tzu." In *Chinese Texts and Philosophical Contexts: Essays Dedicated to Angus C. Graham*, edited by Henry Rosemont Jr., 129–42. LaSalle, IL: Open Court, 1991.

Raz, Joseph. "Multiculturalism: A Liberal Perspective." *Dissent* 41, no. 1 (1994): 67–79.

Rorty, Richard. *Contingency, Irony, and Solidarity*. New York: Cambridge University Press, 1989.

Sennett, Richard. *The Craftsman*. New Haven, CT: Yale University Press, 2008.

Van Norden, Bryan W. *Introduction to Classical Chinese Philosophy*. Indianapolis: Hackett, 2011.

———. *Mengzi: With Selections from Traditional Commentaries*. Indianapolis: Hackett, 2008.

———. "Zhuangzi's Ironic Detachment and Political Commitment." *Dao: A Journal of Comparative Philosophy* 15, no. 1 (2016): 1–17.

Watson, Burton. *The Complete Works of Chuang Tzu*. New York: Columbia University Press, 1968.

Wong, David. *Natural Moralities: A Defense of Pluralistic Relativism*. New York: Oxford University Press, 2006.

———. "Zhuangzi and the Obsession with Being Right." *History of Philosophy Quarterly* 22, no. 2 (April 2005): 91–107.

Ziporyn, Brook. *Zhuangzi: The Essential Writings, with Selections from Traditional Commentaries*. Indianapolis: Hackett, 2009.

Chapter Five

Elusive Masters, Powerless Teachers, and Dumb Sages

Exploring Pedagogic Skills in the Zhuangzi

Romain Graziani

"You must keep quite still," her inspiration told her. "You cannot leave room for any land of desire; not even the desire to question. You must also shed the judiciousness with which you perform tasks. You must deprive the mind of all tools and not allow it to be used as a tool. Knowledge is to be discarded by the mind, and willing: you must cast off reality and the longing to turn to it. You must keep to yourself until head, heart, and limbs are nothing but silence. But if, in this way, you attain the highest selflessness, then finally outer and inner will touch each other as if a wedge that had split the world had popped out!"

—Robert Musil, *The Man without Qualities*, 531–32

Jamais l'homme ne se possède plus que dans le silence: hors de là, il semble se répandre, pour ainsi dire, hors de lui-même et se dissiper par le discours; de sorte qu'il est moins à soi qu'aux autres.

—Abbé Dinouart, *L'Art de se taire*, 38

吾安得忘言之人而與之言哉？
How shall I find someone oblivious to words, and how shall I speak with him?[1]

—*Zhuangzi* 莊子, "External Realities" ("*Wai wu*" 外物)

This chapter examines the question of skills in the *Zhuangzi* through the lens of the very peculiar relationships between master and disciples that are developed across a wealth of stories and dialogues centred on the possibility—and the limits—of verbal instruction.

The most recurrent type of human relationship in the *Zhuangzi* is made of encounters and conversations between people who are held as sages and people who come to pose questions or ask to be instructed in the Way. Lucid or ludic, iconic or ironic, comic or cosmic, parodic or parochial, the guises that masters and sages take are manifold, and, as we will see, this unsettling variety can be seen as the consequence on the narrative plane of the *Zhuang-zi*'s lessons on the pitfalls of pedagogy, the dangers of public recognition, and the futility of verbal instruction.

We can subsume these encounters under the generic category of the "master-disciple relationship," though, properly speaking, most characters in the category of masters are just persons who are supposed to be knowledge-able or spiritually more advanced, while the characters in the position of disciples are not necessarily involved in a steady or long-term learning rela-tionship with the superior person they approach. Indeed, we only find a scarcity of scenes portraying masters and disciples in the literal sense of these terms. In spite of the overwhelming number of pedagogic dialogues, in the whole *Zhuangzi* there are only nine regular relationships between masters and disciples, among which a good many are just alluded to but never de-scribed or represented.[2]

Aside from a few ideas and aphorisms from the *Laozi*, there are no posi-tive instructions based on a repository of texts or a set of codified norms and patterns of conduct. Relationships between masters and disciples are charac-terised by a systematic tendency either to ignore or to disparage education centred on the rote learning of texts, the memorisation of moral precedents, and the acquisition of ritual manners. Zhuangzi's freely recreated Confucius happens to lament about his failure to instruct and transform people through writings from the past and ritual manners. After being lectured by Zi Sanghu 子桑雽, he dumps all his books—thereby eliciting intense affection from his disciples (chapter 19, "*Da sheng*" 達生).

Virtue (*de* 德) itself appears not as the expected result of a moral educa-tion but as the by-product of actions undertaken for other ends than attaining virtue.[3] In chapter 32, "*Lie Yukou*" (列禦寇), the author alerts to the danger of cultivating virtue while being aware of what one is doing. The *Zhuangzi* has a knack for turning the wisdom of his age upon its head with the flick of a few aphorisms:

> There is no greater evil than for the mind to be aware of virtue, and to act as though it were a pair of eyes. For when it starts acting like a pair of eyes, it will peer out from within, and when it peers out from within, it is ruined. There are five types of dangerous virtue, of which inner virtue is the worst. (trans. Watson, *Complete Works*, 359)

Here is the first paradox about the figure of the master in the *Zhuangzi*: we keep seeing people in the position of teaching urging their listeners to dispense with everything they have learned so far and to revert to a state of ignorance, oblivion, or stupidity. Yi Erzi 意而子 refuses to teach Xu You 許由 on the grounds that he has been distorted and amputated by his Confucian education. Hong Meng (Vast-Veiled, 鴻蒙) in chapter 11, "*Zai you*" (在宥), urges Jiang Yun (General of Cloud, 將雲) in the most infuriating way to destroy all his knowledge, his awareness of things, and his sense of identity. The same kind of personal annihilation is urged by Xu Free-of-Daemons (徐無鬼) on Marquis Wu of Wei（Wei Wuhou 魏武侯) in chapter 24, "*Xu Wugui*" (徐無鬼). This harsh rejection of positive knowledge and traditional education[4] is not even the object of an explanation, as if this truth could only dawn on someone, all of a sudden, without any resort to reasons and arguments.

Some of the greatest lessons delivered in the *Zhuangzi* are put in the mouth of unconventional or unseemly figures of mastery: in chapter 18, a skull gives a nightly sermon to Master Zhuang on the royal felicity of being dead, free from hierarchy and oppression, and on the misfortunes of human life. In chapter 4, a gigantic tree upbraids carpenter Shi (Jiang Shi 匠石) for his ignorant arrogance. In chapter 5, amputated persons, hence former criminals, are in the position of instructing their interlocutor (as will be dealt with below). In chapter 29, "*Dao zhi*" (盜跖), the feral criminal and warlord Zhi 跖, who plagues the whole country, forcefully incriminates Confucius for employing ritual niceties and sophisticated words to tart up his moral debauchery. In chapter 24, a child on Mount Tai Wei 太隗 proves able to provide an answer to crucial questions, whereas the seven sages are lost and at their wits' end.

Most judicious observations and helpful advice in the *Zhuangzi* are not part of a pedagogic plan: they are just wise or penetrating words given on a specific occasion, in the context of a singular encounter. The instruction dialogues are most of the time written against the expectation readers may expect from the wise guidance of a master. The numerous episodes dealing with the awakening of the mind or with the sudden liberation from worries and anxiety, all suggest that what nurtures the mind is not so much to be found in texts or in wise sayings from the past as in observing and listening to people from all walks of life who do not have any particular ambition to instruct. Such are the Butcher Ding who chops up an ox in front of Lord Wen Hui, the Wheelwright Bian, the man who swims in the perilous waterfalls of Lüliang, the ferryman handling his oar at Goblet Deeps (Shang shen 觴深), the old fisherman (Yu fu 漁父), the man who will not use a crank wheel to draw water from the well and who protests against the detrimental effects of technological inventions on human nature (chapter 12, "*Tian di*" 天地); such are the Carpenter Qing, the cicada catcher, and the tax collector, ironically called Free-Spending from the Northern Palace (Beigong she 北宮奢). Different as they may be, all these characters, when describing what they do, how they work, or how they cope with things, exert an elating or enlightening effect on their interlocutor. Their words, often preceded by a demonstration of their craftsmanship, have the virtue of a great lesson for the reader, miles away from the classical scene of instruction that casts a revered master surrounded by a legion of pious and zealous disciples. They give a lesson "in passing," without any deliberate or assertive tone. We can see in these episodes how authentic mastery shifts from a textual knowledge to various forms of know-how, from theoretical rules to practical skills, from ancient writings to a "live performance." We have here the intimation of an idea that was at the time certainly hard to admit: that mastery and knowledge can be acquired without a master and a proper education.[5] And yet people need a master like Bohun wuren or Calabash (Huzi 壺子) in order to understand that they hardly need a master in the conventional sense. In the few regular scenes of instructions we have mentioned above, a straightforward and positive teaching that can serve as a direct lesson (for the disciple and for the reader) is rather the exception. I have found only ten cases of masters or sages who kindly answer and advise those who come to enquire.[6] Indeed, in the majority of pedagogic episodes where one is credited to know and the other is willing to learn, something irregular happens, and the encounter takes an unexpected turn, far from a clear scene of instruction in which the demonstration of knowledge and mastery would take place for the benefit of the student. Xu You, after refusing to take Yi Erzi as his disciple, finally changes his mind after hearing his metaphoric argument about the possible regrowth of his amputated nose (chapter 6, "*Dazongshi*" 大宗師). Confucius, after hearing of his student Yan Hui's 顏回 progress in the art of forgetting, asks him to become his disciple (chapter 6). In chapter 5, "*De chong fu*," Confucius scornfully rejects Shushan Wuzhi (Calm-Mountain No-Toes, 叔山無趾) and, after listening to his response, apologises and tries to retain him, but to no avail. In the same chapter, Confucius aspires to become Wang Tai's (Wang Broken-Down, 王駘) disciple, a rival master in the state of Lu. In chapter 11, "*Zai you*," Guang Chengzi (Vast-Accomplishment, 廣成子), after rebuffing the Yellow Emperor, rejoices at his spiritual reform that results from a prolonged ascetic retreat and begins to instruct him. Even Master Zhuang, after his famous lesson on the great use of uselessness, is embarrassingly belied by his host's decision to put to roast the goose that cannot sing and spare the one who can; when asked by his disciples for an explanation, Master Zhuang only gets away with a rhetorical parade.

In most pedagogic episodes, pupils or disciples end up mystified or bemused. The stances taken by many characters portrayed as sages or as masters do not follow any clear line but seem perfectly calibrated to unsettle, confuse, humiliate, or silence their interlocutors. What is, then, the purpose of these short fictions?

To provide a set of partial answers to these questions, I will now examine the various ways in which the authors annihilate and reinvent the possibility of instruction, specifically how they promote new figures of mastery and how they distribute roles between sages, masters, teachers, and disciples. Often the real lesson for the reader diverges from what is said in the conversation with a sage: it is rather the personal reflection on the failure of the encounter, the master's refusal to spell out his views about the Way, or the brutal flustering of the questioner that constitute the pedagogic gain for the reader.

1. THE SAGE WHO WOULD NOT TEACH

Since the relationships between those who know and those who want to learn are fraught with obstacles, misunderstandings, and tensions, we can surmise that it is precisely these conflicts that form the lessons imparted to readers, who must thus ask themselves how to decipher and construe these encounters.

Our first working hypothesis is that if the exchanges are so problematic between masters and disciples, it is because the very conversations bear on the limits of teaching and teachers, as is evidenced by the recurring conversations about the impossibility of saying something sensible about the Way (though in fact a lot is said). Because of the initial discrepancy between the expectations of disciples and the perspective of masters, there can hardly be any unproblematic continuity between the master-disciple relationship and the author-reader relationship. [7]

It should be here reminded that in any reading of fiction, there is an ongoing (though often implicit) dialogue between author, narrator, characters, and readers. The axis between the author and the reader can run parallel to the one between the narrator and the characters, or it can be tangential. For instance, when, in the *Analects*, Confucius is depicted in a scene in which he instructs his disciples, the teaching is also valid in the same terms for the readers, who stand, so to speak, at the periphery of his circle of listeners.

In contradistinction to this classical pedagogic pattern, in the *Zhuangzi* the recurrent failures of the instruction, marked by the refusal of the master to say anything, become for the reader a "meta-lesson" bearing on the possibility and the limits of instruction. But even so, we as readers hardly get positive guidance from the author: there is no direct authoritative intervention to control the beliefs or the comprehension of the reader. The anonymous authors of these pedagogic episodes leave their characters to work out their own fates, and readers, or scholars, may often disagree on the ultimate meaning of a story. For instance, in chapter 7, *"Ying di wang"* (應帝王), in the story of the encounter between the evil charlatan Ji Xian 季咸 and Master Calabash, should we understand Liezi's three years of seclusion and service to his pigs and his wife as a self-inflicted punishment, or just as an ethical choice to conquer his autonomy? In chapter 22, *"Zhi bei you,"* is Master Non-Being (Wu You 無有) a complete hoax, or is he the paradoxical image of absolute perfection? And then how should we interpret the abstruse, if not absurd, praise that Bright-Dazzlement (Guang Yao 光曜) gives him? In chapter 5, did Bohun wuren deliberately provoke the bickering between his two disciples, the former criminal Shentu Jia and Prime Minister Zi Chan, by simply having them seated on the same mat? We are often left without the guidance of explicit authorial evaluation; we can only eavesdrop on the characters and assume that in such and such situations they say something serious and important and that, at other times, the authors are just playfully puzzling us. The defining traits of authentic mastery are all the harder to perceive and define. When, in chapter 21, Bohun wuren praises the archery of non-archery (*bu she zhi she* 不射之射), or when in chapter 7 Master Calabash describes the nine abysses (*yuan* 淵), are they jokingly mystifying Liezi? We cannot easily infer what the author's own judgement is. In pedagogic dialogues, the narrators rarely tell us what to think, they seldom employ direct judgement, and readers teeter between philosophical puzzlement and comic delight, as if, morally speaking, the authors refused to exert definite control over their readers' range of conclusive judgement about each instruction scene.

Hence the question: what kind of mastery characterises these sages who manage to transform without instructing or give lessons without teaching? This question is inextricably tied to the literary skills and schemes implemented by the authors of these stories, who faced the challenge of denouncing the limitations of verbal communication and textual knowledge while maintaining the possibility of imparting a genuine lesson to the readers. In particular, the authors had to wrestle with difficulties in the portrayals, descriptions, and dialogues of eminent figures whose superiority lies precisely in the fact that they are reluctant to speak and remain hardly visible.

The recursive and paradoxical rejection of language is in keeping with the general tendency in the *Zhuangzi* to depict sages as unwilling to enroll, train, or teach disciples. Teaching is almost never a way of life and least of all a livelihood; there are, as we mentioned, several exceptions, but they all remain problematic insofar as the content of the teaching is barely explicit and as the master's economic relationship with his disciples is never mentioned. Often the mastery a character is credited with remains unseen or unproved. Most sages have nothing to say, or will say nothing; they dodge issues and deflect questions, or only give confusing methods for self-improvement. In chapter 11, *"Zai you,"* Hong Meng, depicted as a raving lunatic, hops around like a sparrow and slaps his thighs; when questioned for the first time by

General of Cloud, he blurts out evasive syllables and then whisks off. In chapter 21, "*Tian Zifang*," Wenbo Xuezi (Master-Snow-Warm-Uncle, 溫伯雪子) refuses to meet up with some gentlemen of Lu. He finally obliges but ends up weary and bitterly disappointed with the petty ritual experts he saw. In the first story of chapter 22, "*Zhi bei you*," in which the author facetiously creates an effect of semantic confusion and sonic saturation by the obsessive repetition of the three characters *zhi* 智, *wei* 謂, and *dao* 道, the conceptual character Consciousness (*zhi* 知) asks Meaning-of-Non-Action (Wuwei wei 無為謂):

> What sort of pondering, what sort of cogitation does it take to know the Way?
> What sort of surroundings, what sort of practices does it take to find rest in the Way? What sort of path, what sort of procedure will get me to the Way? (trans. Watson, *Complete Works*, 234)

Meaning-of-Non-Action proves unable to answer these questions. "It wasn't that he just didn't answer—he didn't know how to answer!" (trans. Watson, ibid.). Then, Mad Hump (Kuang Qu 狂屈) is asked the same questions, but "as he was about to say something, he forgot what he was about to say" (ibid.). These two supposed sages appear as senile dimwits until the Yellow Emperor, met shortly afterwards by Consciousness, explains to him that only Meaning-of-Non-Action is in the right. This remark finally gives us a hint of the author's view on the characters. The puzzling advice the Yellow Emperor gives to Consciousness[8] could lead us to hold him as a sage—albeit a strange sage—but, surprisingly, he confesses being nowhere near the Way insofar as he is still subjected to the logic of analysis and explanation. Drawing on the aphorisms of the *Daodejing* about speaking and knowing, the story of these three encounters shows that sages and teachers are in an irreconcilable position: those who teach have no communication with the Way, and those who enjoy the Way can neither communicate nor teach. In this regard, there can be no direct lesson from a sage. And if the author did not make a comment through the Yellow Emperor for Consciousness, to whom the reader can but identify, the episode of the encounter with Mad Hump and with Meaning-of-Non-Action would remain wholly unintelligible. It is the literary creation of a scene in which is intimated the impossibility for the sage to impart a lesson that provides the real occasion of a lesson for the reader. In other words, the sage cannot teach, but the literary skills of the anonymous authors take this impossibility as the object of a narrative that becomes a didactic episode. The string of scenes which use this narrative pattern show how sages are unable to provide a direct lesson; only teachers situated at an inferior level can give an inkling of how sages see the world and act accordingly. As Confucius concludes after seeing Wenbo Xuezi: "With that kind of man, one glance tells you that the Way is there before you. What room does that leave for any possibility of speech?" (*Zhuangzi* 21; trans. Watson, *Complete Works*, 223).

The narrative device that draws on the necessary dissociation between the silent sage and the teacher who speaks and instructs is again implemented in chapter 21. Tian Zifang often quotes the wise sayings of a certain Qi Gong 谿 工, who struck him as a judicious man when speaking about the Way. But when asked by his lord if he regards this Qi Gong as his master (*shi* 師), Tian Zifang explains that his real master is Master Going-Along from the Eastern Wall (Dongguo Shunzi 東郭順子), whom he usually never mentions for the following reason:

> He's the kind of man who is True—the face of a human being, the emptiness of Heaven. He follows along and keeps tight hold of the True; pure, he can encompass all things. If men do not have the Way, he has only to put on a straight face, and they are enlightened; he causes men's intentions to melt away. But how could any of this be worth praising!

> Zifang retired from the room, and Marquis Wen, stupefied, sat for the rest of the day in silence.

Finally, after hearing Zifang, the lord summons his ministers and confesses:

> I used to think that the words of the wisdom of the sages and the practices of benevolence and righteousness were the highest ideal. But now that I have heard about Zifang's teacher, my body has fallen apart, and I feel no inclination to move; my mouth is manacled, and I feel no inclination to speak. (trans. Watson, *Complete Works*, 221–22)

This brief didactic episode draws its dynamic from the constant switch between the merits of speech and the higher virtue of remaining silent. Tian Zifang as a learned man and court adviser entertains his lord with wise words, and, in their conversations, he often happens to quote a perceptive man he knows from his neighbourhood. But when it comes to genuine superiority, he admits that his real master cannot be properly quoted or described. The irrepressible power of his holy presence transforms people and can hardly be expressed. Not a single word is reported from this Master Shun; the sage here again will not be heard. As to Lord Wu, he remains speechless and loses the desire to talk after hearing of this extraordinary man. Mastery is cleaved between silent sages and speaking masters. In a didactic setting and in the context of an economic relationship with his lord, Tian Zifang is happy to speak, quote, and teach, but he remains aware that superior communication and moral influence take other channels, such as a radiant, vibrant, and disarming presence. Those who instruct, advise, and teach have certainly social skills, but they embody an inferior form of mastery. The greatest merit of this story perhaps is not to prompt to silence those who speak and teach, but on the contrary to make silence speak of itself as it were: Tian Zifang explains why he has always remained silent about Master Shun and how the latter deeply moves other people with his eloquent and silent presence. As to Lord Wu, after being dumfounded upon hearing his adviser's words, he explains to his ministers why he does not feel like talking any longer.

In chapter 13, "*Tian dao,*" Laozi, when attacked by the arrogant Shi Chengji who tries to unsettle him by denying him the quality of a sage, opposes a silence that exerts an uncanny therapeutic effect. The headstrong man comes back to the old master the next day without any aggression. Now Laozi can begin to give him a piece of his mind because the man has no more defences to oppose. The sage's pedagogy here again consists in abstaining from starting a quarrel or engaging in disputation: his peaceful and passive silence is enough to disarm his opponent.

2. THE SKILL OF HIDING ONE'S SKILLS

The sage is stupid and blockish (*shengren yu chun* 聖人愚芚).
—*Zhuangzi*, chapter 2 ("*Qiwulun*" 齊物論); trans. Watson, *Complete Works*,
16

2.1. The Strategy of Insanity and Senility

The first two characters visited by Consciousness in chapter 22 ("*Zhi bei you*"), Meaning-of-Non-Action and Mad Hump, appear as senile persons struck with amnesia (trans. Watson, *Complete Works*, 234). Other sages come across as being embarrassingly stupid. If they ever deserve to be called masters (*zi* 子), that which they master remains invisible in their language and can only be inwardly experienced. As we saw above, Hong Meng appears in his first encounter with Jiang Yun as a crazed loner (chapter 11). In chapter 23, "*Gengsang Chu,*" the eponymous character, after dismissing his smart and perceptive attendants, "shared his house with drabs and dowdies and employed the idle and indolent to wait on him" (trans. Watson, *Complete Works*, 248). In chapter 1, Jie Yu 接輿, "the madman of Chu," frightens and confuses Jian Wu 肩吾 with his unhinged (*jing ting* 逕庭) words and speeches wide off the mark (*bu jin ren qing*不近人情). When Jian Wu asks Lian Shu (Uncle-Who-Links 連叔) for an explanation, he comes to realise that he is the one who lacks a proper understanding, and that his failure to grasp Jie Yu's words only reveals how blind and deaf he is. Here again, we witness a necessary dissociation between the figure of the sage (Jie Yu) and that of the teacher Lian Shu: someone who masters the workings of life leaves ordinary people dumbfounded, and he who wants to learn can only benefit from someone able to decipher the superior man and translate his attitude and utterances into the didactic form of a lesson, just like the Yellow Emperor interpreted the attitude of the two apparently senile masters Meaning-of-Non-Action and Mad Hump for the perplexed wanderer Consciousness.

If we met people like Mad Hump or Jie Yu in real life, we would obviously judge them mentally unfit to impart anything worth our while. But the implicit message conveyed by the author is that we should hold them as sages, thanks to the insertion of another character who speaks for them and provides a rationale for their disturbing outlook. The same didactic narrative device is used in chapter 6 when Zigong asks Confucius about the unseemly behaviour of two friends who sing in front of the corpse of their late companion Zi Sanghu. Confucius extols the superhuman capacities of the two uncouth lads and confesses that he is himself trapped in the realm of human conventions just as a convict remains in his chains and shackles. Confucius can only be a teacher; he can only provide the exegesis of a sage's conduct while remaining himself unable to achieve an optimal state of blissful detachment. In the same chapter, another story of a funeral casts Confucius explaining to his disciple Yan Hui the superior capacities of a certain Mengsun Cai 孟孫才 behind his apparently shocking lack of ritual propriety.

2.2. Sages Who Would Not Serve

The imperative of keeping one's talents and skills invisible is one of the most consistent themes in the *Zhuangzi*. A common feature of sages is their reluctance to publicise or promote their talents. Some uncanny figures of sagehood tend to live hidden, keeping away from the predatory greed of men, thereby avoiding to be exploited or instrumentalised. In chapter 20, "*Shan mu*," Ren 任 reports to Confucius the words he heard from an accomplished man:

> Who can rid himself of success and fame, return and join the common run of men? . . . Wiping out his footprints, sloughing off his power, he does not work for success or fame. So he has no cause to blame other men, nor other men to blame him. The Perfect Man wants no repute. (trans. Watson, *Complete Works*, 224)

Some characters embodying a form of supreme mastery are associated with wild places and solitary locations. Guang Chengzi is described as quietly meditating on the Kongtong Mountains. Xu Free-of-Daemons (Xu Wugui) is said to lead a poor solitary life in a forest up in the mountains. Mad Hump is spotted alone on the hill of Dispelled-Doubt; the hunchback who proves a virtuoso in the art of catching cicadas on a stick, and who stirs Confucius's admiration, is also alone in a forest (chapter 19, "*Da sheng*"). So is Hong Meng when Jiang Yun bumps into him (chapter 11, "*Zai you*").

When sages or people endowed with a superior skill do not live as hermits, they still endeavour to remain unknown, if not invisible. In chapter 21, King Wen spots an old man fishing, but fishing as though he were not fishing for anything (*qi diao mo diao* 其釣莫釣), rather as if fishing were his constant occupation in life (*you diao zhe ye, chang diao ye* 有釣者也，常釣也). He detects in him a sage and manages to hand over to him the government. But when, after three years of peace and order, King Wen begins to bow to the fisherman as a great teacher and asks him to extend his methods of government to the whole world, the old man just mumbles an excuse and runs away at nightfall, never to be seen again (trans. Watson, *Complete Works*, 228–30).

One of the longest narratives in the *Zhuangzi* (chapter 23) describes the itinerary of a certain Gengsang Chu, a former disciple of Laozi who settles in a remote northern mountain region where his discrete but pervasive influence benefits all the inhabitants. After three years of bountiful harvests, people acknowledge him as a great sage and worship him, which Gengsang Chu considers as a personal catastrophe.

> So the man who would preserve his body and life must think only of how to hide himself away, not minding how remote or secluded the spot may be. (trans. Watson, *Complete Works*, 249)

Gengsang Chu even has a hard time convincing his disciples that gaining a reputation and being considered as a model is something baleful and dangerous and means, among other things, losing one's quietness and security. Sadly, even the position of the hidden sage is untenable since his talent, his influence, or his skills always end up achieving something which gets recognised and valued by others. Gengsang Chu managed to get rid of the kind of people who might immediately single out his talents or exhaust his vital forces (smart servants and concubines); he seems to have the stuff and the skills of a sage, but he does lack the skill to keep his skills hidden! The end of the story seems to suggest that the moment a sage is turned into a renowned master is the beginning of his downfall.

In chapter 32, "*Lie Yukou*" (列禦寇), Liezi explains to his master that he called off his journey to Qi because he could not hide his inner potency from the gaze of people:

> If you can't dispel the potency inside you, it oozes out of the body and forms a radiance that, once outside, overpowers men's minds and makes them careless of how they treat their own superiors and old people. And it's from this kind of confusion that trouble comes.[9]

But after that noble explanation, Bohun wuren reproaches Liezi with frittering time and energy for the sake of playing the sage for a herd of worthless admirers. These people do not merit any instruction and should be dismissed like so many banes that end up poisoning the mind (*jin ren du ye* 盡人毒也). "Since no one understands and sees clearly, how would it be possible to get to know each other?" (*mo jue mo wu, he xiang shu ye* 莫覺莫悟，何相孰[熟]也！) concludes Bohun, the most eminent figure of mastery in the *Zhuangzi* along with Lao Dan.

In chapter 24, the recurring character Nanpo Ziqi confesses to Yan Chengzi 顏成子 the great mistake of letting oneself be known by a prince and thereby becoming the author of one's own misfortune.

> Once I lived in a mountain cave. At that time, Celestial Harmony (Tian he 天禾) came to pay me one visit and the people of the state of Qi congratulated him three times. I must have had hold of something in order for him to find out who I was; I must have been peddling something in order for him to come and buy. . . . Ah, how I pity those men who destroy themselves! (trans. Watson, *Complete Works*, 271)

His error was not to keep silent. If masters become public models or popular teachers, they are bound to lose what little they have cultivated. The injunction to stop talking and remain secluded can be viewed both as an instruction about the optimal psychological state and an invitation to social prudence. Yet, the tragedy is, as Bohun wuren explains to Liezi, that "even if you stay at home, people are going to flock around you."

2.3. Abashed by Calabash

The problematic relationship between a master who keeps his powers hidden and a disciple who is eager to "obtain the Way" lies at the heart of many pedagogic episodes in the *Zhuangzi*. In the encounter between Master Calabash and the evil shaman Ji Xian,[10] the tendency to keep one's art hidden or one's Way veiled is at odds with the necessity of demonstrating one's skills, were it only for the sake of the gullible Liezi, who, like Truffaldino in Goldoni's play, acts for a while as the servant of two masters.

Calabash is the archetype of the master whose skills stay deliberately hidden, even to his own and unique disciple Liezi, whom he does not hold to be mature enough, or sufficiently "hatched." We have an inkling of Calabash's powers through what he does in the story, but we also have an intimation of the extent of his potency through his negative capacity to keep it to himself. Genuine mastery cannot be dissociated from the ability of not using one's powers. It is the mastery over the desire to flaunt one's skills that sets a sage like Huzi apart from a trickster[11] like Jixian.

And yet, since a master only exists because his disciples acknowledge him so, he must be forced sooner or later to show his knowledge or his powers, though in doing so he jeopardises the authentic way of life from which he should never stray. Calabash feels forced at some stage to show a few tricks to Liezi at the expense of Ji Xian. The latter proves four times unable to decipher the ploys set up by Calabash, who can simulate and stimulate whatever life processes he fancies.

By putting himself under the scrutiny of Ji Xian, Calabash lays bare, as a backlash, the wizard's lack of penetration. While Ji Xian thinks he is demonstrating his mastery, each encounter with Calabash is an occasion for Liezi to get an inkling of the hidden skills of his master, and also an occasion to realise Ji Xian's self-deluding attitude, who cannot see beyond what he is given to look at.

Huzi and Jixian test each other; they stand for Liezi—and for the readers likewise—in a relationship of confrontation, in a struggle for supremacy and the recognition of that supremacy. In this string of four confrontations, the multiple roles and positions assigned to each character always go by pairs in a game of symmetry: we have two masters, Calabash and Ji Xian; two of the characters can be seen as patients who are diagnosed and tested: Huzi plays the apparent patient while Liezi, inebriated by the shaman, is secretly tested by Huzi. Both Huzi and Liezi are tricked by Calabash and end up defeated and ridiculed. Liezi finally realises he has been blinded by the powers of Ji Xian, who appears just as blind, since he figured he could see through Calabash. Finally, there are two endings: first when Ji Xian runs away, and then when we pass to the description of Liezi's new life.

How Calabash manages to control his physiological or mental workings remains a mystery; the magic of fictions rapidly takes over the verisimilitude of a didactic tale. But the gist of the story is that one should not use one's skills in order to impress or dominate other people, and one should be able to learn under the guidance of a master without the intention of gaining power. In other words, inner potency should not be turned into external powers and used as a weapon. The best swords are kept in their sheath, just as the best master keeps his power out of sight.

In this cautionary tale, the mastery that Huzi harbours inside him can be seen as the ultimate quest of Daoist self-cultivation: the total control of one's vital workings, the perfect mastery of inner activities and energetic cycles within the body. Calabash's powers are used in a ludic manner: they are for the reader an occasion for mocking the complacent Ji Xian, whereas the evil wizard's powers are used only to impose himself and frighten other people. What singles out Calabash's real mastery is the fact that his knowledge of inner workings does not differ from his capacity to act upon himself.

Whereas Ji Xian figures he is diagnosing and curing Calabash, his presumption and his ridicule help Liezi make a diagnosis on the severity of his own ignorance and foolishness. The therapeutic pedagogy works backwards for Liezi and for the reader: Calabash, who has willingly put himself in the position of a dying patient, unveils Ji Xian's defects and thereby puts Liezi in the position of a witness who realises, in moral terms, his severe condition, which requires a drastic diet.

In chapter 19, Master Bian Qing scolds a certain Sun Xiu who comes to him for advice but repines at his fate in terms akin to the lesson imparted by Calabash to his immature disciple Liezi.

> Now you show off your wisdom in order to astound the ignorant, work at your good conduct in order to distinguish yourself from the disreputable, going around bright and shining as though you were carrying the sun and moon in your hand! (trans. Watson, *Complete Works*, 207)

Not only does the general ethical orientation in the Zhuangzi run afoul of traditional ways of ensuring a master his legitimacy through public recognition of his skills, but it also disregards economic considerations when dealing with masters and disciples.[12]

3. THE SILENCE OF THE SAGE

The *Zhuangzi* is very wordy about the importance of keeping mum. The many lessons bearing on the impossibility of getting an intellectual comprehension of the Way, on the fallacy of logic, or on the impotence of language can also be read as so many skilful explorations and exploitations of the possibilities of language. It is as if the fallacious and fictitious nature of ordinary speeches could only be convincingly denounced by way of a fictional representation of silence.

Language and logic remain at the periphery of the sage's way of life, and this ethical choice of keeping *logos* at bay in favour of *bios* can be held as a general feature of Chinese thought.[13] What singles out the *Zhuangzi* is that the consummate mastery of rhetoric and the profligacy of literary inventions serve to intimate the superiority of non-discursive practices of the self. Hence the portrayal of sages who enlighten or inspire without a word or without being heard by the reader. Wenbo Xuezi is endowed with a presence so expressive as to leave Confucius in a posture of silent admiration; he does not utter a word lest he should trouble the sage's intimacy with the Way (chapter 21). Master Dongguo Shunzi causes human plans, worries, or intentions to melt away by dint of his pure presence (chapter 21). Bohun wuren is praised for his bounty by Shen Tujia in front of Zi Chan, prime minister of Zheng, while their master stays in the backdrop as a silent but efficient presence (chapter 5). It is not so much the words said by the sage as the description of the sage himself, without ever hearing a word from him, that constitutes the most resounding lesson and exerts a deep effect on the characters and on readers simultaneously. Just think of Wang Tai, the charismatic master, amputated of one foot (thus a former convict), who attracts half the population of the state of Lu. One of Confucius's disciples, Chang Ji (Eternally Immature 常季), reports to his master his amazement at seeing the popularity of Wang Tai outshining that of Confucius: "When standing, he does not teach: when seated, he does not expatiate.[14] People come to him empty and are well sated when they leave. Is there really a way to teach without speaking and an indiscernible way to bring the mind to its completion? What sort of man is that?"

What is the skill of this sage who does not teach nor discuss but fulfils his listeners and imparts to them something substantial (*shi* 實)? As with so many other figures of sagehood in the *Zhuangzi*, we do not hear what Wang Tai has to say. We do not even have a glimpse of what he thinks. We only hear of the powerful effects he produces on other people. Like Confucius, we are given to hear how his mastery works, but not what stuff it is made of. The literary technique of having witnesses speak or disciples report (Tian Zifang, Shen Tujia, Chang Ji, etc.) is the only way to approach the silent mastery of sages.

4. SAGES AND THE ART OF SHOCK THERAPY

In the *Zhuangzi* and in the *Liezi* 列子, which exploits materials expunged from or inspired by the *Zhuangzi*, as shown by the following extract from chapter 1, we can find a recurring narrative pattern in which he who draws near a sage and questions him winds up rebuked and excoriated, if not humiliated.

> Ten times, when Lieh-tzǔ was not busy, he (i.e. Yin Sheng) took the opportunity to beg for his secrets; and each time Lieh-tzǔ turned him away and would not tell him. Yin Sheng was indignant and took his leave; Lieh-tzǔ made no objection.
>
> A few months after Yin Sheng withdrew he had not renounced his aim, and went to join Lieh-tzu again.
>
> "Why do you keep coming and going?" Lieh-tzǔ asked him.
>
> "Not long ago I made a request to you, but you would not tell me. It is true that I felt some rancour against you, but now it is all gone. So I have come again. I used to think you intelligent; are you really as vulgar as all that?"
> (*Liezi*, chapter 1; trans. Graham, *The Book of Lieh-tzǔ*, 36)

We would be at a loss to show in the characters of masters any evident sign of a benevolent or a humanistic attitude. Though the stances taken by the various masters under consideration do not follow any clear pedagogical line, most of the time they seem inclined to annoy, bewilder, or confuse their interlocutor. Some characters credited with a superior mastery put their listeners in a state of disarray, catch them off guard, and impart delirious injunctions as pieces of wisdom. We see sages turning down students or aspiring disciples and fending off questions they are implored to answer. In chapter 22, Ran Qiu 冉求 who comes to meet Confucius is left flabbergasted by the master's string of compelling paradoxes. Every so often one can see masters or sages who, far from relieving their "patients," perpetuate and intensify their anxiety and discourage any sort of exchange that might resemble a conversation.[15] Should we appraise this attitude as a negative phase before a possible positive instruction, as a way to sift out people who do not have the right stuff? Or should we suspect we have here the disturbing display of a peculiar pedagogy?[16]

Many are the anecdotes or dialogues that follow this narrative pattern. In chapter 4, the spirit of a giant and twisted tree gives a piece of his mind to Carpenter Shi. In chapter 5, Confucius rebukes Shushan Wuzhi (though it must be stressed here that the master's scornful attitude is clearly a blunder, and that Shushan Wuzhi's refusal to continue the conversation after Confucius's sudden about-face is evidently not part of a pedagogic strategy). In chapter 6, Xu You 許由 initially refuses to instruct Yi Erzi 意而子, whom he sees as incurably distorted and defiled by his "Confucian" education. But his rejection appears as a probation, and Yi Erzi's witty retort makes him change his mind. Still in chapter 6, Nü Yu 女偊, Dame-Twisted, or Woman Crookback, refuses to instruct Nanpo Zikui 南伯子葵, but the way (s)he[17] argues her refusal takes the form of an indirect instruction. By recalling how she instructed an old student of hers, a certain Buliang Yi 卜梁倚 who attained under her guidance a state of mystical ecstasy, she gives an insight into the personal experience of the Way.[18] In chapter 11, Guang Chengzi rebuffs the Yellow Emperor and heaps opprobrium on him for his hubris, until the latter sets out to reform himself and comes back purified of his former predatory ambitions. In chapter 18, "*Zhi Le*" (至樂), a skull on the road is mockingly questioned by Zhuangzi who uses it as a pillow overnight. The skull appears in the sleeper's dream, flays his arrogant ignorance, and lectures him on the royal felicity of being dead. In chapter 22, Master Zhuang is riled by Master Dongguo's questions and retorts with offending terms—but instructs him nonetheless. In chapter 27, Laozi taunts Yang Ziju 陽子居 for his haughty countenance and disdainful air and rejects the possibility of instructing him. Yang Ziju benefits from this harsh treatment and stops acting as someone superior to others. In chapter 13, "*Tian dao*," Laozi refuses to engage in a conversation with the peevish Shi Chengqi (Mister Handsome-Successful 士成綺) and the following day reproaches him for his petulance, arrogance, and rash manners. Aside from Confucius's disastrous encounter with Shushan Wuzhi, only once does a master feel remorse for having harshly treated someone who came to ask advice from him, namely Master Bian Qingzi with Sun Xiu in chapter 19, "*Da sheng*." One of Bian Qingzi's disciples tries to convince his master he was right to behave that way and kindly reassures him. Bian Qingzi's feeling of remorse is yet justified, seeming to conclude the story, for that was not the kind of lesson that poor Sun Xiu needed. This anecdote can be seen as an antidote to the temptation of reading all the aforementioned encounters like so many exemplifications of a pedagogic skill to be used at all times with everyone.

Though far from being systematically implemented, the "pedagogic nasti-ness" of the master may prove a useful resource to help the interlocutor make headway. It appears that people who are rebuked by a sage are those who want to get something directly, something they imagine will make them more powerful or more knowledgeable (Liezi, the Yellow Emperor, Confucius, Nanpo Zikui). They hope to get it from someone else and thereby spare efforts and time; the strong refusal to teach in these conditions suggests each time that the first thing to do is to change the disciple's current dispositions and frame of mind before carrying out anything further.

Most of the time, it is impossible for he who enquires to get a straight answer or to be immediately accepted as a disciple. In the *Liezi* (chapter 2), even the eponymous character does not seem to have exchanged a single sentence with his master Old Shang (Lao shang shi 老商氏) for years, as he recounts his experience to a new disciple who shows a most inappropriate and irritating impatience. After three years, recalls Liezi, he was graced with a glance from the master. After five years of spiritual progress, the master's face relaxed in a smile. After seven years, when he had apparently reached a peak, he was allowed to sit on the master's mat beside him. One should notice however that Liezi's description of his own progress is, to say the least, at odds with what one could expect, for externally the reader can only see the attitude of an immature person who does not think before speaking and acting. The following passage can be read as a variation on the theme of the sage in the guise of an old gaga. Put in another context, and in someone else's mouth, it could be held as evidence of foolishness:

> After nine years, I thought without restraint of whatever came into my mind and said without restraint whatever came into my mouth without knowing whether the right and wrong, benefit and harm, were mine or another's, with-out knowing that the Master was my teacher.[19]

The mental confusion experienced by Liezi, which is expressed further in the same story in one of the most poetic passages of the whole book, blurs once again the differences between an accomplished individual inwardly enlight-ened and a senile person losing his basic faculties of awareness and recogni-tion. Mastery seems a regressive process of loss and dispossession.

How should we receive and understand this brutal way of dealing with people eager to learn, to improve, and to change? It may be a fair bet that the negative phase in the encounter between the person in the position of the disciple and the person enacting the sage is not a test of sorts prior to positive

teaching: it is the typical non-didactic, non-humanistic way of giving someone a lesson. The negative emotions aroused by these inhospitable manners
are a way of exploring in the *Zhuangzi* the upsides of feeling bad about
oneself or about failure, against the deception of self-protective thoughts.

In chapter 11, Guang Chengzi's vehement remonstration against the Yellow Emperor and his refusal to instruct him[20] prove a salutary intervention. It
enables the power-hungry ruler to realise the destructive nature of his desire
and turn his power of awareness onto himself. The violent reproaches have
acted like a cue to set off a silent and solitary period of meditation. This
counterintuitive attitude, which many a student today might feel and de-
nounce as an insufferable instance of moral harassment, enables masters to
protect themselves while forcing disciples to reconsider their ambitions and
desires.

5. PERMUTING ROLES, MIXED IDENTITIES

The art of exploiting negative situations in the *Zhuangzi* is often displayed at
the expense of those characters who find themselves in an ambivalent role,
that of a master or a supposed expert who winds up remonstrated and treated
as someone smug, ignorant, or stupid. In chapter 4, Carpenter Shi is remonstrated by the useless tree that he was fool enough to disparage when walking
past with his apprentice. In chapter 5, Confucius loses face in front of his
disciples when Shushan Wuzhi exposes his petty and intolerant reaction. In
chapter 12, Emperor Yao is remonstrated by a simple man who shows him
how ridiculous is his supposedly disinterested grandeur, before flying away.
In chapter 20, Confucius is beleaguered somewhere between Chen and Cai;
he is famished and fears for his life, at which point a certain Ren lectures him
for being vain and superficial. In chapter 29, Confucius intends to persuade
Robber Zhi to amend his ways but suffers a humiliating diatribe from his
menacing and blustering host. And, as we have seen, the charlatan Ji Xian
after meeting four times Master Calabash ends up running away just like the
people from Zheng he used to frighten.

Many pedagogic episodes in the *Zhuangzi* are characterised by the un-
steady nature of relationships, positions, and statuses between masters and
disciples. Some characters, like Confucius, the Yellow Emperor, or Liezi, are
sometimes depicted as powerful masters, sometimes as immature men in
need of further learning. For instance, Confucius instructs his historical disciples but takes lessons from many men, such as Laozi (see their three dialogues in chapter 14), the old fisherman (chapter 31), Master Sang Hu
(chapter 19), and a certain Ren (chapter 20). In chapter 6, after probing his
old disciple's progress, Confucius even asks Yan Hui to act as a master for
himself.

Liezi is also a complex figure, who exemplifies the ambiguities of the relationship between masters and disciples. He is treated as an immature pupil by Master Calabash (chapter 7) as well as by Dark-Count Non-human, but he is also mentioned as a superior man (chapter 1, "*Xiao yao you*" 逍遙遊) or a sage living quietly in a state of arrant poverty (chapter 28). In chapter 32, as we saw earlier, he plays an ambivalent role: a guru of sorts for common people, but an immature person to the eyes of Bohun wuren. As to the Yellow Emperor, he approaches Guang Chengzi as a submissive disciple would do in chapter 11; in chapter 24, he is instructed by a young boy in a remote region and after listening to his political advice calls him Heavenly Master (*tian shi* 天師), but he is also depicted as a wise and knowledgeable person in chapter 22; in chapter 14, he appears as a divine music master able to perform the very movements and rhythms of the cosmos. The character Nanguo Ziqi is subjected to similar changes and inversions: he figures as a sage in chapters 2 and 24, and, if he can reasonably be seen as the same person as Nanpo Zikui in chapter 6, he appears as an immature disciple turned down by Nü Yu.

There is a last string of scenes to blend in this strange mosaic: those in which the severing of one's relationship with one's master or with one's disciples proves the essential condition for spiritual progress. Confucius, after being lectured by Ren, leaves his friends, dismisses his disciples, and retires to a swamp, living among animals, feeding on chestnuts and acorns, and wearing only coarse cloth and furs. In chapter 7, Liezi makes at last some real progress and reaches out to his true nature after leaving his master and living secluded from the world. In chapter 6, Yan Hui keeps progressing by forgetting what Confucius taught him. In chapter 14, Confucius, remonstrated by Laozi, stays at home cooped up for three months and finally becomes enlightened. In chapter 20, the superiority of solitude is once again pitted against the miserable fate of rulers: Yi Liao from the South-Market (Nanshi Yiliao 南市宜僚) gives advice to Prince Lu, who is in a state of exhaustion and keeps repining at his fate. He talks the ruler into renouncing his possessions, leaving the world, and dwelling in poverty in a remote corner of the earth.

6. BY WAY OF A CONCLUSION

The relationship between masters and disciples is nowhere disparaged, but the most fruitful relationships take the form of face-to-face conversations preceded or followed by personal exercises, the nature of which remains mysterious. In the rare mentions of regular relationships between masters and disciples, we can barely imagine what kind of instructions are imparted, what exactly disciples learn, do, hear, or perform. That which is consistently

evoked or described is the series of optimal states that result from the exercises or that constitute the goal of the lessons. On the other hand, people who
speak easily and openly about their skill or their craft do not claim to be
masters or sages, just ordinary workers who happen to give a lesson fortui-
tously.

The canonical relationship between master and disciple is moreover sub-
verted by the frequent reversal of roles, by the elusive identity of sages, by
the unexpected choice of people or creatures who give a lesson, and by the
condemnation of verbal teaching and textual transmission.

The most persuasive lessons in the *Zhuangzi* cannot be reduced to messages made of wise injunctions and advice; they also lie in the thought-
provoking portrayals of imaginary sages who are credited with skills that
tend to remain hidden or unshared. The many mentions of the elating impact
exerted by masterly figures on certain characters who become dumbfounded
and enchanted and who undergo a spiritual conversion is inextricably associated with the literary skills of the anonymous authors who found a way to
convey or imprint in the reader the intuition of certain optimal states akin to
the Way.

Among all the texts from the Warring States centred on the figure of
masters and sages, only in the *Zhuangzi* (and in the *Liezi* for that matter) do
we find ourselves in the presence of accomplished masters who shun disciples and like to appear devoid of any skills, if not mentally retarded; the
reader witnesses situations in which masters happen to be upbraided like
immature pupils, in which masters and disciples switch roles, or in which
some students and disciples make decisive progress once they find themselves alone and are not fettered any longer by what they have learned,
thereby promoting the pioneering idea of skills of oblivion or mastery in
blissful confusion. The elusive presence of the sage, the striking variety of
characters who possess a kind of mastery, and the constant warnings about
the fallacies of language and logic, along with the fact that so many eye-
opening lessons subvert the didactic setting of regular instruction, can be
seen as so many devices that prevent readers from turning messages and
personal advice into a doctrine, into universal truths delivered by an unques-
tioned and unique master. The ultimate skill of masters in the *Zhuangzi* lies
in their capacity to lead their interlocutors to realise the failings of a pedagogic relationship based on a theoretical form of instruction. Now, it appears
that the literary representation of these skills give the readers a compelling
lesson on the art of staying away from a traditional relationship between
masters and disciples. The figure of the sage is reinvented in the *Zhuangzi*
against the traditional setting of a revered authoritative figure whose culture
and sayings prompt the deference of inferiors eager to listen to what he has to
say. It is, perhaps, against the risk of sacralising the sage and turning his

words into a doctrine that the following story was written, which leads the evasive figure of supreme mastery to a deep and farcical paroxysm:

> Bright Dazzlement asked Nonexistence (Wuyou 無有), "Sir, do you exist, or do you not exist?" Unable to obtain any answer, Bright Dazzlement stared intently at the other's face and form—all was vacuity and blankness. He stared all day but could see nothing, listened but could hear no sound, stretched out his hand but grasped nothing. "Perfect!" exclaimed Bright Dazzlement. "Who can reach such perfection? I can conceive of the existence of nonexistence but not of the nonexistence of nonexistence. Yet this man has reached the stage of the nonexistence of nonexistence. How could I ever reach such perfection!" (*Zhuangzi* 22; trans. Watson, *Complete Works*, 244)

We have seen how the non-discursive universe of the sage impacted on the literary techniques of depiction of mastery in the *Zhuangzi*. Questions on how to attain the Way or how to transform people may be rejected as absurd and silly by various sages, but precisely if such questions were not posed and cast in a dialogue, there would be no lessons for the readers, not even a negative instruction. Hence the paradoxical position of these authors, who are forced, in order to promote their values, to ignore them.

Indeed, if a small number of thinkers had not taken the trouble of talking and writing about the virtues of silence and the inefficiency of verbal transmission, there would be nothing left to instruct the readers and perpetuate a lesson. In this sense, the art of remaining silent does not antagonise the art of opening one's mouth or holding one's brush; it is just another chapter in the history of rhetoric. The authors of the *Zhuangzi* have not lost sight of the practical goals of rhetoric: their accomplishment lies not so much in their capacity to remain silent against the temptation of speaking, as in their art of opening the readers's minds to the virtues of silence by dint of an exceptional mastery of literary techniques.

Though ultimate sages seldom give clear, positive, and regular instructions as masters do, and though their mastery can only be hinted at through the powerful effect they produce on people who meet them (since some of them keep appearing stupid, inert, or non-existent), readers as well as protagonists constantly benefit from explanations, testimonies, and exegeses from a host of different "inferior masters." The authors of the *Zhuangzi* are in a relationship with us similar to that of the Yellow Emperor with Consciousness (Zhi 知) in chapter 22 or to that of Confucius expatiating on the élan vital of ultimate men in front of his disciples. Their achievements partly lie in the art of giving imaginative access to the silent skills of superior sages. The reader is always shuttled between the ideal point of view suggested by these episodes, namely the silence of the sage and his own perspective as a reader, who relishes the exhilarating wordiness of these stories about sages and students.

Many characters in the *Zhuangzi* prove unable to make a clear difference between the quest for the Way and the search for secret arts liable to increase their personal power and their control over other people. Various chapters illustrate this initial fallacy by casting figures of masters and disciples who waver, hesitate, are led astray, and often fail. Those who finally accomplish something undergo a series of sudden inner changes, often characterised by a state of confusion in which all the core oppositions created by our perceptive habits and our use of language (between oneself and others, between the inner and the outer, etc.) suddenly disappear, to such an extent that the will to power and domination, which initially triggers the process of finding a master and attaining the Way, becomes irrelevant. From this perspective, one may finally come to understand why masters can appear so reluctant to speak, and why some sages are adamant that they will remain unknown, without disciples, and keep their mastery hidden. Authentic mastery implies dispensing with external powers in favour of a personal cultivation of inner potency that cannot become instrumentalised by others. The logical implication is that mastery cannot be taught and that teachers are masters who cannot hold a candle to real sages. The *Zhuangzi* conveys these tensions when casting various forms of interaction between sages, masters, teachers, and pupils, with shifting roles and sudden reversals. The authors behind these stories could justify their flamboyant wordiness about silent skills and unproved mastery by concluding, in the style of Coleridge:

> And we did speak only to break
> The Silence of the Sage[21]

NOTES

1. Translations are mine unless otherwise indicated.
2. The "regular" masters are as follows: (1) Master Nanguo Ziqi 南郭子綦, lost in a catatonic ecstasy, is questioned by his disciple in attendance, Yancheng Ziyou 顏成子游 (chapter 2, "*Qiwulun*" 齊物論). (2) Huzi (Master Calabash壺子) with his disciple Liezi 列子, pits his master against Ji Xian 季咸. (3) Master Zhuang 莊子 and his (anonymous) disciples (chapter 20, "*Shan mu*" 山木). (4) Bohun wuren (Dark-Count Non-Human 伯昏無人) with Shen Tujia 申徒嘉 and Zi Chan 子產, prime minister of Zheng (chapter 5, "*De chong fu*" 德充符). (5) Confucius and some of his historical disciples (many episodes casting Yan Hui 顏回, Zigong 子貢, Zilu 子路, Zengzi 曾子, passim). (6) Yancheng Ziyou 顏成子游 recounts his nine years of training and progression to his master Dongguo Ziqi 東郭子綦 (chapter 27, "*Yu yan*" 寓言). (7) A-he Gan 婀荷甘 and the Divine Labourer (Shen Nong 神農) study together under Auspicious Old-Dragon (Lao-long Ji 老龍吉) (chapter 22, "*Zhi bei you*" 知北遊). (8) A certain Zi Bian Qingzi 子扁慶子 is mentioned with his disciples, but we don't know what exactly the nature of his teaching is (chapter 19, "*Da sheng*" 達生). (9) Gengsang Chu 庚桑楚 speaks to his disciples and instructs Nanrong Chu 南榮趎 in particular (chapter 23, "*Gengsang Chu*" 庚桑楚).
3. This point is shrewdly denounced by Wang Bi 王弼 (226–49) in his *Laozi zhilüe* 老子指略, which offers a commentary on the aphorisms of the Old Master about the moral fallacy lying in behaviours that are intentionally moral.

4. For a criticism of Confucian teaching and ancient institutions deemed superannuated or archaic, see chapter 14 *"Tian Yun"* (天運).

5. On the silent efficiency of nature and the profit from going along with the flow of things, see, for instance, chapter 13, *"Tian dao"* (天道) (Watson, *Complete Works*, 149–50).

6. (1) Confucius advises Gao, duke of Ye (Ye Gongzi Gao 葉公子高), who is brimming with anxiety before his imminent mission to Qi 齊 (chapter 4, *"Renjianshi"* 人間世). (2) Qiu Bo Yu 蘧伯玉 (close to Confucius) advises the fearful Yan He 顏闔 who is tasked with instructing the bloodthirsty Duke Ling of Wei's son and heir (chapter 4, *"Renjianshi"*). (3) Confucius patiently advises Yan Hui 顏回 against a self-imposed quixotic moral crusade to the state of Wei 衛. He begins by making his disciple aware of his absence of solid plans and of his self-defeating preconceptions (chapter 4, *"Renjianshi"*). (4) Confucius instructs Ran Qiu 冉求, though in the end he leaves him flabbergasted (chapter 22, *"Zhi bei you"*). (5) Confucius instructs Yan Hui (in two dialogues of chapter 4 and also in chapter 28, *"Rang wang"* 讓王). (6) The old fisherman instructs Confucius (chapter 31, *"Yu fu"* 漁夫). (7) Xu Wugui comes down from his forest to bring solace to Marquis Wu of Wei (chapter 24). (8) Laozi cautions Cui Qu (Soaring-Sweeping 崔瞿) against the inconsistencies of the human mind and the violence that plagues the world (chapter 11, *"Zai you"*). (9) Emperor Shun 舜 questions one of his advisers, who entertains him about the illusion of personal identity and the anonymous workings that make each person live (chapter 22, *"Zhi bei you"*). (10) Lao Dan kindly responds to a string of questions asked by Confucius (chapter 21, *"Tian Zifang"* 田子方).

7. This discrepancy is exemplified in other situations in which a disciple figures that sagehood is a skill that can be acquired by external means just like a secret art. Another source of misunderstanding lies in the disciple's ignorance that he cannot reach an optimal state of bliss or supreme detachment in an intentional way. Optimal states that are akin to the Way cannot be *willed* (see Romain Graziani, "Optimal States and Self-Defeating Plans," 440–66).

8. *Wu cong wu dao shi de dao* 無從無道始得道. "Follow nothing, don't look for a way, and you'll begin to find your way."

9. Watson, *Complete Works*, 353. I have emended the translation of *cheng* 誠 from "sincerity" to "potency." In this passage, sincerity does not make sense. *Cheng* obviously designates a sort of personal charisma.

10. Among the wealth of *Zhuangzi* stories regularly commented and analyzed by scholars, this episode from chapter 7 has elicited the most interesting commentaries and the most valuable ideas. See, among others, Billeter, *Etudes sur Tchouang-tseu*, 29–35; Defoort, "Instruction Dialogues in the *Zhuangzi*," 459–78; Moeller, "Liezi's Retirement," 379–92.

11. About "trickster": I borrow this most apposite qualification to Moeller, "Liezi's Retirement."

12. The economic aspect of the relationship between a master and his disciples cannot be overlooked since the master's economic needs have a bearing on his teaching and his pedagogy, while some disciples visibly expected a profitable return from their years of training in economic and political terms. Disciples vested a master with authority and invested in him; their loyalty and earnestness could gain them a position for the state or at the service of a powerful family. On the economic solidarity between a master and his disciples, and on the historical evolution of their relationships, see Oliver Weingarten, "What Did Disciples Do?," esp. 67 et seq.

13. On this perennial aspect of Chinese thought beyond the sole case of the *Zhuangzi*, see Graziani, "The Subject and the Sovereign," 485–87.

14. *li bu jiao, zuo bu yi* 立不教，坐不議.

15. Zen masters, too, show in their cryptic, shrewd, and unsettling style a ruthless lack of response, a refusal to offer any support or assistance, thereby maintaining the thrum of anxiety and sense of loss in their disciples at a high level.

16. Even in the *Mengzi* which antagonises so many views contended in the *Zhuangzi*, the eponymous philosopher asserts that teaching can proceed by way of remaining silent and that this refusal to instruct someone is also a form of instruction (cf. *Mengzi zhengyi* 1A, *"Liang Hui Wang"* 梁惠王, 46; 6B, *"Gaozi xia"* 高子,下, 416).

17. Nü 女 could mean here "Woman," or it could just be the name of a male character. The female connotation is associated to the underlying image of birth giving in the story, whereas the character Yu 偊, which can also mean "Solitary," refers to the One attained by Buliang Yi.

18. For an exhaustive study of this dialogue, see Graziani, *Fictions Philosophiques*, 227–70.

19. Graham, *The Book of Lieh-tzŭ*, 36. See also in chapter 20 what Ren explains to Confucius about the Accomplished Man: "Vacant, addled, he seems close to madness" (*chunchun changchang, nai bi yu kuang* 純純常常，乃比於狂) (trans. Watson, *Complete Works*, 214).

20. Though the reader rapidly understands that this remonstration is in itself a powerful lesson.

21. "And we did speak only to break / The silence of the sea." Coleridge, *The Rime of the Ancient Mariner* (2:26).

REFERENCES

Abbé Dinouart. *L'Art de se taire: principalement en matière de religion*. Edition de 1771.

Billeter, Jean François. *Etudes sur Tchouang-tseu*. Editions Allia, 2016.

Coleridge, Samuel. *The Rime of the Ancient Mariner*. 1798.

Defoort, Carine. "Instruction Dialogues in the *Zhuangzi*: An 'Anthropological Reading.'" *Dao: A Journal of Comparative Philosophy* 11, no. 4 (2012): 459–78.

Goldoni, Carlo. *The Servant of Two Masters*. Translated by Stephen Mulrine. New Yiork: Nick Hern Books, 2014.

Graham, Angus Charles. *The Book of Lieh-tzu*. New York: Columbia University Press, 1990.

Graziani, Romain. *Fictions philosophiques du Tchouang-tseu*. Edition Gallimard, 2006.

———. "The Subject and the Sovereign: Exploring the Self in Early Chinese Self-Cultivation." In *Early Chinese Religion, Part One: Shang through Han (1250 BC–220 AD)*, edited by John Lagerwey and Marc Kalinowski. Leiden: Brill, 2008.

———. "Optimal States and Self-Defeating Plans: The Problem of Intentionality in Early Chinese Self-Cultivation," *Philosophy East and West*, 2009. 59.4: 440–66.

Mencius: Corrected Interpretations (Mengzi zhengyi 孟子正義). Edited by Jiao Xun 焦循. Beijing: Zhonghua, 1987.

Moeller, Hans-Georg. "Liezi's Retirement: A Parody of a Didactic Tale in the *Zhuangzi*." *Dao: A Journal of Comparative Philosophy* 15, no. 3 (2016): 379–92.

Musil, Robert. *The Man without Qualities*. Vol. 2, from *The Posthumous Papers*. Translated by Sophie Wilkins and Burton Pike. New York: Vintage, 1961

Watson, Burton, trans. *The Complete Works of Chuang Tzu*. New York: Columbia University Press, 1968.

Weingarten, Oliver. "What Did Disciples Do? Dizi 弟子 in Early Chinese Texts," *Harvard Journal of Asiatic Studies*, 2015, 75.1: 29–75.

Chapter Six

Skill and Embodied Engagement

Zhuangzi *and* Liezi

Steven Coutinho

In Daoist philosophy, the pinnacle of human life is to live in tune with nature—from a Cosmic perspective (天 *tian*)—with skilful ease. In part, this implies successful engagement with complex and precarious circumstances. Traces of the idea can be found in the *Laozi*, but more explicit reflection on the nature of skill is explored in narrative form in stories in the *Zhuangzi*.[1] The most famous are the story of Cook Ding in chapter 3 (*Yangsheng Zhu* 養 生主) and the collection of stories in chapter 19 (*Da sheng* 達生). Versions of several of these can be found in the *Liezi*, which also contains other anecdotes that develop the Daoist philosophy of skill in more detail. I would argue that the political narratives of chapter 4 (*Ren Jian Shi* 人間世) should also be understood as contributing to the philosophy of skill. In these stories, it is the dispositions of a tyrannical ruler that constitute the medium with which we must learn to engage skilfully.

Daoist philosophy of skill has two aspects: an overarching existential philosophy that brings human life into attunement with the *dao* of the Cosmos, and, within this broader context, a philosophy of action that advocates the cultivation of specific modes of embodied engagement with particular media and through particular types of actions. In the following, I provide an overview of this philosophy of skill in the *Zhuangzi*, supplementing the explanation where appropriate with ideas developed in the *Liezi*. But as this is a philosophical exercise and not an essay in the history of ideas, I interpret and elaborate these philosophies with my own Zhuangzian reflections.

In section 1, I discuss some preliminary questions about the use of the term "skill" and whether it is to be understood as a type of 'knowledge'. In section 2, I situate the philosophy of skill within its broader existential and cosmological context. In sections 3.1, 3.2, and 3.3, I discuss the role of discipline and training in the cultivation of our perceptual sensitivity and responsiveness as discussed in many stories in both the *Zhuangzi* and the *Liezi*. In section 4, I discuss the conditions of preparation for performance once the relevant skills have been honed and refined. In section 5, I consider the conditions of skilful performance itself, as described by the swimmer, Wheelwright Bian, and Master Charioteer Tai Dou (in the *Liezi*). I draw readers' attention in advance to two notable contrasting and complementary elements that recur through all stages of acquisition, training, and performance: concentrated awareness, on the one hand, and oblivious familiarity (or forgetting), on the other. In section 6, I end by raising two questions that remain unresolved: the first about the relationship between skill and wisdom, and the second about whether ethical considerations can play any part in the Daoist cultivation of skill. It is unclear whether the conceptual resources of Zhuangzian philosophy of skill are adequate to address this second question in an ethically satisfactory manner.

1. PRELIMINARY ISSUES

While the *Zhuangzi* does clearly extol the abilities of skilful people, it is sometimes critical or dismissive of *qiao* (巧), a term that is sometimes translated as "skill." Analysis of the text reveals that there are two senses in which the term is used negatively in the *Zhuangzi*: to refer to mere technique and to trickery or sleight of hand, intended to deceive. But the skilful action that is admired by Daoist philosophers goes beyond mere technique and has nothing to do with trickery or deception. It is a matter of interacting with materials and negotiating obstacles carefully, efficiently, and successfully. In its highest and most revered form, when performance is accomplished with subtle artistry, it is not usually given a name but is sometimes referred to as *shu* (術) or "art", for example, by Woodcarver Qing (19.11) and in the *Liezi* stories of the charioteer Zao Fu (5.15) and the archer Ji Chang (5.14). In these stories it is also referred to as *qiao* (巧), and Confucius uses the same term to describe the ferryman's extraordinary ability.

Since Gilbert Ryle, we have become accustomed to thinking of skill as a kind of knowing—'knowing how' as opposed to 'knowing that'—but it is not explicitly discussed this way in Daoist texts. In fact, there is no equivalent expression to the English "know how" that would classify this sort of ability as a kind of knowledge. The term closest in meaning to "knowing" is *zhi* (知). Analysis of its philosophical usage in the *Zhuangzi* reveals that it has primary senses of 'being aware', 'knowing that something is so', and 'understanding why it is so'. In fact, what is emphasised is our *inability* to understand where skill comes from, our *not knowing* how we do what we do.

As we shall see, the epistemological terms that arise most often have to do with concentrating, forgetting, sensing intuitively, and responding (acting, interacting, following, cooperating, and even controlling). I shall refer to this combination of embodied sensing and responding as "epistemological engagement" to highlight the embodied interplay between sensing and acting.

2. EXISTENTIAL PHILOSOPHY

Both chapters 3 ("The Principle of Nurturing Life") and 19 ("Deep and Expansive Insight into Life") begin with a general philosophy of life. This can be understood as expressing a distinctively Daoist type of 'stoic' attitude, insofar as it teaches how to achieve a tranquil life in tune with the Cosmos by distancing ourselves from entanglements in worldly affairs. In chapter 3, however, we are also advised to avoid the twin social dangers of fame and punishment in order to preserve life, if we are unable to extricate ourselves from worldly affairs. Indeed, after Cook Ding describes his philosophy of skill, Lord Wen Hui interprets it as the secret of nurturing life: Lord Wen Hui said, "Marvellous! I hear Chef Ding speak, and from him learn how to nurture life!" (trans. Hagen and Coutinho, *Philosophers of the Warring States*, 371). In context, this would imply that he sees it as advice for negotiating the difficulties in a life of social entanglements. [2]

The characters admired by Daoists of the Zhuangzian [3] strand of Daoist thought often live on the outskirts of society, away from the dangers of social artifice, or in the lower ranks of society (a woodcarver, a ferryman, or a wheelwright, for example). Zhuangzian sages immerse themselves joyfully in the Cosmos, living harmoniously with the natural world, remain unperturbed by the unavoidable disasters of natural circumstance, and are able to preserve their lives to their fullest natural completion. But, as we are embodied beings, embedded in the natural world, living well must also entail dealing skilfully with our environments and circumstances, overcoming obstacles that may prevent us from succeeding or surviving. We develop extraordinary levels of non-verbal embodied skill through the cultivation of our natural capacities. Cosmic wisdom is thus manifested in practical adeptness in negotiating our environments without being harmed.

3. DISCIPLINE AND TRAINING IN THE CULTIVATION OF PERCEPTUAL SENSITIVITY

3.1. Discipline

For the swimmer at Lüliang Falls, his initial (*shi* 始) conditions (*gu* 故) arise from the fact that he was "born on dry land and was comfortable on dry land"

(19.10; trans. Hagen and Coutinho, *Philosophers of the Warring States*, 374). We have these basic skills just as a matter of being living organisms: we can see with our eyes, move our bodies through our environments, and interact with or evade moving objects. They are a precondition for our living engagement; we live through them, allowing them to function without being consciously in control of them. In addition to the initial conditions (*gu* 故) that we are born with, there are also conditions of practice that must be fulfilled first (*xian* 先) so that we may develop higher degrees of expertise. While a small minority of people may have the capacity to acquire astonishing degrees of dexterity with little practice, most people need a long period of apprenticeship for non-routine or ordinary tasks, often lasting many years.

We could theoretically attempt to master the new skills from scratch, but we tend to apply other skills that we have already acquired if they are closely similar in relevant ways. We modify pre-existing skills that we have already learned to new materials, situations, and changing conditions that are similar to those we are able to negotiate in an expert manner. As the swimmer puts it, he grew up in the water and became comfortable in the water. And he attributes this ability to his *xing* (性), his natural tendencies. Natural tendencies are thus understood as inherently flexible capacities: they can be applied to new circumstances and allow radical acquisition of new abilities.

The ferryman also explains how ferrying skills can be acquired by swimmers and divers:

> Excellent swimmers quickly develop the ability. As for divers, they may never have seen a boat before but will know how to handle it. (19.4; trans. Hagen and Coutinho, *Philosophers of the Warring States*, 373)

In the *Liezi* version of the story, there is an extra line: the ferryman says, "Anyone who can swim may be taught it; a good swimmer picks it up quickly," and Confucius explains, "it is because he takes the water lightly" (2.8; trans. Graham, *The Book of Lieh-tzu*, 43). That is, they are so familiar with the water, they can take it for granted. Both versions of the story go on to say that excellent swimmers have great ability to learn because they can forget the water. (I say more about this below.) Divers can acquire ferrying skills with ease because they are so familiar with the water that they are able to *see* it *as* land: the water is now as familiar to them as land, and the difficulties of water appear as variations of difficulties on land. It is as though they are applying the same skills to the situation in the water.

If we don't already have applicable skills, then we must first develop skills that can be cultivated in more controlled conditions to enable us to deal with situations that are more spontaneous and less predictable. The cicada catcher, for example, says that he first learns to balance (or sustain) balls in the air before he applies this skill to catching live cicadas. In *Liezi* 5.15, master charioteer Tai Dou instructs Zao Fu, quoting an ancient poem, "The child of an excellent bowsmith must first (*xian* 先) bend baskets; the child of an excellent metalsmith must first mend furs" (trans. Graham, *The Book of Lieh-tzu*, 113).

After the new preparatory skills have been mastered, training in the skill itself must begin. Cook Ding describes many years of training involving three stages, which I call the stages of the novice, apprenticeship, and expertise. These stages can be compared with the stages of learning a language: the first the stage of foreignness, the second the stage of immersion, the third the stage of fluency. These three stages apply not only to third-level skills, which involve control of a specially designed instrument, but even to the earliest acquired skills, such as walking and grasping. To a toddler in training, walking is the most extraordinarily difficult skill: at first it is an altogether unfamiliar activity. Then comes the stage of intense concentration and control of balance. Finally comes the stage of mastery, in which they no longer pay close sensory attention to the activity. It is comfortable and familiar and flows by itself; they are able to 'forget' (*wang* 忘) the activity and live through it in order to engage in other activities. One forgets when one is completely at home in the medium or skilful activity: it is a sign of fluency and expertise that one no longer needs to concentrate. *Zhuangzi* 19.13 says, "When our engagements fit comfortably 事會之適, we have no inward disturbances 不內變, and do not follow after externals 不外從" (trans. Hagen and Coutinho, *Philosophers of the Warring States*, 375).

3.2. Epistemological Engagement

The three stages of discipline discussed by Cook Ding are explained in terms of what I call "epistemological engagement," the interplay between how we sense a medium and how we respond to it. Ding says that his initial perception is only of the whole ox. This is our ordinary everyday way of seeing things for ordinary everyday interactions. His understanding did not go much further than taking the animal as a whole to be what we call an ox. Of course, we know that it is an animal, that it eats grass, that is has a head, eyes, legs, and a tail, and so on. But without any specialised kind of interaction, we have a limited ability to make any further discriminations that are specific to the nature of the ox's body as a medium. Only extensive, practical experience with any specific kind of material can result in the relevant specific understanding and responsiveness.

Ding reports that after three years of training, he no longer saw the whole. The deeper we become involved in a discipline, skill, or practice, the closer our attention focuses on the details of the task at hand. When we pay closer attention, what we once took to be familiar reveals itself to be unfamiliar; it turns out to be so complex that several years of concentration are required in order to learn to be familiar and forgetful in the new medium. Ding doesn't elaborate on this stage of his training, but the cicada catcher provides more detail about his own practice: it proceeds through graded degrees, each stage increasing the degree of difficulty (the number of balls he can sustain in the air simultaneously), but under regulated conditions. We find still more detail about these sorts of training drills and exercises, especially the training of our perceptual and intuitive responsiveness, in the *Liezi*, discussed in the section below.

At the time of Ding's interview with Lord Wen Hui, he has had many years of practice and has been so skilful that he hasn't needed to sharpen his blade for nineteen years (though he doesn't tell us how long it took to reach this stage). As Ding says, "Right now, at this time, I'm not looking with my eyes, but encountering it with *shen* 神 (spirit)" (trans. Hagen and Coutinho, *Philosophers of the Warring States*, 370). In the *Liezi*, master charioteer Tai Dou tells apprentice Zao Fu that he will eventually learn to 'see' without having to rely on his eyes (Hagen and Coutinho, *Philosophers of the Warring States*, 377). Although Ding refers to *shen*, which in some contexts can be translated as "spirit," there is no good reason to insist that it must be interpreted here in referential terms as naming an independent entity or epistemological faculty. Too little is said to provide any justification for such a literally referential reading. Indeed, what Ding is describing can more readily be understood phenomenologically; the capacities he is talking about are after all available to anyone who has attained such degrees of skill. In fact, almost everyone attains this kind of intuitive responsiveness with regard to our most basic abilities. (I shall say more about the cultivation of this intuitive capacity in the section below.)

But flawless artistry is not infallible. We can never claim to have mastered all possibilities of any material. Because of its complexity, and that of the environmental context in which engagement takes place, natural variations can accumulate to the point where new properties emerge: uncharacteristically awkward regions, hard and knotty places. A lake may often be calm and easy to cross, but there will be times when the waves are unpredictable, and a skilled ferryman will have to become extra vigilant to changing circumstances. The grain of familiar wood will not always have its typical texture. And as Zhuangzi's Confucius says in chapter 4, words can quickly become as treacherous as wind and waves. In encountering these unanticipated novelties, the expert, no longer in familiar conditions, must slow down, withhold expectations, and concentrate, acutely and pointedly aware of the new formations of the medium, adjusting the approach accordingly. In this way, the artist acquires not only new experience and familiarity with the nature of the material in unusual circumstances, but also new practice in negotiating novelty skilfully. The development of skill itself becomes skilfully developed.

However, the swimmer at Lüliang Falls makes a remarkable claim. The pool at the base of the falls is not only forceful and violent; it is almost entirely turbulent. Now, the very nature of turbulence is that it is constituted of *unpredictable* swirls and eddies. But the swimmer claims to be able to negotiate these unpredictable conditions with utmost ease and without risk of being harmed—indeed, without having to concentrate at all. In effect, he claims to be *completely familiar* with the *completely unpredictable*. Now, certainly one can become familiar with what was previously unfamiliar through extensive practice. But it is hard to understand how one could possibly become familiar with the completely unpredictable. In the absence of corroboration from other experts with similar skills, it is hard to know how to assess what appears to be a hyperbolic claim.

3.3. Refinement of Perception

Methods and procedures, which require relatively low levels of skill, involve macroscopic levels of awareness and categorisation, and may be teachable verbally. The written instructions on a box, for example, are sufficient to enable us to open the box without practice specifically dedicated to box opening, so long as we have already acquired the necessary first- and second-level skills. We can often succeed in such endeavours, paying little attention to the subtleties and complexities of the medium we engage with. We can even impose our plans on it, ignoring its own tendencies and inner makeup. This sort of cutting without sensitivity to subtle internal structures and striations of a medium is what Ding would call "hacking away." Such actions, guided by crude concepts, may be described as clumsy.

Now, ontologically speaking, the innermost subtle aspects of nature that are responsible for the production, constitution, and development of phenomena are minuscule beyond the limits of perceptibility and as such would not be able to appear determinately to our senses. *Liezi* 4.11 says, "The eye can discern the tip of an autumn hair just as it is about to lose its sight. The ear can hear a gnat flying just as it is about to lose its sense of hearing. The palate can distinguish between water from the Zi and Sheng rivers just as it is about to lose its taste."[4] That is, there is a level of hypersensitivity to the subtlest tendencies just before the threshold of perceptual awareness; I believe this capacity for hypersensitivity is what is being referred to as *shen*. In fact, this natural capacity is itself a subtle tendency that our ordinary perceptions, concepts, and reflections normally overlook. It is only in our quieter, more reflective moments, especially under the guidance of an expert teacher,[5] that we become aware of this degree of sensitivity.

Practice is required in order to cultivate this sensitivity and responsiveness. To do so, we must create conditions in which we attempt to sense, respond to, and eventually anticipate the subtle tendencies of things. Archer

Ji Chang takes two years of training before he can control his eyelids and prevent them from blinking (*Liezi* 5.14). After this, he is ready to train his eyesight to become more sensitive to minutiae. He practises observing minute things: suspending a flea in his window and observing it from a distance. After three years of training, it appears to loom large in his vision. That is, he is now clearly aware of the minuscule details that were previously invisible to him. The story is, of course, exaggerated, but it remains true that our perceptual sensitivity can be improved through training. Of course, merely staring at an object doesn't improve eyesight. Practised concentration, paying closer attention to our visual field, especially under the guidance of an expert, increases our awareness of its subtler structures.

In *Laozi* chapter 11,[6] it is the emptiness that makes successful functioning possible. Windows, doors, rooms, and wheels are able to function only because of the empty spaces that allow for movement. In the *Yangsheng Zhu*, even what appears to be solid is actually permeated with empty spaces (*xi* 郤, *kuan* 窾, *jian* 間). These form the natural patterning (*li* 理) of things and are understood as indicating possible directions of responsive movement. Ding says,

> Following the natural striations (*tian li* 天理), lunging into the vast cavities (*xi* 郤), and guided through the vast openings (*kuan* 窾). According with what is simply so (*gu ran* 固然), I don't even sense the sinews, joints, and tendons, never mind the massive bones. . . . The joints have spaces (*jian* 間), and the blade has no thickness: when you enter these spaces with what has no thickness, there'll be vast expanses through which the knife edge may roam, and there'll still certainly be room to spare. (trans. Hagen and Coutinho, *Philosophers of the Warring States*, 370)

To engage successfully with a medium, we must become sensitive to these channels, follow them, and respond in anticipation of new directions of possibility that open up as we proceed. As they become more familiar, they loom larger in our awareness and appear as vast empty spaces.

We also find something similar in our awareness of temporal processes. As we concentrate on the subtleties of processes of transformation, we become increasingly aware of the details that previously escaped our attention. The cicada catcher describes the ability to catch the cicadas: "It will be as though I pluck them precisely with my fingers" (19.3; trans. Hagen and Coutinho, *Philosophers of the Warring States*, 372). Those who are experienced at juggling eventually find that the balls appear almost motionless: it feels as though you are reaching up and 'plucking' the ball from air like an apple from a tree. Again, in 19.4, Confucius explains the ferryman's claim about divers: "As for divers, they may never have seen a boat before but will know how to handle it, because they see the surging water of the abyss as a mound, and the tipping of the boat as like a cart slipping backwards." As we

become more familiar with the complex interweaving changes in the movement of waves, it is as though our perception, and even time itself, appears to
slow down. What used to be a fast-moving wave now appears as a mound.
We can now respond with the same spontaneity as we would to a cart on a
hill: while movement feels slow and careful to the skilful practitioner, it
appears as demonic speed and accuracy to an outside observer.

4. PREPARATION FOR PERFORMANCE

For our everyday skills, our continuous engagement and interaction itself
constitutes sufficient practice and preparation. For skills requiring higher
than normal accuracy, precision, speed, or swift responsiveness, however, we
must be in a state of hyper-alert awareness to perform successfully, and this
state must be stimulated through a series of preparatory exercises. This is a
state of intense focused concentration on the task at hand. The cicada catcher
says that he is able to be aware (*zhi* 知) only (*wei* 唯) of cicadas' wings
because his attention is unwavering (*bufan buce* 不反不側), and Confucius
comments, "He uses his undivided attention (*zhi bu fen* 志不分), and concentrates (*ning* 凝) his spirit (*shen* 神)" (trans. Hagen and Coutinho, *Philosophers of the Warring States*, 372).

But to be able to concentrate in this way, one must be free from all
distractions. In a different context, Xunzi, in chapter 21 (*Jie Bi*), also comments on the importance of focused concentration. He says that in order for
our minds to be able concentrate they must be tranquil (*jing* 靜), focused with
single-minded attentiveness (*yi* 壹), and empty of distractions (*xu* 虛), especially those that arise from our aspirations (*zhi* 志) (*Xunzi* 21.5d, in Hagen
and Coutinho, *Philosophers of the Warring States*, 205–6). These distractions include emotional states and external factors. *Zhuangzi* 19.4 says,
"When you play for tiles you are skillful; when you play for trinkets you are
anxious; when you play for gold you are witless! . . . Whenever you overval-
ue externals, you will be inwardly clumsy" (trans. Hagen and Coutinho,
Philosophers of the Warring States, 373). Externals may be material (wealth
or social status), or they may even be immaterial (praise or blame). Both
kinds of external considerations can cause anxiety, and excessive anxiety can
interfere with smooth performance.

Woodcarver Qing discusses his procedure of psychophysical preparation
before he can carve an awe-inspiring bell stand (19.11). He is careful to
conserve his energy and fasts (*zhai* 齊; equivalent to 齋) to still (*jing* 靜) his
xin (心; mind-heart). We can infer from his subsequent remarks that this is a
kind of meditative practice in which external cares, for reward, praise, criticism, and so on, are weakened until they become insignificant. Even worry-

ing about being skilful or clumsy, without concern for reward or praise, still counts as an 'external' distraction.

In fact, distracting externals even include one's own body. Ultimately, Qing is ready to proceed only when he is able to 'forget' that he has four limbs and a body. Our bodies can distract us from perceiving the richness and potential of our environments. To forget one's own body is for it to recede from being an object of awareness separate from its environment. Of course, this is our natural state for most of our ordinary everyday actions. We simply live in the world through our bodily engagements; we do not treat it as an object of awareness. Qing says that it is only at this point that his skill (*qiao* 巧) is concentrated (*zhuan* 專). The term *zhuan* here has a similar significance to *yi* (壹), single-minded attentiveness, in the Xunzi passage above. It is only when he is completely empty of self that he is fully present in his environment and so may become more receptive to natural tendencies he would otherwise have been unable to sense. Concentration and forgetting thus play complementary roles. To concentrate is to lose oneself in the medium or the activity itself. Qing's body thus slips away from his attention as he immerses himself in direct embodied integration with his environment. He is then able to observe (*guan* 觀) the natural tendencies of the Cosmos (*tian xing* 天性) and match nature with nature. Phenomenologically speaking, the phenomenon of worldly presence is manifested as a single process of interactive engagement. All that is left is a 'clearing' in which the phenomenon is itself manifested without obstruction. This does not entail that he sees everything as it really is, only that obstacles to perceiving more detail and subtlety are removed.

5. PERFORMANCE

Once trained experts have undergone preparations, they are now ready for the performance to begin: swimming in a turbulent pool, ferrying a raft across a whirlpool, drawing a circle, carving a bell stand, or driving a chariot. These are all very different skills, but they have their conditions of performance, some specific to each skill, some shared with others.

Confucius is singularly impressed with the swimmer at Lüliang Falls and asks if he has a *dao*. He replies that he has none but simply 'follows' (*cong* 從) the *dao* of the water without imposing himself on it (*bu wei si yan* 不為私焉) (19.10). To simply impose one's own personal path on a medium is, as Ding would put it, to hack away across the grain. This advice is especially important in turbulent conditions. A creature may try to fight the turbulence in order to maintain its path, but if the currents are too strong the creature may well be damaged by the excessive resistance. But this raises the question as to the difference between following the current and simply being thrown around by it. Surely the swimmer is not recommending simply doing nothing in the water, like a branch tossed by the flow. Indeed, being thrown around by a strong current is not necessarily less likely to result in harm.

In fact, the swimmer goes on to say, "I go under in tandem *with* (與 . . . 俱 入) the swirls and come out together *with* (與 . . . 偕出) the eddies" (trans. Hagen and Coutinho, *Philosophers of the Warring States*, 374). Carpenter Chui is described in similar ways: "his fingers transformed *with* things (*yu wu hua* 與物化), undetained by his mind" (19.13; trans. Hagen and Coutinho, *Philosophers of the Warring States*, 375). Chui is perhaps the Daoist equivalent of a Mohist worker: an artisan rather than a mere technician, he is able to do what the Mohists are able to do with their precise distinctions, models, and standards, but without any artificial tool to regulate him. Chui draws a perfect circle without the help of artificial devices, by following the nature of the material; he does not produce a random accidental scribble. So, clearly there is a difference.

Birds can maintain balance amidst turbulent flows, but they achieve this by sensing and responding swiftly to rapid changes in environmental conditions, not simply by ignoring the currents altogether and either forcing a path through them or being thrown around by them. There must be degrees of cooperation: one yields, but not completely. Maintaining one's wholeness requires responding to the rapidly changing currents in appropriate ways: not firmly standing stiff against the onslaught, but always slipping out of danger between lines of force, the vast empty channels in the airflow that manifest in concentrated attention. A bird hovering in strong gusts of wind is not doing nothing but engages in a complex and gentle choreography of twisting, shifting, tilting, turning, loosening, lifting, and dropping: multiple and simultaneous manoeuvres throughout its whole body, continuously readjusting in seemingly instantaneous response not only to environmental flow but also in response to one another, always returning to an ever-shifting centre of balance.

It is hard to phrase this sort of engagement without implying a misleading ontology. "Interaction" and "cooperation" can be understood so as to imply two separate entities; "control" also implies that one entity imposes its actions on another. These terms should instead be understood as emphasising the process *between*: a simultaneously bidirectional process of interactivity. Still, even though the performance is a holistic phenomenon, we can *conceptually* distinguish the bidirectional process of skilful performance from its two directions; we can also distinguish two distinctive types of directions: from a skilfully responsive performer to a medium of engagement, and vice versa. The 'medium' of engagement may be still, moving, or transforming, passive, active, or even aware: it may be a piece of wood; a constantly transforming vortex; a creature with awareness, feelings, and intentions (Zao

Fu's horses); or even another skilfully responsive performer (the tyrannical rulers in chapter 4).

From the perspective of the performer, these two directions may be thought of as "getting" (*de* 得) and "responding" (*ying* 應), to use the terminology of Wheelwright Bian: "You just 'get it' in your hand, and respond from your *xin*" (13.9; trans. Hagen and Coutinho, *Philosophers of the Warring States*, 376). In the *Lie Zi*, Master Tai Dou explains to his student Zao Fu that in leaping across poles successfully, he is responding (*ying*) with his mind-heart to what he is 'getting' (*de*) in his feet (5.15). In the same way, this must apply to a skill with a tool: one learns to extend one's body into an external medium: a raft or a bridle, perhaps. Tai Dou points out that this sensitivity continues to extend outwards in a chain: from the bridle to the bit. Here, there are two extra stages to the chain of responsiveness: the heart-mind responds to the information provided by the hand; the hand responds to the information provided by the bridle; the bridle responds to the information from the bit.[7] A driver of a modern vehicle is familiar with sensing the grip of the wheel against the ground through a chain of connections from the tire to the hands and body of the driver. But a charioteer's sensitivity extends still further: the bit itself is also responding to the horse's emotional state. If the horse is relaxed or anxious, this will manifest in its head and mouth movements, and this will have an effect on the bit, and this effect will be transmitted through the bridle to the charioteer's hands, and from there to their own *xin*.

I could add that the charioteer is simultaneously aware of information coming from the wheels through the chariot to his or her feet, and from the movement of the vehicle to his or her sense of balance. Visual and auditory information, and other kinds of sensory information, are all involved and interconnected in a continuous complex flow of mutual responsiveness. Extending the argument further, one might say that the whole environmental complex is an extension of one's body. In that case, driving a horse and chariot through a terrain is simply an extension of moving one's own body, and so one ought, at least in principle, to be able to charioteer as precisely as if one were controlling one's own steps: advancing and retreating in a perfectly straight line, swerving and circling in a perfect circle as effortlessly as Carpenter Chui.

6. TWO QUESTIONS

I end with a discussion of a discussion of two questions: one about the relationship between skill and Daoist wisdom, the other about the role of ethical considerations. Because of the Daoist scepticism regarding evaluative concepts, it is unclear on what grounds a Zhuangzian Daoist can distinguish between wise and unwise skilful actions, and also between ethical and unethical skilful actions.

I noted at the beginning that living wisely in tune with the Cosmos would entail interacting skilfully with our environments. The question arises, then, whether all such practical skill is a manifestation of Cosmic wisdom. Are all those who cultivate skill sagely models to be emulated? Would Alex Hannold, the fearless free rock climber, be admired as a Daoist sage? Would an athlete such as Serena Williams? What about the artist Andy Goldsworthy, who displays consummate skill in understanding the transformations of natural materials. What about a student who can throw a line of sharpened pencils into a high vaulted ceiling with even spacing and precision? It seems unlikely that all skilful people would be regarded as sagely, but the texts do not make clear what the distinguishing criteria would be.

Regarding the second question, ethical questions arise when our actions can impact others by causing them harm in some way. The Utopian strand of Daoist philosophy has the capacity to deal with this question, as preserving life and avoiding harm are explicitly expressed as fundamental values. Things are not so easy for the Zhuangzian strand, however. The introductory paragraph to chapter 3 says, "If you act virtuously (*shan* 善), keep away from fame; if you act badly (*e* 惡), keep away from punishment. Follow the guiding channels, and you will be able to protect your person, keep your life whole, nurture what is close to you (*qin* 親), and live your years to the fullest extent" (trans. Hagen and Coutinho, *Philosophers of the Warring States*, 369). The term *qin* can sometimes include reference to one's parents, but this would be a forced interpretation in this context: less ambiguous evidence is necessary to settle the issue. Self-preservation, while not itself an unethical principle, is insufficient by itself to rule out action that causes unnecessary harm to others.

Mengzi (1A7)[8] explicitly acknowledges the suffering of a cow that is taken to slaughter; he is even aware that human artifice damages the nature of wood, when we chop down trees and denature the material to shape it into useful utensils. The Utopian Daoists[9] value human life and disapprove of harming our natural tendencies. In some passages of the Utopian strand, this concern for caring for life and preventing harm extends to other people, though there are no explicit signs that this concern should extend to animals. This would mark the limits of ethical skill for the Utopian strand of Daoist philosophy in the *Zhuangzi*, but it is unclear whether anything comparable can be found in the Zhuangzian strand of the anthology. Indeed, in chapter 3, the concern for nurturing life does not extend to the life of the animal that is being butchered by Cook Ding. And sensitivity to its inner tendencies does not extend to its capacity to experience suffering. This leaves interpretation wide open, unless ethical boundaries can be deduced from other Zhuangzian concepts.

NOTES

1. For my analyses of original texts, I used the searchable electronic editions on Donald Sturgeon's Chinese Text Project archive: https://ctext.org. Most translations are my own, including chapter titles. They have been published in Hagen and Coutinho, *Philosophers of the Warring States*.

2. Further applications of this kind of skilful political negotiation can be found in chapter 4 (*Ren Jian Shi* 人间世), but I do not include them in this investigation.

3. With this term I refer to the overall philosophical attitude of the Inner Chapters together with broadly compatible passages in the Outer and Miscellaneous Chapters. I include them under the same rubric because these philosophical strands are so closely interconnected that it is hard to prise them apart with any certainty. Even where they differ, it is not easy to be sure which passages were written earlier, given Guo Xiang's editorial rearrangement of the text. Linguistic evidence does not always help to settle the issue either. Although I do not explicitly include the *Liezi* in this category, the skill stories are so close in spirit to those of the Zhuangzian school that they help to throw light on deeper elements of this philosophy of skill. (I prefer the loose adjective "Zhuangzian" to the term "Zhuangist" in order to avoid implications of an unnecessarily reified Zhuang*ism*.)

4. My translation. Compare Graham, *The Book of Lieh-tzu*, 84.

5. It is noteworthy that the skill stories in the *Zhuangzi* make no explicit reference to a teacher, as several contributors to this volume note. Some of the skills are traditionally acquired through apprenticeship with a master (ferrying, woodcarving, carpentry), but no mention is made of a teacher in these stories. It is unclear whether this should be taken to imply that no guidance under an expert is ever necessary, or whether this sort of apprenticeship is so obvious that it is presupposed. The ferryman, for example, says that ferrying can be learned (*xue* 學). Etymologically, the graph implies a child receiving instruction. Arguably, the concept simply means receiving instruction (from people or texts with authority). Indeed, A. C. Graham translates the passage in terms of whether ferrying can be *taught* (which the ferryman answers affirmatively). The *Liezi*, however, does make explicit reference to the students' apprenticeship under a master. Zao Fu, the charioteer, for example, studied under Tai Dou; and Ji Chang studied archery with Fei Wei, who in turn studied under Gan Ying.

6. Hagen and Coutinho, *Philosophers of the Warring States*, 289.

7. Michael Polanyi discusses this sort of extension of perception in terms of "subsidiary awareness". These are the aspects of our experience of engagement that are so familiar that we no longer focus on them; they recede from our attention, which derives its new focus in the extended instrument (Polanyi, *Personal Knowledge*).

8. Hagen and Coutinho, *Philosophers of the Warring States*, 140–41.

9. This is the strand of Daoist thought represented by chapters 8, 9, 10, 28, 29, and 31 of the anthology. Liu Xiaogan refers to them as the Anarchist school, while A. C. Graham divides them into two factions, the Primitivist (chapters 8 to 10), and the Yangists (chapters 28 to 31) (Liu, *Classifying the* Zhuangzi *Chapters*). I refer to them as "Utopian" as they express a shared utopian vision of a flourishing human life. See Coutinho, *An Introduction to Daoist Philosophies*, 128–39.

REFERENCES

Coutinho, Steve. *An Introduction to Daoist Philosophies*. New York: Columbia University Press, 2014.

Graham, Angus Charles. *The Book of Lieh-tzu*. New York: Columbia University Press, 1990.

———. *Chuang-tzu: The Inner Chapters; A Classic of Tao*. Indianapolis: Hackett, 2001.

Hagen, Kurtis, and Steve Coutinho. *Philosophers of the Warring States: A Sourcebook in Chinese Philosophy*. Peterborough: Broadview Press, 2018.

Liu, Xiaogan. *Classifying the* Zhuangzi *Chapters*. Translated by Donald Munro. Michigan Monographs in Chinese Studies 65. Ann Arbor: University of Michigan, 1994.

Polanyi, Michael. *Personal Knowledge: Towards a Post-Critical Philosophy*. New York: Harper Torch Books, 1964.

Chapter Seven

The Unskilled Zhuangzi

Big and Useless and Not So Good at Catching Rats

Eric Schwitzgebel

Zhuangzi—by which I mean the Zhuangzi of the Inner Chapters of the book that is traditionally attributed to him—does not especially value spontaneous, skilful responsiveness. He criticises skill more than he praises it. He does not see skill as particularly worth aiming for, and he does not particularly admire people who display skilful mastery of their arts.

In saying this, I mean to be disagreeing with the mainstream tradition in Anglophone Zhuangzi interpretation. A. C. Graham portrays Zhuangzi as celebrating the "spontaneous aptitude" of skilful craftsmen, which cannot be conveyed in words. Zhuangzi's "Taoist sage", Graham writes, responds to the world with "unthinking dexterity" and like such artisans in their best moments "is spontaneous from the very centre of his being" (Graham, *Disputers*, 191). Chad Hansen characterises Zhuangzi's "practical advice" to be pursuit of the highest level of skill mastery in any arena, to the point where "skill responses appear to us as natural responses" (Hansen, *Daoist*, 302). Philip J. Ivanhoe writes that Zhuangzi's "view of the world takes as its paradigms individuals who *know how* and shuns those who merely *know that*. Most important of all are skilful individuals like [master ox carver] Cook Ding" (Ivanhoe, "Zhuangzi on Skepticism," 650). Graham, Hansen, and Ivanhoe disagree on important points, but they agree that skilled responsiveness, like that of an expert craft worker, is central to Zhuangzi's positive vision. Many other interpreters follow Graham, Hansen, and Ivanhoe.[1]

My main observation is this: almost all of the celebrations of skill in the *Zhuangzi* are in the Outer Chapters, not the Inner Chapters, and are thus dubiously related to the Zhuangzi of the Inner Chapters.[2] A close reading of the Inner Chapters finds Zhuangzi criticising skilfulness at least as often as he celebrates it, and even the famous passage about the ox-carving cook permits an interpretation that does not emphasise the value of skill.

1. PASSAGES CONCERNING SKILL IN THE INNER CHAPTERS

Let me attempt a catalogue of the passages in the Inner Chapters that most directly concern skill, especially spontaneous skilful responsiveness that seems to go beyond words. It would beg the question in favour of skilfulness interpretations to treat *every* successful action as a result of skill in the intended sense, without clear textual evidence that success requires something analogous to the spontaneous skill of a practised artisan. It would similarly beg the question to treat wisdom itself, or flexibility, or the magical powers that Zhuangzi sometimes appears to celebrate, as involving skilfulness in the intended sense, without clear textual evidence. Success, wisdom, flexibility, or magic might, for example, be innate, or based merely on attention to the right things, or due to chance, or due to not being interfered with, or due to avoiding certain sorts of mistakes, or due to having an easygoing or open-minded personality. I will confine my analysis to passages in which skilfulness is either explicitly discussed or the presence or absence of something like artisanal, athletic, or musical skill is especially striking.[3]

The cicada, the dove, the quail, the giant bird, and Liezi. Flying might be seen as an athletic skill. Three clumsy, limited flyers appear near the beginning of the Inner Chapters: the cicada and the dove, who can't even reliably make the leaps from tree to tree, and the quail who can barely get a few yards before dropping to the ground (1/5/4[4]). Zhuangzi contrasts these small creatures with a giant bird who can soar ninety thousand miles and with the sage Liezi, who "rode forth upon the wind, weightlessly graceful" (1/7/5; cf. "Spirit-Man," 1/11/7). The small animals laugh at the giant bird, absurdly insisting that their own way of flying is better. Although Zhuangzi appears to be portraying the cicada, dove, and quail as in some way inferior to Liezi and the giant bird, a straightforward skill interpretation of the passage isn't especially natural. Zhuangzi does not appear to be urging the cicada, dove, and quail to improve their flying techniques so that they can respond spontaneously without thought, as a great athlete might. Instead, Zhuangzi's emphasis is the absurdity of the small laughing at the big—their lack of perspective, their failure to appreciate the huge and marvellous. Regarding Liezi, the focus appears to be on how chasing merit, good fortune, and good name leads one to "depend on" things—and that even graceful Liezi, who did not anxiously aim at good fortune, still fell short of the ideal because he had to depend on the wind (1/7–8/5–6).

The skilled balm maker and Huizi smashing gourds. Zhuangzi describes a man who is "skilled at making balm to keep the hands from chapping" (1/13/

7).⁵ His family never earns more than a few pieces of gold from this, so they sell the formula to a customer who finds a military use for it and earns a fiefdom. In this passage, Zhuangzi appears to be criticising the use of skill in a small, conventional purpose, compared to creative "thinking outside of the box". This interpretation harmonises with the broader context of this passage in which Zhuangzi is criticising his friend Huizi for smashing giant gourds because he couldn't find a conventional use for them.

The yak and the weasel. Chapter 1 ends with Zhuangzi contrasting a yak and a weasel. The weasel leaps high and low, dashes east and west, catching mice—and dies in a trap. The yak, however, is "good at being big—but of course it cannot catch so much as a single mouse" (1/14/8). Likewise, Zhuangzi says, a giant useless tree will "never be cut down by ax or saw", and "you can loaf and wander there, doing lots of nothing there at its side, and take yourself a nap" (cf. 4/17–18/30–31). In broader context, Huizi has just criticised Zhuangzi for his "big but useless" words, and the parable of the yak and weasel is Zhuangzi's defence against Huizi's complaint. To be big and useless, Zhuangzi seems to be saying, has some benefits. Arguably, the weasel is a paradigm of spontaneous skilful activity. It is talented at dashing around, catching rodents! What Zhuangzi appears to celebrate instead is loafing, lazy bigness and *lack* of skills—"doing nothing" in the common-sense understanding of that phrase. Similarly, later, Zhuangzi points out that a dog's ability to catch rats is liable to "bring on leashes that bind" it (7/4/51).

Zither playing, baton waving, and desk slumping. Zhuangzi describes two masters of music and one of logic—the master of logic being his "desk slumping" friend Huizi (2/26–27/15). He says that "the understanding these three had of their arts flourished richly", and they wanted to share their delight with others. However, because they could not successfully share their delights they ended up debating obscurities and unsuccessfully attempting to force others into their practices. Presumably, this bad result derives from their evangelism rather than the skills themselves. However, it can hardly be said that this passage is a celebration of the benefits of skilfulness.

The cook and the ox. This passage (3/3–6/22–23) is the most famous skill passage in the Inner Chapters. I defer its treatment until section 2.

People testing skills against each other. Zhuangzi writes, "When two people test their skills against each other, it starts out brightly enough, but usually ends darkly; when it really gets extreme, they end up engaging in all sorts of outrageous tactics to defeat each other" (4/14/28).⁶ As with the zither-playing passage, probably it is not skill per se that is to blame. Nonetheless, skill is again associated with something negative rather than celebrated.

The mantis flaunting its talents. Zhuangzi describes a mantis with such a high opinion of its talents that it attempts to stop a carriage. Analogously, he suggests, if you irritate powerful people by flaunting your talents, you risk being killed (4/16–17/29–30, cf. 4/3/25). If what is being flaunted or counted upon here is skill of the relevant sort (it's not clear whether it is), then again Zhuangzi is associating skill with something negative rather than celebrating it.[7] In this passage, Zhuangzi appears to be suggesting that instead of parading your talents you merely follow along with the behaviour and preferences of the powerful. (Although it is possible that appropriately following along with the behaviour and preferences of the powerful itself involves a kind of spontaneous skilful responsiveness of the sort seen in artisanal and musical skills, the passage does not give us particular reasons to think so.)

Horsehead Humpback. In chapter 5, Zhuangzi describes a man who seems to lack any skills, Horsehead Humpback (5/13–14/35–36). Horsehead Humpback "has never been heard to initiate anything of his own"; he has "no position of power", no "stash of wealth"; he is "ugly enough to astonish all the world"; and he "achieves nothing". Despite this, women would rather be his concubine than another man's wife, people crowd around him, and Duke Ai of Lu asks him to be prime minister of the state (from which obligation Horsehead Humpback flees). One might argue that Horsehead Humpback has some artisan-like spontaneous skilfulness that is hard to describe in words and remains implicit in the passage. But a more straightforward interpretation is that Horsehead lacks any artisan-like skills at all. Instead, Zhuangzi says, he has kept his "innate powers whole and intact".

Skill is merely salesmanship. Zhuangzi writes that for the sage, "understanding is merely a bastard son, obligations and agreements merely glue, virtue[8] a mere continuation of something received, skill[9] mere salesmanship. . . . He is not for sale as a commodity, so what use would he have for salesmanship?" (5/20/38).

My teacher supports heaven and earth without being skilful. Xuyou says of "my teacher" that "he covers and supports heaven and earth and carves out all forms, but without being skilful.[10] It is all the play of his wandering, nothing more" (6/51–52/48–49).

If we take these passages at face value, it seems that, overall, Zhuangzi is at best ambivalent about the value of artisanal, athletic, and musical skill. He does not celebrate such skills, much less privilege them as his ideal. His ideal appears instead to be something like lazing about, doing nothing, mastering nothing, and serving no purpose. I have not cherry-picked these passages to make my point. They are something close to a complete list of the explicit discussions of artisan-like skill in the Inner Chapters, excepting the passage about the ox-carving cook, to which I now turn.

2. THE COOK WHO TEACHES THE KING TO "NOURISH LIFE"

Friends of skill interpretations rely heavily upon this passage from the Inner Chapters:

> The cook was carving up an ox for King Hui of Liang. Wherever his hand smacked it, wherever his shoulder leaned into it, wherever his foot braced it, wherever his knee pressed it, the thwacking tones of flesh falling from bone would echo, the knife would whiz through with its resonant thwing, each stroke ringing out the perfect note, attuned to the "Dance of the Mulberry Grove" or the "Jingshou Chorus" of the ancient sage-kings.
>
> The king said, "Ah! It is wonderful that skill can reach such heights!"
>
> The cook put down his knife and said, "What I love is the Way, something that advances beyond mere skill. . . .[11] When I first started cutting up oxen, all I looked at for three years was oxen, and yet I was still unable to see all there was to see in an ox. But now I encounter it with the spirit instead of scrutinising it with my eyes. . . . A good cook changes his blade once a year: he slices. An ordinary cook changes his blade once a month: he hacks. I have been using this same blade for nineteen years, cutting up thousands of oxen, and yet it is still as sharp as the day it came off the whetstone. For the joints have spaces within them, and the very edge of the blade has no thickness at all. . . .
>
> "Nonetheless, whenever I come to a clustered tangle, realising that it is difficult to *do* anything about it, I instead restrain myself as if terrified, until my seeing comes to a complete halt. My activity slows, and the blade moves ever so slightly. Then all at once, I find the ox already dismembered at my feet like clumps of soil scattered on the ground. . . .
>
> The king said, "Wonderful! From hearing the cook's words I have learned how to nourish life!" (3/3–6/22–23)

This is a beautiful passage—one of the most striking passages of the Inner Chapters. It is easy to see the temptation to build one's interpretation of Zhuangzi around it.

The passage clearly celebrates someone with impressive artisanal skill. And his skill is in some way connected with "nourishing life". Yet I see four reasons not to stand this passage at the centre of one's Zhuangzi interpretation.

First: As I argued in the previous section, high levels of artisanal, athletic, and musical skill do not earn Zhuangzi's praise elsewhere in the Inner Chapters and indeed seem to be targets of criticism.

Second: The Inner Chapters are full of contradictions. Indeed, self-contradiction is central to Zhuangzi's style. Elsewhere I've argued that if Zhuangzi's aim is to jar us out of dogmatism, without installing a new dogma in place of the old dogmas, then embracing contradictory standards in different portions of the text might be an effective technique that he intentionally employs (Schwitzgebel, "Death, Self, and Oneness" and "Zhuangzi's Attitude"). If this is correct, it would be bad interpretative policy to accept any one passage at face value without checking to see whether it is contradicted elsewhere in the Inner Chapters. This passage, to the extent that we read it as a celebration of artisanal or athletic skill, is among those that do appear to be contradicted. Skill is mere salesmanship (5/20/38). The sage covers heaven and earth without being skilful (6/51/49). It is better to be a useless, unskilled yak than a skilled catcher of rodents (the weasel [1/14/8], the dog [7/4/51]). (Zhuangzi does not contradict himself on all points. He never seems to say that the small is better than the big, for example, nor that it is a good idea to ruin one's health in pursuit of fame and accomplishment.)

Third: It is plausible to read Zhuangzi as dubious about the types of ideals that philosophers articulate and defend, whether those are ideals of Confucian virtue; of Mohist virtue; of "usefulness", wealth, reputation, or political power; or even the Yangist ideal of achieving a long, healthy life. The ideal of developing artisan-like skills—or even developing one's ability to react with spontaneous artisan-like skilfulness to whatever arises in one's life situation—is another ideal of which Zhuangzi, at least in his sceptical moments, might be similarly dubious.

Fourth: It is not clear that the cook's skill is the thing that teaches King Hui how to nourish life. It might be the knife's passivity instead. I do not insist on this interpretation. It is perhaps not the most natural one. However, I think this interpretation has something to be said for it. Consider, first, that there's another obvious way that the cook's knife could have remained as "sharp as the day it came off the whetstone": The cook might have done nothing with it. He might have carved no oxen at all. He might have laid the knife in a drawer or lazed around with it beneath a giant tree in the field of the bright and boundless. The yak survives by (approximately) doing nothing, the trees by doing nothing. If one is good at something, one gets yanked into service like a dog on a leash (7/4/51) or like an able-bodied man facing military conscription (4/18/31). Maybe what's good about the knife, or at least what leads to its healthy longevity, is that it simply follows along through empty spaces, rather than hacking and slicing. The knife itself has no skills. Due to the *cook's* skill, the knife itself needs to do almost no cutting at all. It is this inactive knife, following along into the empty spaces, doing as little as a knife can do, that is praised for its longevity, not the active, skilled cook. Indeed, one might worry about the fate of the cook: his talents have come to the attention of a king (whether by choice or not is unclear from the passage)—a worrisome thing if one values one's life and freedom.

Zhuangzi is presenting the cook's skill for our admiration, celebrating that skill and associating it, in some way, with nourishing life. I don't mean to deny that obvious interpretation of this passage. But in the context of the Inner Chapters as a whole, this passage is an outlier. Considering what Zhuangzi says elsewhere, we might do better to take the knife as our model rather than the cook.

3. CONCLUSION

If we base our understanding of Zhuangzi on the Inner Chapters, we should reject the commonly held view that Zhuangzi especially values spontaneous skilful activity of the sort that is characteristic of highly skilled artisans and athletes. Most discussions of skill in the Inner Chapters are neutral or even negative about the value of skills of this sort.

I suspect that skill interpretations are partly motivated by passages from the Outer Chapters, partly by the vivid beauty of the passage about the ox-carving cook, partly by how Zhuangzi was received by the later Daoist tradition, and partly because it gives an appealingly simple answer to the question of what Zhuangzi wants people to aim for, given that Zhuangzi is undeniably suspicious of fixed words and doctrines. However, at best, this interpretation is poorly grounded in the Inner Chapters. At worst, seeking spontaneous wordless skill as the highest goal becomes exactly the sort of driving dogma that Zhuangzi hoped to resist. He might rather laze around incompetently beneath a tree than become a skilful master at catching rats. [12]

NOTES

1. For example, Barrett, "*Wuwei* and Flow"; Eno, "Cook Ding's Dao"; Fox, "Concrete Ethics"; Fraser, "Wandering the Way"; Huang, "Respecting Different Ways"; Kohn, *Zhuangzi*; Slingerland, *Effortless Action*; and Yearley, "Zhuangzi's Understanding."

2. On the relation of the Inner Chapters to the rest of the text, see Graham, *Disputers*; Klein, "Were There 'Inner Chapters'"; McCraw, *Stratifying Zhuangzi*; and notes in Graham's Zhuangzi translation (Chuang-tzu, *Seven Inner Chapters*). I will assume that the Inner Chapters come from one hand or one closely related group of people and that they are more closely textually related to each other than they are to the Outer and Miscellaneous Chapters, thus constituting the core "Zhuangzi" outlook. Despite textual problems, most interpreters still accept this much.

3. Quotes and references will be to the Ziporyn translation (Zhuangzi, *Essential Writings*), except where indicated. Where details of translation are relevant, I will also cite the original Chinese and/or translations by Watson (*Complete Works*), Graham (*Seven Inner Chapters*), and Kjellberg (*Zhuangzi*).

4. References are chapter/part/page number in Ziporyn's translation.

5. 宋人有善為不龜手之藥者. Watson has "skilled at making" (*Complete Works*, 34). Graham has "expert in making" (*Seven Inner Chapters*, 47). Kjellberg has "were good at making" (*Zhuangzi*, 212).

6. 且以巧鬥力者，始乎陽，常卒乎陰. Qiao (巧), here translated as "skill," is also translated with a negative valence as "tactics" and "cunning" later in the passage. Watson and Kjellberg both have "pit their strength in games of skill" (*Complete Works*, 60, and *Zhuangzi*, 230, respectively). Graham has "competitors in a game of skill" (*Seven Inner Chapters*, 71).

7. Watson also interprets the passage as about "parading your store of talents" (62–64). Graham interprets it as pride in your nobility (72). Kjellberg omits the passage.

8. I have replaced Ziporyn's translation of *de* (德) as "Virtuosity" with the more standard "virtue".

9. *Gong* (工) is translated here as "skill" by Ziporyn as well as by Watson (75). However, Kjellberg translates it as "effort" (234) and Graham as "deeds" (82).

10. Again, *qiao* (巧) is translated as "skill". Watson has "he doesn't think himself skilled" (90). Graham has "it is not skill" (91). Kjellberg says he "is not handy" (241).

11. I have replaced Ziporyn's translation of *dao* (道) as "Course" with the more standard "Way". Although Zhuangzi here says that the Way goes "beyond mere skill" (進乎技矣), I see this phrase as ambiguous between devaluing skill or ability (*ji* 技) and claiming skill so much beyond ordinary skill that to call it mere skill is to underappreciate it. (Compare reacting to a great concert by saying, "That is not mere music, it's the very turning of the heavens!") The character *ji* (技) also appears in two other passages in the Inner Chapters: the passages about the skilled balm maker and the rat-catching dog, discussed above. Thus, it does not appear that Zhuangzi is distinguishing between *ji* (技) and *qiao* (巧) as good versus bad types of skill.

12. For helpful discussion, thanks to Kelly James Clark, Julianne Chung, Steven Coutinho, P. J. Ivanhoe, Lisa Raphals, Mary Riley, and Kwong-loi Shun.

REFERENCES

Barrett, Nathaniel F. "*Wuwei* and Flow: Comparative Reflections on Spirituality, Transcendence, and Skill in the *Zhuangzi.*" *Philosophy East and West* 61 (2011): 679–706.
Chuang-tzu. *The Complete Works of Chuang Tzu.* Translated by B. Watson. New York: Columbia, 4th c. BCE/1968.
———. *The Seven Inner Chapters and Other Writings from the Book Chuang-tzu.* Translated by A. C. Graham. London: Allen and Unwin, 4th c. BCE/1981.
Eno, Robert. "Cook Ding's Dao and the Limits of Philosophy." In *Essays on Skepticism, Relativism and Ethics in the* Zhuangzi, edited by P. Kjellberg and P.J. Ivanhoe. Albany, NY: SUNY Press, 1996.
Fox, Alan. "Concrete Ethics in a Comparative Perspective: Zhuangzi Meets William James." In *Varieties of Ethical Reflection,* edited by M. Barnhart. Lanham: Lexington, 2002.
Fraser, Chris. "Wandering the Way: A Eudaimonistic Approach to the *Zhuangzi.*" *Dao* 13 (2014): 541–65.
Graham, A. C. *Disputers of the Tao.* La Salle, IL: Open Court, 1989.
———. *Studies in Chinese Philosophy and Philosophical Literature.* Albany, NY: SUNY Press, 1986/1990.
Hansen, Chad. *A Daoist Theory of Chinese Thought.* New York: Oxford, 1992.
Huang, Yong. "Respecting Different Ways of Life: A Daoist Ethics of Virtue in the *Zhuangzi.*" *Journal of Asian Studies* 69 (2010): 1049–69.
Ivanhoe, Philip J. "Zhuangzi on Skepticism, Skill, and the Ineffable Dao." *Journal of the American Academy of Religion* 61 (1993): 639–54.
Klein, Esther. "Were There 'Inner Chapters' in the Warring States? A New Examination of Evidence about the *Zhuangzi.*" *T'oung Pao* 96 (2011): 299–369.
Kohn, Livia. *Zhuangzi: Text and Context.* St. Petersburg, FL: Three Pines, 2014.
McCraw, David. *Stratifying Zhuangzi.* Taipei: Academica Sinica, 2010.
Schwitzgebel, Eric. "Death, Self, and Oneness in the Incomprehensible Zhuangzi." In *Oneness in Philosophy, Religion, and Psychology,* edited by P. J. Ivanhoe, O. Flanagan, R. Harrison, H. Sarkissian, and E. Schwitzgebel. New York: Columbia University Press, forthcoming.
———. "Zhuangzi's Attitude toward Language and His Skepticism." In *Essays on Skepticism, Relativism and Ethics in the* Zhuangzi, edited by P. Kjellberg and P. J. Ivanhoe. Albany, NY: SUNY Press, 1996.
Slingerland, Edward. *Effortless Action.* Oxford: Oxford University Press, 2003.
Yearley, Lee H. "Zhuangzi's Understanding of Skillfulness and the Ultimate Spiritual State." In *Essays on Skepticism, Relativism and Ethics in the* Zhuangzi, edited by P. Kjellberg and P. J. Ivanhoe. Albany, NY: SUNY Press, 1996.
Zhuangzi. *Zhuangzi: The Essential Writings.* Translated by B. Ziporyn. Indianapolis: Hackett, 4th c. BCE/2009.
———. *Zhuangzi.* Translated by P. Kjellberg. In *Readings in Classical Chinese Philosophy,* 2nd ed., edited by P. J. Ivanhoe and B. W. Van Norden. Indianapolis: Hackett, 4th c. BCE/2005.

Part II

The Stories

Chapter Eight

Butcher Ding

A Meditation in Flow

James D. Sellmann

Butcher Ding was butchering an ox for Lord Wen Hui. His hands danced as his shoulders lunged with the step of his feet while his knees bent. With a hiss and a thud, the brandished blade never missed the rhythm as it sliced, now in time with "The Mulberry Grove" dance, now as if an orchestra were playing "The Managing Chief" symphony.

"Oh my, this is excellent, that a person's skill can attain such heights!" Lord Wen Hui said.

Setting aside his blade, Butcher Ding replied, "What your servant cares about is the course of action (*dao* 道), which goes beyond mere skill. When I first began to butcher oxen, I saw nothing but the whole ox wherever I looked. After three years, I stopped seeing the whole ox. Nowadays, I am in touch through my daemonic 神 insight, and I do not look with my eyes. With the senses I know where to stop; with the daemonic I desire to run its course. I rely on Nature's Patterns (*tian li* 天理), cutting along the main seams; I let myself be guided by the cavities, going by what is inherently so. A vein or artery, a ligament or tendon the blade never touches, not to mention bone. A good butcher changes his blade once a year because he hacks. A common butcher changes it once a month because he smashes. Now I have had this cleaver for nineteen years, and have butchered several thousand oxen, and the blade's edge is as sharp as though it was fresh from the grindstone. Each joint has an opening, and the blade's edge has no thickness. When you insert what has no thickness where there is an opening, then what more could you ask; of course, there is ample room to move the edge about. That's why after nineteen years my blade's edge is as sharp as though it were fresh from the grindstone.

"However, whenever I come to something intricate, I see where it will be hard to handle and cautiously prepare myself, my gaze settles on it, action slows down for it, you scarcely see the flick of the blade—and with one stroke the tangle is unravelled, as a clod of earth crumbles to the ground. I raise my

111

blade; assess my work until I'm fully satisfied. I clean the blade and put it away."

Lord Wen Hui said, "Excellent! By listening to Butcher Ding's words, I have learned from them the means to nurture life (*yangsheng* 養生)."[1]

1. THE EXPERIENCE OF FLOW

The *Zhuangzi*'s influence cannot be overstated. Its impact on Chinese Chan (Japanese Zen) Buddhism has been documented (Wu, *Golden Age*, 23–29). The *Zhuangzi*'s images of naturalism and spontaneity influenced Chinese poetry, music, and painting, especially landscape painting. It also influenced the martial arts with the idea of imitating the natural movements of animals and natural phenomena. Zen and the art of archery and Zen swordplay are early examples of achieving selfless flow activities in the Zhuangzi style. Zhu Xi proposed that the narrative of Butcher Ding carving up an ox with his stages of progression over the first three years and then nineteen years of practice was an example of the importance of gradual self-cultivation or gradual enlightenment over the sudden approach, which was popular at that time and is still popular today (Ching, *Religious Thought*, 156). Frank Lloyd Wright and Abraham Maslow are among the many that were influenced by the *Zhuangzi* (Thompson, "Fallingwater," 2017; Maslow, *Motivation and Personality*, 208).

In this chapter, I argue that the performance stories in the *Zhuangzi*, and the Butcher Ding story, emphasise an activity meditation practice that places the performer in a mindfulness flow zone, leading to graceful, efficacious, selfless, spontaneous, and free action. These stories are metaphors showing the reader how to attain a meditative state of focused awareness while acting freely in a flow experience. From my perspective, these metaphors are not about developing practical or technical skills per se. My argument challenges a strict instrumental reading. Although instrumental reasoning can easily lead one to focus on the pragmatic outcomes depicted in these stories (see Eno, "Cook Ding's Dao"; Callahan, "Cook Ding's Life"; and Robins, "Beyond Skill"), the proposed pragmatic outcomes are merely a kind of collateral result of effortless, free actions in the flow experience. The metaphors of Butcher Ding, the Lüliang rapids swimmer, the Wheelwright Bian, the Woodcarver Qing, the cicada catcher, the naked artist, and so on are used to show the reader a way to engage in free and graceful action in the flow experience. Zhuangzi is not concerned about developing labour skills. He criticises such skills, seen above when the butcher claims to have "left skill behind" (進乎技矣) (Graham, *Chuang-tzu*, 63), and chapter 5 notes that "skill is a peddler" (工為商) (Watson, *Complete Works*, 75). For Zhuangzi, specialists who deploy instrumental reasoning are "trying too hard and want too much," and the "teaching dialogues do not seem to convey practical techniques any more than a moral code or philosophical system" (Defoort, "Instruction Dialogues," 475).

Although it may be easy to interpret these performance narratives instrumentally, I propose that they are used as metaphors to show the reader a way to act freely in an effortless (*wuwei* 無爲), natural, and spontaneous (*ziran* 自然) flow experience. Attaining freedom of action in the flow experience could be a pragmatic outcome itself, but that would be a different kind of "practical goal" from a skill per se.

The teaching pedagogy depicted in these performance metaphors is a form of non-instruction in which learning still occurs (Defoort, "Instruction Dialogues," 474–77). Victor Turner describes these kinds of performances as being in the liminoid *communitas* zone (Turner, *From Ritual*). Mihaly Csikszentmihalyi gives a detailed analysis of what he calls the experience of flow (Csikszentmihalyi, *Flow*). Sports psychologists developed his flow idea and have identified the meditative or mindfulness state of awareness that accompanies being in the flow.[2] Neurophysiologists have analyzed the conditions of effortless action and effortless concentration (Bruya, *Effortless Attention*). Eliot Deutsch employed the terms "grace" and "acting freely" to describe these kinds of performances (Deutsch, *Personhood* and *Creative Being*). Thus, I think of them as graceful, free actions in the flow performance.

Christopher Kirby reframes the *Zhuangzi* as advocating a kind of naturalistic moral expertise (Kirby, "Naturalism and Moral Expertise," 14). Carine Defoort lists possible interpretations of what kind of philosophy Zhuangzi is doing to include being "a primitivist, relativist, individualist, hedonist, pessimist, nihilist, fatalist, naturalist, mystical negativist, transcendentalist, evolutionist, pre-Zen Buddhist, cynic, sceptic, contemplative, metaphysician, idealist or materialist, and so forth," which she then dissolves in her essay (Defoort, "Instruction Dialogues," 462). Eric Nelson breaks down the artificial distinctions of philosophy, scepticism, religion, mysticism, health, and so on when interpreters try to mislabel the *Zhuangzi* as merely representing one of these options (Nelson, "Questioning Dao"). For example, Buddhism is based on a health-care or "medical cure" model to alleviate suffering (*dukkha*), and the teachings are presented in a religious-philosophical "way of life" manner because too much metaphysical, theoretical, or philosophical "thinking" can obstruct the practice of mindfulness or meditation and the insights needed for liberation from such suffering. The *Zhuangzi*, and Daoism in general, have similar concerns of offering "ways of life" that are based on a "medical cure" model in a religious-philosophical manner. Among the reasons Buddhists deployed Daoist terminology to translate their concepts was the medical cure approach shared by the two teachings.

The two most popular academic interpretations of the *Zhuangzi*, namely scepticism and mysticism, are only part of the focus for nurturing life. The *Zhuangzi* recognises the limits of language, which cannot adequately describe our experience of the world (*tiandi* 天地), or the unsummed totality (*dao* 道), the experience of acting freely in the flow zone of selfless, spontaneous performance, or the panenhenic experience of being united with the continuous transformation of things "by entering the silent oneness of the sky" (乃入於寥天一) or the "Great Pervade" (大通) (Zhuangzi, *Concordance*, 18/6/82 and 19/6/93). The *Zhuangzi* contains a kind of linguistic scepticism, but this approach is used to avoid offering another teaching based on the questionable veracity of propositional knowledge. Zhuangzi is not a sceptic per se; rather, he employs a form of linguistic scepticism as a method to liberate the reader from the limitations of language. He deploys a limited methodological linguistic scepticism and still uses language, especially metaphors, poetry, humour, anecdotes, and narrative, as "goblet words" (*zhiyan* 巵言) to show how to gain an experience of losing the ego or self in a flow performance or in the panenhenic experience of oneness. He is trying to give the reader the experience itself or at least an insight into the experience; he is not concerned about the accuracy of the linguistic denotations or their truth value. If there is a philosophy in the Zhuangzi, it is profoundly holistic and not easily characterised (Kirby, "Naturalism and Moral Expertise," 14).

In the context of the philosophy of religion and the history of religions, mysticism refers to the experience of unity or oneness with an ultimate reality as it is variously understood in different teachings. R. C. Zaehner differentiated three general types of the mystical experience, namely, (1) total and complete oneness in the (Hindu) Brahmanic teachings; (2) limited or partial oneness in the monotheistic teachings where the creator/created dichotomy will not allow for complete unity; and (3) experiencing oneness with an aspect or force of nature or the entire natural world, that is, nature mysticism or the panenhenic experience of unity with nature (Zaehner, *Mysticism*). The type of nature mystical experience in Daoism and the *Zhuangzi* promotes active participation in the world, not merging with a philosophical absolute or otherworldly transcendent experience.[3] Even the practice of sitting in oblivion (*zuowang* 坐忘) is used to awaken a person to participation in the natural processes and transformations of life. Zhuangzi withdraws from imposed ritual norms, embracing active participation in living life with engaged enjoyment. If by "mysticism" we mean that the *Zhuangzi* attempts to describe the experience of an active or lived unity with an aspect of nature or the unsummed totality or *dao* (道), then that will be adequate for my purposes in this chapter.

Chapter 2 of the *Zhuangzi* is concerned with avoiding stress to live well, linguistic scepticism, and unity with nature—"the myriad things and I are one" (Graham, *Chuang-tzu*, 56). The text is also concerned with overcoming death anxiety and being able to live out one's natural life span, which entails physical and psychological health. Chapter 3 of the *Zhuangzi* is especially concerned with the health-care issue of mastering the means to nurture life.

Chow Tse-tsung argues that the title and theme of chapter 3 is derived from *The Yellow Emperor's Classic of Internal Medicine, the Huangdi neijing* (黃帝內經).[4] Graham proposed that Zhuangzi was likely following Yang Zhu's idea "that the life and health of the body are more important than worldly possession" (Graham, *Chuang-tzu*, 117).

To claim, as Watson does, that the *Zhuangzi* is advocating a complete break with all social norms or conventional values would be an exaggeration (Watson, *Complete Works*, 17). The opening passage of the chapter "The Master of Nurturing Life" (*Yangsheng zhu* 養生主) clearly describes the expected outcomes of practising Zhuangzi's way of life and worldview.

> Our lives are limited, but knowledge has no limit. If we use what is limited to pursue what has no limit, there is danger that the flow will cease. When the flow ceases, the one who still tries to use knowledge will be in danger for certain!
>
> Good doer, stay away from fame (*ming*).
>
> Wrongdoer, stay away from punishments (*xing*).
>
> Tracing the central controlling meridians (*du* 督), making them your standard (*jing*)
>
> can protect your body (*sheng*),
>
> keep life whole (*sheng*),
>
> nurture your parents (*jin*), and
>
> live out your years (*nian*).[5]

Graham has hit the mark in his translation by noting that "there is danger that the flow will cease." The flow here is primarily the flow of life energy (*qi* 氣), which is connected to the flow experience when a person acts freely, which is described in the Butcher Ding metaphor in the next passage of the chapter. Victor Mair's translation of the second to the last line is "nourish your inmost viscera," translating *qin* (親) as the "inmost viscera," has merit, fitting well with the medical model being advanced here (Mair, *Wandering*, 26). However, his translation assumes that nurturing parents is only a Confucian value. This overlooks the common ground shared by both Daoist and Ruists; it also goes against most of the commentarial precedent that interpret *qin* to refer to "immediate family or parents."

The above opening passage to chapter 3 outlines some basic norms that are found in ancient pre-Qin, state of Song, and many other cultures. It especially mentions the norms of taking care of our parents and being able to complete our natural life span. I intentionally refer to our parents and our lives because Zhuangzi is not advocating an impersonal or abstract philosophy; rather, he proposes a way of living that requires a person's unique and actual engagement—"so that each particular can be itself" (而使其自已也) (Zhuangzi, *Concordance*, 3/2/9). Zhuangzi accepts that there are some basic natural norms, such as nurturing your life and caring for family members, that we want to and naturally should follow.

Some might think that Daoists are always hermits, but this is not the case. Liezi and Zhuangzi were married with families, and many of the Daoist characters in the stories have good friends who attend funerals, even though they break the social norms at the funeral.[6] Zhuangzi acknowledges that imposed social and ritual norms promote unhealthy expectations and psychological and physical stress that tend to make life uncomfortable and shorter. He is sceptical and critical about the value of those imposed norms, especially court and social ritual norms, but not the natural norms such as a healthy life and family. He is sceptical and critical about the veracity of statements, but he is willing to use metaphor and narrative to provide instruction on what can be learned but not taught directly—a teaching on non-teaching. The mystical panenhenic experience is an important goal but not the only one. People must live well enough to sustain their own lives and those of family members to flourish and have panenhenic and other experiences as well.

Zhuangzi and his namesake text do advocate several values that point a way towards a this-worldly and life-affirmative optimism by engaging the world and life with joy (Kohn, *Zhuangzi*, 11–22). The various characters in the text are exemplar role models, especially those who "suffer" some physical deformity either from birth or punishment-amputation. Those role models are depicted as being at one with their own radical transmutations and the transformations of the myriad things of the world in the recognition that change is the natural constant course of things. This "go with the flow" or "go with the creative-transformative process" (造物者) approach to living promotes a healthy attitude of releasing oneself from the anxiety of living up to ritual norms or other socially imposed expectations, and even from death anxiety. This radical worldly optimism is articulated in the expression "make it be spring with everything."[7]

Butcher Ding's free-flow performance "shows how" even a somewhat difficult task of manual labour can be an opportunity to engage the world and our performance in it with joy. That is an enjoyment forged in forgetting excessive self-consciousness by merging with an activity in the present moment. Joy is derived from meditative mindfulness in action. To be able to perform daily tasks requiring a high level of proficiency in challenging situations accompanied by mindful concentration, creativity, selfless awareness, and satisfaction, and the ability to transform what might appear to be mundane, repetitive tasks into challenging, creative, aesthetic performances are key points of the flow experience at work or on the job, so to speak (Csikszentmihalyi, *Flow*, 143–63).

It is interesting how Zhuangzi's healing religio-philosophy seems to anticipate the findings of developmental psychology. Taylor and Marienau review and compare three constructive-developmental models, showing how mature people can multi-frame and hold on to contradictions without confusion, are independent, and construct knowledge and values based on the context or situation. These self-actualising values fit well with what Zhuangzi is doing, trying to lead the reader to a new and improved or more balanced way of living as an adult (Taylor and Marienau, *Facilitating Learning*, 273–83).

In this manner we can agree with Zhuangzi that language is limited; we make things so by saying they are so, based on the consensual, social construction of linguistic meaning. Social expectations have imposed rituals, economic requirements, norms, and mores on us that create unnatural, unhealthy, and stressful outcomes. We can reframe our mindset and transform those unnatural expectations, replacing them with this-worldly optimism derived from engaged enjoyment. In a sense, Zhuangzi is a master teacher of transformative learning and the use of disorientating dilemmas. Jack Mezirow uses the term "disorientating dilemmas" in his groundbreaking work on transformative learning to describe an unexpected situation that forces a person to think differently about something taken for granted up to that point in life (Mezirow, *Transformative Dimensions* and *Learning as Transformation*). Zhuangzi's philosophy, in a sense, provides the reader with several disorientating dilemmas by focusing on the stories and metaphors, like "goblet words" (*zhiyan* 卮言), that break down our preconceived ideas and put us in touch with the processes or transformations in nature, in society, and especially within our own persons. Defoort's study of Zhuangzi's "teaching of non-teaching" fits well with Mezirow's transformative learning and disorientating dilemmas. Her analysis of the anti-teaching is instructive in the conventional sense in trying to explain the unconventional anti-teaching style.

> The second aspect of anti-teaching shows, moreover, that this Zhuangzian attitude cannot be consciously adopted for the sake of being an inspiring teacher. Teaching [in the conventional sense] concerns to a large extent a transmission of knowledge, insights, and skills, but the *Zhuangzi* stories remind us of the fact that it should also contain a measure of not teaching, letting go, undoing, liberating or undermining . . . while Zhuangzi's masters . . . do have some intentions, namely, to notice the force and value of their energetic underflow, and to let it proceed without obstruction. Their training lies in removing obstacles, including those of fixed norms, elegant theories, clear judgments, good intentions and efficient techniques. All such certainties ultimately impede the formless force that, powerfully but beyond our apprehension, flows within us. (Defoort, "Instruction Dialogues," 476)

Zhuangzi's meditation practices are designed to teach the reader to empty the heart-mind and experience the flow within us. The practice of passive (sitting, reclining, or standing) or active (swimming, carving wood, or butchering an ox) meditation opens up the practitioner to a different experience of the world. This is a world founded on a direct experience that is not mediated by linguistic or other social trappings. Hence the position of no-ordinary position can be achieved by focusing on the meaning of the experience, rather than the meaning of the words used to express the experience—see the end of *Zhuangzi*, chapter 26: "Where can I find a man who has forgotten words, so I may have a word with him" (Watson, *Complete Works*, 302). This kind of self-emptying meaning also fits with the "goblet words" further developed below. If we can agree that we need to find people who have forgotten the meaning or precise denotation to establish a word's referential meaning so that we may converse with them using metaphor, poetry, or anecdote, we might then overcome our limited, constructed, linguistic categories and expressions to use language differently and thereby express the unique, graceful, free action in the flow performance and other spontaneous, natural performance experiences. In this case, I claim that the text has philosophical, religious, and health content derived from both passive (*zuowang* 坐忘) sitting in oblivion mediation and active (the flow performance activities) meditative practices that lead people to an experience of being one with the performance in particular, and with the unsummed totality of *dao* or *tiandi*—the natural world—in general.

2. THE PASSAGE

Concerning Butcher Ding cutting up an ox, some translators and interpreters want to place emphasis on the use of the term *shen* (神), the spirit or the daemonic, as a type of "supernatural efficacy" (Slingerland, *Effortless Action*, 7) or as spiritual or daemonic forces that can "possess a person and therefore they help bring to a person the highest possible spiritual fulfilment" (Yearley, "Zhuangzi's Understanding of Skillfulness," 154). These kinds of interpretations seem to assume a type of dualism of spirit and body that is not present in the *Zhuangzi*. The alleged separation of spirit and body does not fit with what is being described. What Ding means by "with the daemonic I desire to run its course" is not supernatural possession or supernatural efficacy but the attainment of the selfless, autotelic flow experience of acting freely and gracefully. The flow experience is often described as having an almost "magical" quality to it (Csikszentmihalyi, *Flow*, 54). If these interpreters proposed that it is "as if" a supernatural or magical force were at work or "as if" a person were possessed, then it would be a closer fit to what is really going on in the description. In Zhuangzi's terms, when people empty themselves of themselves, as in the practice of sitting in oblivion or fasting the heart-mind, they embody the *dao* as void, generating spontaneous, creative acts. In cutting lose (*jie* 解) from imposed social norms and awakening (*jue* 覺) to the natural course of transformation, people flow or wander free and easy (*you* 遊) in "the silent oneness of nature" or "pervade and unify" (*tongweiyi* 通為一) their actions and everything else in the world. This is how Zhuangzi describes acting and living freely in the flow experience.

3. FREE ACTIONS IN FLOW

Ancient agriculturalists and modern vegetarians might propose that the ox working in the fields better facilitates the cosmic flow than to serve as an example of optimal performance on the bloody chopping block. For Daoists, however, death is part of the natural transformations and optimal performances can be illustrated in activities in what might be considered less than optimal conditions such as a butchering or catching bugs. In this sense the butcher metaphor is instructive.

The butcher's performance describes an artful or aesthetic expression of what Deutsch refers to as free and graceful action (Deutsch, *Personhood* and *Creative Being*). Turner's description of being in the *communitas* zone (Turner, *From Ritual*) and Csikszentmihalyi's flow experience (Csikszentmihalyi, *Flow*) all fit nicely to explain what is being described in this story. The story is a metaphor for attaining states of spontaneous, natural action in which the performer loses excessive self-awareness to achieve a state of unity with the performance-action. Turner noted six points of comparison between his social concept of *communitas* and Csikszentmihalyi's individual flow experience (Turner, *From Ritual*). Allow me to tie into the discussion Deutsch's concept of free and graceful action.

Turner's first two elements of flow correlate with Deutsch's notion of skilfulness; they are (1) a merging of action and awareness that is made possible by (2) a centring of attention.[8] Because much of the performance is presented as efficacious action, it has the appearance of being a mere habit or a form of instinctual "ritualization" that an anthropologist may study. The behavioural event is only a necessary condition for acting freely. If we stop our investigation at the level of apparent behaviour, then there are no truly free acts, only behavioural events. Lord Wen Hui perceives Ding's actions to reflect a consummate behavioural event. The butcher denies the surface skills, leading the reader to a deeper experience. After three years of training, the butcher was able to merge awareness and action and see beyond the whole ox. The training taught the butcher to concentrate and unify his thought and action. Spontaneous actions are causally efficacious such that they free human actions from being mere behavioural events. "The actor must be a master of the conditions of his action and not as with behavioural events, their victim," and this spontaneity "is grounded in the deepest structures of one's being and is . . . a non-egoistic expression of one's spiritual potentiality" (Deutsch, *Personhood*, 117). It is interesting to note the similarity of expression between Deutsch's use of "spiritual potentiality" and "spiritual domain" and Butcher Ding's use of the "daemonic or spiritual" (神) apprehension of the ox (Deutsch, *Personhood*, 118).

This description correlates with the next two elements of the flow experience, namely, (3) loss of ego and (4) control of one's actions and control of the immediate environment. Turner emphasises this point in the following comment about the performer: "He may not know this at the time of 'flow' but reflecting on it he may realise that his skills were matched to the demands made on him by ritual, art, or sport" (Turner, *From Ritual*, 57). This spontaneity is expressed symbolically in rituals of creation or renewal through the reenactment of cosmic creativity, and it can be seen in rites of passage where the initiate in the liminality of betwixt and between is free to act without constraint of social status or taboo (Turner, "Betwixt and Between" and "Social Drama and Ritual"). The performance itself requires spontaneity as part and parcel of its efficaciousness. The performance of the actions provides a context in which there is an overwhelming emphasis placed on the proper performance of the acts themselves. This care for the appropriate performance of the action is a recognition of the "natural grace," "inherent order," "natural rhythm," or way of performing the action in its most fitting manner (Deutsch, *Personhood*, 117). All performances require an appropriation of natural grace. What Butcher Ding is concerned with is the natural course of action (*dao* 道), which has a spiritual or daemonic (*shen* 神) quality to it for him. Ding is dancing his butcher performance in a trance-like, egoless state while being in complete control of his actions and the ox.

Although a vegetarian would object to the killing of the ox, the metaphor "works" in that optimal performances with natural grace can occur in challenging situations. By discussing and clarifying "natural grace" in terms of artistic creativity, two points become clear. These acts have an "autochthonous ordering of elements under a controlling sense of rightness which results in the achievement of what, when the work is successful, appears to be inevitable" (Deutsch, *Personhood*, 118). Butcher Ding's dance-like performance exhibits this natural grace while acting freely, as cuts of meat fall to the ground. This concept of "autochthonous ordering" clears up a problem concerning the meaning of "rules" in the flow model. The last two elements of flow are (5) non-contradictory demands for action and clear unambiguous feedback for a person's actions. This element requires the actor to believe or at least suspend disbelief in the *rules* that govern a culturally designed game, art, or ritual. When the butcher confronts an intricate spot, he briefly returns to use his senses, his gaze settles on it, and his action slows down; then, suddenly with a flick of the blade, the ox falls apart like dry dirt. Finally, (6) flow is autotelic, an end in itself; it has no goal or reward outside of itself (Turner, *From Ritual*, 57–58). The Butcher finally assesses his work, is satisfied, and cleans and sheaths the blade. Turner proposes that what he calls *communitas* "has something of a 'flow' quality, but it may arise, and often does arise spontaneously and unanticipated—it does not need rules to trigger it off" (Turner, *From Ritual*, 58). Here the concept of "autochthonous order" captures both the meaning of "rule" in the flow experience and the spontaneity of *communitas*. Turner notes that the flow experience is individual, whereas *communitas* is a social group experience. I propose that the individual and social dichotomy fuse in Zhuangzi's non-dual or correlative logic. Just as Lord Wen Hui can learn from the butcher, the readers of the performance metaphors can identify with the characters in the stories and gain insight into the optimal flow experience being depicted such that the self-other dichotomy dissolves. Self-other, individual-society, person-world are linguistic conventions that are overcome or released in the flow experience.

For Deutsch, free actions, like works of art, "involve a timing that is right for them" (Deutsch, *Personhood*, 118). The timely performance of free action reflects a person's achievement of personhood. "It (a properly timed free action) will thus be obedient to what is called for by the situation and it will reflect wholly the rhythm of the actor's own achieved persona" (ibid.). In addition to the loving care and concern that is needed to embody natural grace, a kind of "wonderment" is also required. This wonder is not an absent-minded gaping at the world; "rather it is a kind of joyful harmony. Wonder involves . . . an awareness of belonging to a spiritual domain of being; it involves a sense of shared participation" (ibid.). Barrett uses the flow experience to analyze different cultural understandings of spirituality in the *Zhuangzi*'s performance stories (Barrett, "*Wuwei* and Flow," 685–91). Wonderment as a "joyous accompaniment" dissolves Turner's distinction between flow as individual experience and *communitas* as group experience because within the context of acting freely, the person, the group, and the environment are all harmoniously interpenetrating, such that even the observing audience achieves personhood by vicariously participating in the flow activity—for example, in the manner that the observer, Prince Wen Hui, realises how Ding's flow performance can be used to nurture life in the above narrative. Finally, the actor achieves and experiences a *power* in action through efficaciousness, spontaneity, and wonder-filled action (Deutsch, *Personhood*, 119). This effortless power is promoted by performances that elicit the flow experience. The degree to which people achieve effortless power in their performance displays their achievement of personhood. The more contrived people's actions are, the less authentic and sincere they appear to be.

4. GOBLET WORD METAPHORS: FLOW IS FUNDAMENTALLY DISCURSIVE

As noted above, Zhuangzi's linguistic scepticism does not have him retreating into silence, at least not immediately. Zhuangzi is willing to deploy language as a teaching tool, without concern for precise referential meaning or veracity. Zhuangzi's discourse itself is a form of flow. Kim-Chong Chong appeals to the story of Butcher Ding as a metaphor for finding a free-flowing, non-rigid, or spontaneous dance-like performance that cannot be reduced to a set of rules (Chong, *Zhuangzi's Critique*, 59). As we saw above, the autochthonous character of the performance displaces the notion of rule-governed behaviour. Embracing the radical transformation of things, Zhuangzi can counter the Confucian world view of a fixed moral character to *tian* (天) or nature with an alternative world view of the rapid transformation of ephemeral things, constantly changing, coming into and going out of existence. Zhuangzi's use of metaphor evokes a sense of the unity of all things (Chong, *Zhuangzi's Critique*, 45, 63–64). That sense of unity or that which "pervades and unifies (*tongweiyi* 通為一)" is also found in the flow experiences of Butcher Ding and the other performance stories in the *Zhuangzi*.

In what sense are the mores of ritual action contrived or unnatural? The apparent dichotomy between artificial or constructed experiences formed by culture and society versus natural or authentic experiences is itself a distinction that needs to be ameliorated by Zhuangzi. In the opening passage of the *Zhuangzi*, chapter 6, Dazongshi (大宗師), the Great Venerable Master, proposes that there must be a sublimely transforming person (*zhenren* 真人) before there can be sublimely transforming knowledge (*zhenzhi* 真知) by focusing on the *zhenren*'s equanimity of experience, that is, not feeling wet in water or hot in fire and not feeling anxiety in daily life or in sleep-dreams. In this sense the dichotomy between the artificial and the natural dissolves for the self-actualising person. Everything that comes from nature is natural, even the human, and everything thought of by human beings is contrived by them, so let it be.

Human knowledge is based on human bodily experiences. Neurophysiology can help philosophers better understand the brain's organic operations and its use of metaphor to learn (Taylor and Marienau, *Facilitating Learning*, 51–55). Zhuangzi's use of metaphor consciously or unconsciously hits the mark in how the brain learns. We can see in it an enlightened master-teacher's pedagogy to awaken the reader to a new perspective on life, to different ways of nurturing and caring for our short life spans that can be made even shorter by stress, dis-ease, and other forms of illness. Zhuangzi's metaphors help us identify with these types of acting freely in flow experiences, leading us towards them. In this sense, the Butcher Ding story is a metaphorical example of a self-actualising person who exhibits sublimely transforming "knowledge" or "know-how" that is performed for others to see. Either literally or metaphorically we see the butcher's flow experience. There is a medical or health-care aspect to Zhuangzi's religious-philosophical teachings, and this is especially the case in the Yangsheng Zhu chapter.[9] The term *jie* (解) is commonly used in ancient medical texts, such as in the *Yellow Emperor's Classic of Internal Medicine, the Huangdi neijing* (黃帝內經), to mean "to cure," "to cut loose" the patient from the affliction, and in the butcher story, *jie* (解) is a metaphor for cutting oneself lose from the restrictions of socially constructed norms. The free-flowing movements of Butcher Ding are grounded in the concrete reality of being in the natural flow zone, acting freely and spontaneously like the natural flow of *qi* (氣) energy within us. It is also a general metaphor for how one can live and nurture one's life in a natural manner that is focused, mindful, and free of anxiety or any imposed sense of strain, even while working in a dirty, bloody butcher shop.

Rur-bin Yang argues that Zhuangzi's performances bring about a state of "'synesthesia' commonly found in religious and artistic experience."[10] Yang's use of synesthesia fits well with the flow experience of graceful free actions. Yearley's description of these kinds of "performances" achieving a state of "intraworldly mysticism" that "differs from most Western and many South Asian forms of mysticism" hits the mark, and he accurately describes the mental mindset as "effortless concentration, lack of fatigue, quick passage of time, and a disinterest in doing anything other than what is now being done" (Yearley, "Zhuangzi's Understanding of Skillfulness," 160, 168). The flow of optimal, effortless action is expressed in the mysterious (*shen* 神) glow and dexterity of the cultivated person. The flow of *qi* energy is hylozoistic. If someone thinks that the psychological experience of being in the free-flow zone is distinct from a panenhenic nature mysticism experience, then I propose that this is because our artificial focus depicts the psychological experience as being different from the religious or mystical experience. "Synesthesia" provides a bridge between the religious and the aesthetic experience. From my perspective, being in the flow zone is strongly similar if not essentially the same as the nature mysticism experience of engaging in the "pervading unity" with some aspect of nature or the unsummed totality of cosmic transformations.

There is no discernible difference between being at one with the free, graceful, flow-zone performance and being at one with some other aspect of nature. It is the experience that matters, not the limitations of our description or the limits of language in general. This is what Zhuangzi is trying to show us, namely that we need to forget the words after we have grasped the meaning. Chong makes a similar point, saying, "Zhuangzi warns against being attached to absolute distinctions and having fixed conceptions" (Chong, *Zhuangzi's Critique*, 82). Moreover, the sublimely transforming person can harmonise the natural and the human by maintaining a calm attitude, a still, reflective, and empty heart-mind as exemplified by Butcher Ding (ibid.).

In this sense the Butcher Ding story is "empty" and leaves us with nothing more than a picture of, or a pointer towards, the free-flow-zone performance. It is a metaphor for the "just do it" attitude that is free, easy, natural, spontaneous activity, such as rambling (*you* 遊), body surfing in the rapids, catching bugs, carving wood, painting, or butchering. The function of the metaphor of Zhuangzi's goblet words (*zhiyan* 巵言) is to empty the words, the story, and the mindful reader of attachment to artificial constructs, especially true and false or right and wrong (*shi fei* 是非). The *Zhuangzi* uses language not to make claims or to state propositions that can or should be tested for their veracity; Zhuangzi uses words in "a spontaneous and non-judgmental nature that resists being pinned down to any position" (Chong, *Zhuangzi's Critique*, 108).

The non-judgemental mindset of being able to hold a position of no ordinary position is further developed by Zhuangzi in two ways. First, the "natural heart-mind" (what Zen refers to as the "everyday mind"), *chang xin* (常心) or constant mind, as opposed to the preconceived socialised heart-mind, *cheng xin* (成心), operates like a mirror or calm water, reflecting without storing what is present. Second, the metaphorical function of the goblet words is itself empty and free flowing. The *Zhuangzi* uses both approaches to present a position of no ordinary position. Shuen-fu Lin proposes that "*Zhi yan*, then, is speech that is natural, unpremeditated, free from preconceived values, always responding to the changing situations in the flow of discourse, and always returning the mind to its original state of emptiness as soon as a speech act is completed."[11]

The flow experience is fundamentally discursive. Lin shows us that the Butcher Ding story and the other performance stories in general are in a sense "empty." They are especially devoid of any theory of truth per se. Hans-Georg Moeller comes to a similar conclusion by using Wittgenstein's own admission that his approach to writing philosophy is based on discourse as "criss-crossing" flow; that is, Wittgenstein's writing became a carefree meandering (*you* 遊) rather than systematic theory (Moeller, "Rambling without Destination"). In a similar fashion, the performance stories lead the reader to engage in a free-flow activity, first, vicariously in reading the story, and then to engage the world in our daily lives with the ability to ramble freely, beyond effort in mindful concentration. Such is the outcome of Zhuangzi's bimodal, non-dual, correlative thinking coupled with passive and active meditation.

The free-flow-zone experience and other forms of meditation depicted in the *Zhuangzi* offer ways to get beyond the limitations of one's perspective by merging with the Great Pervade, the ongoing process of transformation. Getting beyond the limitation of one's own perspective opens new horizons for experiencing oneself and the world differently. This kind of personal transformation puts the practitioner in touch with a wider perspective and a different way of experiencing the world and its creatures. "This cognition is the culmination of an apophatic practice" (Roth, *Original Tao*, 154). Daoist meditation practices continued to develop after the *Zhuangzi*, with inner alchemy and other forms of mediation.[12] The narrative of Butcher Ding is best understood as a metaphorical guide to enter the free-flow zone ourselves.

ACKNOWLEDGEMENTS

A special thank you is due to Sharon Rowe, Roger Ames, Graham Parkes, and James Giles for helpful comments on drafts. Editors Wai Wai Chiu and Karyn Lai and fellow authors, especially Kim-Chong Chong, helped improve the chapter. Any remaining errors are my responsibility.

NOTES

1. Adapted by the author from the following translations: Zhuangzi, *Concordance*, 3/7–8/ 2–12; Graham, *Chuang-Tzu*, 63–64; Mair, *Wandering*, 26–27; Hamill and Seaton, *Essential Chuang Tzu*, 19–20; Graziani, "Princes Awake in Kitchens," 63.
2. Kaufman, Glass, and Arnkoff, "Evaluation of Mindful Sport"; Martinez and Scott, "Trail and Ultra-Running."
3. Jochim, "Say No to No Self," 62; Yearley, "Zhuangzi's Understanding of Skillfulness," 160.
4. Cited in Chong, *Zhuangzi's Critique*, 7. Chow, "Original Meaning of Yangsheng zhu."
5. Zhuangzi, *Concordance*, 7/3/1–2; modifying Watson, *Complete Works*, 50; Graham, *Chuang-tzu*, 62; Mair, *Wandering*, 25–26; Hamill and Seaton, *Essential Chuang Tzu*, 19.
6. See *Zhuangzi*, chapter 6, for example.
7. Watson, *Complete Works*, 19, 74; Chong, *Zhuangzi's Critique*, 128.
8. Turner, *From Ritual*, 56, and see Barrett, "*Wuwei* and Flow," 692.
9. Graziani, "Princes Awake in Kitchens," 63–65; Velleman, "Way of the Wanton," 187–88; Nelson, "Questioning Dao," 12; Kohn, *Science and the Dao*.
10. Yang, "From 'Merging the Body,'" 97; Chong, *Zhuangzi's Critique*, 80.
11. Lin, "Language of the Inner Chapters," 65; Chong, *Zhuangzi's Critique*, 109.
12. Kohn, *Healing Exercises*, "Forget or Not Forget," *Science and the Dao*; Eskildsen, *Daoism, Meditation*.

REFERENCES

Ames, Roger T., ed. *Wandering at Ease in the* Zhuangzi. Albany, NY: SUNY Press, 1998.
Ames, Roger T., and Takahiro Nakajima, eds. *Zhuangzi and the Happy Fish*. Honolulu: University of Hawai'i Press, 2015.
Barrett, Nathaniel F. "*Wuwei* and Flow, Comparative Reflections on Spirituality, Transcendence, and Skill in the *Zhuangzi*." *Philosophy East and West* 61, no. 4 (Winter 2011): 679–706.
Bruya, Brian. *Effortless Attention: A New Perspective in the Cognitive Science of Attention and Action*. Cambridge, MA: MIT Press, 2010.

Callahan, William A. "Cook Ding's Life on the Whetstone: Contingency, Action, and Inertia in the *Zhuangzi.*" In *Wandering at Ease in the* Zhuangzi, edited by Roger T. Ames, 175–96. Albany, NY: SUNY Press, 1998.

Ching, Julia. *The Religious Thought of Chu Hsi.* New York: Oxford University Press, 2000.

Chong, Kim-Chong. *Zhuangzi's Critique of the Confucians: Blinded by the Human.* Albany, NY: SUNY Press, 2016.

Chow, Ts'e-tsung 周策縱. "The Original Meaning of the Yangsheng zhu Chapter of the *Zhuangzi* 《莊子。養生主》篇 本義 复原." *Bulletin of the Institute of Chinese Literature and Philosophy* 中國 文 哲 研究 集刊 2 (1992): 13–50.

Csikszentmihalyi, Mihaly. *Flow: The Psychology of Optimal Experience.* New York: Harper and Row, 1990.

Defoort, Carine. "Instruction Dialogues in the *Zhuangzi*: An 'Anthropological' Reading." *Dao* 11 (2012): 459–78.

Deutsch, Eliot. *Creative Being: The Crafting of Person and World.* Honolulu: University of Hawai'i Press, 1992.

———. *Personhood, Creativity, and Freedom.* Honolulu: University of Hawai'i Press, 1982.

Eno, Robert. "Cook Ding's Dao and the Limits of Philosophy." In *Essays on Skepticism Relativism and Ethics in the* Zhuangzi, edited by Paul Kjellberg and Philip J. Ivanhoe, 127–51. Albany, NY: SUNY Press, 1996.

Eskildsen, Stephen. *Daoism, Meditation, and the Wonders of Serenity: From the Latter Han Dynasty (25–220) to the Tang Dynasty (618–907).* Albany, NY: SUNY Press, 2015.

Graham, Angus C. *Chuang-tzu: The Seven Inner Chapters and Other Writings from the Book Chuang-tzu.* London: George Allen and Unwin, 1981.

Graziani, Romain. "When Princes Awake in Kitchens: *Zhuangzi's* Rewriting of a Culinary Myth." In *Of Tripod and Palate*, edited by Roel Sterckx, 62–74. New York: Palgrave Macmillan, 2005.

Hamill, Sam, and J. P. Seaton. *The Essential Chuang Tzu.* Boston: Shambhala, 1998.

Jochim, Chris. "Just Say No to 'No Self' in *Zhuangzi.*" In *Wandering at Ease in the* Zhuangzi, edited by Roger T. Ames, 35–74. Albany, NY: SUNY Press, 1998.

Kaufman, K. A., C. R. Glass, and D. B. Arnkoff. "Evaluation of Mindful Sport Performance Enhancement (MSPE): A New Approach to Promote Flow in Athletes." *Journal of Clinical Sports Psychology* 4 (2009): 334–56.

Kirby, Christopher C. "Naturalism and Moral Expertise in the *Zhuangzi.*" *Journal of East-West Thought* 7, no. 3 (Autumn 2017): 13–27.

Kohn, Livia. *Chinese Healing Exercises: The Tradition of Daoyin.* Honolulu: University of Hawai'i Press, 2008.

———. "Forget or Not Forget? The Neurophysiology of *Zuowang.*" In *New Visions of the* Zhuangzi, edited by Livia Kohn, 161–79. St. Petersburg: Three Pines Press, 2015.

———. *Science and the Dao: From the Big Bang to Lived Perfection.* St. Petersburg: Three Pines Press, 2016.

———. *Zhuangzi, Text and Context.* St. Petersburg: Three Pines Press, 2014.

Lin, Shuen-fu. "The Language of the Inner Chapters of the *Chuang Tzu.*" In *The Power of Culture: Studies in Chinese Cultural History*, edited by W. J. Peterson, A. H. Plaks, and Ying-shih Yü, 47–69. Hong Kong: Chinese University Press, 1994.

Mair, Victor H. *Wandering on the Way: Early Taoist Tales and Parables of Chuang Tzu.* New York: Bantam, 1994.

Martinez, C. T., and C. Scott. "Trail and Ultra-Running: The Impact of Distance, Nature, and Personality on Flow and Well-Being." *Psi Chi Journal of Psychological Research* 21, no. 1 (Spring 2016): 6–15.

Maslow, Abraham H. *Motivation and Personality.* New York: Harper and Brothers, 1954.

Mezirow, Jack. *Transformative Dimensions of Adult Learning.* San Francisco: Jossey-Bass, 1991.

Mezirow, Jack, and Associates. *Learning as Transformation: Critical Perspectives on a Theory in Progress.* San Francisco: Jossey-Bass, 2000.

Moeller, Hans-Georg. "'Rambling without Destination': On Daoist '*You*ing' in the World." In *Zhuangzi and the Happy Fish*, edited by Roger T. Ames and Takahiro Nakajima, 307–19. Honolulu: University of Hawai'i Press, 2015.

Nelson, Eric Sean. "Questioning Dao, Skepticism, Mysticism and Ethics in the *Zhuangzi*." *International Journal of the Asian Philosophical Association* 1 (January 2008): 11–22.

Robins, Dan. "It Goes beyond Skill." In *Ethics in Early China*, edited by Chris Fraser, Dan Robins, and Timothy O'Leary, 105–23. Hong Kong: Hong Kong University Press, 2011.

Roth, Harold D. *Original Tao: Inward Training (Nei-yeh) and the Foundations of Taoist Mysticism*. New York: Columbia University Press, 1999.

Slingerland, Edward. *Effortless Action: Wu-Wei as Conceptual Metaphor and Spiritual Ideal in Early China*. Oxford: Oxford University Press, 2003.

Taylor, Kathleen, and Catherine Marienau. *Facilitating Learning with the Adult Brain in Mind*. San Francisco: Jossey-Bass, 2016.

Thompson, Kirill O. "'Fallingwater': Daoist Inklings about Place, Strategy, Design, and Space." *International Communication of Chinese Culture* 4, no. 1 (February 2017): 5–23.

Turner, Victor. "Betwixt and Between: The Liminal Period in *Rites de Passage*." In *Proceedings of the American Ethnological Society: Symposium on New Approaches to Religion* (1964): 4–20.

———. *From Ritual to Theatre*. New York: Performing Arts Journal Publications, 1982.

———. "Social Drama and Ritual Metaphor." In *Ritual, Play and Performance*, edited by Richard Schechner and Mady Schuman, 97–120. New York: Seabury Press, 1976.

Velleman, J. David. "The Way of the Wanton." In *Practical Identity and Narrative Agency*, edited by Kim Atkins and Catriona MacKenzie, 169–92. New York: Routledge, 2008.

Watson, Burton. *The Complete Works of Chuang Tzu*. New York: Columbia University Press, 1968.

Wu, John C. H. *The Golden Age of Zen*. New York: Doubleday, 1996.

Yang, Rur-bin 楊儒賓. "From 'Merging the Body with the Mind' to 'Wandering in Unitary Qi 氣': A Discussion of Zhuangzi's Realm of the True Man and Its Corporeal Basis." In *Hiding the World in the World: Uneven Discourses on the Zhuangzi*, edited by Scott Cook, 88–127. Albany, NY: SUNY Press, 2003.

Yearley, Lee. "Zhuangzi's Understanding of Skillfulness and the Ultimate Spiritual State." In *Essays on Skepticism, Relativism, and Ethics in the* Zhuangzi, edited by Paul Kjellberg and Phillip J. Ivanhoe, 152–82. Albany, NY: SUNY Press, 1996.

Zaehner, R. C. *Mysticism, Sacred and Profane*. London: Oxford University Press, 1961.

Zhuangzi. *A Concordance to Chuang tzu*. Harvard-Yenching Index Series 20. Cambridge: Harvard University Press, 1956.

Chapter Nine

Wheelwright Bian

A Difficult Dao

Lisa Raphals

Duke Huan was reading a book in the upper part of his hall. Wheelwright Bian was cutting a wheel in the lower part of the hall. Putting down his hammer and chisel, he went up and asked Duke Huan:

"I venture to ask what words Your Highness is reading?"

The duke replied: "The words of the sages."

The wheelwright said: "Are the sages still alive?"

The duke replied: "They're already dead."

The wheelwright said: "If that is so, then what My Lord is reading is the ancients' dregs and leavings."

Duke Huan replied: "How can a wheelwright offer comment on what I am reading? If you have an explanation, very well, but if you have none, you shall die."

Wheelwright Bian said: "Your servant will observe it from the perspective of his own occupation. Now in cutting a wheel, if the spokes are loose, they'll fit sweet as a whistle, but the wheel won't be solid. If they're too tight, you won't be able to insert them, no matter how hard you try. To make them neither too lose nor too tight is something you 'get' in your hands and respond to in your mind. The mouth cannot put it into words, and there is a knack to it. I cannot explain it to my son, and my son cannot receive it from me, which is why I am seventy years old but am still cutting wheels. The ancients and that which they could not transmit have both died, so as a result, what My Lord is reading is only ancients' dregs and leavings."[1]

The story of Wheelwright Bian is unusual for three reasons. First, Bian is a master of a clearly defined skill that is in addition technically difficult, and this difficulty distinguishes his skill from others that can be easily mastered to at least a moderate degree. Second, his skill is linked to broader attitudes to *dao*, by its content, by the chapter title (*Tian dao* 天道) and by his explicit opposition of his "wordless" expertise to the reading of texts. Finally, the rhetoric of the story is a virtual inversion of that of Cook Ding, one "skill" story in the Inner Chapters and its account of the relation between skill and *dao*. Both are teaching narratives in which a skill expert instructs a ruler. But unlike the story of Cook Ding, which begins and ends with praise of Ding's skill, this story is structured around a threat of death if Bian does not explain himself adequately, and we are not told what happens to him.

To examine the peculiarities of this story, I begin with the framing of the chapter. I then turn to the account of Bian's skill. The remaining sections turn to the interpretation of this skill and its relation to other skill stories in the *Zhuangzi*.

1. THE FRAME

The story of Wheelwright Bian making a wheel (*Lun Bian zhuo lun* 輪扁斲輪) occurs at the end of "The Way of Heaven," the thirteenth chapter of the *Zhuangzi*. I begin by looking at the framing of the story, both through the initial framing of the chapter itself and through the passage immediately preceding it.

The chapter begins:

> The *dao* of heaven revolves and wheels but holds nothing, and causes the myriad things to come to completion. The *dao* of the emperors revolves and wheels but holds nothing, and causes all under heaven to return. The *dao* of sages revolves and wheels but holds nothing, and causes all within the seas to submit. Those who are clear about heaven, conversant with sages, and who understand how the efficacy of emperors and kings penetrates the six directions and four quarters act of themselves, but without seeming to be so, are never not still. The stillness of sages is not so because stillness is said to be good and so they are still. It is because the myriad things can get no foothold in disturbing their minds that they are still. When water is still, it clearly reflects [every hair of] a man's whiskers and eyebrows. It is such a perfect level that great artisans take their standard from it. If the stillness of water is so bright and clear, how much more so are essence and spirit [*jing shen*]! The stillness of sages' minds is the mirror of heaven and earth; it is the lens of the myriad things.[2]

This framing passage praises three things: the efficacy of stillness (*jing*); the power of essence and spirit (*jing shen*), presumably of properly cultivated individuals; and the mirror-like stillness and clarity of the minds of sages who practise stillness and cultivate their essence and spirit. All three are important themes that appear elsewhere in the *Zhuangzi*.

A passage in the Outer Chapters links nourishing the heart-mind with cultivating or releasing the spirit and with stillness (*jing*). In a discourse between Yun Jiang 雲將 (Cloud General) and Hong Mang 鴻蒙 (Vast Obscurity), the latter gives advice on self-cultivation:

> Nourish the heart-mind. Only abide in *wuwei*, and things transform of themselves. Slough off the body [*shenti*]; cast out hearing and vision . . . release the heart-mind; free the spirit; be as still as if without a soul.[3]

Another describes stillness and the complex acting by not acting (*wuwei* 無為) as necessary for the "*dao* of nourishing spirit" (*yang shen zhi dao* 養神之道):

> To be pure and unadulterated, to be still and unified without changing, to be mild and [to act by] *wuwei*, in motion to walk with Heaven, this is the *dao* of nourishing spirit.[4]

Stillness, unity, and nourishing the spirit are also linked with fasting the heart-mind (*xin zhai* 心齋).[5] The *Zhuangzi* describes the clarity of the fasted heart-mind as clear like a mirror:

> When water is still, its clarity mirrors the [observer's] whiskers and eyebrows. It is fitting and accurate, so the great craftsman takes it as his standard. If still water is clear like this, how much more so is a pure spirit! The heart-mind of the sage is still thus! Heaven and earth mirror it and it is a looking glass for the ten thousand things.[6]

Here the metaphor of the mirror illustrates the stillness of *wuwei*. The image of the heart-mind as a mirror is particularly important in the *Zhuangzi*, where the (fasted) heart-mind becomes a mirror that clearly reflects things outside it.[7] For example, when an interlocutor asks Confucius about the special ways the cripple Wang Tai 王駘 uses his heart-mind, Confucius responds:

> he does not take cognizance of what the ears and eyes are appropriate for, but his heart-mind wanders in the knowledge of Power.[8]

He looks on the loss of his feet as only the loss of so much earth because

> he is entirely occupied with his self; he uses his wits to get hold of his heart-mind, and he uses his heart-mind to get hold of his unchanging heart-mind [*chang xin*].[9]

The passage continues:

People never find a mirror in flowing water, for a mirror [we look] into still water. Only the still can still whatever is stilled. [10]

Here, acting as a mirror (*jian* 鑑) is a deliberate activity and one that is elsewhere associated with perfected persons (*zhi ren* 至人) who "use their heart-minds like mirrors; they do not escort things out or welcome them in; they respond but do not store." [11]

Comparison to the *Xunzi* illustrates the importance of *wuwei* in the *Zhuangzi* account of the "mirror-like" mind of a realised person. The *Xunzi xin*-mirror metaphor resembles the imagery of *Zhuangzi* 13, but with opposite conclusions. The *Xunzi* also deploys the image of still water as mirror, but he uses it of the *junzi* who is bright and clear and thus able to understand *dao*. As he puts it:

Hence, the heart-mind may be compared to a pan of water. If you place the pan upright and do not stir the water up, the mud will sink to the bottom, and the water on top will be clear and pure [*qing ming*] enough to see your beard and eyebrows and to examine the lines on your face. But if a slight wind passes over its surface, the submerged mud will be stirred up from the bottom, and the clarity and purity of the water at the top will be disturbed so that it is impossible to obtain the correct impression of even the general outline of the face. Now, the heart-mind is just the same. [12]

But unlike the *Zhuangzi*'s natural water, Xunzi's is held still in a pan, and his metaphor emphasises clarity over stillness. More important, as David Nivison points out, the clear mirror is a means to an end: a means to clear thinking and correct judgement, rather than an end in itself. The clear mind mirror makes it possible to order the mind and understand *dao* (Hutton, *Xunzi*, 231).

2. THE *DAO* OF ANTIQUITY IN TRANSMITTED TEXTS

The section of *Zhuangzi* 13 before the Wheelwright Bian passage is explicitly concerned with both language and texts, and it is one of the relatively few passages in the *Zhuangzi* that seem to closely paraphrase the language of the *Daodejing*. It reads:

Writing is the means by which the world values *dao*, but writing does not go beyond words and words also have value. Meaning is the means by which words have value, but meaning has that upon which it depends. That upon which meaning depends cannot be transmitted by language, yet the world nonetheless values language and transmits writing. And although the world values it, I myself consider it not sufficient to value, because what is valued is not what is valuable. Therefore, that which we can see when we look is form and color; that which we can hear when we listen is names and sounds. Alas, that the people of the world should consider form, color, name, and sound to be sufficient to grasp the inherent nature of that! But given that form, color, name, and sound are not sufficient to grasp the inherent nature of that:

> Those who know do not speak
> Those who speak do not know.

But how could the world recognise this?[13]

This passage reaffirms the limitations of writing, language, and sensation to understand the true nature of things, but it also stresses the limits of sense perception. It is here that the skill of Wheelwright Bian enters the narrative.

3. WHEELWRIGHT BIAN'S SKILL: HOW TO CHIP A WHEEL

The Wheelwright Bian story contrasts—conceptually and even spatially—the reading of Duke Huan and the artisanship of Wheelwright Bian, the one reading a book above, the other chipping a wheel below. The story ends with Bian's explanation and does not say what happened to him. Various interpretations have been given of this interaction. Gu Ming Dong views it as a presciently early (pre-postmodern) account of the "death of the author" (Gu, *Chinese Theories*, 23). As Asaf Goldschmidt has shown, the story has been used to problematise the ability of Chinese physicians to transmit their accumulated clinical knowledge, in addition to their theoretical expertise (Goldschmidt, "Reasoning with Cases," 19–20).

One point that has received little discussion is *why* Wheelwright Bian cannot teach his skill to his son. Bian's wheel cutting conspicuously does not use any of the implements that are pervasively associated with the work of skilled artisans. In particular, he does not use a compass. By contrast, several Warring States sources attest to the use of the compass by wheelwrights. The earliest is a passage in the *Mozi* that compares the intentions of heaven (*tian zhi* 天志) to the wheelwright's compass and the carpenter's square:

> Mozi said: "As for me having the [concept of] the will of Heaven, the metaphor [example, *bi*] is like the wheelwright having a compasses and the carpenter having a carpenter's square. The wheelwright and carpenter use compass and square to measure all square and circular things and say: those that hit the mark [*zhong*] are right [correct]; those that don't hit the mark are wrong [incorrect]."[14]

This is a metaphor of accurate fit, and it clearly refers to wheelwrights using a compass to "hit the mark" *(zhong* 中).

Xunzi also attests the use of compasses to make wheels in his famous analogy about human nature:

> Through steaming and bending, you can make wood as straight as an ink-line into a wheel. And after its curve conforms to the compass, even when parched under the sun it will not become straight again, because the steaming and bending have made it a certain way.[15]

Elsewhere, Xunzi analogises the certainty they provide about squareness and roundness to the *junzi*'s use of the rites:

> If the state lacks ritual, then it will not be set straight. As for the way ritual sets for the state, one can compare it to the relation of scales to the heavy and the light, the relation of the ink-line to the curved and the straight, and the relation of compass and square to the round and the rectangular. When they have been set out properly, then no one can deceive you about these things.[16]

Finally, he distinguishes the standards they provide from the fluid arguments of Hui Shi and Deng Xi. In his "Discourse on Ritual" (chapter 19), he expounds on the depth of the patterns of ritual, that "investigations into the hard and the white, the same and the different drown when they try to enter into it."[17] This refers to Hui Shi and Deng Xi. The passage continues:

> And so, when the ink-line is reliably laid out, then one cannot be deceived by the curved and the straight. When the scale is reliably hung, then one cannot be deceived by the light and the heavy. When the compass and carpenter's square are reliably deployed, then one cannot be deceived by the circular and the rectangular. . . . Thus, the ink-line is the ultimate in straightness, the scale is the ultimate in balance, the compass and carpenter's square are the ultimate in circular and rectangular, and ritual is the ultimate in the human way.[18]

All these texts clearly show that wheelwrights used compasses to measure their wheels, nor is there any suggestion in them that there is an "unteachable" element to wheelmaking independent of measurement. Wheelwright Bian appears not to do so. He is first described as cutting a wheel and putting down his hammer and chisel, with no mention of a compass. Had he used one, there would be no obvious reason he could not teach his son to chip wheels. But instead, he seems to operate "freehand" with a hammer and chisel. He is not an ordinary wheelwright.

How do we know this and rule out the possibility that the text simply didn't mention the compass? Four passages in the *Zhuangzi* repeatedly and explicitly criticise the use of compass and square. The first appears in chapter 8:

> To depend on the carpenter's curve, inked cord, and compass and square to make things straight is to pare away your nature. To depend on cords, knots, glue, and lacquer to hold together is to violate virtuosity [*de*]. To bow and crouch for rites and music and smirk and simper over benevolence and rectitude [*ren yi*] to soothe the world's heart-minds is to lose the constant.[19]

The context is a claim that constancy does exist in the world (*tianxia you chang ran* 天下有常然). But the argument continues that real constancy is not bent by the carpenter's curve, straightened by the inked cord, rounded by the compass, or squared by the carpenter's square.[20]

These passages admit multiple interpretations. According to a weak view, rejecting measurement tools is not a rejection of the standards they measure. Rather, the claim is that crafts masters can work without them as precisely as if they were using them. In one version, compass, square, and so on are useful, but the true expert does not need them, for example:

> The potter says: "I'm good at managing clay; my circles are true to the compass, my squares to the [carpenter's] square." The carpenter says: "I'm good at managing wood; my bends are true to the [carpenter's] curve, my straight edges correspond to the plumb line."[21]

But other passages take a stronger view and explicitly reject the use of measuring instruments:

> Smash the carpenter's curve; snap the plumb line, throw away the compass and square. Crush the fingers of Craftsman Chui and at last throughout the world people will have their skills [*qiao*].[22]

This passage clearly prefers some kind of genuine skill (*qiao*) to the misguided (some pun intended) precision of artisans' instruments. A fourth passage makes this point explicit by associating Carpenter Chui with the ability to draw without reference to precision instruments:

> When carpenter Chui drew a figure it was true to compass and square; his finger shared in the transformations of things and he did not use his heart-mind to calculate.[23]

Here the deliberative use of the heart-mind is analogised to precision instruments. The combined force of these passages is threefold. First, all reject—in different ways—the use of precision instruments. Second, this rejection includes an association of these mechanical aids with conventional norms. This point is especially important because the term *guiju* 規匠—"compass and square"—lost its literal meaning and became a metaphor for moral regulation. For example, Mencius analogises the perfect squares and circles they produce to sages' mastery of human relationships: "Compass and square produce perfect squares and circles; sages are the perfection of human relations."[24] Finally, they recommend a different kind of perception—arising from inner nature (*xing*) or virtuosity (*de*). And it is this, not the mechanical ability to chip a round wheel, that Wheelwright Bian cannot teach his son.

4. COMPASS AND SQUARE, LANGUAGE AND THE HEART-MIND

The absence of compass and square is significant for three other reasons that bear more broadly on the philosophical stances of the *Zhuangzi* text. First, the "compass and square" issue further substantiates the *Zhuangzi*'s argument against language. Second, the *Zhuangzi* rejects not only compass and square but regulation by the (non-fasted) heart-mind. In this sense, the "compass and square" approach stands in contrast to the "heart-mind approach" of many Warring States texts. Finally, it bears on our understanding of teaching in the *Zhuangzi*.

Wheelwright Bian's rejection of compass and square parallels the claim, throughout the *Zhuangzi* but in the *Qiwulun* especially, that true understanding of *dao* cannot be expressed directly in words. Words and language are mechanical and inflexible in the same kind of way as are compass and square. This attitude also parallels Bian's rejection of Duke Huan's texts, which cannot transmit the knowledge of the sages of antiquity because they lack the live teaching of their authors. Because real knowledge of *dao* cannot be put into words directly, texts cannot teach how to acquire skills.

Another important point in Wheelwright Bian's account of his own skill is the role of the heart-mind (*xin* 心). He takes a distinctive attitude towards the heart-mind in that he neither puts it at the centre nor entirely rejects its guidance. On his account, the exact balance necessary to chip a wheel correctly involves a complex interaction between embodied skill and mental response:

> To make them neither too lose or too tight is something you "get" in your hands and respond to in your mind. The mouth cannot put it into words, and there is a knack to it. [25]

Wheelwright Bian's method can be contrasted to the "mechanical" approach of using a compass to guide the formation of a wheel. But the problem is that the "compass and square" approach cuts short what is constant by nature:

> Furthermore, if we must depend upon the hook, ink-line, compass and square to align things correctly [make things correct], that would be to slice away their nature. If we must depend upon cords, twine, glue, and lacquer to make things solid, that would be to invade their integrity [*de*]. Bending and scraping in rites and music, simpering and smirking with humaneness and righteousness to console the heart-minds of all under heaven, this is to forfeit constancy. All under heaven have constancy. But constancy implies making angles without a hook, making straight lines without an ink-line, making circles without a compass, and making squares without a [carpenter's] square. [26]

This passage clearly contrasts the use of compass and square with a "free-hand" practice that relies on a very different use of the heart-mind from standard measurement and standard norms.

Recent *Zhuangzi* scholarship has called attention to the importance of teaching in the *Zhuangzi*.[27] Another possible view of the story of Wheelwright Bian (and Cook Ding and all the other skill masters of the text) is to read it as a teaching story, but of a special kind. It is special because what is being imparted is not knowledge—pieces of information or the memorisation of a transmitted text—but an intangible skill, or even an approach to skill in general (these stories have an audience beyond those who aspire to chip wheels or carve oxen). It is striking that both the story of Wheelwright Bian and the story of Cook Ding (discussed in the next section) are teaching stories in which a skilled artisan instructs a ruler, as with the discourse on swords in *Zhuangzi* 30.[28]

Other stories instruct aspiring sages, such as Liezi and even Confucius. But these two figures respond very differently. Chapter 7 describes Liezi's interactions both with the *wu* spirit medium Jixian and with his own teacher, Master Calabash, whose "emptiness" ultimately terrifies Jixian. But as the story progresses, Liezi realises that he has not understood his master's teaching, and to do so he must reverse his life to really learn. He stops studying with Master Calabash, remains at home, and abandons conventional hierarchies and boundaries, cooking for his wife and feeding his pigs as if they were people. Eventually he becomes like an "uncarved block" and "remained whole to the end."[29] By contrast, although the swimmer of chapter 19 gives an account of how he swims in the treacherous waters, Confucius opts to instruct his followers by words rather than by experience.[30]

5. WHEELWRIGHT BIAN AND COOK DING

The story of Wheelwright Bian is unusual for three reasons. First, Bian is a master of a clearly defined skill that in addition is technically difficult, and this difficulty distinguishes his skill from others that can be easily mastered to at least a moderate degree. Second, his skill is linked to broader attitudes about *dao*, by its content, by the chapter title (*tian dao*), and by his explicit opposition of his "wordless" expertise to the reading of texts. Finally, the rhetoric of the story is a virtual inversion of that of Cook Ding (Pao Ding 庖 丁), one "skill" story in the Inner Chapters and its account of the relation between skill and *dao*. Both are teaching narratives in which a skill expert instructs a ruler.

But what is Wheelwright Bian arguing here (assuming he survives the interaction)? Especially taken together with the preceding section, Bian is arguing against an assumption—elsewhere voiced by Confucius—that the wisdom of the ancients is accessible to those of the present day. Here the *Zhuangzi* ridicules any such attempt. And as Rudolph Wagner points out, in doing so, the *Zhuangzi* argued against what remained a common assumption until the end of the third century CE, namely that "classics" were "texts of a special kind coded in a highly sophisticated manner, which managed to purvey a glimpse of the *Dao* to those who knew how to read them" (Wagner, *Language, Ontology*, 15). As such, we can also align Bian—a craftsman—with the history of Chinese debates about innovation, though he himself is making no claims about it.

Part of this story's claim to fame is its espousal—and description—of "knack." As such, it has been taken as a "knack" story by A. C. Graham and others, including in extended discussions of "know-how" knowledge.[31] As Aaron Stalnaker has pointed out, it is surprising how rarely the Inner Chapters—or the *Zhuangzi* in general—describe or recommend any sustained course of instruction or training or promote the expertise of teacher figures. Instead, they repeatedly endorse notions of skill or knack (Stalnaker, "Mastery, Authority," 270–74).

The figure of Wheelwright Bian also has this reputation in China. He reappears in a poem by the great Yuan landscape painter Wu Zhen 吳鎮 (1280–1354):[32]

> [One day] I suddenly forgot that I held a brush in my hand.
> Do Cook Ding and Wheelwright Bian still remember this process of evolution?[33]

This poem links together two figures from the *Zhuangzi*, the skilful butcher Pao Ding from *Zhuangzi* 3 and Wheelwright Bian. Both seem to have moved from conventional measurement and mechanical assessment to a teaching that goes beyond trivial skill. Ding presumably assessed his oxen with his eyes before he was able to use his *shen*. Bian presumably learned to chip wheels with a compass before he learned how to make them without one.

But Pao Ding is praised for his teaching, while Wheelwright Bian is threatened with death, and we do not know the upshot. They key difference is that Ding's demonstration does not challenge alternate hierarchies of knowledge, and praising him costs Lord Wen Hui nothing. By contrast, Bian explicitly challenges Duke Huan by fundamentally questioning the authority of the "classics" he is reading and the many assumptions that lie behind them.

6. CONCLUSION

It has been argued in chapter 7 of this volume by Eric Schwitzgebel that the *Zhuangzi* is, overall, critical of skill in the Inner Chapters. On this line of reasoning, praise of skill is an "Outer Chapters" matter, and therefore (on

Schwitzgebel's account) not central to the *Zhuangzi*, which he defines as the Inner Chapters. A different way to approach the question of the skill stories in general, and specifically "knack" stories such as Wheelwright Bian and Pao Ding, is to ask what rhetorical purpose they serve, and further, to ask whether the rhetoric of the Outer Chapters skill stories is consistent with the broader arguments of the Inner Chapters.

I argue that the story of Wheelwright Bian is consistent with the attitudes of the Inner Chapters because it underscores two of their important and related themes: one is a claim about language, the other a claim about the nature and value of distinctions and discriminations (which include the distinctions and discriminations of language).

The language claim is the claim that "real" knowledge, or knowledge of *dao*, is veiled by words and words' distinctions. This is a central issue in the *Qiwulun*. In the story of Wheelwright Bian, the claim is pursued by a different strategy, the rejection of the knowledge of the sages of antiquity as transmitted through texts. But here a question arises: why are Duke Huan's books only "dregs and leavings"? At issue here is whether Bian is making a claim about timeliness and innovation or a claim about language. Viewed as an argument about timeliness and innovation, the knowledge of the sages of antiquity addressed the needs of a different time, and their wisdom, while valuable for their own time, is not valid for this one. On this reading, in their own time, their teachings were valid, and there is no inherent problem about their being written down and transmitted in texts.

A stronger claim (and not incompatible) is the language claim, that real knowledge or wisdom cannot be transmitted directly or "mechanically" through texts. On this view, Duke Huan's texts are "dregs and leavings" because they are written down and divorced from the live teaching of their authors. Thus even in their own time, they would have been partial and inadequate because real knowledge of *dao* cannot be put into words directly. In this sense, any book can be no more than the "dregs and leavings" of genuine teachings. The passage seems to clearly make the claim about timeliness and innovation because of its emphasis on the sages being dead. But it also may be making the language claim. On this interpretation, the significance of the sages being dead is not that their knowledge is too old, but that it is no longer possible to transmit it in a valid way, by teaching. In summary, reading Wheelwright Bian in the stronger terms of the claim about language reinforces parallels between the Outer and Inner Chapters.

The second theme, the rejection of conventional distinctions and discriminations, is also a central theme in the Inner Chapters. But in the Outer Chapters it takes an additional and very specific form in the rejection of "compass and square." If we put aside the conventional reading of this term as a metaphor for morality and rectitude and read it literally, we see another dimension of the *Zhuangzi*'s rejection of discriminations by opposing reliance on mechanical instruments to an "inner compass" that allows the skilful expert to chip a wheel freehand.

NOTES

1. 桓公讀書於堂上。輪扁斲輪於堂下，釋椎鑿而上，問桓公曰：「敢問，公之所讀者何言邪？」
公曰：「聖人之言也。」
曰：「聖人在乎？」
公曰：「已死矣。」
曰：「然則君之所讀者，古人之糟魄已夫！」
桓公曰：「寡人讀書，輪人安得議乎！有說則可，无說則死。」
輪扁曰：「臣也以臣之事觀之。斲輪，徐則甘而不固，疾則苦而不入。不徐不疾，得之於手而應於心，口不能言，有數存焉於其間。臣不能以喻臣之子，臣之子亦不能受之於臣，是以行年七十而老斲輪。古之人與其不可傳也死矣，然則君之所讀者，古人之糟魄已夫！」(*Zhuangzi jishi* 13:490–91; Mair, *Wandering*, 128–29).

2. 天道運而无所積，故萬物成；帝道運而无所積，故天下歸；聖道運而无所積，故海內服。明於天，通於聖，六通四辟於帝王之德者，其自為也，昧然无不靜者矣。聖人之靜也，非曰靜也善，故靜也；萬物无足以鐃心者，故靜也。水靜則明燭鬚眉，平中準，大匠法焉。水靜猶明，而況精神！聖人之心靜乎！天地之鑑也，萬物之鏡也。(*Zhuangzi jishi* 13:457). Translation is my own but is indebted to Mair, *Wandering*, 119–20. I am grateful to Karyn Lai and David Machek for comments on this chapter.

3. 心養。汝徒處无為，而物自化。墮爾形體，吐爾聰明 . . . 解心釋神，莫然无魂。(*Zhuangzi jishi* 11:390; cf. Mair, *Wandering*, 99).

4. 純粹而不雜，靜一而不變，惔而無為，動而以天行，此養神之道也。 (*Zhuangzi jishi* 15:544; cf. Mair, *Wandering*, 146).

5. E.g., *Zhuangzi jishi* 4:147.

6. 水靜則明燭鬚眉，平中準，大匠取法焉。水靜猶明，而況精神！聖人之心靜乎！天地之鑑也，萬物之鏡也。 (*Zhuangzi jishi* 13:457–58). Similarly, *Zhuangzi jishi* 7:307 describes the heart-mind of a realised person as like a mirror: 至人之用心若鏡.

7. Harold Oshima argues that the earliest known uses of the metaphor of the heart-mind as a mirror are found in the *Zhuangzi* and that the mirror metaphor is fundamental for several of the *Zhuangzi*'s ideas about the *xin* (*A Metaphorical Analysis*, 75). For mirror metaphors in early China, see Demiéville, "Le Miroir Spirituel"; Reding, "Light and the Mirror"; and Slingerland, *Effortless Action*.

8. 不知耳目之所宜, 而游心於德之和 (*Zhuangzi jishi* 5:191, trans. after Graham, *Chuang tzu*, 77).

9. 彼為己, 以其知得其心, 以其心得其常心 (*Zhuangzi jishi* 5:192, trans. after Graham, *Chuang tzu*, 77).

10. 人莫鑑於流水, 而鑑於止水, 唯止能止眾止 (*Zhuangzi jishi* 5:193, trans. after Graham, *Chuang tzu*, 77).

11. 至人之用心若鏡, 不將不迎, 應而不藏, 故能勝物而不傷 (*Zhuangzi* 7:307, trans. after Graham, *Chuang tzu*, 98).

12. 故人心譬如槃水, 正錯而勿動, 則湛濁在下, 而清明在上, 則足以見鬚眉而察理 矣. 微風過之, 湛濁動乎下, 清明亂於上, 則不可以得大形之正也. 心亦如是矣 (*Xunzi* 21:401; Knoblock 3:107).

13. 世之所貴道者書也，書不過語，語有貴也。語之所貴者意也，意有所隨。意之所隨者，不可以言傳也，而世因貴言傳書。世雖貴，我猶不足貴也，為其貴非其貴也。故視而可見者，形與色也；聽而可聞者，名與聲也。悲夫，世人以形色名聲為足以得彼之情！夫形色名聲果不足以得彼之情，則知者不言，言者不知，而世豈識之哉！ (*Zhuangzi jishi* 13:488–89; cf. Mair, *Wandering*, 128).

14. *Mozi* 26/41, translation my own; cf. Mei, *The Ethical and Political*, 140. See also *Mozi* 4/2–3, 27/63–67, and 28/44–45 (Mei, *The Ethical and Political*, 13, 149, and 156) and Graham, *Later Mohist*, Canons: 316.

15. 木直中繩，輮以為輪，其曲中規，雖有槁暴，不復挺者，輮使之然也。 (*Xunzi* jijie 1:2, trans. Hutton, *Xunzi*, 1).

16. 國無禮則不正。禮之所以正國也，譬之：猶衡之於輕重也，猶繩墨之於曲直也，猶規矩之於方圓也，既錯之而人莫之能誣也。 (*Xunzi* jijie 11:209–10, trans. Hutton, *Xunzi*, 104).

17. 禮之理誠深矣，「堅白」「同異」之察入焉而溺 (*Xunzi* jijie 19:356; trans. Hutton, *Xunzi*, 130).

18. 故繩墨誠陳矣，則不可欺以曲直；衡誠縣矣，則不可欺以輕重；規矩誠設矣，則不可欺以方圓
故繩者，直之至；衡者，平之至；規矩者，方圓之至；禮者，人道之極也。(*Xunzi* jijie 19:356; trans. Hutton, *Xunzi*, 130).

19. 且夫待鉤繩規矩而正者，是削其性者也；待繩約膠漆而固者，是侵其德者也；屈折禮樂，呴俞仁義，以慰天下之心者，此失其常然也。(*Zhuangzi jishi* 8:321; cf. Graham, *Chuang tzu*, 201).

20. 曲者不以鉤，直者不以繩，圓者不以規，方者不以矩。(*Zhuangzi jishi* 8:321; cf. Graham, *Chuang tzu*, 201).

21. 陶者曰：「我善治埴，圓者中規，方者中矩。」匠人曰：「我善治木，曲者中鉤，直者應繩。」(*Zhuangzi jishi* 9:330; Graham, *Chuang tzu*, 204).

22. 毀絕鉤繩而棄規矩，攦工倕之指，而天下始人有其巧矣。(*Zhuangzi jishi* 10:353; cf. Graham, *Chuang tzu*, 209).

23. 工倕旋而蓋規矩，指與物化而不以心稽。(*Zhuangzi jishi* 19:662; cf. Graham, *Chuang tzu*, 138).

24. 規矩，方員之至也；聖人，人倫之至也 (*Mengzi zhengyi* 4A: 490 (4A2), translation my own). Cf. 4A1, 6A20, and 7B5. For further examples of these metaphors, see Raphals, "A 'Chinese Eratosthenes' Reconsidered."

25. 不徐不疾，得之於手而應於心，口不能言，有數存焉於其間。 (*Zhuangzi jishi* 13:490–91; cf. Mair, *Wandering*, 128–29).

26. 且夫待鉤繩規矩而正者，是削其性；待繩約膠漆而固者，是侵其德；屈折禮樂，呴俞仁義，以慰天下之心者，此失其常然也。天下有常然。常然者，曲者不以鉤，直者不以繩，圓者不以規，方者不以矩。(*Zhuangzi jishi* 8:321; cf. Mair, *Wandering*, 77).

27. See, in particular, Defoort, "Instruction Dialogues"; Graziani, "Rhetoric That Kills"; and Lai, "Skill Mastery, Cultivation."

28. For further discussion, see Graziani, "Rhetoric That Kills."

29. For discussion, see Defoort, "Instruction Dialogues."

30. For discussion, see Lai, "Skill Mastery, Cultivation."

31. See Fraser, "Skepticism and Value"; Jochim, "Just Say No"; and Raphals, *Knowing Words*, 67, 77, 231.

32. Wu Zhen was one of the Four Great Painters of the Yuan dynasty. His style name was Zhonggui 仲圭, as well as Meihua Daoren 梅花道人 (Plum Blossom Daoist Priest); see Wang Tzi-cheng, "Wu Zhen's Poetic Inscriptions."

33. 初童不自知，忽忘箏在手。

庖丁及輪扁，還識此意否？

(*Meihua Daoren yimo*, juan A, 6, trans. Wang Tzi-cheng, "Wu Zhen's Poetic Inscriptions," 233).

REFERENCES

Defoort, Carine. "Instruction Dialogues in the *Zhuangzi*: An 'Anthropological' Reading." *Dao* 11 (2012): 459–78.

Demiéville, Paul. "Le Miroir Spirituel." *Sinologica* 1, no. 2 (1947): 112–37.

Fraser, Christoper. "Skepticism and Value in the Zhuāngzi." *International Philosophical Quarterly* 49, no. 4 (2009): 439–57.

Goldschmidt, Asaf. "Reasoning with Cases: The Transmission of Clinical Medical Knowledge in Twelfth-Century Song China." In *Antiquarianism, Language, and Medical Philology:*

142   *Lisa Raphals*

From *Early Modern to Modern Sino-Japanese Medical Discourses*, edited by Benjamin Elman, 19–51. Leiden: Brill, 2015.
Graham, Angus C. *Chuang tzu: The Inner Chapters*. London: Unwin, 1981.
———. *Later Mohist Logic, Ethics and Science*. Hong Kong: Chinese University Press, 1978.
Graziani, Romain. "Rhetoric That Kills, Rhetoric That Heals." *Extrême-Orient, Extrême-Occident* 34 (2013): 41–77.
Gu, Ming Dong. *Chinese Theories of Reading and Writing: A Route to Hermeneutics and Open Poetics*. Albany, NY: SUNY Press, 2005.
Hutton, Eric L. *Xunzi 荀子: The Complete Text*. Princeton, NJ: Princeton University Press, 2014.
Jochim, Chris. "Just Say No to 'No Self' in *Zhuangzi*." In *Wandering at Ease in the* Zhuangzi, edited by Roger T. Ames, 35–74. Albany, NY: SUNY Press, 1998.
Lai, Karyn. "Skill Mastery, Cultivation and Spontaneity in the *Zhuangzi*: Conversations with Confucius." In *The Oxford Handbook of Chinese Philosophy*, edited by Justin Tiwald. Oxford: Oxford University Press, forthcoming.
Mair, Victor. *Wandering on the Way: Early Taoist Tales and Parables of Chuang Tzu*. New York: Bantam, 1994.
Mei, Yi-pao. *The Ethical and Political Works of Motse*. London: Arthur Probsthain, 1929.
Mencius: Corrected Interpretations /Mengzi zhengyi 孟子正義]. Edited by Jiao Xun 焦循. Beijing: Zhonghua, 1987.
Mozi: A Concordance [*Mozi yinde* 墨子引得]. Shanghai: Shanghai Guji, 1986.
Nivison, David S. "Xunzi and Zhuangzi." In *Virtue, Nature, and Moral Agency in the Xunzi*, edited by T. C. Kline III and P. J. Ivanhoe, 176–87. Indianapolis: Hackett, 2000.
Oshima, Harold H. "A Metaphorical Analysis of the Concept of Mind in Chuang-Tzu." In *Experimental Essays on Chuang-tzu*, edited by Victor H. Mair, 63–84. Honolulu: University of Hawai'i Press, 1983.
Puett, Michael J. *The Ambivalence of Creation: Debates Concerning* Innovation *and Artifice in Early China*. Palo Alto: Stanford University Press, 2002.
Raphals, Lisa. "A 'Chinese Eratosthenes' Reconsidered: Chinese and Greek Calculations and Categories." *East Asian Science, Technology and Medicine* 19 (2002): 10–61.
———. *Knowing Words: Wisdom and Cunning in the Classical Traditions of China and Greece*. Albany, NY: Cornell University Press, 1992.
Reding, Jean-Paul. "Light and the Mirror in Greece and China: Elements of a Comparative Metaphorology." In *Comparative Essays in Early Greek and Chinese Rational Thinking*. Burlington: Ashgate, 2004.
Slingerland, Edward T. *Effortless Action: Wu-wei as Conceptual Metaphor and Spiritual Ideal in Early China*. Oxford: Oxford University Press, 2003.
Stalnaker, Aaron. "Mastery, Authority, and Hierarchy in the 'Inner Chapters' of the Zhuāngzǐ." *Soundings* 95, no. 3 (2012): 255–83.
Wagner, Rudolph G. *Language, Ontology, and Political Philosophy in China: Wang Bi's Scholarly Exploration of the Dark (Xuanxue)*. Albany, NY: SUNY Press, 2003.
Wang Tzi-cheng. "Wu Zhen's Poetic Inscriptions on Paintings." *Bulletin of SOAS* 64, no. 2 (2001): 208–39.
Wu Zhen 吳鎮 and Fen Qian 錢棻. *Daoist Plum Blossoms* [Wu Zhen's Posthumous Writings] [*Meihua Daoren yimo* 梅花道人遺墨]. Siku quanshu edition.
Xunzi: Collected Explanations [Xunzi jijie 荀子集解]. Edited by Wang Xianqian 王先謙. Beijing: Zhonghua, 1988.
Zhuangzi: Collected Annotations [*Zhuangzi jishi* 莊子集釋]. Edited by Guo Qingfan 郭慶藩. Beijing: Zhonghua shuju, 1961.

Chapter Ten

The Cicada Catcher

Learning for Life

Karyn Lai

When Confucius was on his way to Chu, he passed through a forest where he saw a hunchback catching cicadas with a sticky pole as easily as though he were grabbing them with his hand. Confucius said, "What skill you have! Is there (a) *dao*?" "I have (a) *dao*", said the hunchback. "For the first five or six months I practise balancing two balls on top of each other on the end of the pole and, if they don't fall off, I will lose very few cicadas. Then I balance three balls and, if they don't fall off, I will lose only one cicada in ten. Then I balance five balls and, if they don't fall off, I know it will be as easy as grabbing them with my hand. I position my body like a stiff tree trunk and hold my arm like an old dry limb. No matter how expansive heaven and earth are, or how numerous the ten thousand things, I'm aware of[1] nothing but cicada wings. Not wavering, not tipping, not letting any of the other ten thousand things take the place of those cicada wings—how can I help but succeed in taking them?" Confucius turned to his followers and said, "He keeps his will undivided and concentrates his spirit—is this not what we say about the venerable hunchback?" (*Zhuangzi* 48/19/17–21, adapted from the translation by Watson, *Complete Works*, 199–200)[2]

1. INTRODUCTION

The cicada catcher seems an unlikely Daoist. He comes across as being focused and organised, as he has a clear sense of his task and what he is required to do. He confidently and lucidly articulates how he has mapped out and undertaken his training for cicada-catching, giving readers the impression that he has himself successfully followed through with his plans to become an excellent cicada catcher—so impressive are his actions that Confucius stands in awe. This story runs against the grain of representations of Daoist philosophy as being wary of words and language (*yan* 言) and as advocating action guided by intuition rather than reason.[3] Especially in the *Zhuangzi*, a text with a chapter entitled "Free and Unfettered Wandering" (*Xiaoyaoyou* 逍遙遊), the cicada catcher's noticeable meta-level awareness of his task and the practice required appear ill fitted to some of the fundamental concerns of Daoism as represented in the literature.

A focal point of this story is the learning process, planned and undertaken by the cicada catcher. What are his goals, and how does he plan to achieve them? How does learning to balance balls on the end of a pole prepare him for catching cicadas? And why does he need to attend (only) to cicada wings? This chapter explores these questions in order to understand more about Zhuangzian skill and mastery from the angle of what is learned and how it is learned. Can its views on knowledge and action be aptly captured in terms of some of the conceptual frameworks and terms provided by Western philosophical discussions in epistemology, philosophy of action, or philosophy of mind? I suggest that the explanatory frameworks and angles used in recent work on embodied cognition theory (ECT)—broadly speaking, that cognition is dependent on or shaped by bodily and sensorimotor capacities and exercised by engaging with what is presented in the environment—capture many important elements of mastery in the *Zhuangzi*. The second objective of this chapter is to draw insights from the *Zhuangzi*'s views on learning in order to shed light on the notion of *dao* in the *Zhuangzi*'s intellectual context. What are the skill masters learning? When approached by Confucius on his awe-inspiring performance, the cicada catcher claims he has *dao*. What is *dao*? Do each of the *Zhuangzi*'s masters have (a) *dao*? The mastery stories focus on single, *ordinary* activities. Hence, should we live like the masters? How are their reflections relevant to life, and how do these views speak to a contemporary audience? I propose that our grasp of *dao* may be illuminated through a fuller understanding of the cicada catcher's learning program. From that angle, in the cicada catcher's story, *dao* refers to preparedness, yet openness, in one's engagement with the world. The fundamental claim here is that the cicada catcher's approach to learning can inform our thinking about preparedness for encountering and dealing with practical matters in life.

To support my argument about learning and *dao*, the discussion in the following section, section 2, examines the cicada catcher story to illuminate how learning must be structured, yet allow room for openness in one's encounters with the world. I discuss some possible ways in which we may explain what it is the cicada catcher hopes to learn and how he does it. Section 3 dwells on how some existing characterisations of the *Zhuangzi*'s views on knowledge and action—for example, as know-how, intuition, or spontaneity—fail to capture the cicada catcher's empirically-based approach.

As an alternative, I suggest in section 4 that some aspects of ECT can provide a more fitting explanatory framework for understanding the story. The point here is not to establish or defend ECT but to demonstrate that this more recent approach to knowledge, action, and cognition can help cast our gaze on the integration between a person's capabilities and actions and therefore better illuminates the *Zhuangzi*'s empirical approach. Finally, in section 5, I consider how the *Zhuangzi*'s views of learning, articulated in the cicada catcher story, may be instructive for how we can pursue a good life.

2. LEARNING, AS A DAOIST LEARNS

In the story, the cicada catcher's learning process involves only the cicada catcher himself and the activity of cicada-catching. There are no references to a teacher or a model, or to other cicada catchers who might share in his practices. There would have been other cicada catchers as part of this cicada catcher's community of practice, but in this story we encounter only him, in conversation with Confucius. Some of Confucius's followers are present, but they are only recipients of Confucius's instructions and do not have a voice in this story. At the scene, Confucius is intrigued by the cicada catcher's expertise and requests more information about his skill (*qiao* 巧). "What skill you have! Is there (a) *dao*?" (*you dao ye* 有道邪), Confucius asks. The portrayal of the craftsman engaged in learning, without a teacher, is a common theme in the skill stories in the *Zhuangzi*. The butcher, Pao Ding, tells of how he has learned to carve an ox effortlessly (*Zhuangzi* 7/3/2–8/3/12); the swimmer enlightens Confucius on how he has developed skill to swim at the foot of dangerous cascades (*Zhuangzi* 48/19/22–26); the wheelmaker, Bian (扁), says that has tried teaching his son how to make wheels but has failed to do so (*Zhuangzi* 36/13/68–74). In fact, *none* of the *Zhuangzi*'s stories on expertise directly involve a teacher! Moreover, although there are passages where instruction occurs, they advocate non-conventional ways of teaching (see Defoort, "Instruction Dialogues in the *Zhuangzi*"). For example, Liezi's teacher scares away a shaman simply by manifesting vacuity (*xu* 虚; *Zhuangzi* 20/7/15–21/7/31). In the final section, I will explain how the *Zhuangzi*'s aversion to teaching is an important part of its rejection of conventional views on government and society. Here, I focus on the text's discussions on the *transmission* of ideas to illuminate our understanding of the cicada catcher's learning processes. Verbal instruction, a commonly used mode of teaching, is a recurrent theme in some of the mastery stories. In fact, the text is wary of it. For example, the wheelwright singles out words as an ineffective mode of teaching and learning. He draws parallels between his attempt to teach his son how to make wheels and Duke Huan's reading of books on past sages:

I cannot put it into words, and yet I figure it out in the midst of the activity. I cannot teach this to my son, and he cannot receive it from me. . . . When the men of old died, they took with them the things that couldn't be handed down. So what you are reading there must be nothing but the chaff and dregs of the men of old. (adapted from the translation by Watson, *Complete Works*, 152–53)

The point here is not that *no* knowledge or skill can be transmitted, but rather that the kind of capability the *Zhuangzi* sought (*qiao* 巧; *ji* 技) cannot be transmitted, especially not in words. Is this a reason why these ordinary men have acquired mastery without a teacher? But—aren't these masters themselves attempting to impart instructions when they converse with Confucius and others about their skills? Is it their intention to teach? On closer scrutiny, it appears that these masters are perhaps only describing how *they themselves* have learned their skill in response to the questions they have been asked. In other words, the format of the masters' response in quite a few of the stories runs like this: you've asked me how I do this (butchering, swimming, ferrying, etc). Well, let me tell you how *I* did it. First, it was like this, and I did that. Then I proceeded to do this. Now, at this point (years later), this is what I do. (I'm not telling *you* how to do it!) The use of first-person self-references by these masters in their stories supports this claim that the masters are telling their personalised stories rather than providing generalised accounts of learning: across the mastery stories, the characters *chen* (臣), *wo* (我), and *wu* (吾) are used. These self-referential terms signify how the masters, by and for themselves, have developed and cultivated their different skills and capabilities. Therefore, in the stories where Confucius seeks to hear from the masters, there is an ironic twist: what these individual masters have articulated as personal experiences, Confucius appropriates and generalises for his followers to learn from. Confucius attempts to transmit (*dao* 道) what is not transmittable. In giving verbal instructions to his followers to do as the master does, Confucius has failed to see the point, that is, to learn as the master learns! Such attempts by Confucius to teach occur not only in the cicada catcher story but also in the stories of the swimmer at the dangerous cascades and of the ferryman (*Zhuangzi* 48/19/22–49/19/26). If we follow this line of reasoning, the lesson of the skill stories is not so much to urge readers to *do* as a Daoist master does, but to *learn* as a Daoist master learns. In other words, the stories engage at a meta-level discourse on learning. Their point is not for us readers to imitate the cicada catcher's actions or to internalise his words, as Confucius attempts to get his followers to do. The cicada catcher has *dao* (*wo you dao ye* 我有道也), and our task is not to acquire his *dao* but to develop our own. This is one reason the text self-reflexively refers to its teaching as "teaching without words" (*bu yan zhi jiao* 不言之教; in *Zhuangzi* 12/5/1–13/5/13; 57/22/1–57/22/5). In this light, Confucius is spurned twice: first, as the novice Daoist learning from a master (who, as a craftsman, would undoubtedly be of lower social rank than Confucius) and, secondly, as one who misses the point entirely about what can be learned and how it should be learned.[4] In the style of the *Zhuangzi*, we could express scepticism about learning from instructions, as: "Can skill be learned? Can skill not be learned?"[5]

3. PHILOSOPHISING KNOWLEDGE AND ACTION

The cicada catcher articulates a self-designed training program that he has undertaken in order to develop his abilities in cicada-catching. This training is arduous and sounds fantastical—as if anyone could balance five balls, or even three, at the end of a pole! But there is more: with his body, he needs to imitate trees, the familiar habitat of cicadas. What underpins the design of this training program? The cicada catcher needs to observe cicadas, to see how sensitive they are to movements in their environment. For example, how do cicadas detect threats? Will an onrush of air caused by a moving object (the pole or the hand) be likely to send them flying off? What is the tree environment of cicadas like? How does a human (body) position itself so as to be like a tree, in relevant ways, for cicadas? How might balancing balls on a pole help develop cicada-catching skills?

Evaluations of the *Zhuangzi*'s stories and the mood and style of the text often highlight its distinctive views of knowledge and action. Accounts have described the *Zhuangzi*'s epistemological approach as more closely aligned with knowing-how rather than knowing-that,[6] and its views on mind (if it had views on "mind", broadly conceived) and action in terms of the intuitive, spontaneous, and non-rational. With regard to the latter, for example, an early twentieth-century sinologist, Henri Maspero, proposes that, in the story of the wheelwright, "reasoning itself must be abandoned, for it obscures the true knowledge which is intuitive" (Maspero, *China in Antiquity*, 307). The assessment of the *Zhuangzi*'s departure from reason is echoed by another influential sinologist, Angus C. Graham, who characterises Zhuangzi as "anti-rationalist".[7] Further, specifically in relation to the skill stories, Graham situates his analysis of the *Zhuangzi*'s philosophy comparatively, in the terms of Western epistemological debate:

> The many stories about craftsmen in [the *Zhuangzi*] are always especially illuminating to a Westerner grappling to understand [Daoism]. He learns from them that the [Daoist] art of living is a supremely intelligent responsiveness which would be undermined by analyzing and choosing between alternatives, and that grasping the Way is an unverbalizable "knowing how" rather than "knowing that." (Graham, *Unreason within Reason*, 186)

These characterisations of the *Zhuangzi* as "anti-rational", or as abandoning reasoning, or as "know-how" sit within a Cartesian framework that dichotomises body and mind and which elects the mind as the distinguishing feature of the self. Closely associated with this conception of mind is the promotion of its foremost *capacity*, that is, to *reason*. In defence of these *Zhuangzi* studies in Anglophone literature, it should be noted that their aim is often to defend the distinctiveness, and legitimacy, of the kind of reasoning the *Zhuangzi* seems to uphold. These discussions are well intentioned in their attempts to carve a place for the *Zhuangzi* in comparative Chinese-Western discourse. Unfortunately, this strategy has its limits because it aligns the text's epistemology with *anti*-reason, irrationality, or know-how, all of which take second place to reason and intellectual knowledge in dominant strands of Western epistemological discourse.

The unsatisfactoriness of the projects described above may be illuminated by drawing attention to an analogous scenario in George Orwell's *Animal Farm*. In *Animal Farm*, the downtrodden and disgruntled animals are led by the pigs to overthrow their human masters. When they succeed, the animals devise new standards, agreeing to uphold the dictum "Four legs good, two legs bad"—a simple overturning of the values associated with their human masters. The animals also create a set of "Seven Commandments" that merely overturn the practices and beliefs of the overthrown humans, such as "3. No animal shall wear clothes", and "4. No animal shall sleep in a bed".[8] These decisions taken by the animals remain locked in the entrenched animal-human dualism. Sadly, the animals have failed to take advantage of their newly established opportunity to explore new possibilities.

How does this analogy inform our understanding of the underlying epistemological assumptions in the *Zhuangzi*'s cicada catcher story? I propose that, to characterise the *Zhuangzi*'s views on reasoning, or its style of reasoning, as anti-rational, or intuitive, or as know-how, implicitly accepts the dichotomies entailed by the philosophical vocabulary. This is akin to how the animals' new creed of "Four legs good, two legs bad" implicitly accepts the dualism inherent in this framework.

If we examine the cicada catcher's story, we realise that *both* what we call "knowing-how" *and* "knowing-that" are involved in this *one* activity of cicada-catching. If we were to persist with the entrenched dichotomy, how do we represent this activity using the language of knowing-how and knowing-that? We may say:

> The cicada catcher *knows-that* after he can balance three balls, he needs to develop his skill by balancing five balls. When he *knows-how* to balance three balls, he needs to *know-that* he *knows-how* to balance three balls (i.e., a higher-order knowledge). This higher-order *knowledge-that* engenders (or is linked in a causal way to) the belief that he is ready to attempt to balance five balls.

And so it goes. This cumbersome rendition of the cicada catcher's story is intended to highlight the potential overlaps between knowing-how and knowing-that, not as two mutually exclusive types of knowledge but, indeed, working together at relevant points in the learning process such that the cicada catcher is able to say, "Then I balance five balls and, if they don't fall off, I know it will be as easy as grabbing them with my hand." (I will revisit this issue of the integration of knowing-how and knowing-that later in this section.)

Just as importantly, the analysis of knowing-how and knowing-that in Western epistemology is often embedded in a framework whose primary concern is to understand knowledge's nature. From this angle, the approach is typically to set out what it means to know-how and to know-that, prior to investigating how individuals may be said to have knowledge-how or knowledge-that. This concept of knowledge (whether in propositional form or as capacities or skills) is grounded in the assumption of a person's—*any* person's—*possession* of a particular (type of) knowledge, According to this view, interest in the cicada-catching story might include raising questions such as "What kind of knowledge is needed to catch cicadas?" and "Can Confucius and his disciples learn this knowledge?"

However, this mindset detracts from what actually happens in the story. The cicada catcher articulates a personalised account of his way of cicada-catching, hunchback and all. *This* is the way (*dao*) he succeeds at cicada-catching. He is *not* offering a generalised explanation of the know-hows of cicada-catching, as one might if one were answering a question relating to knowing-how, conceived in the way described in previous paragraphs. Ironically, and in contrast, Confucius assumes that the cicada catcher imparts a body of teaching that his followers may appropriate and call their own. He misunderstands the fact that *this* cicada catcher's knowledge is not transferable, and he attempts to convey the teaching to his followers. But, we have to ask, how can the cicada catcher's learning program—the lessons designed for and undertaken by a hunchback—be useful for Confucius and his followers who, as far as we know, are not hunchbacks? Confucius has failed to grasp that the cicada catcher, as the knower, is not intersubstitutable with other knowers.

The cicada catcher's *dao*—his ability to catch cicadas—holds *only* for him because *dao* is subject dependent. There may be others who can catch cicadas, but perhaps not as though they were grabbing cicadas with their hands, or perhaps even more skilfully! His capacity to catch cicadas is personal and not transmittable. The cicada catcher is very much *in* his cicada-catching world, attuned to cicadas and their environments. The emphasis in this story is not on how a cognisant subject encounters the inert world (although the cicada catcher is very aware of what he is doing and how he executes his task).[9] Rather, it centres on his preparation for his performance and his performance itself. Here, I highlight two pertinent aspects of cicada-catching performance in the story.

First, upon seeing the cicada, the cicada catcher's capacities are engaged *at once*: physically positioning his body and his limbs, dispositionally attuned to the cicada's bearings, understanding how the cicada is situated relative to his own position, flexing the right muscles in a particular way with appropriate swiftness, and so on. To say that these capacities are engaged at once is not to say that they must all happen at the same time. Rather, it is intended to convey the coordination of the different capacities that, *in working together in a specific context*, are constitutive of masterful cicada-catching performance. He observes cicadas—for example, to understand that they are comfortable in particular tree environments—in order to develop a course of action so that he can *be* part of the tree environment. There is no "correct" sequencing of thinking before acting, as for instance, where the cicada catcher *first* seeks to understand that the cicada is in a certain position and then, *secondly*, to catch it, he needs to crouch in a particular way and act accordingly.[10] "I position my body like a stiff tree trunk and hold my arm like an old dry limb. No matter how expansive heaven and earth are, or how numerous the ten thousand things, I'm aware of nothing but cicada wings", says the cicada catcher. His performance draws on knowledge-how, knowledge-that, physical ability, and appropriate dispositions, all at once. Surely the cicada catcher's performance is not anti-rational. Note the self-aware way he has taken into account the habitat and habits of cicadas and accordingly planned his practice. Nor, indeed, is it lacking in knowledge-that, given his discursive, step-by-step articulation of how he develops skill for catching cicadas. In the words of Gilbert Ryle, cicada-catching in this story is *one* intelligent activity, not *two* (the thinking and the doing):

> When I do something intelligently, i.e., thinking what I am doing, I am doing one thing and not two. My performance has a special procedure or manner, not special antecedent. (Ryle, *The Concept of Mind*, 32)

This brings to mind, secondly, that in the cicada catcher story, there is no clear boundary between the cicada catcher's *thinking* self and his *doing* self. His views and thoughts are shaped by his perceptions of the cicadas and their environments. But the story says more than just that body and sensorimotor experiences influence thought.[11] Consider how the cicada catcher holds his body like a stiff tree trunk: this must be excruciating. Yet, could it be less so for Zhuangzi's cicada catcher because he is a hunchback? Did he *become* a hunchback from his cicada-catching practice, or does his being a hunchback render him particularly well suited to catching cicadas? Or is his being a hunchback a mere coincidence with his special abilities for catching cicadas? The last scenario is possible though not plausible, as the text is playfully knowing in its choice of words and images; consider, for example, how the wheelwright's name is "Flat" (*Bian*; *Zhuangzi* 36/13/68–74). The cicada catcher story does not tell us more about the connection between hunchback-ness and cicada-catching, but it prompts us to ponder the fascinating possibil-ities suggested by its imagery. Whether being hunchbacked is an enabling capacity for cicada-catching or an unintended consequence, we are left to wonder whether the cicada catcher's *being* in the environment of cicadas is constitutive of his cognitive processes. This is a much more significant claim than that made previously, which was that experiences shape thought. Here, the suggestion is that the cicada catcher's positioning of himself and acting within the cicada-catching environment could, or maybe should, be seen as cognitive processes. Perhaps, for this reason and more, we need to move beyond the conceptual framework of traditional classifications of rational/ anti-rational, mind/body, and knowing-that/knowing-how.

4. KNOWING, AS A DAOIST KNOWS

The discussion in this section highlights a few themes that have arisen in the context of debates in embodied cognition theory. The aim is to show that dimensions of ECT and its implications for how we think about mind and knowledge will help draw out the performance orientation of the *Zhuangzi* in a much more pertinent way than the dominant epistemological frameworks in Western philosophy do. In some ways, it is not a coincidence that we can detect in the cicada catcher story some similar lines of thought that have informed ECT. Both have empirical bases. In the case of the *Zhuangzi*, its focus is on the performance of the cicada catcher. In the case of ECT, many of its arguments draw from what it means for people or subjects to encounter situations and act responsively.[12] In brief, both approaches focus on the performative or participatory aspects of human action; their objective is not to theorise the mind.

An important note to make here is that this section in no way assumes or suggests that ECT is a unified theory.[13] Nevertheless, a core emphasis in ECT is the involvement and integration of a range of human capabilities in cognition. For example, vision, bodily movement, and the feedback generat-ed from the subject's actions in the environment are more tightly integrated than in a traditional picture of mind as the centre of cognitive processing (see, for example, O'Regan and Noë 2001). In the three subsections below, I highlight three points of alignment between ECT and the cicada catcher story: (1) destabilising the mind as the centre of cognition, (2) perception, and (3) performance.

4.1. Destabilising the Mind as the Centre of Cognition

In ECT, cognitive processing is not the sole prerogative of the mind. The body, as well as the environment in which an individual is situated, may have non-reducible contributory roles such that they are integral parts of cognitive processes. Different strands of ECT adopt particular angles on cognition, whether to understand that "mind" is shaped by body within its environment (e.g., Gallagher, *How the Body Shapes the Mind*) or to see that "mind" is manifest in our sensorimotor processes in contexts.[14] Yet, we can say generally that ECT holds an expanded conception of mind (as compared with the traditional view that mind and body are each associated with distinctive processes), undergirded by complicated, yet more empirically realistic, accounts of agency and causation.

How might some of these ideas provide a vocabulary for unpacking the cicada catcher's learning, knowledge, and action? ECT is established on discourse that destabilises mind-body dualism, as well as the role of mind as the independent centre of cognitive processes. In cicada-catching, it is not that the cicada catcher first engages in reflection, "in the mind", with cicada-catching activity following as a result of the reflections. The story provides more details that may be embraced within an explanatory framework of integrated cognition: the cicada catcher holds his arm like a tree limb, he sees only cicada wings, and he manipulates the pole as if it were his hand.[15] Even though we may descriptively carve out the different components of cicada-catching in words, these are not three activities, but one. On one account of ECT, such successful manipulations of the setting of the environment, and of the things therein (such as the pole to grab cicadas with), *are* the cicada catcher's cognitive practice (see Menary, *Cognitive Integration*, and Wheeler, *Reconstructing the Cognitive World*). Cognition operates—in both "body" and "mind"—*while* the cicada catcher observes his environment and acts in it. The upshot of understanding the story in this way is not to reduce cognition to action, but to highlight the *interdependence* of what are typically identified as "cognitive" capacities, on the one hand, and "sensorimotor" processes, on the other. Recall a question raised earlier about the cicada catcher's hunchback: has his hunchback developed because of his cicada-catching activities, or is he a better cicada catcher because of his hunched back? It is not only that his cognitive processes are generated by his doing; he learns, knows, and acts *with his body*.[16]

4.2. Perception: Learning to See

The cicada catcher story focuses on the cicada catcher's encounter with cicadas and his attentiveness to their wings. Why does he focus on their wings? The discussion in this section focuses on the idea that cognitive processes take place within specific environments, and therefore it is necessary to develop perceptive skills to effectively manipulate what is available. Should elements within environments change, performance needs to be adjusted in order to successfully adapt to that change (cf. Varela, Thompson, and Rosch, *The Embodied Mind*; Barsalou, "Situated Conceptualization"). Consider, for example, how the cicada catcher story effectively expresses awareness that the probability of things going wrong is overdetermined: distractions might arise, cicadas might fly off, and so on. It is no wonder, therefore, that arduous practice is necessary for effective cicada-catching. Amongst other things, the demanding training processes described by the cicada catcher aim to hone his perceptive skills, *situated in the environment*. For the cicada catcher, "perception" includes visual perception (e.g., observing cicada habitats), sensorimotor perception (e.g., feeling the movement of the balls stacked at the end of the pole), and even the closing off of some other perceptual capacities (e.g., restricting the distractions of the world (*wanwu* 万物, lit. "ten thousand things")) (cf. Gibson, *The Ecological Approach*; Chemero, "An Outline of a Theory of Affordances").[17]

The cicada catcher is completely absorbed in his activity: "No matter how expansive heaven and earth are, or how numerous the ten thousand things, I'm aware of nothing but cicada wings." What does he perceive in the cicada wings? What does his training help him see that a person not trained in cicada-catching does not see? One branch of the debate in ECT draws on discussions on perception in ecological psychology. An influential account, offered by James Gibson in 1979, understands perception in terms of its functions within the animal's environment (Gibson, *The Ecological Approach*). The perceptive capabilities of an animal are crucial in helping an animal navigate and live in its environment or habitat. However, the distinctiveness of Gibson's account lies not in its provision of a list of perception's functions within the environment. Its key significance was to highlight the opportunities provided within an environment, for which he coined the term "affordance" to suggest that the environment is not inert, nor does it exist as a bunch of representations to be processed by the perceiving subject's "mind". Gibson writes: "The affordances of the environment are what it offers the animal, what it provides or furnishes, either for good or for ill" (Gibson, *The Ecological Approach*, 127). The word "affordances", the nominal form of the verb "afford", highlights the richness of the environment and what is made available to animals.[18] For perceiving subjects, different possibilities may arise from the same environment: rotten fruit on the forest floor "afford" food for the rhinoceros beetle, whereas they might present the likelihood of slipping for the bushwalker. Cicadas present cicada-catching affordances for the cicada catcher. But why does he focus on cicada *wings*? To catch cicadas, one end of the pole had strong adhesive to which cicada wings would stick and the cicada would be caught. In the language of affordances, we may say that the cicada catcher concentrates on cicada wings because they present sticking affordances for the sticky end of the pole. By focusing his attention on cicada wings, the cicada catcher aligns his perceptive capabilities with cicada habitats, hence *enacting* the cicada-catching affordance. One advantage of this explanatory framework is its aversion from an approach that both elevates the intellectual capacities of perceiving subjects and deflates the status of the environment by objectifying it.

Is there more we can say about what the cicada catcher perceives in the environment? In general, from the angle of a person's engagement within the environment, it is important to ask the question of what it is she attends to when she looks, listens, feels, and perceives more generally. Given the situatedness of human action in contexts that present manifold opportunities, and given that there is no limit to what we perceive in each of these contexts of action, our perceptive capabilities need to be fine-tuned to new kinds of information (Ingold, *The Perception of the Environment*, 166). We see that the cicada catcher learns by doing: first balancing one ball at the end of the pole and attending to what is required for him to do that successfully. During the learning process, the cicada catcher must cultivate activity-appropriate behaviours and skills and also acquire an understanding of conditions that might impact on the activity in significant ways. This familiarisation process allows a learner to understand patterns in *typical* contexts, perhaps akin to the kind of activity Hubert Dreyfus refers to as "habitual activity". One example of habitual activity is driving to the office (*Being-in-the-World*, 93). Another is pegging clothes on a line.

Learning to operate in formulaic ways is necessary, though not sufficient, for activities that are not merely habitual. Many activities we engage in require us to take into account context-based factors which impact on the activity. In the case of cicada-catching, for example, this might include cognisance of the damp undergrowth in *this* environment, or of the denseness of *that* forest. These elements could constitute the "new kinds of information" Ingold alludes to, as discussed above. Through his learning practices, the cicada catcher must come to understand salient factors that are more or less stable, and others that vary more significantly, in different contexts where cicada-catching happens. Learning in this way alerts the learner to the important focal points of a particular activity, helping her understand what she needs to attend to when taking action so that she can be just as successful in atypical scenarios. This aspect of learning may be identified as an "education of attention", as suggested by Gibson (Gibson, *The Ecological Approach*, 188, 254; cited in Ingold, *The Perception of the Environment*, 167).

Back to the cicada catcher story: perhaps a cicada catcher trained to catch cicadas in a "habitual" way may be able to catch some cicadas. However, the cicada catcher in our story knows in a qualitatively different way: he knows not to be distracted by the range of situational particularities, focusing only on those that *matter*, in relevant ways, to cicada-catching. The position and movement of cicada wings seem critical to the cicada catcher's success; perhaps they indicate that the cicada has come to rest on this branch, or that it is unsettled, or that it is about to fly off. The cicada catcher's attentiveness to cicada wings helps him pre-empt possible exigencies associated with the activity.

In the language of ECT, we could say that the cicada catcher is perceptively attuned to a dynamic cicada-catching environment and that his cognitive processes involve his movement through the environment, including his control of his attention, to focus on cicada wings. In this light, we may perhaps more accurately describe the *Zhuangzi*'s underlying epistemological commitments as "agentive knowledge", which focuses on apt practice. One account of agentive knowledge helps to illuminate the discussion here: it is "not a general knowledge that can be taught, but a knowledge that shows itself in individual praxis, in the course of doing something right in a given situation".[19]

4.3. Performance

By focusing on performance, we move away from the emphasis on mind and its computational capacities. Instead, we attend to how the cicada catcher catches cicadas or, more generally, how people get things done in real time (cf. Clark, *Being There*, 1997) . The cicada catcher story requires readers to step back and take in the performance of the cicada catcher within his cicada-catching environment. That cicadas might fly off suddenly, whether because there has been an onrush of wind or a change in temperature, or because they have sensed a predator, seems to be written in the fine print of the story. Indeed, the emergent environment demands the cicada catcher's complete attentiveness to the task at hand. The view that environments are dynamic, hence requiring a systems approach, is a line of debate arising in the ECT literature. Here, mind and world operate as an integrated system; intellection works interdependently with sensorimotor experiences, *situated* within specific environments. In this explanatory framework, a person's engagement with the world comes to the forefront. An influential account of a dynamic systems approach, proposed by Anthony Chemero, characterises affordances in terms of the relation between individuals and the environment (Chemero, "An Outline of a Theory of Affordances").[20] As relations, specific affordances enable particular behaviours: soil affords nest-building behaviours for the Australian apostle bird, and earth that is sufficiently deep affords burrow-digging behaviours for wombats. This view of affordances creates room for attention to *action*, drawing our gaze to the individual's behaviour in context. The account builds on the Gibsonian emphasis on a system-based approach—an *ecological* one—that seeks to understand the psychology of perception more accurately, in terms of what an individual perceives and how the individual behaves within the environment.[21] Chemero's ecological approach, a "form of realism about the world as it is perceived and experienced" (Chemero, *Radical Embodied Cognitive Science*, 150), allows us to locate an organism's activities in a rich, varied, and often unpredictable environment and to arrive at a more realistic picture of its behaviours and capabilities in context. From this ecological angle, the cicada catcher's performance may be understood in terms of appropriate physicality, awareness, concentration, percipience, and responsiveness, each of which is necessary, though insufficient, for catching cicadas.

We may build on this picture to provide a richer account of the cicada catcher's performance. Here, consider the way in which the cicada catcher uses the pole as if he were "grabbing" the cicadas with his hands. In other words, the pole may be considered a vehicle—an "extra-bodily vehicle"—in his cicada-catching (Menary, *Cognitive Integration*, 4–6). It enables him to engage in this activity more effectively. We could say that the pole is an "epistemic tool", in the same way that a calculator is an epistemic tool for a person performing mathematical calculations (Menary and Gillett, "Embodying Culture", 74). This conceptual framework brings together epistemological acumen and physical capabilities in a way that helps highlight the centrality of performance in the *Zhuangzi*. *As a hunchback*, the cicada catcher's successes occur at the *intersection* of his capabilities and the environment; appropriate matching of these two elements of affordances is a prerequisite to success.

5. *DAO*: LIVING, AS A DAOIST LIVES

What is the relevance of the cicada catcher story to life more generally? Cicada-catching is such a specific activity, after all. In its intellectual milieu, this story, and indeed many sections of the *Zhuangzi*, questioned existing approaches to quelling unrest. Some of these texts reflect the intentions of court officials at that time to address sociopolitical unrest by implementing standards for human behaviour. Standards for correct behaviours were upheld and affirmed especially in the creation of norms, perpetuated in words (language). There was the so and not-so (*ran* 然, *buran* 不然); possible and not possible (*ke* 可, *buke* 不可); correct and permissible, and wrong and impermissible (*shi* 是, *fei* 非); and so on. From the *Zhuangzi*'s point of view, life was impoverished by these standards because they reduced its plurality to uniformity by simplistically drawing distinctions according to these seemingly straightforward categories.

The cicada catcher story, and others like it, offers snapshots of ordinary, yet *masterful*, lives. Is it plausible that the lives of these ordinary folk are more enriched than those led by court officials? And would these masters not be better off familiarising themselves with prevailing norms and abiding by them? As noted previously, the *Zhuangzi* addresses both the lives of the officials as well as their misconceived views of government. In relation to the former, the text wonders about the preparedness of these officials to deal with contingencies thrown up in exigent situations. In a passage where Confucius has a conversation with his favoured follower, Yan Hui, some strands of the *Zhuangzi*'s hesitations about official life are expressed. The story appears in a chapter titled "Worldly Business among Men", where Yan Hui announces to Confucius that he is ready to take on a difficult task, that is, to work with the notorious prince of Wei (*Zhuangzi* 8/4/1–9/4/24). Instead of applauding Yan Hui on his commitment to a worthy mission (as we would expect a Confucian to do), Confucius—here a spokesperson for the *Zhuangzi*—attempts to persuade Yan Hui not to take up the post. Yan Hui reassures Confucius, noting that he has devised plans to deal with this difficult prince, at which point Confucius says, "Goodness, how could that do? You have too many policies and plans and you haven't seen what is needed. You will probably get off without incurring any blame, yes. But that will be as far as it goes. How do you think you can actually convert him? You are still making the [heart-mind] your teacher!" (*Zhuangzi* 9/4/23–24; trans. Graham, *Chuang-Tzu*, 66–67). In the eyes of the *Zhuangzi*, the cultivated heart-mind (*xin* 心) is a symbol of Confucian accomplishment: it is a heart-mind that stands firm on Confucian ideals.[22] Such *acculturation* to a fixed way of thinking was deemed unacceptable to the *Zhuangzi*, as it foreclosed on issues even before a person encountered them, just as Yan Hui was proposing to do in his dealings with the prince of Wei.

The insidiousness of such an approach to life would be compounded if the *people* were expected to live by standards devised by officials who upheld such conceptions of a flourishing life. Such a *dao*, one that is prescribed for everyone, restricts rather than enables. This also helps explain why there are different accounts of mastery in the *Zhuangzi*. They are each a model of how learning and mastery are possible and, *because* norms are activity-specific, we must in life refrain from recommending any one set. It is only in this way that the cicada catcher story, even though it tells us about *one ordinary activity*, reveals important lessons for life. We should not learn to be *like* the cicada catcher, but rather, learn in the way he learns. To learn like he does, we may develop our perceptive capabilities so that we can understand the world's regularities and patterns and its activity-specific norms, as well as its contingencies. In the *Zhuangzi*, the plurality in the world should not be quelled as it offers many possibilities. There is much it has to offer, but we need simultaneously to be attuned to it, and open to its possibilities, in order to thrive. The cicada catcher has *dao*. Do you and I each have (a) *dao*?

158 Karyn Lai

ACKNOWLEDGEMENTS

Chris Fraser provided many insightful comments on an earlier version of this chapter, for which I am extremely grateful.

NOTES

1. The character *zhi* 知 in this phrase *wei tiao yi zhi zhi* 唯蜩翼之知 may be translated as "to be aware of", but it may also be translated as "to comprehend".

2. 仲尼適楚，出於林中，見痀僂者承蜩，猶掇之也。仲尼曰：「子巧乎？有道邪？」曰：「我有道也。五六月累丸，二而不墜，則失者錙銖；累三而不墜，則失者十一；累五而不墜，猶掇之也。吾處身也若厥株拘，吾執臂也若槁木之枝，雖天地之大，萬物之多，而唯蜩翼之知。吾不反不側，不以萬物易蜩之翼，何為而不得！」 孔子顧謂弟子曰：「用志不分，乃凝於神，其痀僂丈人之謂乎！」 (*Zhuangzi* 48/19/17–21). All references to the Chinese-language *Zhuangzi* text are taken from the *Zhuangzi Yinde*, the Harvard Yenching index (1956).

3. I discuss some of these characterisations in later sections of this chapter.

4. See, for example, Dufresne's discussion ("The Illusion of Teaching and Learning," 2017).

5. In the *Zhuangzi*, this style of questioning, first to frame a question, then to pose its contrapositive, is interesting. If only one question were posed, e.g., "Can skill be learned?", a possible interpretation is that the text is in fact making a statement by posing a rhetorical question. (It could, of course, be a genuine question, seeking an answer for its query.) However, to first frame a question and then to follow it up immediately with its contrapositive expresses an open-ended scepticism. The effect of this is to prompt readers to further consider the issue at hand.

6. See, for example, Philip Ivanhoe's "Zhuangzi on Skepticism", 648, and Harold Roth's "Bimodal Mystical Experience", 24, 27.

7. Graham writes, "Like all great anti-rationalists, [Zhuangzi] has his reasons for not listening to reason . . . all reasoning depends on making distinctions, and to reach the conclusion that we should abandon reason for the immediate experience or an undifferentiated world, transforming 'All are one' from a moral into a mystical affirmation. It is in 'The sorting that evens things out' that [Zhuangzi] takes this step" (Graham, *Chuang-Tzu*, 9).

8. Orwell, *Animal Farm*, chapter 2.

9. This picture unsettles a dominant conception of propositional knowledge in Western philosophy, that it is the foundational element of epistemology. Gilbert Ryle challenged the prioritisation of knowledge-that over knowledge-how in Western analytic epistemology more than half a century ago ("Knowing How and Knowing That," 1946). The debate on the status of knowledge-that remains contentious; for example, the "intellectualist debate" centres on whether knowledge-how is primarily a kind of knowledge-that, with the "intellectualists" holding the affirmative view. Jason Stanley and Timothy Williamson's defence of intellectualism is an influential view ("Knowing How," 2001). See the discussion by Jeremy Fantl ("Knowing-How and Knowing-That," 2008) and John Bengson and Marc Moffett (*Knowing How*, 2011).

10. Timothy Ingold, bringing the insights of ecological psychology to bear on his anthropological work, comments that the idea of knowledge detached from action in context and independent of bodily engagement is problematic. He argues, "To think in these terms, however, is to treat performance, such as that of the English speaker or the bowler in cricket, as nothing more than the mechanical execution, by the body, of a set of commands generated and placed 'on line' by the intellect" ("From the Transmission of Representations," 135).

11. Ellen Fridland presents an interesting account of the *chronological priority* of skill learning to conceptual thought. She suggests that "it is through the processes of skill learning that intentional actions break free from their domain-specific instantiation environments and begin to exhibit increasing degrees of distinctness and abstractness" ("Skill Learning and Conceptual Thought," 77–78). This account is not about the priority as such of skill over

conceptual thought, nor is it attempting to reconfigure what Ryle tried to do. However, it harks back to Ryle's aim to address the unequal weights of knowing-that and knowing-how as well as how they are conceived in explaining knowledge and action. Ryle sought "to turn the tables and to prove that knowledge-how cannot be defined in terms of knowledge-that and further, that knowledge-how is a concept logically prior to the concept of knowledge-that" ("Knowing How and Knowing That," 4–5).

12. Some of this research considers data from experiments in the cognitive and neurological sciences, as well as on robotics. Work on robotics allows researchers to construct robots that appear responsive to environments and that seem to engage in adaptive behaviours, yet without a "mind" to explain such behaviours (see, for example, Webb and Consilvio, *Biorobotics* (2001), and the brief discussion in Wilson and Golonska, "Embodied Cognition is Not What You Think It Is," 3–4). This research has significant implications for philosophy, include expanding our understanding of adaptive behaviour (and how that compares with existing explanatory accounts) and challenging views of mind that defend the centrality of representational content in cognitive processes (see the discussions by Alva Noë (*Varieties of Presence*; "Experience without the Head"), who rejects the centrality of representations in knowledge, and Susanna Siegel (Siegel and Silins, "The Epistemology of Perception"; Siegel, *The Contents of Visual Experience*), who defends it.

13. There are many positions on what it means to say that cognition is *embodied*; these views are shaped in part by which philosophical problem ECT is used to address. Some influential versions of ECT include Mark Johnson's *Embodied Mind, Meaning and Reason*; Andy Clark's *Supersizing the Mind*; Shaun Gallagher's *How the Body Shapes the Mind*; Richard Menary's *Cognitive Integration*; and Andy Clark and Alan Chalmers's "The Extended Mind." Views that challenge ECT include Jakob Howhy's "The Self-Evidencing Brain" and Frederick Adams and Kenneth Aizawa's *The Bounds of Cognition*. For an overview of different positions, see Shapiro, *Routledge Handbook of Embodied Cognition*, and Wilson and Golonka, "Embodied Cognition Is Not What You Think It Is."

14. Menary discusses these strands in *Cognitive Integration*, 3–5. He draws on both strands in his proposal for cognitive integration, the view that our manipulations of the environment have a normative dimension, embedded in cognitive practices (ibid., 6; see also Menary and Gillett, "Embodying Culture").

15. I discuss the idea of cognitive integration later, in section 4.3, which focuses on performance.

16. For support for this view, refer to Gallagher, *How the Body Shapes the Mind*; Varela, Thompson, and Rosch, *The Embodied Mind*; and Clark, *Being There*. See also Noë, "Experience without the Head", and the collection of papers edited by Richard Menary in *The Extended Mind*, in response to Clark and Chalmers's article of the same title, "The Extended Mind."

17. Contrast this picture of learning with that implied Confucius's actions, revealing the latter's assumption that learning primarily involves the internalisation of knowledge or ideas. Confucius's simplistic conception of learning threatens to reduce it to "an unproblematic process of absorbing the given, as a matter of transmission and assimilation" (Lave and Wenger, *Situated Learning*, 47). The thesis of situated learning is not simply that one learns by doing but that all learning, even in the formation or acquisition of an abstract principle, is "a specific event in specific circumstances" (ibid., 34).

18. For Gibson, these possibilities given in the environment—affordances—would be perceived directly by the animal (think, for example, of an animal foraging for food) and not mitigated by inference or the processing of information received through visual and other sources (Gibson, *The Ecological Approach*). On direct perception, Gibson notes that: "when I assert that perception of the environment is direct, I mean that it is not mediated by retinal pictures, neural pictures, or mental pictures" (Gibson, *The Ecological Approach*, 147). The assertion that perception is direct is not unproblematic. This debate centres on whether the mind works with *representations* or directly on the details presented in the environment, as articulated in Gibson's account. Anthony Chemero and his collaborators draw on Gibson's work to defend an account of direct perception. For Chemero, however, direct perception does not involve inferences, whereby the animal first makes inferences about the environment (or

mental representations of it) before acting on it. Calling his view "radical embodied cognitive science", Chemero argues that "direct perception is perception that does not involve mental representations" (Chemero, *Radical Embodied Cognitive Science*, 114). In a subsequent analysis of direct perception, Chemero and his collaborator, Withagen, argue that "direct perception is a coupling between the perceiver and its environment, via information in the array" (Withagen and Chemero, "Affordances and Classification," 532). See further discussion of this in note 20 of this chapter.

Refer to Berit Brogaard, *Does Perception Have Content?*, for a collection of papers on the topic of representation. Finally, refer to Clark, *Being There*, for a discussion on how artefacts and representations shape cognitive operations.

The articulation of the cicada catcher's story need not delve into the intricacies of the representationalist debates. Clearly, the Zhuangzi would not have had the level of sophistication to discuss the nature of representation and mind. The aim here is just to draw out the relation between perception and the environment.

19. Stegmaier, "Was heist: Sic him Denken orientieren?," 11, cited in and translated by Johanna Seibt, "Intercultural Dialogue and the Processing of Significance," 95.

20. A significant difference between Chemero's and Gibson's accounts is that, for Gibson, affordances are *possibilities* provided by the environment, whereas for Chemero, affordances are *relations*. In Chemero's formulation of affordances, he states, "Translated more loosely and colloquially, this means 'The environment affords behavior ϕ for the organism'" (Chemero, "An Outline of a Theory of Affordances," 187). This suggests that affordances are *relations*, rather than just relational. Yet in a later formulation, Chemero seems to align affordances more closely with the environment(al features) rather than with the relation between the individual and the environment. In considering the question, "Do Affordances Exist without Animals?," he writes, "Affordances do not disappear when there is no local animal to perceive and take advantage of them" (Chemero, *Radical Embodied Cognitive Science*, 150). In my view, *because* affordances are relations, they do not *exist* when there is no animal in the environment to perceive and act within that environment.

21. These relations, Chemero asserts, are *real* and not simply a projection of the animal's impressions (of the world) (Chemero, *Radical Embodied Cognitive Science*, 150).

22. One important example of the centrality of the heart-mind in the Confucian tradition is Mencius's heart that does not waver (*budongxin* 不动心), in the notable passage Mencius 2A2 (Bloom, *Mencius*, 29–32).

REFERENCES

Adams, Frederick, and Kenneth Aizawa. *The Bounds of Cognition*. Malden, MA: Blackwell, 2007.

Barsalou, Lawrence. "Situated Conceptualization: Theory and Applications." In *Foundations of Embodied Cognition*, edited by Y. Coello and M. H. Fischer, vol. 1, *Perceptual and Emotional Embodiment*, 11–37. East Sussex, UK: Psychology Press, 2016.

Bengson, John, and Marc Moffett, eds. *Knowing How: Essays on Knowledge, Mind, and Action*. Oxford: Oxford University Press, 2011.

Bloom, Irene, trans. *Mencius*. Edited and with an introduction by Philip J. Ivanhoe. New York: Columbia University Press, 2009.

Brogaard, Berit, ed. *Does Perception Have Content?* Oxford: Oxford University Press, 2014.

Chemero, Anthony. "An Outline of a Theory of Affordances." *Ecological Psychology* 15, no. 2 (2003): 181–95.

———. *Radical Embodied Cognitive Science*. Cambridge, MA: MIT Press, 2009.

Clark, Andy. *Being There: Putting Mind, Body, and World Together Again*. Cambridge, MA: MIT Press, 1997.

———. *Supersizing the Mind: Embodiment, Action, and Cognitive Extension*. New York: Oxford University Press, 2008.

Clark, Andy, and David Chalmers. "The Extended Mind." *Analysis* 58, no. 1 (1998): 10–23.

Defoort, Carine. "Instruction Dialogues in the *Zhuangzi*: An 'Anthropological Reading.'" *Dao: A Journal of Comparative Philosophy* 11, no. 4 (2012): 459–78.

Dreyfus, Hubert. *Being-in-the-World: A Commentary on Heidegger's Being and Time*. Cambridge, MA: MIT Press.

Dufresne, Michael. "The Illusion of Teaching and Learning: Zhuangzi, Wittgenstein, and the Groundlessness of Language." *Educational Philosophy and Theory* 49, no. 12 (2017): 1207–15.

Fantl, Jeremy. "Knowing-How and Knowing-That." *Philosophy Compass* 3, no. 3 (2008): 451–70.

Fridland, Ellen. "Skill Learning and Conceptual Thought: Making Our Way through the Wilderness." In *Contemporary Philosophical Naturalism and Its Implications*, edited by Bana Bashour and Hans Muller , 77–100. New York: Routledge, 2014.

Gallagher, Shaun. *How the Body Shapes the Mind*. Oxford: Oxford University Press, 2005.

Gibson, James J. *The Ecological Approach to Visual Perception*. 1979. Reprint, Boston: Houghton Mifflin, 1986.

Graham, Angus C. *Chuang-Tzu: The Inner Chapters*. Indianapolis: Hackett, 1981.

———. *Unreason within Reason: Essays on the Outskirts of Rationality*. La Salle, IL: Open Court, 1992.

Hohwy, Jakob. "The Self-Evidencing Brain." *Nous* 50, no. 2 (2016): 259–85.

Hurley, Susan. "Perception and Action: Alternative Views." *Synthese* 129, no. 1 (2001): 3–40.

Ingold, Timothy. "From the Transmission of Representations to the Education of Attention." In *The Debated Mind: Evolutionary Psychology versus Ethnography*, edited by Harvey Whitehouse, 113–53. Oxford: Berg, 2001.

———. *The Perception of the Environment: Essays in Livelihood, Dwelling and Skill*. London: Routledge, 2000.

Ivanhoe, Philip J. "Zhuangzi on Skepticism, Skill, and the Ineffable Dao." *Journal of the American Academy of Religion* 61, no. 4 (1993): 639–54.

Johnson, Mark. *Embodied Mind, Meaning, and Reason: How Our Bodies Give Rise to Understanding*. Chicago: University of Chicago Press, 2017.

Lave, Jean, and Etienne Wenger. *Situated Learning: Legitimate Peripheral Participation*. Cambridge: Cambridge University Press, 1992.

Maspero, Henri. *China in Antiquity*. Translated by Frank A. Kierman Jr., from *La Chine antique*. Les Presses universitaires de France, 1927. Amherst: University of Massachusetts Press, 1978.

———. *La Chine antique*. 1927. 2nd ed., Paris: Les Presses universitaires de France, 1965.

Menary, Richard. *Cognitive Integration: Mind and Cognition Unbounded*. London: Palgrave Macmillan, 2007.

———, ed. *The Extended Mind*. Life and Mind: Philosophical Issues in Biology and Psychology Series. Cambridge, MA: MIT Press, 2010.

Menary, Richard, and Alexander Gillett. "Embodying Culture." In *The Routledge Handbook of Philosophy of the Social Mind*, edited by Julian Kiverstein, 72–87. Abingdon: Routledge, 2016.

Noë, Alva. "Experience without the Head." In *Perceptual Experience*, edited by Tamar Gendler and John Hawthorne, 411–33. Oxford: Oxford University Press, 2006.

———. *Varieties of Presence*. Cambridge, MA: Harvard University Press, 2012.

O'Regan, J. Kevin, and Alva Noë. "A Sensorimotor Account of Vision and Visual Consciousness." *Behavioral and Brain Sciences* 24, no. 5 (2001): 883–917.

Orwell, George. *Animal Farm*. 1945. Penguin edition, London: Penguin, 2008.

Roth, Harold D. "Bimodal Mystical Experience in the 'Qiwulun' Chapter of the *Zhuangzi*." In *Hiding the World in the World: Uneven Discourses on the Zhuangzi*, edited by Scott Cook, 15–32. Albany, NY: SUNY Press, 2003.

Ryle, Gilbert. *The Concept of Mind*. Chicago: Chicago University Press, 2002. First edition published 1949 by Hutchinson's University Library (London).

———. "Knowing How and Knowing That." *Proceedings of the Aristotelian Society* 46 (1946): 1–16.

Seibt, Johanna. "Intercultural Dialogue and the Processing of Significance: Cognition as Orientation." In *How Is Global Dialogue Possible?—Foundational Research on Values, Conflict, and Intercultural Thought*, edited by Johanna Seibt and Jesper Garsdal. 85–115. Berlin: Walter de Gruyter, 2015.

Shapiro, Lawrence, ed. *Routledge Handbook of Embodied Cognition*. Oxford: Routledge, 2014.

Siegel, Susanna. "Affordances and the Contents of Perception." In *Does Perception Have Content?*, edited by Berit Brogaard, 51–75. Oxford: Oxford University Press, 2014.

———. *The Contents of Visual Experience*. New York: Oxford University Press, 2010.

Siegel, Susanna, and Nicholas Silins. "The Epistemology of Perception." In *The Oxford Handbook of Philosophy of Perception*, edited by Mohan Matthen, 781–811. Oxford: Oxford University Press, 2015.

Stanley, Jason, and Timothy Williamson. "Knowing How." *Journal of Philosophy* 98, no. 8 (2001): 411–44.

Stegmaier, Werner. "'Was heisst: Sich im Denken orientieren?' Zur Möglichkeit philosophischer Weltorientierung nach Kant." *Allgemeine Zeitschrift für Philosophie* 17, no. 1 (1992): 1–16.

Varela, Francisco, Evan Thompson, and Eleanor Rosch. *The Embodied Mind: Cognitive Science and Human Experience*. 1991. Rev. ed., Cambridge, MA: MIT Press, 2016.

Watson, Burton, trans. *The Complete Works of Chuang Tzu*. New York: Columbia University Press, 1968.

Webb, Barbara, and Thomas Consilvio, eds. *Biorobotics*. Cambridge, MA: MIT Press, 2001.

Wheeler, Michael. *Reconstructing the Cognitive World: The Next Step*. Cambridge, MA: MIT Press, 2005.

Wilson, Andrew, and Sabrina Golonka. "Embodied Cognition Is Not What You Think It Is." *Frontiers in Psychology* 4 (2013): 1–13.

Withagen, Rob, and Anthony Chemero. "Affordances and Classification: On the Significance of a Sidebar in James Gibson's Last Book." *Philosophical Psychology* 25, no. 4 (2012): 521–37.

Zhuangzi Yinde 《莊子引得》 [*A Concordance to* Zhuangzi]. Edited by Hong Ye 洪業主編. Harvard-Yenching Institute Sinological Index Series, Supplement No. 20. Cambridge, MA: Harvard University Press, 1956.

Chapter Eleven

The Ferryman

Forget the Deeps and Row!

Chris Fraser

Yan Yuan asked of Confucius, "I once crossed the depths at Goblet Deeps. The ferryman handled the boat like a spirit. I asked him, 'Handling a boat, can it be learned?' He said, 'It can. Good swimmers are quickly able, and as to divers, without having seen a boat, they can handle one.' I asked him about this but he didn't tell me. May I ask, what was he referring to?"

Confucius said, "Good swimmers are quickly able—it's that they forget the water. As to divers' handling a boat without ever seeing one—they regard the depths as like land and the boat's capsizing as like their cart rolling backward. Boats could capsize and carts roll backward all around them without it penetrating their chest. Where could they go and not be at ease?

"Shooting for tiles, you're skilled. Shooting for silver buckles, you're uneasy. Shooting for gold, you're flustered. Your skill's the same, but there's something you're worried about—this is putting weight on the external. Anyone who puts weight on the external gets clumsy with the internal." (19/22–26)[1]

What interferes with learning and performing skills well? The *Zhuangzi* story of the ferryman who steers a sampan through treacherous deeps with preternatural skill highlights one crucial factor: anxiety. Managing or eliminating anxiety is a pivotal step in acquiring and performing skills and, the discursive context of the story suggests, in living a flourishing life. To fare well, in life as in boat handling, we must learn to forget the deeps and row.

The ferryman is one of several skill stories included in *Zhuangzi* chapter 19, a collection of short writings that an unknown ancient editor entitled "Mastering Life" (*Da sheng* 達生), borrowing the first two words of the brief essay with which the chapter begins. The story was probably included under this theme because in the *Zhuangzi*, performance anxiety has a broader significance than merely how to pilot a sampan safely. One aim of the present chapter is to explore how salient motifs in the ferryman story illustrate broader themes in Zhuangist ethics concerning the flourishing life. The main such theme from the ferryman is that adept performance in any field rests partly on psychological attitudes. To perform well, agents must overcome fears or worries about their circumstances and the stakes of their action—no matter how dangerous or intimidating—and focus on the task before them. By doing so, as I will explain, they may experience an efficacious and fulfilling mode of agency characteristic of one Zhuangist vision of the well-lived life.

Since managing one's emotions is crucial both to skills and to the good life, a second aim of the chapter is to examine what guidance the ferryman and thematically related passages offer about exactly how to overcome anxiety. I will suggest that the texts collectively present two complementary approaches. One is to focus attention on the task at hand, leaving no room for extraneous concerns; the other is to defuse potential sources of anxiety by reframing our view of what matters. Is this guidance persuasive? I suggest it can be, provided we understand it as an attractive ideal, not an imperative one.

Before examining the ferryman story in detail, let me briefly explain the approach to reading the *Zhuangzi* pursued here. My discussion accepts the results of recent philological research arguing that the *Zhuangzi* is a diverse anthology of brief writings of unknown authorship, probably composed over many decades and most likely written, edited, and compiled by a variety of hands.[2] One important implication of this research is that the writings in the so-called "inner chapters" (*pian* 篇) have no privileged authorial, historical, or doctrinal status. Material from chapters such as "Mastering Life," a so-called "outer chapter," may be as informative and valuable in understanding important strands in Zhuangist discourse as the "inner chapters" are. Another implication is that neither the *Zhuangzi* as a whole, nor the seven "inner chapters," nor even the individual chapters themselves constitute unified works. With few exceptions,[3] even at the level of the individual "chapter," we are interpreting collections of discrete, short writings, which may relate to each other in various ways.

Given these features of the source material, I approach the individual passages that make up the *Zhuangzi* as discrete contributions to a range of loosely coherent discourses which overlap and intersect with each other in various respects. The specific relation between any particular pair or set of passages is an open question, to be explained through interpretive work. A provisional hypothesis adopted here is that the skill stories and other *Zhuangzi* material bearing on agency and performance are parts of a broad discourse addressing how agents can transform themselves to live more adeptly. In the discussion that follows, I will explore how ideas that different passages contribute to this discourse might be combined to form a hypothetical aggregate position. Such a position is not intended to represent the unified or overall standpoint of the *Zhuangzi*, however, for the texts are simply not organised in such a way as to present such a standpoint. It is simply one way of weaving together Zhuangist ideas to form a position that may be philosophically instructive.

1. THE FERRYMAN

The ferryman story is presented as an exchange between the literary figures of Confucius and Yan Yuan, Confucius's favourite student. Yan asks Confucius to explain the cryptic remarks a skilled ferryman made to him once while crossing a famously intimidating stretch of water. Confucius's response frames these remarks as primarily about anxiety and its effects on performance. Most likely, many people at the time—probably including Yan—could not swim and were distressed at the thought of falling off the ferry sampan into the deeps. To a fearful passenger such as Yan, the aplomb with which the ferryman perched on the stern, steering and sculling with the single oar, would have seemed astonishing, even superhuman.

Whether the ferryman's performance is indeed beyond the reach of normal people is precisely the point of Yan's question. Is his spirit-like skill due to innate, exceptional features that set him apart, or is boat handling something others can learn? The ferryman's answer suggests that many of us could achieve a similarly high level of competence. Those who are comfortable in the water can easily learn boat handling, he says, while those truly at home in the water probably grasp it already. To be sure, the latter claim seems an exaggeration. Expertise in swimming underwater may be relevant to boat handling, but it hardly translates directly into proficiency. Still, perhaps the point is the plausible one that being at home in a situation is a crucial prerequisite for acquiring related skills—and it could be true that, without having seen a boat, expert divers can teach themselves how to steer one.

In itself, the ferryman's remark could be taken to concern only familiarity with the water and how to move around in it. But Confucius's exposition gives it a psychological twist, tying ease of learning to the absence of anxiety. Good swimmers can learn boat handling quickly, he says, because they forget the water, which for non-swimmers looms as an omnipresent, overwhelming object of fear. Clearly, this forgetting cannot imply being oblivious to or unheedful of the water. Expert swimmers are acutely sensitive to the water as they pull against and glide through it. The point is rather that good swimmers are unconcerned by the water. They forget about it in that they don't attend to it as a source of anxiety. Worries about it don't enter their mind.[4]

Confucius's description of divers explains one reason the adept can forget about what for novices is an oppressive source of fear. They are wholly at ease with the circumstances in which they perform their skill. Conditions that intimidate others are as unstressful to them as their home environment. A boat capsizing is a minor inconvenience, not a life-threatening calamity, so the possibility of an accident doesn't unsettle them. They calmly proceed with the task at hand, their psychological equilibrium undisturbed.

The final paragraph generalises Confucius's point about anxiety and performance. The higher the stakes, the more anxious participants in an archery competition tend to become, and the more their performance suffers, because they worry about the prize—what's "external" or extraneous—rather than attending to the task at hand. The result is that for them the "internal" becomes clumsy—they lose their composure and blunder in what they're doing.

The gist of the passage, then, is that attaching importance to things extraneous to our actual performance renders us inept and ill at ease, because—unlike expert swimmers and divers—we attend to, rather than forget, potential sources of anxiety. The implication is that if we can forget or unweight sources of stress external to a task, we can relax and perform at our best, learning skills and perhaps progressing to spirit-like competence.

The ferryman passage makes two prominent, complementary claims: putting weight on the external produces clumsiness, and good swimmers avoid this because they "forget the water." The passage interweaves these two themes with several other motifs that recur prominently in Zhuangist discourse about skilled performance and living well. These include the depiction of skilled adepts as at ease in all circumstances, the link between ease and the agent being unaffected by stressful events, and the spirit-like character of the agent's performance. The next several sections explore the two main claims and the implications of these other motifs.

2. WORRYING ABOUT THE EXTERNAL

Given the structure of the ferryman passage, its main point is the concluding slogan, based on the example of increasingly high-stakes archery competitions: "Anyone who puts weight on the external gets clumsy with the internal."

The word "internal" (*nei* 內) here is often taken to refer specifically to the performer's psychological state or the heart-mind (*xin* 心).[5] By implication, the word "external" (*wai* 外) then refers to whatever is outside the agent's heart-mind. On this interpretation, the import of the slogan is that attaching too much importance to matters external to a healthy psychological equilibrium, such as the material consequences of our actions, disrupts our internal functioning. The internal being clumsy refers to how, in the archery example, shooters become increasingly nervous and flustered as their worries intensify over the increasingly valuable prizes. Since the example specifically mentions psychological states—being uneasy or worried and flustered or disconcerted—the psychological reading offers a plausible interpretation of at least one dimension of the internal/external contrast.

The import of the slogan probably goes beyond this interpretation, however. In Classical Chinese, the *nei/wai* contrast has a wide semantic scope, and the precise reference of these paired terms depends heavily on context. Generally, what is *nei* (internal) can be whatever is core, primary, or vital versus what is peripheral, secondary, or relatively insignificant. So the slogan can also be read in a general sense as implying that anyone who places undue weight on what is secondary becomes clumsy at what is important. More specifically, in the ferryman passage, *nei* probably refers principally to one's performance in the task at hand. The notion of putting weight on what is *wai* (external) is introduced as an explanatory label for cases in which, although our level of skill hasn't changed, our performance suffers because we're worrying about something extraneous—namely, the silver and gold. The specific contrast invoked by the *nei/wai* pair is thus between our poor performance and the prizes. A reasonable inference is that what is *nei* is our performance, along with anything directly pertinent to it. So the internal being clumsy refers simply to blundering the matter at hand.

These three ways of interpreting *nei* largely converge. On the assumption that the activity we are engaged in is significant to us, the general interpretation—what's vital or important—picks out the same referent as the specific interpretation in the ferryman passage, namely, our performance in archery. Since the major theme of the passage is that psychological composure is crucial for competent performance, the psychological interpretation, too, surely picks out an important aspect of "internal clumsiness." However, there is no reason to think one's psychological state is the whole story. Proficient technical execution of one's skill is also needed, for example.

The passage presents "putting weight on the external" as an explanation for cases in which worry or concern interferes with skill. "The external" thus refers to sources of anxiety. The implication is that to avoid anxiety, we need to remove the weight we attach to the external. The implicit proposal is that we can unweight the external by "forgetting" it.

3. FORGETTING THE WATER

What, then, is "forgetting"? Forgetting (*wang* 忘) is a pivotal notion in numerous *Zhuangzi* passages that treat personal cultivation and adept performance, which collectively present several distinct dimensions or conceptions of forgetting. Since this chapter focuses specifically on the ferryman passage, I will consider only aspects of forgetting directly relevant to the passage's implications about expert swimmers and nervous archers.[6]

In the ferryman story, swimmers and divers forget the water in the sense that it doesn't weigh on their minds as a source of anxiety. But they must continue to perceive it, for they need to feel and react to it in order to swim. So forgetting something, in the sense intended here, cannot entail being insensible or blind to it. Rather, as the description of divers shows, forgetting is associated with being comfortable, at home, unworried, and competent.[7] Swimmers and divers perceive the water, but it isn't a focus of worry for them. So in learning boat handling they place no weight on the external, here understood as the risk of falling into the water.

A passage coupled with another skill story, that of Artisan Chui, introduces a further dimension of forgetting that overlaps the case of expert divers who are comfortable in the water. We forget things, the passage declares, when they fit well. They create no discomfort or impediment to smooth functioning and hence draw no attention. "Forgetting your feet is your shoes fitting well; forgetting your waist is your belt fitting well; your awareness forgetting right and wrong is your heart-mind fitting well." More generally, when we achieve "good fit with affairs and encounters," we "neither alternate internally nor follow along externally" (19/62–63). As in the ferryman story, if we fully fit into our circumstances, as the divers do, nothing extraneous can pull us off balance.

In another respect, the belt and shoe examples might seem to contrast with that of forgetting the water. Swimmers cannot be oblivious to the water, I suggested, since they must feel it to swim. By contrast, it might seem that we do become oblivious to a well-fitting belt or shoes. They seem to slip from awareness, reemerging again only if they cease to fit or we deliberately attend to them. Might expert swimmers forget the water as we forget a comfortable pair of shoes? Might this mean they are indeed oblivious to it?[8]

Without question, swimmers may fit into their watery environment extremely well—perhaps as well as we fit into comfortable shoes. But in both cases, I suggest, we retain peripheral awareness of the objects we interact with—the water, the shoes, the ground we use the shoes to walk on. We do not genuinely become oblivious to these objects. To the contrary, the more comfortable or at home we are with something, the more sensitive we are to it. Expert swimmers or runners feel the flow of the water or the shape of the ground more keenly than novices do. Hence I suggest that forgetting, in a sense that covers both the swimmers and the shoes, pertains not to perception or heedfulness but to attention, particularly attention associated with anxiety or disturbance. Expert swimmers perceive the water without specifically attending to it; worried archers cannot stop nervously attending to the prizes and so are clumsy. Well-fitting shoes are comfortable, cause no disruption, and so draw no attention.

The proposal that forgetting pertains mainly to attention also helps to explain an important difference between the swimming and archery examples. Not all forgetting of fears or distractions can be due to comfort or good fit in the way that, for example, expert swimmers might forget fear of the water because of how comfortably they fit into the watery environment. Seasoned archery competitors who forget the prizes do so not by achieving good fit with them but by setting thoughts of them aside to concentrate on their shooting. They devote no attention to them.

The belt and shoes examples are paired with a description of Artisan Chui, who could draw perfect circles or squares because he let his fingers transform with things without his heart-mind examining his actions, thus keeping his "spirit platform" (the chest) unified and unfettered (19/62). Perhaps because Chui's fingers fit so well with things, his heart-mind had no need to attend to them. The implication is that good fit and forgetting occur when action need not be monitored or supervised by the heart-mind (*xin*), normally regarded in early Chinese thought as the organ of cognition and action guidance. This interpretation coheres well with conceiving of forgetting as an absence of attention, since it is the heart-mind that attends to things. A tentative implication of the Chui story is that masterful performance proceeds not from the *xin* but from a unified, unimpeded spirit (*shen* 神). I will suggest below that this description reflects an important view in Zhuangist discourse about the locus of adept agency.

When stress-inducing matters are wholly extraneous to the performance of a skill, perhaps forgetting could indeed entail becoming oblivious to them, at least temporarily. This point is illustrated by Qing the woodcarver, who sculpts bell stands of uncanny beauty (19/55–59). Before starting a new piece, Qing fasts for seven days to still his heart-mind by emptying it of distractions. Step by step, all thoughts of praise or reward, rank or salary, honour or condemnation, and skill or clumsiness slip away. Ultimately, he claims, he forgets even his limbs and body. Emptying himself of these sources of potential interference, he suggests, allows him to "match nature with nature," aligning his natural capacities and fully concentrated skill with the natural grain of the finest timber. To commence work, of course, Qing must recover cognitive awareness of the aim of his project and kinaesthetic awareness of his limbs. But perhaps he might really become wholly unmindful of factors such as praise and criticism. He does not cease to think or be aware—he still critically evaluates the quality of the timber, for example. But he lets extraneous concerns vanish, such that his skill becomes fully focused and attuned to its object. Arguably, what he describes is a process of removing attention from irrelevant matters and focusing it more fully on what he is doing.

4. FROM FORGETTING TO SPIRIT-DRIVEN ACTION

Motifs associated with forgetting in the ferryman story link the concept not just to skill but to other traits characteristic of the Zhuangist sage or adept and the well-lived life. They also hint at a complex conception of adept agency distinctive of Zhuangist discourse.

One such motif is ease. Good swimmers and divers forget the water because they are deeply at ease in it, Confucius says. This description is echoed in the story of the whitewater swimmer who deftly glides through rapids too treacherous even for fish and turtles. Having grown up in the water, the swimmer says, he is at peace in it. Gliding along with the flow is second nature to him (19/52–54). The swimmer and Confucius use different words for being at ease—*an* 安 (at peace) versus *xia* 暇 (at leisure)—but both descriptions evoke characterisations elsewhere in the *Zhuangzi* of exemplary agents as maintaining serenity in stressful circumstances.[9] A salient example is Ziyu, a man struck with a disfiguring, fatal disease, whose "heart-mind was at leisure (*xian* 閒), without anything amiss" (6/49). Gain and loss follow from inevitably changing circumstances, Ziyu remarks; the adept is "at peace (*an*) with the times while dwelling in the flow" and is thus "released from bonds" rather than tied down to things (6/52–53)—as we are tied down when we put weight on the external.

A related motif shared with the ferryman is that agents who achieve this sort of ease maintain equanimity by becoming impervious to disruptive emotions: "sorrow and delight cannot penetrate them" (6/52). A view found across numerous *Zhuangzi* passages is that psychological disturbances occur when stressful events or the emotions they incite penetrate the chest or heart-mind and disrupt the equilibrium of the spirit (*shen* 神) or vital vapor (*qi* 氣) in the centre of the body. Hence Confucius describes divers as so at ease that boat and cart accidents are unable to penetrate their chest—literally, their "dwelling" (*she* 舍)—where the heart-mind is and the spirit resides. The imagery of the adept or the person of *de* 德 (power, agency) being impenetrable by such disturbances is common in the *Zhuangzi*.[10] Of particular note is an association some passages draw between affective imperviousness and the wholeness or integrity of the spirit (*shen*)—the source of psychological functioning and agency—within the chest. For example, those whose "spirit is whole" are said to have no gaps or fissures through which things can get in to disrupt them, and so "death or life, shock or fear do not penetrate their chests" (19/12–14).

Such references to the spirit highlight a third motif that, as I will explain, draws the others together: Yan Yuan's description of the ferryman's boat handling as "like a spirit (*shen*)." The ferryman is one of several passages that associate skilled expertise with the efficacy of spirits or ghosts. In the story of the whitewater swimmer, Confucius initially mistakes the swimmer for a ghost (19/51). Woodcarver Qing's works are so striking that viewers are astounded, as if they'd seen a ghost or spirit (19/55). Elsewhere, the perfected person is said to be spirit-like (*shen*) (2/71), and indeed one synonym for the perfected or sagely person is the "spirit-person" (1/22). Besides denoting the vital spirit within human beings, the word *shen* can also refer to superhuman denizens of the cosmos, who are in effect personified agents of Heaven or nature (*tian* 天) and so directly reflect the workings of nature. By extension, *shen* is also used to describe the wondrously efficacious agency characteristic of spirits or of Heaven. Thus one implication of the comparison of skilled performances to the agency of ghosts or spirits is that through skills we can approach a perfected mode of activity in which our actions align fully with the natural world.

Beyond this point, I want to suggest that the three distinct uses of *shen*—referring to the vital spirit in human agents, to superhuman entities, and to spirit-like efficacy—may be interrelated in a way that can help explain how agents act from a state of forgetting, why such action is marked by affective ease and equanimity, and why it is considered singularly efficacious.

One plausible hypothesis is that concentration and wholeness of the *shen* within—achieved by forgetting extraneous distractions—yield equanimity and facilitate spirit-like levels of performance. Another skill story in "Mastering Life" depicts a hunchback who uses a sticky pole to lift cicadas from trees as deftly as if plucking them with his hand. He attributes this feat partly to his intense stillness and concentration, through which he disregards all the myriad things to focus only on cicada wings, to which he lightly sticks the end of the pole (19/20). Confucius describes him as unifying his intent so well that his *shen* is "condensed" (19/21). Concentration of the *shen* thus facilitates feats of skill.

Given that the *shen* forms part of our psychological make-up, it is only a short step from the hypothesis that a concentrated *shen* facilitates performance to a view presented by Cook Ding the butcher, the most well known of the *Zhuangzi* skill exemplars. Having reached a high level of expertise, Ding says, "I meet the oxen with my *shen*, without looking with my eyes; perceptual knowing ceases, while *shen*-impulse proceeds" (3/6). At advanced levels of skill, according to Ding, the *shen* itself can drive action.

Drawing on this idea, let me suggest a view that goes beyond the conception of *shen* as spirit-like efficacy in the ferryman passage yet may elucidate the notion of forgetting that is the passage's main theme. The view is that efficacious performance and closer attunement to nature can be attained by learning to act from our *shen*, an advanced mode or source of agency that functions most fully when we forget—that is, when we cease using the heart-mind to deliberately attend to or self-consciously control what we are doing.[11] Passages such as the Artisan Chui and Woodcarver Qing stories suggest that adept action follows from stilling or purging the heart-mind (*xin*). *Shen* may be a label for the dimension of agency that then takes over. Mastering skills is a process of expanding the scope of activity that issues from the *shen* rather than being deliberately directed by the heart-mind.[12]

This set of ideas provides a plausible explanation of how good swimmers can forget the water without becoming oblivious to it. The explanation is that forgetting pertains to the heart-mind, while expert performance issues mainly from the *shen*. An expert swimmer's heart-mind forgets the water, but the *shen* continues to respond to it sensitively and intelligently.

The web of concepts just surveyed thus suggests an intriguing composite account of expert performance. This account is not an integral doctrine attributable to any particular *Zhuangzi* passage or passages, but a hypothetical stance constructed from elements partly shared across various passages. For purposes of discussion, it represents one way of tying together ideas from Zhuangist skill discourse into a relatively fine-grained picture of high-performance action.

On this account, expert performance consists largely of spirit-driven activity. Central to this mode of activity is that, through forgetting, the heart-mind is emptied of thoughts, judgements, plans, worries, and fears, and action issues mainly from the spirit (*shen*). Such action is marked by focused concentration; the absence of extraneous, distracting thoughts or emotions; a sense of ease or calm; and freedom from ties to things. It need not be effortless; for all we know, the ferryman, woodcarver, or butcher may work up quite a sweat.[13] The relevant conception of ease is rather an absence of cares, tension, or disturbance. Spirit-driven activity is associated with *de*, the power of agency bestowed on us by nature, and with heightened efficacy, arising from the superior attunement to natural conditions that the spirit can achieve compared with the heart-mind. By implication, characteristic features of spirit-driven activity are at the same time central features of the life of *de*, or the Zhuangist good life.[14]

Is spirit-driven activity an intelligible conception of action? I suggest that it is, at least in outline, and we can plausibly explicate it in terms of contemporary concepts such as procedural memory and the contextual nature of basic actions. A basic action is one we perform without performing any further action. What counts as a basic action may be relative to an agent's competence. For a skilled typist, typing the word "action" may be a single basic action, whereas for a beginner, typing "action" might require a separate basic action for each letter, accompanied by a discrete, conscious intention to type each one. Procedural memory—popularly called muscle memory—refers to the largely unconscious memory system by which we learn and execute skills. Spirit-driven activity is in effect highly competent action in which much of the perception, judgement, and movement required has become automatic, issuing from procedural memory without self-conscious attention or guidance. In such activity, what count as basic actions for the agent may shift to a high, general level. Instead of consciously performing the separate actions of pushing off, balancing, sculling, steering, and landing, for instance, expert boat pilots may be able to simply cross the river as a single, continuous high-level action, requiring little conscious thought, guided largely by their *shen*. Such activity, I suggest, is understandable and even familiar. Many of us experience it daily while performing routine, automatic, yet intelligent actions, such as driving a car or walking to the bus stop, and when exercising expertise in sports, work, crafts, or the performing arts.

Taking this conception of spirit-driven activity seriously need not commit us to accepting early Chinese metaphysical views about the existence of an inner entity called the *shen*, constituted of *jing* 精 (vital fluid) and *qi* (vital vapor). For our purposes, we can simply take *shen* to refer to whatever psychophysiological capacities underwrite the features ascribed to spirit-driven action.[15] Nor need we hold that spirit-driven activity somehow magically resolves thorny normative questions about the appropriateness of various courses of conduct.[16] *Zhuangzi* passages valorise key features of spirit-driven activity, but perhaps an agent could attain spirit-like competence while doing appalling things, as oxen no doubt hold is the case with Cook Ding.[17]

Valorising spirit-driven activity also need not entail what Montero labels the "just do it" view of skills, the popular yet generally unexamined assumption that expert-level performance is characterised by an absence of conscious thought, control, or effort (*Thought in Action*, 14). Montero draws on evidence from professional athletes, dancers, musicians, and chess players to argue that conscious mental processes such as self-reflective thinking, planning, or monitoring of one's actions are often employed in optimal performance (*Thought in Action*, 38). Some *Zhuangzi* passages may present a radical no-thought view of action (for example, 15/10–14), but not all do. The Cook Ding story depicts interaction between spirit-driven activity and the self-conscious cognition associated with the heart-mind. Ding describes handling tough parts in the ox by consciously noticing and preparing for them before again applying spirit-driven capacities to work his way through: "I see the difficulty, cautiously prepare, focus my vision, and slow my action; I move the knife with great subtlety, and suddenly it [the ox] has already fallen apart" (3/10–11). Spirit-driven activity could constitute the foundation or core of optimal performance without thereby leaving no role for self-aware planning, judgement, or control.

5. LEARNING TO FORGET

The concluding moral of the ferryman passage may seem obviously true: putting weight on the external—anxiously attending to factors not directly relevant to the task at hand—hampers performance. In fact, however, the relation between attention, anxiety, and performance is more complex than the passage acknowledges. An established finding in sports psychology is that attaching enough importance to a competition that an athlete experiences some degree of anxiety, along with attendant psychophysiological arousal, tends to improve performance, not impede it. The details depend on a particular athlete's tolerance for anxiety, the athlete's interpretation of anxiety as facilitative (such as pleasant excitement) or debilitative (such as unpleasant stress), and the interaction between somatic anxiety (such as feeling "butterflies in the stomach," which may be facilitative) and cognitive anxiety (such as consciously worrying about failure, which is usually debilitative).[18] Moreover, to attach an appropriate degree of importance to an event and thus generate facilitative excitement about it, the athlete must understand the event's context and its potential consequences. If, as the ferryman story implies, optimal performance requires forgetting the prizes, the relevant type of forgetting should be spirit-driven activity that takes the prizes into account without anxiously attending to or fretting over them, for they are indeed a relevant, albeit peripheral, aspect of the circumstances to which the agent is responding.

Accordingly, rather than placing no weight at all on the external, the most defensible advice may be to place proportionate weight on relevant external factors such that one feels an appropriate, facilitative level of excitement while remaining composed and able to perform well. The lesson of the ferryman story is more compelling if we qualify it: putting *disproportionate* weight on or attending *too anxiously* to extraneous factors hampers performance.

A crucial practical question, then, is how to avoid attaching too much weight to the external. Just how do we forget, in the relevant sense?

The swimming and diving examples suggest that one way to forget sources of anxiety is by attaining sufficient competence that we feel at ease with them. Expert swimmers and divers feel no anxiety in boat handling because for them the consequences of failure are negligible. They know they won't be hurt if they capsize. They place little or no weight on the external— the risk of falling into the water—because it is genuinely trivial to them. The stakes are low; they encounter no appreciable source of stress. An obvious limitation of this solution to anxiety is that it applies only to those with the relevant expertise. Non-swimmers must work their way up from floating in the shallows before they can learn boat handling in the deeps.

The archery example is not directly analogous to that of swimmers and divers. Its point is that when the stakes are indeed high, we become anxious about them, and this concern about matters extraneous to hitting the target undermines our competence. Unless we avoid contests altogether, however, we can't eliminate the stress posed by competition in the way expertise in swimming eliminates the stress posed by the water. The cost of failure—losing the gold—remains. Anxiety about the stakes can be alleviated only by changing our attitudes about them, either by devaluing them or by redirecting attention away from them. Doing so is analogous not to learning boat handling as an expert swimmer but to learning it as a non-swimmer who has found a way to remain calm about the danger of falling overboard. Expert swimmers and divers may illustrate what forgetting the external is like, but they are not necessarily exemplars of how to achieve such forgetting in a high-stress situation.

So what advice do *Zhuangzi* writings offer about how to forget or unweight the external when external factors are unavoidably stressful? On this point, the ferryman story is silent, beyond implying that we must learn to concentrate on the matter at hand. Other passages address the issue in two ways, however, directly and as part of an overall approach to value in life.

The direct approach consists mainly of concentrating on the task at hand and by doing so directing our attention away from extraneous matters. Some passages depict this process as incorporating meditative practices to help clear the heart-mind.

One illustration of a direct approach is the hunchback cicada catcher's regimen for learning to pick the bugs off trees with a pole (19/18–21). He undertakes a course of incrementally more difficult exercises to hone his technique and train his ability to concentrate on the cicadas without distraction. An implication is that by following a disciplined training regimen we can learn to forget the external. Another illustration is Qing the woodcarver's practice of fasting before a new project to still his heart-mind by clearing out extraneous thoughts. The specifics of his routine are probably inessential for our purposes; techniques other than fasting might work equally well. The crux is that he adopts a disciplined psychophysical regimen to focus his skill and direct his attention away from concerns external to his task.

Other well-known passages concerning forgetting and emptying the heart-mind of distractions include the story of Yan Hui making ethical progress by "sitting and forgetting" (6/89–93) and the dialogue in which Confucius admonishes Yan Hui to undertake "heart-fasting" to purge his impractical plans to reform the cruel tyrant of Wei (4/1–34). The first story depicts Yan forgetting conventional values and norms that constitute impediments to aligning with natural processes. The second depicts him emptying his heart-mind of preconceived plans and instead learning to respond fluidly to circumstances by means of *qi* (vital vapor)—in effect, his *shen*. Both stories depict processes of emptying the heart-mind of content that could weigh the agent down through attachment to the external.[19]

The richest direct treatment of anxiety management is Confucius's advice to Zigao, a nobleman debilitated by stress over a high-stakes diplomatic assignment. This passage presents a fourfold approach to reducing stress. One element is cognitive restructuring, as Confucius coaches Zigao to see his situation as a normal, expected part of his social role, observing that from time to time familial and political relationships present all of us with inescapable troubles. Another is affective reinterpretation, as he urges Zigao that the height of *de* 德 (power, agency) lies in finding peace in circumstances he cannot control by seeing them as unchangeable features of his life circumstances (*ming* 命), such as his age or height. A further element is preparation and confidence building. Confucius offers practical advice on human relations and talks Zigao through various scenarios he might encounter. A final, crucial point is attention training. Zigao is to forget the dangers and stresses by absorbing himself in an alternative object of attention, his diplomatic work: "act on the facts of the matter and forget yourself" (4/41–44).

A second major approach to unweighting the external is to reframe the significance of success or failure so that the prospect of failure no longer induces anxiety. Consider the story of Sunshu Ao, who was thrice elevated and then dismissed as premier of his state without feeling either honoured or dismayed. Sunshu maintains equanimity by investing value only in inherent features of the self that are independent of external influences. "Since I regard gain and loss as not me, I wasn't upset." "If [power and status] lie in something else, they're not present in me; if they lie in me, they're not present in something else" (21/64–65). Sunshu has structured his self-understanding and self-worth such that he places little or no weight on the external.

Another example is the amputee ex-convict Wang Tai, whose "constant heart-mind" remains unperturbed even by matters of life and death. Wang understands how not to rely on anything, and so external things cannot pull him this way or that (5/6). Accepting the transformation of things around him as facts of his life circumstances (*ming* 命), he focuses on "preserving his source," or maintaining his nature-given powers of agency (5/6). To maintain a "constant heart-mind," he attends to the respects in which all things are parts of a totality that remains the same regardless of how its parts change or are redistributed (5/7). He thus feels no emotional distress over losing his foot, since to him the amputation is not actually a loss but merely a rearrangement of parts within a whole.

The theme of attaining constancy by identifying with things as a unity appears again in a dialogue in which Lao Dan describes for Confucius the free wandering of the perfected person. Such persons attach no weight to external things, instead adopting the attitude that "value lies in me and is not lost in change" (21/34). Like grazing animals or water-born creatures, they attain "overall constancy" and emotional equanimity by engaging in a flow of activity that remains consistent despite ongoing, minor changes:

> Grass-eating beasts do not fret over a change of pasture; water-born creatures do not fret over a change of waters. They proceed through minor changes without losing their overall constancy, and joy, anger, grief, and happiness do not enter their chests. (21/31–32)

How can we come to live this way? According to the passage, the crux lies in identifying with the world as a unified whole:

> Now as to the world, it is that in which the myriad things are one. If you attain that in which they are one and assimilate to it, your four limbs and hundred parts will be as dust and dirt, and death and life, ending and beginning will be as day and night, nothing being able to disturb you—least of all the distinctions of gain and loss or good and bad fortune! (21/32–33)

One way to interpret these lines is as advocating that we let go of our perspective as individuals and instead identify with the cosmic standpoint of the world as a totality. Overall or high-level constancy then follows, since the totality remains the same whole despite any change or rearrangement of its parts. Once we identify with the totality, it matters little to us whether we as individuals succeed or fail in our endeavours, since from the cosmic perspective there is no net gain or loss.

Let me suggest, however, that the crux of these remarks is less to advocate that we adopt the cosmic standpoint—which may be impractically difficult—than it is to illustrate the idea of overall constancy. Consider again the analogy to grazing or water-born creatures. What they value is the ongoing activity of roaming and feeding in fields or streams. They see no difference between feeding in one place or another; what matters is the overall constancy of their activity. If we identify with the world, considered as the totality of things, we regard it as a single, vast realm within which we roam or wander about. We need not see any difference between wandering in one situation or another. What is of value is our activity, which is wholly internal to us and unaffected by change, since its overall constancy can continue regardless of our particular circumstances.[20]

On this interpretation, both the direct approach and the reframing approach hinge on focusing our intentions and sense of self-worth on our own ongoing activity. In the direct approach, agents mitigate the influence of external factors by concentrating on the task before them. In the value-reframing approach, value is located in the ongoing flow of adaptive activity.

A consequence of both approaches is that in highlighting the importance of unweighting the external, the ferryman story illustrates how the exercise of skills may foster attitudes characteristic of a more general Zhuangist conception of the good life.

6. CONCLUDING REMARKS

The ferryman story weaves together multiple motifs that are shared across numerous *Zhuangzi* passages, thus embedding the story in a web of interrelated conceptions of personal cultivation, adept activity, and the good life. As illustrated by these motifs, feats of apparently preternatural skill can be learned, and doing so offers the possibility of achieving spirit-like attunement with the environment. Pivotal to mastering skills is the ability to forget potential sources of stress, either by becoming expert in dealing with them, directing attention away from them, or reframing one's perception of them so that they cease to be intimidating. Agents who attain such forgetting become at ease with the circumstances in which their skill is performed. Disruptive, extraneous concerns no longer enter the mind, and the agent can adroitly proceed with the task, learning to act from a spirit-like mode of agency available to all of us. The result, I suggest, is an attractive depiction of an important component of mental health and of a fulfilling life.

As we have seen, the topics raised in passages in which these motifs appear reflect how, for many subdiscourses within the *Zhuangzi*, skilled performances function as concrete illustrations of general themes about acting and living adeptly. Forgetting or unweighting extraneous matters, maintaining a mindset of unperturbed ease, and attending to the task at hand may facilitate spirit-like adeptness not only in skills but in the overall course of life. As the medieval scholar Cheng Xuanying commented about the problem of putting too much weight on the external, "How could this apply only to archery?! Everything is so."[21]

The ferryman story focuses on the psychological side of skill performance rather than on technique or the criteria of success. The hunchback story gives examples of technique exercises; the woodcarver attributes his results to alignment between his skills and the natural pattern of the wood; the whitewater swimmer explains how he follows the course of the water. The ferryman passes over such issues. But the text does not imply that the mental side of performance renders the technical side trivial or unnecessary. Swimmers and divers of course rely on technical skill in gliding through water; the point of the archery example is that distractions interfere with technical skill, not that mental composure alone determines success.[22]

The moral of the ferryman story is limited in content yet broad in application. To do anything adeptly—boat handling, archery, or anything else—we need to manage anxiety by setting aside the extraneous or peripheral and directing our attention appropriately. Focus on what you're doing. Forget the deeps and row.[23]

NOTES

1. References to the *Zhuangzi* text cite chapter and line numbers in Hung, *A Concordance to Zhuangzi*. These indices can be used to find the passages cited throughout the online concordance tool at the Chinese Text Project, edited by Donald Sturgeon, https://ctext.org/tools/concordance.

2. For a compact survey of such research, see Klein, "Reading the *Zhuangzi*."

3. The two obvious exceptions are chapter 30, "A Persuasion on Swords," and 31, "The Fisherman."

4. Vavra, "Skilful Practice," 214, agrees that forgetting the water amounts to "getting rid of fear" but maintains—implausibly, in my view—that forgetting rules out any awareness of the water.

5. Most commentators seem to interpret *nei* this way. For example, Chen (*Zhuangzi*, 553, n. 11) and Li (*Zhuangzi*, 360, n. 47) both read it as "the heart-mind within" (*nei xin* 內心), most likely following the medieval commentator Cheng Xuanying (see Guo, *Collected*, 644, n. 6). Wang (*Collated*, 685, n. 13) interprets it as "the heart-mind intent" (*xin zhi* 心志).

6. Fraser, "Heart-Fasting," 205–8, presents a broader account of forgetting.

7. Oshima suggests that perhaps forgetting might just be "some sort of contentment or at-homeness resulting from a lack of conscious concern" ("Metaphorical Analysis," 67). Kohn proposes that the psychological state referred to by *wang* is better interpreted as "never mind" than as "forget"—to *wang* sources of anxiety is to override them by focusing on more important values ("Forget or Not Forget," 180).

8. This seems to be Coutinho's view. With reference to the ferryman passage, he comments that "one is thoroughly at home in a medium only when one simply lives through it, oblivious of its presence" (*Daoist Philosophies*, 186). Similarly, Vavra takes the passage to imply that skilful action requires that a swimmer or ferry pilot be unaware of the water ("Skilful Practice," 214).

9. See, for example, 3/17–19, 4/43, and 5/20.

10. See, for example, 3/18, 5/43–45, 15/9–10, 19/7–17, and 21/30–35.

11. Puett, "Notion of Spirit," 256, suggests the Cook Ding story implies that the impulses of the *shen* produce action that accords with the patterns of nature. Slingerland, *Effortless Action*, 199–201, also regards *shen* as a "normatively positive instantiation of the self" that has a special connection to nature and *dao*. Vavra, "Skilful Practice," 217, questions this link between *shen* as a locus of agency and nature, as he finds that individual passages tend to use *shen* and *tian* 天 (nature) in contrasting ways (207–9). Without denying the significant differences between passages, I suggest that the conceptual associations between the *shen* within agents, the *shen*-like qualities of skilled action, and the *shen*'s responsiveness to natural patterns are strong enough to support the claim that action issuing from the *shen* tends to align with natural circumstances and thus be efficacious.

12. Vavra, "Skilful Practice," 204, notes the widespread use in early Chinese texts of *shen* to refer to highly refined cognitive abilities superior to those of the heart-mind.

13. Contra Slingerland, *Effortless Action*, the *Zhuangzi* skill texts do not emphasise an ideal of effortlessness—not unless we conflate "effortless" in the sense of "fluid" or "graceful" with "effortless" in the sense of "not difficult," "without trying," or "requiring no exertion." Effort per se is generally not a central concern in early Chinese discourse on adept action.

14. Yearley proposes that for the *Zhuangzi*, activity issuing from the *shen* manifests the "ultimate spiritual state," one marked by "a higher kind of ability" that allows the agent to negotiate an easy, efficacious way through the world ("Zhuangzi's Understanding," 176). I agree that *shen*-directed activity illustrates a Zhuangist vision of the fulfilling life. But Yearley packages this view within a framework of what he calls "intrawordly mysticism" (160), accord-

ing to which *shen* activity involves a transformation by "transcendent drives," such that skilled adepts "cease to be normal agents" and are instead possessed by "an alien power" (176). This seems to me an excessively complex interpretation of the skill texts, which I read as implying that a fulfilling life is available to ordinary agents, drawing on resources they already possess and requiring no mystical transcendence.

15. Coutinho (*Daoist Philosophies*, 183) and Yearley ("Zhuangzi's Understanding," 175) both recommend a similar stance.

16. Puett, "Notion of Spirit," 259, argues that the links between spirit and Heaven imply that the Zhuangist adept with a cultivated spirit will inherently follow the proper patterns of the natural world. I am sceptical that the scope of such normative guidance extends very far. Yearley, "Zhuangzi's Understanding," 176, suggests that *shen*-guided activity is amoral by the measure of normal moral standards. I have argued that such activity might facilitate identifying justified ways of interacting with others but cannot ensure that we reliably follow them (Fraser, "Heart-Fasting," 209–12).

17. Ivanhoe, "Relativist," 202, maintains that the *Zhuangzi* skill stories all concern "benign activities." Slaughtering oxen is not benign.

18. Weinberg and Gould, *Foundations*, 85–92.

19. For further discussion of these passages, see Fraser, "Heart-Fasting," 202–8.

20. I offer an interpretation of the Zhuangist good life along these lines in Fraser, "Emotion and Agency" and "Wandering the Way."

21. Guo, *Collected Explications*, 644, n. 6.

22. Hence I suggest that Vavra exaggerates in proposing that the ferryman passage presents a conception of "universal skill" requiring only mental composure and attunement to the environment ("Skilful Practice," 214). The reference to archery assumes that the agent already possesses the needed techniques, while swimmers and divers presumably have at least some familiarity with sculling and steering in water. Forgetting might be a crucial, near-universal element in adept performance without itself constituting a "universal skill."

23. I am grateful to Hagop Sarkissian and Lisa Raphals for helpful comments that improved many details of this chapter.

REFERENCES

Chen Guying 陳鼓應. *Zhuangzi: Modern Notes and Paraphrase* [*Zhuāngzǐ jīnzhù jīnyì* 莊子今注今譯]. 2 vols. Beijing: Commercial Press, 2007.
Coutinho, Steve. *An Introduction to Daoist Philosophies.* New York: Columbia University Press, 2013.
Fraser, Chris. "Emotion and Agency in the *Zhuangzi.*" *Asian Philosophy* 21, no. 1 (2011): 97–121.
———. "Heart-Fasting, Forgetting, and Using the Heart Like a Mirror: Applied Emptiness in the *Zhuangzi.*" In *Nothingness in Asian Philosophy*, edited by J. Liu and D. Berger, 197–212. New York: Routledge, 2014.
———. "Wandering the Way: A Eudaimonistic Approach to the *Zhuangzi.*" *Dao: A Journal of Comparative Philosophy* 13, no. 4 (2014): 541–65.
Guo Qingfan 郭慶藩. *Collected Explications of Zhuangzi* [*Zhuāngzǐ Jíshì* 莊子集釋]. Emendations by Wang Xiaoyu 王孝魚. 3 vols. Beijing: Zhonghua, 2004.
Hung, William, ed. *A Concordance to Zhuangzi* [*Zhuāngzǐ yǐndé* 莊子引得]. Harvard-Yenching Institute Sinological Index Series, Supplement No. 20. Cambridge, MA: Harvard University Press, 1956.
Ivanhoe, Philip J. "Was Zhuangzi a Relativist?" In *Essays on Skepticism, Relativism, and Ethics in Zhuangzi*, edited by Paul Kjellerg and P. J. Ivanhoe, 196–214. Albany, NY: SUNY Press, 1996.
Klein, Esther. "Reading the *Zhuangzi* Anthology." In *Having a Word with Angus Graham*, edited by Carine Defoort and Roger T. Ames, 11–26. Albany, NY: SUNY Press, 2018.
Kohn, Livia. "Forget or Not Forget? The Neurophysiology of *Zuowang*." In *New Visions of the Zhuangzi*, edited by Livia Kohn, 165–83. St. Petersburg, FL: Three Pines Press, 2015.

Li Mian 李勉. *Zhuangzi: A General Study and Section by Section Commentary* [*Zhuāngzǐ zǒnglùn jí fēnpiān píngzhù* 莊子總論及分篇評注]. Rev. ed. Taipei: Commercial Press, 1990.

Montero, Barbara. *Thought in Action*. Oxford: Oxford University Press, 2016.

Oshima, Harold. "A Metaphorical Analysis of the Concept of Mind in the *Chuang-tzu*." In *Experimental Essays on Chuang-tzu*, edited by Victor Mair, 63–84. Honolulu: University of Hawai'i Press, 1983.

Puett, Michael. "'Nothing Can Overcome Heaven': The Notion of Spirit in the *Zhuangzi*." In *Hiding the World in the World*, edited by Scott Cook, 248–62. Albany, NY: SUNY Press, 2003.

Slingerland, Edward. *Effortless Action*. Oxford: Oxford University Press, 2003.

Vavra, Dusan. "Skilful Practice in the *Zhuangzi*: Putting the Narratives in Context." *Asian Studies* 5, no. 1 (2017): 195–219.

Wang Shumin 王叔岷. *Collated Interpretations of Zhuangzi* [*Zhuāngzǐ jiàoquán* 莊子校詮]. 3 vols. Taipei: Academia Sinica, 1999.

Weinberg, Robert S., and Daniel Gould. *Foundations of Sport and Exercise Psychology*. 6th ed. Champaign, IL: Human Kinetics, 2015.

Yearley, Lee. "Zhuangzi's Understanding of Skillfulness and the Ultimate Spiritual State." In *Essays on Skepticism, Relativism, and Ethics in Zhuangzi*, edited by Paul Kjellerg and P. J. Ivanhoe, 152–82. Albany, NY: SUNY Press, 1996.

Chapter Twelve

The Unresponsive Fighting Cocks

Mastery and Human Interaction in the Zhuangzi

Wim De Reu

Ji Shengzi was training fighting cocks for the king. [After] ten days, [the king] asked: 'Are the cocks ready?' [Ji Shengzi] replied: 'Not yet. At present, they are vain and confide in vigour'. [After] ten days, [the king] asked again. [Ji Shengzi] replied: 'Not yet. They still respond to echoes and shadows'. [After] ten days, [the king] asked again. [Ji Shengzi] replied: 'Not yet. They still look around fiercely and are swollen with vigour'. [After] ten days, [the king] asked again. [Ji Shengzi] replied: 'Near enough. Even though some may crow, the cocks are by now without change. Looked at from a distance, they resemble cocks made of wood. Their virtue is complete. As for other cocks, none will dare to respond. They will turn and run'.[1]

The fighting cocks story is one of a collection of so-called skill stories in chapter 19 of the *Zhuangzi* (莊子). Despite being included in the single most relevant chapter of such stories, it is rarely given much attention, even among studies that focus on the topic of skill and mastery in the *Zhuangzi*.[2] This lack of discussion in itself already justifies the inclusion of this story in the present volume.

More important, however, are two substantial reasons why the story warrants our attention. First is that mastery in the fighting cocks story is not a matter of skill. The cocks are *un*responsive. Instead of enhancing their fighting skills, the cocks are trained not to be emotionally-behaviourally impacted by the sight of rival cocks. Evidence from another 'skill story' included in *Zhuangzi* 19 suggests that the composer(s) of this chapter conceptually distinguished between skill on the one hand and the ability to resist the subjective impact of external conditions on the other. There is, in other words, more to mastery than mere skill or technique.

183

Second, the fighting cocks story casts doubt on the view that *dao* practices as advanced in the *Zhuangzi* are value neutral and hence compatible with malicious-actor scenarios. A cockfight is an intrinsically violent situation. We have every reason to expect the cocks to be trained as efficient, skilful killers. In this light, it is surprising to see that the selected course of action in the fighting cocks story is one of non-violence. The cocks are trained not to be impacted, that is, to show control, on the assumption that their resulting ring presence will compel their rivals to withdraw. In the fighting cocks story, winning *does not* depend on fighting, harming, and being harmed. Here and in other conflict situations in the *Zhuangzi*, the optimal course of action (*dao* 道) defuses conflict and eschews harm; or, put differently, it favours sustainability. These values are built into what defines an optimal course of action. It is this state of affairs that makes the development of malicious-actor scenarios unlikely.

The outline of the chapter is as follows. I start with two fairly straightforward sections. Section 1 addresses two basic textual issues. Section 2 describes the more formal aspects of the story: the setup, the framing, and the characters and their relations; it also identifies the relation between rivalling cocks as the primary locus of interaction. Section 3 holds a pivotal position. It analyzes the dynamics of cockfighting as presented in the fighting cocks story by proposing two interpretive keys—impact reduction and ring presence. Sections 4 and 5 build on this analysis and draw conclusions that will be supported by additional material. Section 4 shows that mastery in the *Zhuangzi* should not be exclusively understood in terms of skill. Section 5 examines two more conflict situations to argue that optimal courses of (inter)action are not value neutral but are instead selected on the basis of a concern with defusing conflict and avoiding harm.

1. BASIC TEXTUAL ISSUES

Any translation of the fighting cocks story must face at least two basic textual issues. The first issue is whether to render *ji* (雞, cock) as singular or plural; the second issue is whether the first instance of *ji* in the final reply refers to the master cock(s) raised by Ji Shengzi (紀渻子) or to other, rival cock(s). As we will see later on, answering these issues will prove helpful in making some projections about the cock(s)' training and in understanding the nature of their progress, respectively.

Existing translations are split on the first issue: while some offer a singular reading, others go for the plural.[3] I believe there is a solid argument in favour of the plural. The argument hinges on the 'S *you/wu* V *zhe*' (S 有/無 V 者) construction that appears twice in the final reply. The second case (the *wu* case) clearly points to the plural: it does not make sense to say of a single cock (S) that, rendered literally, "there is no one / there are none that dare(s) to respond" (*wu gan ying zhe* 無敢應者). The preceding *yi ji* (異雞, other cocks) must therefore refer to a *group* of cocks. By virtue of parallel construction, the same holds true for the first case (the *you* case): the phrase "even though there is one / there are some that crow(s)" (*sui you ming zhe* 雖有鳴者) only makes sense if the *ji* (S) that precedes it is thought of as plural.

There is more of a consensus on the second issue. To the best of my knowledge, the first instance of *ji* in the final reply is always taken to refer to the other cocks (*yi ji*) mentioned at the end of the reply rather than to the master cocks raised by Ji Shengzi. Nevertheless, I believe there are two arguments to reverse this reading. The first argument concerns the flow of Ji Shengzi's reply. If the first instance of *ji* is read as referring to *other* cocks, then the flow of the reply shifts from 'other cocks' to 'cocks trained by Ji Shengzi' (next three clauses), and back to 'other cocks'. This is cumbersome. The text suggests a more elegant solution. Since the other cocks are first mentioned only towards the end of the reply, we could read all preceding clauses as statements about the cocks raised by Ji Shengzi. The core part of the reply would then start with a series of four statements about the cocks (*ji*) trained by Ji Shengzi and end with statements about the other cocks (*yi ji*).

The second argument concerns the initial assessment *ji yi* (幾矣, near enough) in conjunction with the following two clauses. The initial assessment implies, first, that there is room for further progress and, second, that any imperfection is inconsequential for the purpose at hand. Both aspects are taken up in the '*sui* X *yi* Y' (雖 X 已 Y) twin-clause construct that follows the initial assessment: "even though some may crow" (*sui you ming zhe*; *sui* X) signals an imperfection, and "they are by now without change" (*yi wu bian yi* 已無變矣; *yi* Y) implies that X is inconsequential because of Y. While the precise meaning of the Y component awaits further discussion, it is clear that these two clauses form a single pattern that is closely tied up with the initial assessment about the cocks trained by Ji Shengzi and that the concessive clause (*sui* X) makes explicit the minor imperfection of those cocks. Since the first instance of *ji*, whose identity we need to ascertain, is the topic of the concessive clause, we have good reason to conclude that it refers to the cocks raised by Ji Shengzi.

2. SETUP, FRAMING, AND THE PRIMARY LOCUS OF INTERACTION

The setup of the story is fairly straightforward: it consists of an opening line and a plot. The opening line sets the scene. It introduces two (human) characters and their relation to each other: Ji Shengzi raises/trains (*yang* 養) fighting cocks for the king. These two characters carry the plot in a series of four exchanges set at regular intervals. At each step, Ji Shengzi reports on the cocks' progress in response to the king's repeated question about their readiness to fight.

Neutral as its setup may seem, the story frames a reality. It hides and highlights. Most obviously left out of the picture is any description of how Ji Shengzi prepares the cocks. Presumably, this is because the process of training is of little interest to the king. His question, "Are the cocks ready?" (*ji yi hu* 雞已乎), rather enquires about results, and it leads Ji Shengzi to style his answers as progress reports. In effect, we are presented with four snapshots taken from the result-oriented perspective of the king.

Less obvious, perhaps, is that the reports lean towards *observable* progress, that is, progress that can be observed in the cocks' *behaviour*. We are told that the cocks "respond to echoes and shadows" (*ying xiang jing* 應嚮景), that they "look around fiercely and are swollen with vigour" (*ji shi er sheng qi* 疾視而盛氣), and that "looked at from a distance, they resemble cocks made of wood" (*wang zhi si mu ji* 望之似木雞). This bias towards the observable does not mean that the reports are not also suggestive of the cocks' inner dispositions. The reports indeed contain what I will refer to as 'emotion markers'—descriptions that mark inner emotional states. However, it is important to note that whatever can be known about such states must be inferred from how the cocks behave. "Fiercely" (*ji* 疾) marks an emotional state but is first of all used to describe a manner of "looking around" (*shi* 視). Similarly, "vain and confiding in vigour" (*xu jiao er shi qi* 虛憍而恃氣), while suggestive of a particular inner state, is most directly explained as a description of the cocks' physical appearance.[4] Even the rather obscure characterisation that "their virtue is complete" (*qi de quan* 其德全) immediately follows the statement "looked at from a distance, they resemble cocks made of wood". It is attributed to the cocks on the basis of observable features. In general, what is lacking in the reports is any account of the cocks' progress independent of how they behave. One reason for this penchant towards the observable may be the king's concern with concrete, tangible progress. It is on the level of the observable, and perhaps on this level only, that the king and Ji Shengzi can engage in meaningful conversation.

The exchanges between the king and Ji Shengzi frame certain aspects of a more complex reality. Yet their relation is not what the story is about, even though Ji Shengzi may, as we will see later on, still have a message for the king. Neither is the story about the relation between Ji Shengzi and the cocks. If it were, we would expect the story to present us with more details about the training process. Admittedly, Ji Shengzi sets the direction of training. If we agree that he prepares a plurality of cocks, we may further assume that part of the training arrangement involves different cocks being exposed to one another. But this is as far as we can go. The question, then, is: what is the story about and where do we locate its main message?

The story's main message is to be located, I believe, on the level of the interaction that takes place between the fighting cocks trained by Ji Shengzi and the, perhaps hypothetical, rival cocks. Although these rival cocks are first mentioned only at the very end of the final exchange, they are assumed throughout. At the first three stages, the rival cocks probably do not yet "turn and run" (*fan zou* 反走), as they do at the final stage. They are most likely undaunted by the behaviour of the cocks trained by Ji Shengzi, and this may very well be the reason why the latter are at these early stages deemed not yet ready to fight. On this reading, the progress reports describe the cocks' behaviour as it would show and play out in an actual fight with other cocks. It is their relation the story informs us about.

3. INTERPRETIVE KEYS: IMPACT REDUCTION AND RING PRESENCE

Imagine a typical cockfight. Probably what comes to mind is a bloody scene with two rival cocks locked in intense fighting, their movements interrupted only by brief moments of pause. The victorious cock, we may assume, is the one that is superior at anticipating his rival's movements and at striking back at the right times and places. We may further assume that training consists in enhancing technique and in improving reflexes and that progress is measured in terms of overall skill and responsiveness.

Surprisingly, the fighting cocks story sketches a rather different picture. The most striking difference is probably that the master cocks are characterised in static terms: they "are without change" and "resemble cocks made of wood". Despite this inactivity, however, they are victorious: "As for other cocks, none will dare to respond"; they simply "turn and run". This picture of 'unresponsive yet victorious fighting cocks' runs counter to our ordinary expectations. How can these cocks, by apparently just standing there, win the game?

Let us start by setting up a basic structure of interaction. We have two sets of cocks: those raised by Ji Shengzi (hereafter, A) and the other ones (B). Assume that their interaction runs as follows: A, upon facing B, respond in a certain way, which in turn triggers a response in B. Let us further suppose that Ji Shengzi was asked to train the king's cocks because he understands the dynamics of cockfighting. He knows how cocks behave and which responses will trigger what kinds of other responses.

How does this basic structure of interaction apply to the first three reports? Most likely, each report describes how A would respond to B or, if we adopt the training arrangement suggested above, how members of A respond to other members of A, on the assumption that they would likewise respond to B. For Ji Shengzi, each of the first three responses is problematic. He probably expects A's demeanour to trigger a violent response in B or, at the very least, he expects that B will be undaunted by the looks of A. The fourth report can be read along the same lines: A's non-response functions as a response, and it causes B to run off. This common structure allows us to phrase the main issue in more general terms: what is it in A's responses to B that leaves B undaunted in the first three cases and makes them run off in the final case? This expanded question requires an explanation that can account for all four cases. The reading I propose consists of two closely related keys: impact reduction and ring presence.

The first key is to take the reports as offering an impact-reduction view of progress. The cocks in group A are not portrayed as gradually perfecting their fighting technique. With the possible exception of the second report, none of the reports addresses fighting skills per se. Rather, two elements point to impact—the subjective influence of external conditions on one's emotions and actions—and the reduction of impact as the better explanation. One element is the presence of what I referred to before as 'emotion markers'. The first and third reports mainly consist of such markers. While emotion markers do not sit well with discussions of a technical nature, they naturally appear in discussions of high-pressure situations and their impact on an agent's functioning. The presence of such markers in a context of cockfighting, a prime example of a high-pressure situation, suggests that progress is conceived of in terms of impact. Positioned in between reports that contain emotion markers, the second report is also best understood in terms of impact: the impact of B on A is such that A's actions are hyperkinetic and off target.[5] Since 'impact' is in its present usage a subjective notion, one can learn to reduce and resist the impact of external conditions. At each further stage, the cocks shed and overcome the behaviour that is associated with the previous stage. This results in a decrease in activity and a heightened focus. Progress in the first three reports may be paraphrased as follows: vain and overconfident strutting (first report), hyperkinetic and off-target responses (second report), and combative posturing, with A's eyes aggressively following B's every move (third report).[6]

The other element that favours an explanation in terms of impact reduction is the non-response—or, more accurately, the near non-response—described in the final report. If progress were a matter of technique or skill, the fourth report would celebrate the cocks' speed and manner of response. It does not do so. In fact, any residual response, the crowing of some of the cocks, indicates that the cocks are merely 'close to' or 'near enough' (*ji yi*) perfection. What the fourth report seems to convey instead is that members of A are only minimally impacted by the sight of other fighting cocks, be they members of A or B. Though some cocks may crow, "they are by now without change" (*yi wu bian*). We can understand the latter phrase through the description "cocks made of wood" (*mu ji*) in the next line. The cocks are without change in that there is no observable change in their posture: from a distance, one could easily mistake them for cocks made of wood. In contrast to the previous reports, all of which imply a change in posture in response to the sight of B, the final report conveys that members of A are no longer impacted, at least not in a sense which Ji Shengzi would expect to trigger a violent response in B.

This reading of the reports in terms of impact reduction draws support from a fragment attached to the end of another 'skill story' earlier in the same chapter. The fragment first records a negative correlation between performance and the stakes in a contest, possibly a game of archery, and then offers an account of what is observed.

> Those who play for an earthen tile are skilful; those who play for a silver buckle are nervous; those who play for gold break down. Their skill is [ever] the same, but when there is something valuable at stake, they put weight on the outside. In general, whoever puts weight on the outside is clumsy on the inside.
> 以瓦注者巧，以鉤注者憚，以黃金注者殙。其巧一也，而有所矜，則重外也。凡外重者內拙。(49/19/25–26)

Crucial in this fragment is that a difference in performance is not explained in terms of a difference in skill (*qiao* 巧). Indeed, this reading is explicitly ruled out. The reason for the decline is instead the impact of a valuable prize on an archer's focus: he puts weight on the prize (the outside) rather than on his performance (the inside).[7] As a result, his performance gets clumsy. Skill levels being equal, it is the subjective impact of external factors that determines the quality of a performance.

The archery fragment and the fighting cocks story share the same concern and outlook. They make observations about high-pressure situations, and they downplay skill in favour of impact, even though the archery fragment does so more explicitly. Yet they differ in what the absence of impact entails.[8] When an archer is unaffected by external factors, he still displays his native skill, shoots the arrow, and hits the mark. Improved performance is the trademark of an experienced archer. By contrast, the master cocks strictly speaking do not perform at all. They do not display fighting skills that were previously suppressed by the impact of external factors. In their case, the absence of impact does not entail an improvement in performance: it is not that they fight better; they do not fight at all. We therefore need another factor to fully explain why they are successful, that is, why rival cocks run away. The difference between the archery fragment and the fighting cocks story leads us to posit a second key.

As the second key, I propose ring presence, the felt influence of a fighter on his opponent as a direct result of his bearing. Ring presence, just like performance, is inversely proportional to impact: it grows with a decrease in impact, and vice versa. A fighter who is visibly impacted by the sight of his opponent does not have a strong presence. He does not own the ring. Such, I submit, is the case with A as described in the first three reports. Even at the third stage, the cocks are visibly impacted. A combative stance may already constitute an improvement over the behaviour displayed at the first two stages, and we may assume that A's presence has correspondingly grown. Still, as they are impacted, they are not in control. This is obvious to B and will trigger a response on their side. By contrast, at the final stage, members of A no longer display any change. This absence of change is not a weakness, nor does it show a lack of interest. Rather, to the opponent, it signals exceptional focus and control. The ring presence of A is such that they can win a fight without *having* to fight. This is why they are ready to enter a fight.

Ring presence complements impact reduction in accounting for the interaction between A and B. These two interpretive keys jointly explain why, in the final case, B instantly recognise A as superior, that is, why B, not daring to respond, simply "turn and run". They also explain why A in the first three cases will get themselves into a fight. One useful way of thinking about impact and presence is as descriptions of a two-way force-dynamic relation that holds between A and B. 'Impact' refers to the force which B exerts on A, while 'presence' describes the force of A exerted on B.[9] Injecting the semantics of force can help us to understand the characterisation "their virtue is complete" in the final report. The notion of *de* (德, virtue) is here certainly not to be understood in a moral sense. Rather, *de* refers to an agent's strength not to be swayed by external conditions and to the ensuing forceful presence he exerts on those around him. Virtue, moreover, is a matter of degree, and the master cocks, despite the fact that some of them may crow, are assessed as having completed (*quan* 全) their virtue.

In developing my account of the fighting cocks story, I have drawn on the presence of emotion markers to establish impact reduction as an important interpretive key. Not letting oneself be impacted by external conditions is, in turn, a crucial factor in assessing someone's virtue. This chain of connections may lead one to think of impact and virtue as inner qualities located in a mental-emotional realm. Such belief, however, would be incomplete and misleading. The important distinction is not that between the mental-emotional and the behavioural, but between external conditions and one's emotional-behavioural response to these conditions. Of course, different stories may for various reasons put a relative emphasis on the emotional or the behavioural. For the fighting cocks story, it is interesting to note that emotion markers do not serve as entry points into a more elaborate psychological account of what is going on inside the cocks. The focus is on *displayed* emotion. Such relative emphasis on the behavioural is perhaps a more natural way of talking about animals. But there may be story-specific reasons as well. Earlier on, I mentioned the king's impatience and his concern with tangible results as one factor. At this point, we can add one more element: what matters in a cockfight are *observable* clues. Or, to rephrase this point in terms of our interactive model, B's response to A depends on what they observe in A's behaviour. In a cockfight, emotion as it is displayed and observable becomes the obvious focus of attention.

4. MASTERY BEYOND SKILL

We often think of mastery in the *Zhuangzi* as a matter of skill: it is the knack to respond to his surroundings with dexterity that characterises the actions of the exemplary person. The most frequently quoted example of skill mastery in the *Zhuangzi* is probably the Butcher Ding story (7/3/2–8/3/12). It describes a butcher who, after years of training, is able to move his knife in perfect attunement to the physical structure of the oxen he slaughters. He slices through them without meeting the slightest resistance. Butcher Ding, we may say, is superbly skilled. On this view, it is skill, more than anything else, that is key to success. Mastery equals skill mastery.

What makes the fighting cocks story as well as the archery fragment relevant to the topic of mastery in the *Zhuangzi* is that skill is in neither case identified as the main factor for success. The skill of an archer manifests itself only if and when he is no longer impacted by the value of the prize he is shooting for. As for the fighting cocks, skill is not even part of their game. These two scenarios highlight another factor, something that is at least as important as skill, that is, the capacity not to be impacted by external conditions. It is this capacity, more than skill, that defines mastery in these two contexts.

A possible objection to this presentation of ideas may be that the capacity not to be impacted is actually part of a performer's skill set. Indeed, the notion of skill could be enlarged to include subjective resistance to impact. However, note that if we were to enlarge the notion of skill, we would still need to distinguish between different kinds of skill. It takes one kind of skill to shoot at the right angle and speed during a practice session; it takes another kind of skill to stay calm at a shooting contest when the stakes are high. In this article, I use 'skill' in a restricted sense to refer to motor skill or to other equivalent skills that require some kind of activity. The advantage of this conceptual demarcation is that it gives more prominence to the message that the fighting cocks story and the archery fragment aim to bring across: that not being impacted is of crucial importance. Significantly, it also finds support in the archery fragment itself, which demarcates not being impacted from *qiao* (巧), the standard term for skilfulness.

While skill and resistance to impact are here taken to refer to distinct realities, they may relate in a variety of ways, and different contexts may emphasise one over the other, or ignore one to give exclusive attention to the other. Both the fighting cocks story and the archery fragment side with resistance to impact, but they do so in different degrees. The archery fragment maintains that it is composure that allows the archer to manifest his skill, and it conveys this point by emphasising resistance to impact over skill. The fighting cocks story takes a stronger stance: it singles out resistance as the sole factor involved. I will here introduce two more passages that side with resistance to impact. These two passages align in degree with the archery fragment and the fighting cocks story, respectively. At the end of the section, I will briefly return to Butcher Ding.

First, the passage to which the archery fragment is attached (48/19/22–49/19/25) features a ferryman who marvellously steers his boat across treacherous waters. When asked by Yan Yuan (顏淵), a disciple of Zhongni (仲尼, Confucius), whether his trade could be learned, the ferryman replies that a good swimmer could pick it up quickly and that a diver could even steer a boat without ever having seen one. Confucius further explains the two parts of the ferryman's reply. A swimmer, he says, could quickly learn to steer a boat "because he forgets the water" (*wang shui ye* 忘水也). As for a diver, he could steer a boat at his first attempt "because he would look upon a deep current as a gentle hill and the capsizing of a boat as a cart rolling backwards. While he may face wild and violent swings in all directions, they would not get to enter his secluded resting place" (彼視淵若陵，視舟之覆猶其車卻也。覆卻萬方陳乎前而不得入其舍).

This passage outlines what it takes to steer a boat in a high-pressure situation. Similar to the archery fragment, it emphasises the importance of not being impacted. This is most obvious in the description of the diver-ferryman: the disturbance that surrounds him contrasts with his "secluded resting place" (*she* 舍), and the phrase "not get to enter" (*bu de ru* 不得入) directly signals the absence of impact. What we do *not* have here is an outline of a technique or skill, even though skill is obviously important in steering a boat. As in the archery fragment, basic skill is assumed. What is crucial—and what would make him an excellent ferryman—is that the diver would not panic. Deep currents and the forces they exert are plainly ordinary to him. As he has been sufficiently exposed to these powerful forces, he no longer pays special attention to them. The case of the swimmer can be interpreted along similar lines: a good swimmer does not pay special attention to—forgets—the water. He may not have been exposed to the same pressure as a diver, but at the very least, he is not subjectively impacted by the water around him. Some further exposure will do.

The second passage is the opening section of *Zhuangzi* 5 (12/5/1–13/5/13). It describes a mutilated convict named Wang Tai (王駘) who attracts as many followers as Confucius despite the fact that he, unlike Confucius, does not have any teachings to offer. When asked for an explanation by a puzzled disciple, Confucius clarifies that Wang Tai is not impacted by any change of circumstance, be it his own mutilation, his mortality, or a change of a more catastrophic nature. He "acquiesces in the alterations of things" (命物之化) to the extent that "even if heaven were to topple and the earth were to slant, he would still not go down with them" (雖天地覆墜，亦將不與之遺). Other people, Confucius goes on to explain, are naturally drawn to someone with such a stable heart-mind: "Nobody looks for his reflection in running water—we all look for it in still water" (人莫鑑於流水，而鑑於止水).

Similar to the fighting cocks story, Wang Tai does not rely on any special skill. His large following stems from the absence of impact and from the influence he has on others as a result of this. What is interesting and also different from the fighting cocks story is that presence—the felt influence on others—functions here as a force of attraction (pull) rather than as a force of repulsion (push). This difference in dynamics coincides with a difference in contextual factors. Unlike the fighting cocks, who stand in a two-party relation to rivals that are reference points for both impact and presence, Wang Tai moves in a three-party space where impact and presence relate to different things. Whereas impact relates to non-human factors, with the collapse of the natural framework as worst-case scenario, presence points in another direction and relates to people who find in Wang Tai the independence and stability of mind they were probably looking for in the first place.

These additional examples show that the authors of the *Zhuangzi* are, among other things, concerned with cultivating subjective resistance to external pressure. What is particularly relevant, I think, is that this concern surfaces both in so-called skill stories and in passages which we would not ordinarily classify as such, witness the Wang Tai case; it allows us to draw connections that would not be visible if we were to focus on skill per se. Skill, of course, still has a role to play, but perhaps only in situations where an agent unequivocally needs to *act* in order to be successful—an archer can never win a game without actually shooting an arrow, as a ferryman obviously still needs to steer his boat. Yet, note that although such activities may require skill, the composers of the archer and ferryman scenarios identify resistance to external pressure, rather than skill, as the key to success. The fighting cocks story goes one step further and removes skill from the equation. Winning a fight does not require skill at fighting.

There is one more 'skill story' that explicitly downplays skill or technique. Surprisingly, this is the Butcher Ding story, which, as we noted, is often looked upon as the locus classicus of skill mastery (7/3/2–8/3/12). Butcher Ding, we may want to observe, is superbly skilled. Even the onlooking king seems to acknowledge this when he exclaims: "Excellent! Why wouldn't skill reach such level!" (善哉！技蓋至此乎). And yet the butcher himself describes his trade as going beyond skill: "What I treasure is *dao*. It advances beyond skill" (臣之所好者道也，進乎技矣).

We should be careful here, I believe, not to read all 'skill stories' as making the exact same point. There is little evidence that would compel us to read *dao* (道) in the butcher's description as 'the capacity not to be impacted by external conditions'. A more plausible reading is that *dao* refers to the cavities or paths that run along the ox's physical structure. It is by following these paths that the butcher effortlessly cuts up the ox. Part of the butcher's explanation is that he "takes the broader cavities as guiding paths" (*dao da kuan* 導大窾).[10] Through accumulated practice, the butcher has developed a good sense of the internal makeup of an ox. On his own description, he is a master butcher because he relies on what the situation affords him with, not because he has a special technique or skill which he adds to what is already there.

The Butcher Ding story differs from the fighting cocks scenario. Even though both 'go beyond' skill, they offer alternative perspectives on *what* is more relevant than skill—grasping a structure versus not being impacted, respectively. Nevertheless, the Butcher Ding story is helpful in adding a second layer of discussion to the fighting cocks scenario. Adding this further layer requires us to shift attention from the cocks proper to Ji Shengzi and how he relates to the cocks.[11] What I have in mind here is not the training program but rather Ji Shengzi's insight into fighting cock behaviour. His grasp of the dynamic structure of cockfighting is comparable to Butcher Ding's grasp of the physical makeup of an ox. *We* may acclaim Ji Shengzi for being superbly skilled at understanding the game of cockfighting. However, if the Butcher Ding story is any indication, such praise is likely to come from a bystander. Ji Shengzi *himself* may want to argue that he is more concerned with identifying the optimal path to victory.

5. OPTIMAL COURSES OF ACTION

A cockfight is a standard conflict situation. It involves two parties that inflict harm upon one another. In ordinary cases, the party that inflicts the most harm (and suffers the least) wins the fight. The ingenuity of the fighting cocks story—the ingenuity of Ji Shengzi—is that it dissociates winning from fighting. Winning does not *need* to depend on fighting, harming, and being harmed.

Ji Shengzi's approach to cockfighting is relevant in light of one possible reading of the 'skill stories' and of the Butcher Ding story in particular. Despite the overall positive depiction in the *Zhuangzi*, it may be argued that 'attuning oneself to the structure of a situation' may also produce morally repulsive behaviour. Robert Eno, in particular, has observed that "*dao*-practises can be adapted to any end: the *dao* of butchering people might provide much the same spiritual spontaneity as the *dao* of butchering oxen".[12] The

Zhuangzian vision, one may conclude, is morally neutral and is therefore of little value in advising us on how to interact with others in a human, social context.

The fighting cocks story casts doubt on this reading. Note that the story could easily have been developed into a skilful killer scenario. Recalling Butcher Ding, one might even come to expect that such a scenario is indeed the direction a cockfight story in the *Zhuangzi* would take. And yet the opposite is true. The story is crafted to show that one does not need to kill in order to win. Out of the two alternatives—skilful killing and cultivating a strong presence, both of which may lead to victory—Ji Shengzi chooses the path that eschews harm. Both parties remain unscathed, even though one is defeated. The optimal course of action (*dao*), it seems, has a built-in value direction. It is this value direction, an implicit concern with defusing conflict and avoiding harm, which makes the development of malicious-actor scenarios unlikely.

The fighting cocks story is not the only *Zhuangzi* passage where a concern with defusing conflict and avoiding harm seems to determine the proper course of action. I will here briefly introduce two more conflict situations. The study of conflict situations is relevant not only because such situations are thematically equivalent to the fighting cocks story, but also because decisions made in situations of conflict tend to reveal implicit value dispositions.

The first case is the well-known monkey-keeper story in *Zhuangzi* 2 (5/2/38–40). The story centres on how to portion the monkeys' daily amount of nuts. The monkey keeper at first suggests giving the monkeys three nuts in the morning and four at night. This 3/4 allocation angers the monkeys. The monkey keeper then flips the allocation to 4/3, as a result of which the monkeys are pleased. We see here two possible courses of action or *daos* (3/4 and 4/3).[13] The course of action that is settled upon is the one that defuses conflict and avoids harm to either party. The tactics of the monkey keeper may be different from Ji Shengzi's, but in both stories an implicit concern with defusing conflict and avoiding harm defines the optimal course of action.

The second case is the long opening section of *Zhuangzi* 4 (8/4/1–9/4/34). It stages Yan Hui (顏回), a disciple of Confucius, as wanting to embark on a mission to 'cure' the despotic ruler of Wei (衛). Confucius observes that Yan Hui's moral self-righteousness will merely result in conflict. Not only will Yan Hui fail to stop the ruler from harming his people, but he himself will also fall victim to the ruler's anger. The only way to gain access to the ruler is for Yan Hui to stop "taking his heart-mind as teacher" (*shi xin* 師心). Yan Hui, so Confucius argues, needs to empty (*xu* 虛) himself by "fasting [his] heart-mind" (*xin zhai* 心齋). Only after having transformed himself will he be able to transform (*hua* 化) the ruler and save the people from further harm.

Confucius's role is similar to that of Ji Shengzi: he sets out the optimal course of action. Out of a variety of possible courses—Yan Hui's moral self-righteousness being one of them—the chosen path is the one that offers the best chances of survival for both Yan Hui and the people of Wei. Once Yan Hui has given up his insistence on how things *should* be, he can cooperate with the king without being harmed and without becoming complicit in harming others.

Many of the 'skill stories' stage characters who have reached a high level of competence in dealing with inanimate objects (especially wood and water). Conflict situations are closer to the inter-human condition. The conflict situations introduced above suggest that optimal courses of action in the *Zhuangzi* are *not* value neutral, that a concern with defusing conflict and avoiding harm, that is, a concern with sustainability, is built into what counts as an optimal course of action. The fighting cocks story is of particular relevance because a cockfight is intrinsically violent. That we do not see a skilful killer scenario being developed in such a context is revealing. The advice of the *Zhuangzi*, it suggests, is to discover and select those courses of action that promote sustainability, *even when conflict and harm would seem inevitable.*

In two fairly recent studies, Huang Yong has argued for an ethics of difference in the *Zhuangzi* and for the primacy of what he calls 'difference stories' to understand what moral action in the *Zhuangzi* amounts to. According to the ethics of difference as he describes it, "the moral appropriateness of our actions towards others is not determined by our standard as moral agents but that of our moral patients" (Huang, "Respecting Different Ways of Life," 1057). In each of the three 'difference stories' which Huang discusses, a moral agent treats a moral patient on his own (that is, the agent's) standard of what is proper, as a result of which the moral patient is harmed and eventually dies.[14] Even if well intended, such actions are morally inappropriate because they are not in line with how moral patients would like to be treated. Through the use of negative examples, these difference stories describe how we should treat each other—that is, with respect for difference. If everyone subscribes to the ethics of difference, then indeed, as Huang observes, malicious-actor scenarios are ruled out. At the very least, such scenarios are not endorsed by the moral outlook of the difference stories in the *Zhuangzi*.

The conflict situations—or conflict stories—introduced above do not appeal to one's moral intuition that patients are being wronged. Unlike in the difference stories, the 'other parties' in the conflict stories are not passive patients: the monkeys are hot tempered, the king is despotic, and the rival cocks are ready to attack. The conflict stories lay out realistic scenarios in which conflict is likely, or apparently inevitable, and they make suggestions for how best to approach such situations. One's approach, the optimal course of action, is bound to differ with situational constraints and affordances. To appease the monkeys, the monkey keeper simply needs to follow the monkeys' preference. As to the rival cocks, following *their* preference not only will not appease them; it will also result in self-inflicted harm. Ji Shengzi's training follows the dynamics of cockfighting rather than the preference of the other cocks.[15] Despite these differences, however, the conflict stories are united in presenting ways to defuse conflict and avoid harm, not only harm to oneself, but harm to others as well. It is this concern with avoiding harm which also connects the conflict stories with the difference stories. In each of the latter stories, the appeal to respect the other's difference is based on the observation that not doing so *harms* the other. The two sets of stories may be viewed as complementing each other: difference stories stage patients who are mistreated and harmed; conflict stories stage agents who find ways to defuse harmful situations. This concern with avoiding harm may not offer guidance in each and every situation, but as a value that shapes the Zhuangzian view of what counts as an optimal course of action, it does seem at odds with malicious-actor scenarios. Instead of allowing for such scenarios, the *Zhuangzi* seems to encourage its readers to think of innovative ways to prevent conflict and coexist with others in a social context.

Eventually, my interpretation of the fighting cocks story also prompts a different reading of the Butcher Ding story (7/3/2–8/3/12). That story, I submit, has a specific and well-defined target, which is the hacking (*zhe* 折) and smashing (*ge* 割) performed by the less-experienced butchers. These terms function as negative somatic markers that convey harm and destruction, both to the butcher's knife and to the ox's bones. The point of the story is *not* that an ox is slaughtered, but that Butcher Ding's carving keeps both the knife and the bones intact. On this view, it would be a misrepresentation of the story if one were to focus on the killing of the ox and project *that* onto the human domain. One can indeed project the Butcher Ding story onto the field of human interaction, but the features that stand to be projected are the hacking and smashing and the damage they do, on the one hand, and Butcher Ding's following (*yin* 因) of an existing structure on the other. Through Butcher Ding's description, the onlooking king is presented with alternative courses of action, and the difference in somatic connotation directs him to that course of action which defuses conflict and avoids harm. At the end of the story, the king himself exclaims that he has learned how to nurture life (*yangsheng* 養生). Arguably, given his status as king, he has learned that sustainable leadership is best served by accepting the long-established consensual practices—the social skeleton—of local communities.

That the *king* learns something from Butcher Ding leads us back to the fighting cocks story, and more specifically to the relation between the king and Ji Shengzi. Early on, we pointed out that the king's preoccupation with tangible results directs the nature of Ji Shengzi's replies. Conversely, Ji

Shengzi's replies may also be read as containing a message for the king. In the battle game of cross-state relations, not to be impacted by what *other rulers* do may be the optimal course of action—it displays control over the situation. Though rivals would probably not turn and run—that may be an exaggeration for rhetorical purposes—cultivating resistance to impact may deliver victory without bloodshed. Read in this way, it is Ji Shengzi who is directing the king-cock rather than the other way around. And, taking this reasoning one step further, the composer of *Zhuangzi* 19, far from presenting a neutral picture, is directing *his* audience via a story on fighting cocks.

NOTES

1. 紀渻子為王養鬥雞。十日而問：「雞已乎？」曰：「未也。方虛憍而恃氣。」十日又問。曰：「未也。猶應嚮景。」十日又問。曰：「未也。猶疾視而盛氣。」十日又問。曰：「幾矣。雞雖有鳴者，已無變矣，望之似木雞矣，其德全矣，異雞無敢應者，反走矣。」(50/19/46–49; Hung, *Concordance to Chuang Tzu*, page/chapter/line).

2. Robert J. Cutter, who wrote an entire volume on the cockfight in Chinese culture, very briefly comments on the story (Cutter, *The Brush and the Spur*, 15–16). For Albert Galvany, the story reflects a trend towards the feminisation of war (Galvany, "Philosophy, Biography, and Anecdote," 636–38). Other brief references can be found in Graham, *Disputers of the Tao*, 188, and Bruya, "The Rehabilitation of Spontaneity," 246, n. 16. None of these studies gives a full account of the issues at play. Studies that discuss skill and mastery in the *Zhuangzi* generally do not mention the fighting cocks story (e.g., Ivanhoe, "Zhuangzi on Skepticism, Skill, and the Ineffable *Dao*", and Yearley, "Zhuangzi's Understanding of Skillfulness and the Ultimate Spiritual State").

3. For the singular reading, see Mair, *Wandering on the Way*, 181; Ziporyn, *Zhuangzi*, 81; Chen, *Zhuangzi*, 2:505–6. For the plural reading, see Watson, *Complete Works*, 204; Graham, *Chuang-tzŭ*, 135–36.

4. Lu Deming (陸德明, ca. 550–630), in his gloss on *xu jiao* (虛憍), mentions an early comment by Sima Biao (司馬彪, ca. 246–306) that reads, literally, "with the head raised high" (*gao yang tou ye* 高仰頭也). See Guo, *Collected Commentaries*, 2:655.

5. The second report may be read in a variety of ways depending on how one interprets the two graphs (*xiang jing* 嚮景 = *xiang ying* 響影) that follow the verb *ying* (應, respond). Semantically, these two graphs may be read as "sound and image" or "echo and shadow"; grammatically, they may function as objects ("to respond to X") or as post-verbal adverbs ("to respond as X," with X understood as echoes and shadows). I propose to read the report as "responding to echoes and shadows" because this is the reading that best reflects the 'impact' interpretation adopted for the entire exchange. It is also the reading given in a number of recent translations: Graham, *Chuang-tzŭ*, 136; Mair, *Wandering on the Way*, 181; Ziporyn, *Zhuangzi*, 81.

6. The adverb *ji* 急 connotes both aggression and fast movement, the latter probably referring to the quick movement of the cocks' heads and eyes.

7. *Nei* (內, inside) and *wai* (外, outside) shift reference with context. Since *wai* refers to the prizes, the *nei-wai* distinction here does not oppose the mental-emotional to the behavioural. Rather, *nei* should probably be thought of as an archer's overall performance. In the first case, the archer is not impacted by the prize, and the term used plainly refers to his skilful shooting (*qiao* 巧); in the second and third cases, the archers are impacted, and emotion markers are used to describe their inferior performance.

8. Another difference is that impact manifests itself differently. In the archery fragment, impact results in anxiety; in the fighting cocks story, the cocks are described as cocky, kinetic, and belligerent. This difference does not play any further role in my analysis.

9. Some may prefer to phrase this force-dynamic relation in terms of *qi* (氣, vigour, energy, strength). However, while the notion of *qi* does appear in the negative descriptions of the first and third reports, we do not find it in the final report. Reconstructing the entire exchange in terms of *qi* would require substantial background work which would arguably overreach the importance of this notion in explaining the present story. I believe it is possible to give a plausible account of the fighting cocks story without relying on the notion of *qi*.

10. Note the equivalence—phonetically, graphically, and semantically—between *dao* (道, course, path, way, guide) and *dao* (導, to guide, to take as a path or guide). Semantically, "to take X as a guiding path" (*dao* 導 X) implies that X is, or at least functions as, a path (*dao* 道). Within the context of the story, the broader cavities (*da kuan* 大窾) are the obvious candidates for what is meant by *dao* (道).

11. Butcher Ding is his own trainer. His dual role of actor-trainer is taken up by two separate characters in the fighting cocks story. 'Grasping a structure' belongs to the trainer side of things and prompts a change in focus to Ji Shengzi when projected onto the fighting cocks story.

12. Eno, "Cook Ding's *Dao*," 142. Other scholars who have voiced similar concerns include Hansen, *Daoist Theory of Chinese Thought*, 220; Wenzel, "Ethics and Zhuangzi," esp. 119.

13. Provided that the expression *liang xing* (兩行, walking both sides) at the very end of the story refers to the alternative 3/4 and 4/3 allocations, it would seem reasonable to think of these alternative allocations as *daos*. This is because a few lines before the monkey-keeper story, the text reads: "*daos*/paths/courses are formed by walking them" (道行之而成, 4/2/33). For an analysis of the monkey-keeper story and related fragments, see De Reu, "On Goblet Words," esp. 91–94.

14. The three stories are the Hundun story (21/7/33–35), the seabird story (47/18/33–36), and the Bo Le story (22/9/2–23/9/4). They are most clearly introduced in Huang, "The Ethics of Difference," 74–76.

15. The fighting cocks story shows that A does not need to treat B the way B would like to be treated if doing so would encourage B's inclination to mistreat A. Significantly, however, the stand-off does not escalate in conflict. In a cockfight, the best approach to prevent conflict yet still hold on to victory is, at least in Ji Shengzi's analysis, to look unimpressed and in control of the situation.

REFERENCES

Bruya, Brian J. "The Rehabilitation of Spontaneity: A New Approach in Philosophy of Action." *Philosophy East and West* 60, no. 2 (April 2010): 207–50.

Chen, Guying 陳鼓應. *A Modern Commentary and Translation of the* Zhuangzi [Zhuangzi *jin zhu jin yi* 莊子今註今亦]. 2 vols. Rev. ed. Taipei: Commercial Press, 1999.

Cutter, Robert J. *The Brush and the Spur: Chinese Culture and the Cockfight.* Hong Kong: Chinese University Press, 1989.

De Reu, Wim. "On Goblet Words: Coexistence and Writing in the *Zhuangzi*." *NTU Philosophical Review* 53 (March 2017): 75–108.

Eno, Robert. "Cook Ding's *Dao* and the Limits of Philosophy." In *Essays on Skepticism, Relativism, and Ethics in the* Zhuangzi, edited by Paul Kjellberg and Philip J. Ivanhoe, 127–51. Albany, NY: SUNY Press, 1996.

Galvany, Albert. "Philosophy, Biography, and Anecdote: On the Portrait of Sun Wu." *Philosophy East and West* 61, no. 4 (October 2011): 630–46.

Guo, Qingfan 郭慶藩. *Collected Commentaries on the* Zhuangzi [Zhuangzi *ji shi* 莊子集釋]. 3 vols. Beijing: Zhonghua shuju, 1961. Reprint, 2008.

Graham, Angus C. *Chuang-tzŭ: The Seven Inner Chapters and Other Writings from the Book Chuang-tzŭ.* London: Allen and Unwin, 1981.

———. *Disputers of the Tao: Philosophical Argument in Ancient China.* La Salle, IL: Open Court, 1989.

Hansen, Chad. *A Daoist Theory of Chinese Thought: A Philosophical Interpretation.* Oxford: Oxford University Press, 1992.

Huang, Yong. "The Ethics of Difference in the *Zhuangzi*." *Journal of the American Academy of Religion* 78, no. 1 (March 2010): 65–99.
———. "Respecting Different Ways of Life: A Daoist Ethics of Virtue in the *Zhuangzi*." *Journal of Asian Studies* 69, no. 4 (November 2010): 1049–69.
Hung, William, ed. *A Concordance to Chuang Tzu* [*Zhuangzi yinde* 莊子引得]. Harvard-Yenching Institute Sinological Index Series, Supplement No. 20. Cambridge, MA: Harvard University Press, 1956.
Ivanhoe, Philip J. "Zhuangzi on Skepticism, Skill, and the Ineffable *Dao*." *Journal of the American Academy of Religion* 61, no. 4 (Winter 1993): 639–54.
Mair, Victor H. *Wandering on the Way: Early Taoist Tales and Parables of Chuang-tzu.* Honolulu: University of Hawai'i Press, 1994.
Watson, Burton. *The Complete Works of Chuang Tzu.* New York: Columbia University Press, 1968.
Wenzel, Christian H. "Ethics and Zhuangzi: Awareness, Freedom, and Autonomy." *Journal of Chinese Philosophy* 30, no. 1 (March 2003): 115–26.
Yearley, Lee H. "Zhuangzi's Understanding of Skillfulness and the Ultimate Spiritual State." In *Essays on Skepticism, Relativism, and Ethics in the* Zhuangzi, edited by Paul Kjellberg and Philip J. Ivanhoe, 152–82. Albany, NY: SUNY Press, 1996.
Ziporyn, Brook. *Zhuangzi: The Essential Writings with Selections from Traditional Commentaries.* Indianapolis: Hackett, 2009.

Chapter Thirteen

The Swimmer

Panic, Parody, and Pedagogy at the Waterfall: Morality as a Misleading Principle for Moral Actions

Albert Galvany

Confucius was scrutinising Lüliang where the waterfall drops from a height of thirty fathoms and the rapids race and boil along for forty miles, so swift that no giant tortoise, crocodile, fish, or soft-shell turtle can swim in this water. Here, he saw a man swimming and, supposing that the man was in trouble and intended to end his life, he ordered his disciples to line up on the bank and save him. But a few hundred paces downriver the man came out of the water, shaking his unbound hair and singing a little song as he strolled along the riverbank. Confucius went up to him, saying, "At first I thought you were a ghost, but now I see you are human. May I ask you if you have any method for moving in the water?" The man said, "You are mistaken. I have no method. I let it begin and it became the origin, I developed it and it became a natural condition, and I completed it and it became fate. I go under with the swirls and let the force of the water bring me up to the surface, following the way the water goes without any preference whatsoever. That is how I move in the water." Confucius then asked, "What do you mean when you say you let it begin and it became origin, you let it develop and it became a natural condition, and completed it and it became fate?" The man replied, "I was born in these mountains and have accommodated to them so here is the original state. I grew up by the water and accommodated to that too, so here is the natural condition. I don't know why things are like that, so here is fate."[1]

Included in chapter 19 (*Da sheng* 達生) of the *Zhuangzi* 莊子, where one finds the greatest concentration of passages about individuals who reveal to an astonished observer extraordinary prowess in carrying out one or another kind of physical activity, there is the story of an encounter between Confucius and an anonymous swimmer at the foot of a mighty waterfall.[2] Partly because of its position in the work and partly because the anecdote contains shared narrative elements, comparable expressions, similar literary strategies, and concepts linking up with those appearing in other stories about skilfulness which frequently recur in this text, the inclusion of the waterfall vignette in this particular category concerned with skills might seem obvious. However, although the category into which these presumably similar anecdotes are pigeonholed is open to criticism with respect to its coherence and hermeneutic efficacy, in the case of the account of what occurs in the meeting between Confucius and the individual who emerges from the waterfall's turbulent waters there would appear to be additional problems.[3] As I shall show below, the apologue presents several notable departures from the shared framework of the stories about skill and, more importantly, offers lessons that, in terms of ideas, are at variance with that framework. Hence, the reasons for subsuming it into this general category are not so evident and, indeed, there are quite a lot of arguments against it.

Nevertheless, my main aim here is less to challenge this category by contesting its analytical legitimacy than to hold out an alternative reading of the apologue, moving away from the core theme of skilfulness to explore some less hackneyed spaces. The great majority of hermeneutic efforts arising from this brief episode, even if only implicitly, are fitted into the framework defined by the question of prowess with a tendency to assume that the core of this brief story in the *Zhuangzi* is the astonishing ability shown by the anonymous individual as he moves in the water and the subsequent explanation he gives to Confucius who interrogates him about his prodigious swimming technique. In keeping with this interpretive bias, the part containing the dialogue has, with few exceptions, overwhelmingly stimulated and attracted the attention of scholars.

I believe that this conspicuous inertia in readings of the apologue is at least partly due to the influence of two prejudices. First is the assumption that the essential, almost exclusive theme of the story consists in offering the reader, as part of a scene where skill takes the spotlight, a reasoned description of the internal processes which explain this dexterous use of the body. The second, less apparent and vaguer prejudice, is related to the way of understanding what I would describe as philosophical writing or, in other words, what it is that makes a text worthy of consideration as being relevant for thought and, more specifically, where its potential philosophical interest resides and which parts of it concentrate and give priority to its reflective substance. Even a quick glance at the available bibliography on the apologue in the *Zhuangzi* supplies a unanimous answer to the latter question: the dialogue section of the anecdote. It seems evident that it is in the exchange between Confucius and the nameless swimmer that the strictly philosophical content of the story is expressed and unfolded. After all, both in China and the West, there is a solid tradition of philosophical hermeneutics based on a reading of dialogues through which, whether their tone is one of dispute or instruction, thought is articulated. From this viewpoint, the reflective relevance of the apologue tends to be situated in the dialogue section where, moreover (and this is also important), several concepts appear: *gu* (故), *xing* (性), and *ming* (命). These were heavily loaded with philosophical meaning in the intellectual arena typifying the final period of pre-imperial China. As a result, the initial part of the story, in which one does not find—at least not in the strict sense—either conversation or concepts decreed as relevant by the different doctrines or schools of thought, would not, by contrast, be anything more than a mere prelude, a preliminary scene endowed, perhaps, with a certain dramatic or literary quality but lacking any thought-provoking dimension.[4] Its function in the story would thus be limited to setting the scene leading to the dialogue between the anonymous man and Confucius, the key event condensing the philosophical content and embracing all interpretive efforts.

My basic objective is, then, to offer an alternative reading of the apologue, thus departing from the usual line of exegesis which still prevails partly because of the continuing influence of the two aforementioned prejudices whose soundness I also intend to refute. I aspire to understand the anecdote more comprehensively, without projecting onto it any preconceived ideas or establishing within it significant asymmetries with regard to its thought-provoking capacity or the philosophical pedigree of any of its constitutive elements. I shall try to demonstrate that the key to a more coherent understanding of this brief passage from the *Zhuangzi* lies in shifting away from the two gravitational centres around which the more conventional interpretations have revolved. Even if it is assumed that the central part of the vignette is to be found in the dialogue between Confucius and the prodigious swimmer, it still cannot be understood without analyzing what occurs in the beginning of the story. In other words, the first purely narrative section which has no dialogue plays a crucial role in making it possible to understand the story in its entirety. Similarly, rather than skilfulness, certain aspects of moral failure as well as some paradoxes of virtuous action constitute the fundamental theme of the story. In order to achieve my aims, I shall now proceed with an almost line-by-line analysis of the apologue, with attention to the main ingredients and, in some cases, the apparently most trivial details.

1. A QUESTION OF GAZES: PERCEPTION, PLEASURE, AND MORALITY IN WATER

In contrast with what takes place in other stories about skill in the same chapter or scattered in other sections of the work, this particular scene from the *Zhuangzi* situates us in a precise space: a mountainous enclave called

Lüliang in the present-day province of Shanxi, which was probably famous in early times, as references in several ancient documents testify (*Huainanzi jiaoshi*, 2.162). This landscape is crossed through with craggy peaks and tumultuous waterways flowing into two great rivers: the Yellow River (Huang He 黃河) and the Fen River (Fen He 汾河). The first lines of the apologue describe huge heights and torrents of water, since Confucius's encounter with the nameless swimmer occurs at the foot of a magnificent waterfall. The action then takes place in a setting of great beauty, which surely must have delighted someone like Confucius, a man who according to the portrait provided by some ancient written sources had a remarkable aesthetic sensibility and had already revealed his fondness for natural elements.[5] Hence, it is not surprising that so many scholars tend to see, mistakenly, at the beginning of the fragment a contemplative mood in Confucius who then becomes a viewer overwhelmed by the sublime (in an almost Kantian sense) spectacle of this natural setting.[6] In keeping with this interpretation, most exegetes coincide in translating the verb with which the text describes Confucius's first action, *guan* (觀), as "contemplate" or "admire". However, I believe that this is not a wholly satisfactory option.

Once again, this passage is different from the other stories about skill in the *Zhuangzi*, which invariably describe an individual watching or contemplating another individual as the latter carries out a task to an extraordinary degree of perfection. The verb used for this act of perceiving in these other stories is not *guan* but another word: *jian* (見). Although both verbs belong to the semantic field of vision, the fact is that they are not wholly equivalent and, depending on the particular circumstances in which they are used, certain relevant nuances should be taken into account. The meaning of the term *guan* is glossed by the *Shuowen jiezi* as "looking carefully" (*di shi ye* 諦視 也) (*Shuowen jiezi zhu*, 408). In other ancient documents and linked with this attentive gaze, the term *guan* has the meaning of carrying out an inspection, a scrupulous visual examination undertaken in a specific, delimited space.[7] The contrast with the verb *jian* becomes more evident when one attempts to understand the scope and function of this term in the other anecdotes about skill. To my mind, the term *jian* is used in these passages to denote a kind of visual perception that is free of enquiry since it entails an idea more like the emergence of an object into the observer's visual field and, accordingly, as the product of an encounter, a more passive position of the viewer. However, *guan* implies not only greater intensity in the visual examination but also, and still more important, active exploration, an enquiry with minute attention to detail.[8] This is precisely what happens when the two mentioned verbs appear in the opening lines of the apologue: while, to begin with, Confucius is scrutinising (*guan*) the Lüliang landscape, searching for something, exploring it with his gaze, a little later in the course of his visual inspection the anonymous swimmer bursts into his visual field (*jian*) and then comes to be the fixed object of his attention.

This is not, however, the only occasion where the ancient literature describes Confucius as carrying out a similar visual examination.[9] One of these passages, this time from the *Xunzi*, is especially pertinent here:

> Confucius was gazing intently at a waterway flowing eastward. Zigong asked Confucius: "Why is it that whenever a gentleman sees a large waterway, he is sure to gaze intently at it?" Confucius said: "When the waterway is large, it provides for the various living things in an all-encompassing fashion, without interfering with them: this resembles virtue. Its flow is towards sunken and low-lying places, and even through curves and bends it is sure to follow this pattern: this resembles justice. Its gushing current is never depleted or exhausted: this resembles the Way. If someone opens a channel for it to go through, its response is as swift as an echo, and it rushes at crevasses a hundred fathoms deep without fear: this resembles courage. When it pours into a basin, it is sure to achieve a balanced situation: this resembles standards; and one does not need a leveling stick: this resembles adhering to correctness. Being soft and supple, it reaches into even minute spaces: this resembles keen discernment. By going into and out of it, one uses it to become fresh and clean: this resembles being transformed to goodness. Even through ten thousand turns, it is sure to head east: this resembles having settled intentions. For these reasons, whenever a gentleman sees a large waterway, he is sure to gaze intently at it".[10]

A reading of this conversation between Confucius and Zigong clearly shows the nuances of different meanings, and that these two terms belonging to the semantic field of vision must be distinguished. The final sentence in the passage is exemplary in this regard: when a noble man or a superior man (*junzi* 君子) comes across a large waterway, and when this occupies his visual field (*jian*), he must necessarily gaze intently at it or subject it to scrutiny (*guan*). However, Confucius's answer to his disciple in this anecdote from the *Xunzi* not only draws attention to the difference which, as he understands it, exists between "see" or "contemplate" (*jian*) and "scrutinise attentively" (*guan*), but it also explicitly indicates which phenomena are worthier of the probing gaze. The master's intervention in the scene makes it clear that, in his opinion, great watercourses (*da shui* 大水) should be subjected to this superior level of more intense, attentive visual examination since they potentially exemplify an ethical lesson.[11] Insofar as he sees himself as a noble man or, at least, someone who aspires to achieve this ideal, Confucius confesses that if he earnestly inspects the mighty flow of a great river it is because he knows that this apparently purely natural phenomenon treasures inside it features that can potentially be interpreted in moral terms. Meticulous examination of the river with a sensitive eye makes it possible to connect up with a philosophical lesson. Every characteristic feature of these great watercourses has a corresponding series of essential values such as virtue (*de* 德), justice (*yi* 義), courage (*yong* 勇), correctness (*zheng* 正), et cetera. Hence, by way of these analogical equations, one can extract a morally rewarding teaching by means of intent observation of the waterway.

It is possible to find, this time in a passage of the *Han shi wai zhuan* 韓詩外傳, a quite similar idea about the moral power conferred on water by Confucian doctrines:

> Should someone ask: "Just what does a sage find in water to give him pleasure?" I would reply: "Now water moves in accordance with reason, not losing even one little moment. In this it resembles sagacity. In moving it descends, and in this it resembles the observance of rituals. It runs along a deep gorge without any uncertainty: in this it resembles bravery. It keeps itself pure through protective embankments and, in this, resembles the man who knows his fate. Passing through deep gorges, it goes far and achieves its destination without diminution: in this it resembles virtue. Through it heaven and earth are completed, through it all living beings are generated and the state is at peace; through it all affairs are settled and phenomena are rectified. This is why the sage takes pleasure in water". [12]

Any attempt at understanding this passage should be within the framework of the end of the Warring States period and an intense debate in which water metaphors and analogies were wielded. In this context, each of the main doctrines of the epoch expresses part of its proposal for a particular understanding of this common element by way of conflicting analogies conceived with different ideological ends. The two passages quoted from the *Xunzi* and the *Han shi wai zhuan* are no exception to this general rule and point to similar moments in other written sources of antiquity, including the *Analects* in which Confucius shows a fondness for interpreting elements from the natural setting on the basis of a moral standpoint. In this case, one should recall the above-mentioned passage in which the master attributes a value, associated with a certain moral quality, to mountains and watercourses (*Lunyu*, 6.23; *Lunyu huijiao jishi*, 6.523). Still more relevant for grasping the anecdote from the *Zhuangzi* is the dialogue in the *Analects* between one of Confucius's disciples, Zilu, and two anchorites called Chang Ju (長沮) and Jie Ni (桀溺) (appellatives consisting of characters with clear aquatic resonances) (*Lunyu*, 18.6; *Lunyu huijiao jishi*, 18.1620–24). Jie Ni, whose name means, among other things, "Drowned Hero", describes the world's situation as being deluged by great floods of water, suggesting that neither Confucius nor any other sage who aspires to intervene in these circumstances is capable of bringing about change. Through the words of this eccentric individual, who has decided to shun any commitment to the political order, the passage in the *Analects* emphasises, by way of contrast, Confucius's vocation as saviour when faced with tumultuous reality that has lost its way (*dao*), as expressed by means of the aquatic analogy.

But Confucius's tendency to take water as the object of moral considerations also appears, indirectly, in other texts, including the *Mengzi*. In one passage from this work, Mengzi's interlocutor, a man named Xuzi (徐子), asks why Confucius has exclaimed on several occasions, "Ah, water! Ah, water!" (*shui zai, shui zai* 水哉，水哉), and why he deems this element worthy of such attention. Mengzi then teaches him a lesson about the virtues that should be extracted from the distinctive features of this natural element (*Mengzi*, 4B18; *Mengzi zhengyi*, 16.563–64). From a similar standpoint, one should also recall the famous dispute described in the *Mengzi* between an individual named Gaozi (告子), about whom there is very little information,[13] and Mengzi himself about the way in which the inner condition of beings (*xing* 性) should be understood. In effect, this polemical debate concerning one of the core issues of the philosophical scheme of the *Mengzi* is articulated in a discussion about the inherent characteristics of water (*shui zhi xing* 水之性), since this is precisely the analogy employed by Gaozi in his first comment, which Mengzi later takes up in his response (*Mengzi*, 6A.1–3; *Mengzi zhengyi*, 20.735–36). The philosophical and moral relevance of watercourses appears once again in the *Mengzi* when Confucius exhorts his disciples to take note of the wisdom hiding behind yet another aquatic analogy, now in the words of a child who is singing a little song about water, which, according to the master's interpretation, bears within it an invitation to make the most of chances to share experiences with virtuous individuals (*Mengzi*, 4A.8; *Mengzi zhengyi*, 14.498–99). It would therefore seem clear that, at least for the followers of the Confucian school, the natural landscape and, more specifically, watercourses are not only recurring objects of beauty-inspired contemplation, of purely aesthetic delight, but also, and certainly even more so, an occasion for ethical reflection, a privileged opportunity to draw lessons about self-cultivation.

Confucius's attitude in the first line of the *Zhuangzi* about the swimmer is not contemplative and neither is he carried away by the stunning beauty of the landscape, but, rather, he is completely immersed in searching, probing, and engaging in a kind of visual fine-combing. He closely inspects the immense torrent as he searches for elements worthy of being used for moral reflection, phenomena, or happenings that would give him the chance to learn something or teach a lesson on the matter. It is not surprising, then, that in another part of the *Mengzi*, and in keeping with this extraordinary quality the philosophical tradition of ancient China attributes to water as predisposed to becoming both object and wellspring of moral reflection, the text speaks of an "art of scrutinising water" (*guan shui you shu* 觀水有術) (*Mengzi*, 7B.24; *Mengzi zhengyi*, 26.913).

In light of these considerations, it seems evident that the aim of Confucius's first action in the anecdote from the *Zhuangzi*, expressed by means of the verb *guan*, is not aesthetic contemplation of the spectacle offered by the landscape of Lüliang but rather attentive examination of the flow of water turbulently cascading down from the top of the waterfall. But what kind of visual scrutiny is Confucius engaged in here? What are his eyes seeking in the water? There is no question that painstaking observation of the potent watercourse suggests a philosophical challenge, since, as I have just demonstrated, its qualities directly point to some of the more important moral questions. The noble man, then, inspects the water because the values of the moral order to which he aspires are subtly incorporated in the various manifestations of the phenomenon. The vignette from the *Zhuangzi* about what happened at Lüliang is included as part of the same logic, taking it up and extending it, although, as described below, it has critical goals that are not exempt from parodic humour.

2. CONFUCIUS QUIXOTICUS? APPEARANCES, LIFE SAVING, AND FAILURE

The appearance onto the scene of the man who plunges into the wild current of the huge waterfall makes Confucius think he is some unfortunate who, because of his suffering, has decided thus to end his days. This perception is understandable not only because, as the text itself sustains, the idea that anyone would dare to swim in these waters would seem to be automatically out of the question since not even the best-equipped aquatic creatures would be capable of such a feat, but also, at least in part, as I have just noted, because of the moral gaze Confucius projects onto this space. From Confucius's point of view, what happens at the waterfall can only be interpreted in moral terms. The water, as described above, constitutes a privileged object for teaching and also a boundless source of vital lessons. It would not seem far-fetched to imagine that, on seeing this man in the middle of the turbulent flow of the waterfall, he would also consider the possibility that the man is committing suicide for moral reasons. Suicide is generally condemned, but when circumstances situate an individual in the position of having to choose between dying or staying alive at the price of renouncing the virtues of humanity (*ren* 仁) and justice (*yi* 義), several passages of the *Analects* suggest that, in such cases, taking one's own life could be the action that most behoves the morally superior man.[14] Ancient literature offers several episodes in which individuals who, wishing to keep their integrity intact when confronted with circumstances which fly in the face of order and without any chance of modifying this situation of intolerable injustice, have opted to commit suicide by throwing themselves into a great river.[15] Impelled by the urgency of the circumstances, Confucius, believing that he sees someone in difficulties, involves his disciples in an attempt to save him, urging them to run downstream and rescue the hapless man.

It is at this point that the reader cannot avoid imaginatively recreating the scene with certain hilarious touches, even though these humorous aspects are not explicit in the telling of the tale. The contrast between the main characters of the sequence could not be more radical, which explains the comic effect. The disciples, giddy with the sense of emergency and excited by the importance of the mission, rush downstream, along the river bends, bumping into each other, tripping on their long tunics, holding on to their caps as best they can while the supposedly desperate man lets himself be borne away (*you* 遊) by the waves and swirling currents of the river.[16] By contrast with the supreme, autonomous solitude of the anonymous swimmer (whose action obeys no requirement and, indeed, as I shall show below, it might be argued that it does not even obey the dictates of his own will), the herd-like cluster of Confucius's disciples is hierarchically ordered around the tutelary figure of their master[17] and limits itself simply to obeying the moral command to rescue the man. Confucius's behaviour in sending his disciples to save the swimmer while apparently remaining where he was, observing the events from a distance and waiting to see what would happen, presents an irony-laden contrast since, in several passages from early literature, it is stressed that in order to save a drowning person or, in other words, bring an urgent ethical task to a successful conclusion, one must get one's feet wet (*ru zu* 濡足).[18] Finally, it is possible to pick out in this scene from the *Zhuangzi* another element of contrast, which I believe is also significant, namely that the will of those who are on dry land is focused on saving the man in the water, while the swimmer, absorbed in his aquatic activity, is totally removed from any idea of rescue. He would not even be able to save anyone else, if one is to believe a passage from the *Huainanzi* which says that "someone who is swimming cannot save another from drowning since his hands and legs are already occupied enough" (*Huainanzi jiaoshi*, 11.1198). In any case, it is evident that this part of the anecdote revolves around the idea of saving or rescuing (*zheng* 拯) the individual who has dived into the waterfall. Confucius's initial act of scrutiny, of a moral nature, is prolonged in the requirement of this life-saving action, which is equally governed by moral intent.[19] Indeed, if the sequence gives rise to some comic effects, it is because it evokes, for satirical reasons, similar situations in some of the most representative texts of the Confucian school which include the same constitutive elements in which a situation of extreme seriousness prevails.[20] The presence of a person on the point of drowning, the situation of emergency this entails, and the impulse to save him educes or, in fact, takes one back to a number of very popular episodes in the philosophical literature of the day. Among them, one must mention the following exchange between Mengzi and Chunyu Kun (淳于髡):

> Chunyu Kun asked: "Does ritual require that men and women not touch when handing each other something?" And Mengzi replied: "That is ritual". Chunyu Kun then asked again: "If your sister-in-law were drowning, would you rescue her with your hand?" Mengzi answered: "Only jackals and wolves would not rescue their sister-in-law if she were drowning. It is required by ritual that men and women should not touch each other when handing each other something, but if your sister-in-law is drowning, to rescue her with your hand is a matter of emergency".[21]

Mengzi's interlocutor chides him for his lack of engagement or involvement in worldly matters and, with a view to making him understand this point, or perhaps to goad him into some kind of reaction, presents him with a false dilemma. Starting out from an imagined situation, Chunyu Kun obliges Mengzi to choose between scrupulous respect for ceremonial rules setting the standards for life in society and playing a crucial role in the moral order for both the Confucian school and Mengzi himself,[22] and its necessary non-compliance by saving a relative who is on the point of drowning. Mengzi's response to this imagined dilemma is clear: only the worst kind of beast would be capable of letting a person die in these circumstances in order to uphold this ritual integrity which prohibits physical contact between individuals of different genders. His original answer, used as an argument to counter Chunyu Kun's approach to the dilemma, is to make use of the term *quan* (權), which designates part of a set of scales and which has, among other meanings in the ancient literature, the senses of "ponder", "assess" (in the sense of calibrate), and "gauge" a given situation. However, in the context of this specific passage, it seems to signal urgent circumstances, an emergency that requires instant evaluation.[23] This is precisely the situation that occurs in the scene from the *Zhuangzi* in which the man plunges into the waterfall at Lüliang. When they try to save the life of a poor unfortunate, Confucius's disciples overlook for a moment the rules of protocol and basic elementary principles of decorum when, in normal circumstances, they would be severely penalised for unconstrained movements and lack of control over their bodily expressions.

Some of these dramatic elements (imminent danger of death by drowning, moral dilemma, and compassion for others inspired by their fate) appear once again in another well-known episode from the *Mengzi*, which has been widely commented upon and turned into a kind of paradigmatic moral dilemma, even in some contemporary ethical debates, although the source is not always mentioned.[24] This passage proclaims, first, the thesis that "all human beings have hearts that are not unfeeling towards others" and goes on to offer proof of this affirmation in order, finally, to extract a series of corollaries.

The reason for stating that all human beings have hearts that are not unfeeling towards others is this: if someone suddenly saw a child about to fall into a well, this person would, in such situation, have in his heart a feeling of anxiety and compassion. And this is so not because of trying to make a good impression on the child's progenitors, or because of wanting a good reputation among neighbours and friends, or because of disliking the noise the child would make with its cries. From this we can observe that if a person is without the feeling of compassion in his heart, he is not human.[25]

According to this passage from the *Mengzi*, the anxiety and feelings of compassion awakened in our hearts by the child's imminent danger of drowning are in no way a pondered but, in fact, a spontaneous response, which might be expected of anyone in similar circumstances. These immediate emotional reactions, which are not subject to external judgement or, in other words, not motivated by social considerations or any kind of calculation, are an essential sign of our humanity, to such an extent that the text deems that if such feelings are absent in our hearts, then, strictly speaking, it is not appropriate to speak of humanity. In another passage of the same work, halfway through a discussion between Gaozi and Mengzi, the latter once again states that all human beings are endowed with these emotional responses which, moreover, constitute the essence of humanity (*ren* 仁) (*Mengzi*, 6A6; *Mengzi zhengyi*, 22.757), the supreme moral ideal in Confucian doctrines.

This latter anecdote from the *Mengzi*, using for moral purposes the practical example of the child who is in danger of falling into a well, does not so much seek to judge the spectator's action or lack of action when faced with this critical situation as to highlight the essential value of the sentiments awakened by it in any human being. However, beyond this element, the important point is that these emotional responses of commiseration and compassion when confronted with another person's bad situation are, as I have noted, spontaneous. They are not influenced by reflection on the consequences our feelings might have, nor does the possible life-saving action depend on the reproaches or praise others might express with regard to our decisions. As for this latter point, however, some other texts of the time suggest alternative positions, once again within the framework of saving somebody from death by drowning. Hence, a work written towards the end of the Warring States period (although including earlier materials), aiming to elucidate the idea that the sage is capable of apprehending the consequences of a process when it has only just begun to come into being, offers two scenes featuring Confucius and two of his disciples. First, the text mentions the case of Zigong who—despite the fact that the norms of the state of Lu establish that if a woman who is a native of Lu has been a concubine to a feudal lord of another kingdom and is purchased out of bondage, then her rescuer will be repaid the purchase price—declines to accept recompense for the amount he has paid to free such a woman. Confucius considers that

Zigong has erred since with this supposedly generous gesture, he will only dissuade others from paying for the freedom of a concubine born in Lu. His second case has a disciple called Zilu taking the leading role.

> Zilu rescued someone who was drowning, and the man rewarded him with a cow, which he accepted. Confucius said, "The people of Lu will invariably come to the rescue of a person who is drowning." Confucius foresaw the end result of the events in their earliest beginnings since his ability to perceive future developments was far reaching.[26]

In contrast with what happens in the episode featuring Zigong who declines to accept recompense for the amount he has spent to free a woman from bondage, Zilu accepts the reward for his moral action of saving the life of a man who was about to drown. In Confucius's view, Zigong's generosity is harmful to the extent that others would be expected to follow suit, and this would act as a dissuasive factor in similar cases. Yet the apparent self-interest of Zilu when he accepts the reward from the man he has saved would be seen as exemplary and would encourage others to imitate his heroism. Hence, although in the two fragments from the *Mengzi* the emphasis is mainly on the internal, emotional, deliberative processes sparked by a situation of the risk of drowning, the latter story from the *Lüshi chunqiu* stresses the exemplarising value of certain actions. Whatever the case, it would seem evident that saving an individual who is about to drown would constitute a sort of locus classicus, a commonplace in a good part of the moral proposals and discourse of the day. From this standpoint, it is not improbable that the author or authors of the anecdote in the *Zhuangzi* bore in mind this recurrent theme when composing the story. The Confucius who is created in this retelling scrutinises the tumultuous torrent tumbling down in the Lüliang waterfall because he knows that this scene is propitious for moral action. He is aware that he is almost certainly in a situation that will call on him to extract analogies on virtue or that will put to the test his feelings of compassion, his ability to assess urgent circumstances, and his courage when required to embody an exemplarising moral ideal. Nevertheless, the endeavour is a resounding failure.

This abortive moral scene, as told in the *Zhuangzi*, is somehow reminiscent of the misadventures of Don Quixote in Miguel de Cervantes's eponymous novel, where in one very well-known episode, Don Quixote believes he is pitted against some evil giants and, despite the warnings of his squire, Sancho Panza, launches a clumsy attack on some inoffensive windmills with dire results (Cervantes, *Don Quijote*, 186). In the *Zhuangzi* story, Confucius is also presented in a tragicomic light, as a sort of bumbling, slightly scatter-brained hero who errs in his perception of things. The similarity may appear to be somewhat forced and overstated because, after all, Confucius's error at

Lüliang is not the product of dotty delusion but belongs in the spectrum of a much more acceptable representation of reality. Nevertheless, I would argue that, in both cases, although to different degrees, this distorted perception well illustrates the extent to which the way in which we apprehend and value reality largely depends on the prior ideas that shape our subjectivity. As a result of compulsive reading of chivalric romance in the case of Don Quixote, and tireless devotion to contemplation of moral issues, many of which feature scenes of drowning, in the case of Confucius, each character acquires an ethos or heroic nature that will end up forging his destiny. They so thoroughly incorporate these handed-down teachings revolving around constant moral demands that they undergo a radical transformation which makes them perceive the world from this privileged and, therefore, ineludibly partial perspective. Everything that happens around them is invariably interpreted on the basis of these superior ideals acquired through a prior and lengthy educational process and, logically, the actions they undertake will bear a corresponding stamp. The gaze Confucius directs at the waterfall of Lüliang is not neutral. It earnestly seeks elements that are susceptible to being interpreted in moral terms and, naturally, on the basis of this scrupulous zeal, the appearance of a man in the wild waters could only but confirm what was already there as a wish from the very beginning of his visual pursuit: the presence of an event of a moral nature which would be useful for extracting an edifying lesson, or even, as in this case, confronting the challenge of achieving a life-saving act that would confirm his virtue and, with that, his benevolence, as well as presenting an example that could be employed as a reference for others.

3. A GRACEFUL ASSUMED REVENANT INSTRUCTS CONFUCIUS

The failure of Confucius's moral action at the foot of the waterfall is situated, then, on the level of visual acuity. It is not that his moral perception is deficient but, rather, as I have suggested above, precisely the opposite occurs. In Lüliang, the scrutinising gaze (*guan*) of the master is most probably—as an effect of tenacious discipline devoted to studying moral diatribes and teachings set in watery contexts—saturated with precepts, norms, stipulations, and expectations: the error, therefore, is caused by a kind of overdose. Confucius's emotional response to the imagined situation in which another man's life is in danger, his immediate decision to order the urgent rescue of the man and, hence, his ability to carry out an exemplary action are not in any doubt. The problem is that this situation of emergency does not exist; he is totally mistaken in his representation of what is happening to the man who has plunged into the water. In the *Zhuangzi* apologue, Confucius, who is so often represented in the ancient literature as the sage who, after having completed an intensive self-cultivation process, can see what escapes others, who can anticipate what is still in an embryonic state thanks to his gifts of observation,[27] is carried away by his impulses and ambitions of the moral ilk and believes he is seeing a situation which does not square with what is really occurring. Before his disciples reach the supposedly wretched man in difficulties, the selfsame man emerges safe and sound from the water, totally at ease before the almost certainly astonished, incredulous gaze of the group of disciples, and calmly strolls along the riverbank. The contrast between the main characters in the story is so extreme at this juncture that the comical-parodic aspects are maximal. Nevertheless, it is worth dwelling a little more on this analysis in order to focus attention on the terms used by the author or authors of the story when writing up this part of the scene.

According to the text, when the man finished his swim he "came out of the water, shaking his unbound hair and singing a little song as he strolled along the riverbank". The description here of the appearance of this person has some connotations which deserve attention. In effect, "unbound hair" (*pi fa*被髮) suggests, first of all, that he has an uncivilised air because this is how members of barbarian tribes are described in the ancient texts;[28] second, and in relation with this first feature, it means contravening some of the basic ritual norms because, as stated in the *Book of Rites* (*Liji*), noblemen must avoid letting their hair loose;[29] and, finally, precisely because of the value of bound hair as a sign of civilisation and a clear way of discriminating between cultivated and savage populations, and as a way of showing respect for ritual conventions, unbound hair has the function in the *Zhuangzi* of signalling the man who has attained a radically free way of life, a long way from the prejudices of the human, all too human sphere. In relation to this last point, it is worth recalling the meeting between Lao Dan and Confucius described in this same chapter 21 of the *Zhuangzi*. According to the text, "Confucius went to call on Lao Dan. The latter had just finished washing his hair and was lying in the sun with his hair spread out, waiting for it to dry. In his immobile bliss, he did not seem to be human (*fei ren* 非人)" (*Zhuangzi jishi*, 21.711). However, even more important, loose hair is also typical of spirits or ghosts.[30] A fragment in the *Han Feizi* describes what happens to a man named Li Ji (李季), who enjoys going away on long journeys. Making the most of his absence, his wife betrays him with an official. One day, Li Ji returns unexpectedly and, since her lover is still in the bedroom, the wife is terrified. One of her servants suggests that she should tell her lover to leave the house through the window, naked and with dishevelled hair, and assures her that all the servants would deny that anything untoward had happened. The husband enters the house saying that he has seen a naked, unkempt-looking man leaving the house through the window. After questioning all the servants, who insist that they have noticed nothing unusual, Li Ji is convinced by his wife that what he has seen is most probably a ghost. Then, the twice-deceived husband is persuaded to take a bath in urine to cure his malady (*Han Feizi xin jiao zhu*, 31.625). In another passage recorded in some of the manuscripts exhumed in Shuihudi, one finds advice for the traveller who might come upon a demon or ghost blocking his way: he must loosen his hair and walk past it, pretending to be another ghost.[31] This emphasis on unbound hair is why Confucius imagines that the swimmer is a ghost. In contrast with other passages in the *Zhuangzi* about extraordinary skills, where examples of great bodily prowess are invariably described by witnesses with expressions including the term "spirit" (*shen* 神), the story about what happened at Lüliang only uses the term "ghost" (*gui* 鬼).[32]

It would therefore appear that what leads Confucius to err once again when he mistakes the swimmer for a ghost would not only be his extraordinary performance as a swimmer but also his appearance when he comes out of the water. I would venture that the author or authors of the story wish to draw attention to the enormous distance, the radical dissimilarity separating the two key figures of the scene. While Confucius is situated on the "human" side, by which I mean he is a prisoner of moral requirements, the swimmer is like some non-human being since he is depicted as someone who has been able to emancipate himself of this conventional dimension in order to enjoy his freedom from the precepts and codes which burden the existence of his interlocutor. It is therefore possible to affirm that, whatever one might be led to think by Confucius's question about whether the swimmer has a special method or technique for moving in the water, the proficiency the man has shown in the water is not so much the crystallisation of a limited talent as the expression of a different existential modality which embraces all his actions. The author or authors of the text, making use of the polysemy of the term which can denote both an activity of swimming and a leisurely stroll with no aim or precise destination, use the same verb (*you* 游) to refer both to the man's prodigious feats in the water and to his carefree roaming along the riverbank.[33] This, then, is not only about an unusually talented swimmer, someone who is outstandingly gifted in this regard, but, be that as it may, he is a human being who follows principles which in themselves are outside the norms, whether he is in or out of the water.

Nevertheless, impervious to these nuances, the Confucius who appears in the *Zhuangzi* anecdote seems mainly interested in knowing whether the man has a method for moving so skilfully in the water. As I shall try to demonstrate below, the fact is that, more than providing him with a description of his action in the water, the anonymous swimmer, now become something like a superior master, offers Confucius a different sort of lesson. The whole story can therefore be understood as a constant interplay of appearances which end up being dashed. Confucius, influenced by his training and moral aspiration, believes he is seeing a man in difficulties, when in fact the man has merely decided to have a dip. Impressed by his feat as well as by the blitheness of his demeanour, Confucius understands that he has met someone who incarnates a particular form of virtue-virtuosity (*de* 德) or, in other words, a man who has been able to develop precisely what constitutes Confucius's ultimate horizon of inspiration and most intense yearnings. In the hope of taking possession of it for himself, Confucius therefore decides to ask the swimmer about the method that has enabled him to acquire this aptitude. At this point, the story confounds the reader's expectations by subverting the conventional positions of the characters, since the champion of virtue, Confucius, upon whose person the ideal of superior wisdom (*da zhang fu* 大丈夫)[34] is frequently projected, addresses a common man (*yi zhang fu* 一丈夫) in the hope of obtaining from him instruction that will help him to attain virtue. However, the swimmer, who appears to be explaining his skill, takes advantage of the occasion to give a new twist to the matter, going back to the source of Confucius's first mistaken perception and offering him a very particular lesson about some of the fundamental problems which permeate the quest for virtue and morality.

In some way, the apologue in the *Zhuangzi* implicitly reveals and, at least in part, responds to a paradox inscribed in the matter of the pursuit of virtue which runs through all of the ancient Chinese philosophical literature. It is described by David S. Nivison who notes that consciously pursuing virtue in order to benefit thereby from the powers and effectiveness it holds out implies diverging from the end and failing, for in order to possess virtue, one must desire it for its own sake without any interference in the attempt at its acquisition from calculations or intentional strategies of any kind.[35] The paradox takes shape in two problems arising in the anecdote because of Confucius's attitude: first, the moral action of saving the man fails precisely because it is motivated by a previous moral intention, by a will that is aware of showing itself to be virtuous, and this leads him to a completely mistaken understanding of the events; and, second, Confucius again embodies this paradox of virtue when, after his error with the spectacle of the swimmer in the waters, he reveals that he is keen to possess this virtue-virtuosity as well and emphatically enjoins the man to share his technique or method (*dao* 道) with him.[36] The exchange between Confucius and the anonymous swimmer can thus be interpreted as an alternative response to the solutions put forth in other doctrinal sources to these two problems deriving from the virtue paradox.[37] As I shall show below, this response indicates one of the solutions to the paradox of virtue glimpsed by Nivison in his article, although it was not developed in his work, perhaps because he had restricted the paradox and its potential solutions to the framework of Confucian doctrines: in order to act virtuously, it is absolutely necessary to shed the very idea of trying to do something virtuous and to neutralise the intention of attaining this end.

From this standpoint, the acquisition of virtue and the achievement of appropriate virtuous action can be assimilated to other mental processes of a similar type, which, in their essence, also harbour a kind of paradox. As the sociologist and philosopher Jon Elster remarks in his book *Sour Grapes*, some mental states appear to have the property of only being able to come about as the by-product of actions undertaken for other ends (Elster, *Sour Grapes*). They can only occur as indirect results. By-product states, then, are states that cannot be attained by the will. Moreover, some cannot be attained precisely because of the intention to attain them. The effort of trying to make them happen is the reason why their happening is impossible. As Jon Elster puts it: "they can never be brought about intelligently or intentionally because the very attempt to do so precludes the state one is trying to bring about" (Elster, *Sour Grapes*, 43). According to Elster, since some of these states are useful or desirable, it is often tempting to try to make them happen, even though the attempt is bound to fail. This is what Elster calls the *moral fallacy of by-products*, meaning that this moral fallacy occurs when we deliberately try to create a state that is essentially a by-product. A good example of this would be the case of an insomniac trying to get to sleep or someone who tries to will herself to forget something. The mere fact of trying to forget makes the mind focus on the selfsame memory one wishes to wipe out, so the harder one tries, the further one ends up from the desired result, at least for a more or less short period of time. Virtue would represent a similar challenge to these mental states. However, as Romain Graziani has brilliantly demonstrated, Elster's work would seem to neglect a fundamental dimension when it comes to overcoming the difficulties deriving from the paradoxical structure of these mental states, namely time.[38] Hence, for example, the aim of forgetting something that has happened to us obeys the paradoxical framework described by Elster provided that consciousness strives to attain its goal in a very short period of time, or immediately. When the temporal dimension comes into play, the process lengthens, the aporetic condition of these mental states tends to be resolved, and, with that, the obstacles that lie in the way of achieving the goal are removed. This is precisely what the anonymous swimmer offers as an explanation to Confucius regarding his ability in the water: it is a process which develops over a long period of time. If, in the cases studied by Graziani, the temporal dimension emerges as a project and materialises in progressive development aiming at the future, in the meeting between the swimmer and Confucius, this temporal dimension is described retrospectively.

Indeed, the first sentence with which the swimmer tries to account for his ability in the water really consists of a concatenation of phases or stages, guided by certain concepts which appear to emphasise, once again, a lineal process. The words pronounced by the swimmer at this point should have seemed very familiar to a reader of the day, yet also strange. When clarifying how, unlike fish and other aquatic animals, he has so adeptly moved through the waterfall's turbulent waters, the swimmer evokes three notions which form part of a constellation of concepts recurrently employed with a definite moral intention in some of the bamboo-slip manuscripts unearthed in the Guodian archaeological site in 1993, in particular the one titled *Xing zi ming chu* (性自命出), as well as in the *Mengzi* and the *Xunzi*: the original (*gu* 故), the natural condition (*xing* 性), and fate (*ming* 命). In the *Zhuangzi* apologue, each one of these terms is situated inside a stage within a process that is underway. Hence, using the particle *hu* (乎), which in this case would signal a directional shift, the step from one phase to the next in accordance with a set pattern, the phrase put in the mouth of the swimmer, which I have chosen to translate as "I let it begin and it became the origin, I developed it and it became a natural condition, and I completed it and it became fate" indicates three main stages, each one of them in turn divided into two movements: beginning/origin, development/natural condition, and consummation/fate.

Besides these three concepts, repeatedly used in discussion of moral issues in the Confucian tradition, the phrase in the anecdote from the *Zhuangzi* employs the metaphor for the process that is reiterated in the Confucian literature in order to denote self-cultivation and, by this means, the attainment of a virtuous condition. Hence, both with the use of concepts imbued with moral meanings and the fact that they appear in the framework of a process which resembles those described in the passages about self-cultivation, the character of Confucius, which would function here as an emblem of this moralising ideology, is trapped among elements familiar to him (or, more accurately, to the reader) but transformed in the words of the swimmer. In effect, the sequence of concepts totally inverts the order imposed on the three concepts, as happens in the manuscript *Xing zi ming chu*. In this manuscript, one finds, first, destiny or the mandate (*ming*) vouchsafed by heaven (*tian* 天).[39] This generates a natural condition for each individual (*xing*) which, in turn, must be embellished by means of inherited institutions and traditions (*gu*) with a view to rectifying and delimiting it so as to encourage the movement of the more elementary emotions (*qing* 情) in an appropriate direction (*yi* 義).[40] From this standpoint, the achievement of a well-functioning moral consciousness would be the result of a simultaneous intervention of both internal (the natural condition and emotions arising from that) and external elements serving to restrain and refine these emerging impulses.[41] Hence, the term *gu* which, in the anecdote from the *Zhuangzi*, I have chosen to translate as "the original", must be understood in the *Xing zi ming chu* and in other similar texts associated with the Confucian school as referring to the set of norms and institutions created by the sages of bygone times, codified in rites, and transmitted by means of some of the classical texts. In fact, in the *Xing zi ming chu*, the term *gu*, which, in this case, should be translated as "reason(s)", is interpreted as a set of deliberate actions: "Purposeful actions are what we call 'reasons'" (*you wei ye zhe zhi wei gu* 有為也者之謂故).[42]

Nevertheless, far from setting this development in a context of a conscious and arduous exercise in moral improvement, the words pronounced by the swimmer seem to suggest more a process of unconscious accommodation or habituation. When Confucius goes on to ask the man about the meaning of his words, the swimmer offers a supplementary explanation: "I was born in these mountains and have accommodated to them so here is the original state. I grew up by the water and accommodated to that too so here is the natural condition. I don't know why things are like that so here is fate". The first two key expressions here, referring to the original and the natural condition, are composed with a common structure linking the first verbal phrase, which appears as a cause, to the second, which is conceived as a consequence of the first. Hence, since he "was born" (*sheng* 生) and "grew up" (*zhang* 長) in a specific setting, in this case a landscape of high places (*lu* 陵) and watercourses (*shui* 水), the swimmer explains that these circumstances had led him to integrate these elements and to be reconciled with them (*an* 安). The verb used to designate this accommodation or acculturation plays an important role in this and other passages from the *Zhuangzi*[43] and, as I understand it, would designate here a kind of *habitus*: a process of practical familiarisation which does not occur by way of the conscience. In other words, it is an unconscious or, to follow Billeter's concept of "integration", an unintentional assimilation of certain mechanisms that entail appropriation by means of the body of the necessary schemes to produce guidelines for action appropriate for each situation (Billeter, *Un paradigme*, 21). Indeed, the non-intentional dimension of this process of incorporation is explicitly accentuated by the swimmer on two occasions. In his first response, after schematically evoking this slow immersion, after which, in order to explain his competent movements in the water by submerging himself with the swirls and, following the movement of the water, being propelled out again, he says that his action merely obeys the principles of the water without interference from any preference whatsoever. The absence of partiality (*si* 私) is not, in this case, the product of a voluntary effort to be impartial (in another passage of the *Zhuangzi*, Lao Dan warns Confucius, saying that the fact of aspiring to be impartial means falling into a form of partiality[44]), but the consequence of having culminated the process of appropriating the surrounding environment, which means that one's actions become "unthinking", that they are unintentionally adapted to the changing requirements of each situation. It is, in fact, possible to read this passage in an alternative though complementary way. As mentioned above, Confucius interrogates the swimmer, eagerly trying to find out if he has some method or technique that enables him to move so deftly through the water. The swimmer responds with a double denial, saying he has no such thing and that he simply moves with the water's method or way (*cong shui zhi dao* 從水之道). Once again, Confucius is invited to rid himself of partiality, to shun the idea that skilful action depends on some method that an individual imposes on reality, in order, on the contrary, to focus on embracing and adapting himself to the modulations and transformations occurring in the world around him.[45]

In the second response, after the swimmer describes in a little more detail the process of habituation to the landscape where he was born and grew up, he suggests, in answer to Confucius's request for explanation, that the consummation of this process is the acquisition of a destiny with a pronounced basic feature: the force that drives things to happen in a certain way, which leads one to act in a particular manner at any given moment, is not conscious (*bu zhi* 不知) but situated in a framework that is unrelated to self-awareness. Just as, in a good part of the ancient literature, fate is imposed on individuals without their managing to understand why at certain moments the events of one's life are set on a plane that is distant and unreachable for one's manoeuvres and plans,[46] the swimmer, once he has completed the process of habituation, also acts without thinking about what has led him to act necessarily in such and such a way.

From this point of view, one must establish a more than notable concomitance between the skilful movements of the swimmer in the water—characterised by a subjective absence of partiality and seamless adaptation to the demands of the occasion—and certain patterns of action defined as autotelic behaviour and studied by psychologists in recent decades.[47] In both cases, the degree of maximum efficiency arising from the bodily actions of people who attain certain mental states is negatively defined by way of two shared characteristics: an absence of felt effort and an absence of self-consciousness.[48] To sum up, however paradoxical it might appear, in these two models the ideal agent is the person who does not act like a real agent. As Brian Bruya has pointed out, in autotelicity guidance is not tantamount to agency and does not occur at the level of the agent in any normal sense of phenomenal agency: there is no immediate sense of the phenomenal self, and so, although there is action, there is no agent as such (Bruya, "Action without Agency," 352). If one of the possible responses for overcoming the paradox of virtue consists in renouncing it, autotelic forms of behaviour are similarly inclined. Just as it is necessary to shed any aspiration to virtue if one wishes to attain virtue, bodily actions, if they are to be effective, require liquidation of the agent as such. Yet it is necessary to make it clear that this is not in any way a case of two conflicting, polarised ways of understanding subjectivity. Since they are situated within a temporal development, the self-conscious agent and the non-conscious agent are no more than two moments of a process. In fact, voluntary subjectivity or the conscious agent is presented as an unavoidable initial stage, as revealed in the words spoken by the swimmer who invokes this intentional instance by explicitly using the first-person pronoun (*wu* 吾). The active participation of the intentional agent is necessary in the first moments, but then, at least ideally, he fades out to give way to the non-intentional agent once the process reaches its culmination.

Naturally, reflection on these aporias is well beyond the scope of this chapter and its initial aim. Yet it is worth at least taking note of them and indicating the fact that they constitute a key problem running through the *Zhuangzi*. Hence, for example, a significant proportion of the passages containing criticism of intentional consciousness and aspiring to point out the harmful effects of a moralising conception of action, or praising certain mental processes related to forgetting and which play an important role in the construction of the text's main arguments, should be understood as more developed ways of approaching these paradoxes from different standpoints. In the specific case concerning the events at Lüliang, rather than offering, perhaps, a reasoned solution to these paradoxes, the focus is mostly on bringing about a change in Confucius's perception, of making him see—and, with him, the reader of the apologue—the negative consequences of a hyperactive moral conscience, dominated by excessive attention to a virtuous vocation which, far from having the desired effect, embodies in fact an example of ineffectiveness, while at the same time constituting a source of permanent error. The words the swimmer addresses to Confucius should then be understood, first of all, as a response to the latter's initial failure, his inability to interpret the events correctly and to act accordingly. The description of the process of accommodating to one's surrounding landscape, the exhortation to shed any trace of partiality, and the invitation to adopt a nonchalant stance in the face of rigid forms of conduct prescribed in advance suggest an attempt to go beyond Confucius's comportment, which, pervaded with a prejudice-laden perception of things and a self-awareness in a permanent state of alert owing to aspirations of a moral nature, makes him adopt an inflexible, severe, and necessarily inept position. At the same time, the swimmer's intervention also works towards a lesson about Confucius's tenacious perseverance in his zeal to conquer virtue, an attitude that is not only revealed in his mistaken understanding, caused to a great extent by his persistence, but also, and once again, in his belief that it is possible to obtain it by means of a method that can be conveyed directly and immediately by the ostensible holder of this virtue. With his description of this process of non-intentional appropriation, the swimmer defuses the fretful yearning displayed in Confucius's question and, to the extent which—unlike the process of moral self-cultivation ascribed to the Confucian school—these phases of "learning" link up and culminate without the intervention of any figure of authority, he suggests an alternative model of education based not so much on obtaining formulae, or on norms and precepts of obligatory compliance by the aspirant, as on lengthy exposure to a more subtle influence that seems to be very different from the conventional authority of the usual kind of master.

NOTES

This paper has been supported by a research project (FFI2017-83593-P) co-funded by the Spanish Ministry of Economy and Competitiveness (MINECO) and the European Fund for Regional Development (FEDER). I would also like to express my gratitude to Jean Levi, Romain Graziani, Mercedes Valmisa, Michael Ing, Ai Yuan, and Juan Carlos Rodríguez Delgado for their stimulating comments and valuable corrections. Of course, all remaining shortcomings are my sole responsibility.

1. 孔子觀於呂梁，縣水三十仞，流沫四十里，黿鼉魚鱉之所不能游也。見一丈夫游之，以為有苦而欲死也，使弟子並流而拯之。數百步而出，被髮行歌而游於塘下。孔子從而問焉，曰：「吾以子為鬼，察子則人也。請問蹈水有道乎？」曰：「亡，吾無道。吾始乎故，長乎性，成乎命。與齊俱入，與汩偕出，從水之道而不為私焉。此吾所以蹈之也。」孔子曰：「何謂始乎故，長乎性，成乎命？」曰：「吾生於陵而安於陵，故也；長於水而安於水，性也；不知吾所以然而然，命也。」(*Zhuangzi jishi*, 19.656–58).

2. The story of this encounter is also told with some variants in two other ancient textual sources, the *Liezi* and the *Shuoyuan*: *Liezi jishi*, 2.62–64; *Shuo yuan jiaozheng*, 17.426–27. The versions of the tale reported in the *Zhuangzi* and the *Liezi* show few differences, which are irrelevant from the standpoint of ideas. However, this is not the case with the account in the *Shuoyuan*, where a different lesson is drawn and a good part of the concepts featuring in the *Zhuangzi* and *Liezi* versions are replaced by others closer to the so-called Confucian doctrines. This might seem to suggest that the *Shuoyuan* version could have been composed as a response to an earlier criticism of Confucius's followers expressed in the *Zhuangzi* and the *Liezi*. Whatever the case, at least to my mind, there are no definitive arguments, either, for discarding the opposite explanation, which is to say that one might also accept that the version appearing in the *Zhuangzi* and the *Liezi* is, in fact, a parodic response to some earlier story connected with Confucian doctrines and which would have been preserved only in the version consigned to the *Shuoyuan*.

3. One symptomatic fact is that some recent contributions aiming to study these anecdotes about skills as a set have overlooked precisely the story which I shall analyze here. See, for example, Vávra, "Skillful Practice."

4. Some recent academic contributions have challenged this still accepted idea that anecdotes in early Chinese literature are philosophically irrelevant from an argumentative point of view. See, for this instance, Rolf Trauzettel, "Stellenwert und Funktion," and van Els and Queen, *Between History and Philosophy*.

5. See, for example, *Lunyu*, 6.23, 9.17; *Lunyu huijiao jishi*, 6.523, 9.794.

6. See, for instance, Graziani, *Le corps dans le taoïsme ancien*, 43–44. As I shall demonstrate in this chapter, the contemplation of waters is not here an occasion to feel one's finitude, to feel humiliated or humbled by the powers of nature.

7. This meaning is to be found, for example, in a manuscript exhumed in the archaeological site of Mawangdui in 1973. Its title is precisely this term, *guan* (*Huangdi sijjing jinzhu jinyi*, 263). For a more complete account of the function of the term *guan* in the ancient literature, I refer to the study by Wu Zhongwei, "Lun guan."

8. Another passage from the *Zhuangzi* underlines explicitly the value of the term *guan* as expressing a scrutinising gaze which also entails prejudices. In the story, we find a certain Shi Chengqi (士成綺) travelling to Lao Dan's house to have an interview (*jian*) with him. However, during the interview, Shi Chengqi inspects scrupulously (*guan*) the house of Lao Dan and perceives abandoned remains of food in it, which is interpreted by him as a revealing sign confirming (mistakenly) the idea that, contrary to his original expectations, Lao Dan is far from being a sage. See *Zhuangzi jishi*, 13.481–84.

9. The verb phrase *guan yu* (觀於) appears in passages concerning Confucius in the following works: *Xunzi jijie*, 28.520; *Shuo yuan jiaozheng*, 10.242; *Kongzi jiayu shu zheng*, 2.9.55–56, 7.28.181, 7.28.183.

10. 孔子觀於東流之水。子貢問於孔子曰：「君子之所以見大水必觀焉者，是何？」孔子曰：「夫水遍與諸生而無為也，似德。其流也埤下，裾拘必循其理，似義，其洸洸乎不淈盡，似道。若有決行之，其應佚若聲響，其赴百仞之谷不懼，似勇。主量必平，似法。盈不求概，似正。淖約微達，似察。以出以入以就鮮絜，似善化。其萬折也必東，似志。是故見大水必觀焉。(*Xunzi jijie*, 28.524–25. Slightly modified translation of Hutton, *Xunzi*, 322).

11. For a general study of the role of water in the philosophical texts of ancient China, see Allan, *The Way of Water*.

12. 問者曰：「夫智者何以樂於水也？」曰：「夫水者，緣理而行，不遺小間，似有智者；動而下之，似有禮者；蹈深不疑，似有勇者；障防而清，似知命者；歷險致遠，卒成不毀，似有德者。天地以成，群物以生，國家以寧，萬事以平，品物以正。此智者所以樂於水也。」(*Han shi wai zhuan jinzhu jinshi*, 3.128).

13. Some scholars have put forward hypotheses about this figure and his ideological affiliation, among them Nivison, with "Philosophical Voluntarism," and Kwong-loi Shun, with his *Mencius and Early Chinese Thought*, 123–26. Goldin has tried to demonstrate that the character of Gaozi represents a branch of the Confucian school whose basic theses are to be found in the manuscripts unearthed in 1993 at the archaeological site of Guodian. In this regard, see his "Xunzi in the Light of the Guodian Manuscripts."

14. *Lunyu*, 15.9; *Lunyu huijiao jishi*, 15.1372. See also *Mengzi*, 6A.10; *Mengzi zhengyi*, 26.891–92.

15. The paradigmatic case of voluntary death by throwing oneself into the waters of a great river for moral reasons would certainly be that attributed to the poet Qu Yuan (fourth–third century BC). Then again, it seems that death by drowning, perhaps because it is frequently the result of a voluntary action, is severely criticised in some ritual treatises of antiquity and is a reason for suspending the ceremony of presenting condolences (*diao* 吊), one of the most important stages of death rites. See, for example, *Liji jijie*, 3.1.182.

16. Jean Levi brilliantly expatiates on the conceptual contrast between solid dry land and the watery world in his book *Le petit monde du Tchouang-tseu*, 117–18.

17. This contrast has been highlighted by Billeter in his excellent analysis of the anecdote (*Leçons sur Tchouang-tseu*, 32).

18. See, for instance, *Huainanzi jiaoshi*, 20.2109; *Shuo yuan jiaozheng*, 7.165; and *Xin xu jinzhu jinshi*, 7.249.

19. The *Mengzi* describes the moral and political attitude of the great sage Yu 禹 by means of the following sentence: "Yu was concerned in such a way that if there were anyone drowning in the world, it was as if he had drowned her himself" (*Mengzi*, 4B29; *Mengzi zhengyi*, 17.597). In a similar vein, a passage from the *Hou Hanshu* explicitly states that if someone does not rescue a person who is drowning, he cannot be considered properly humane (*Hou Hanshu*, 1739). And the *Shuoyuan* establishes an explicit analogy between ordering the world and rescuing someone from drowning (*Shuo yuan jiaozheng*, 5.95).

20. The *Analects* (*Lunyu*, 6.26; *Lunyu huijiao jishi*, 6.532) have a passage in which a disciple presents to Confucius the case of a man who, falsely informed that someone has fallen into a well, is urged to act.

21. 淳于髡曰：「男女授受不親，禮與？」孟子曰：「禮也。」曰：「嫂溺則援之以手乎？」曰：「嫂溺不援，是豺狼也。男女授受不親，禮也；嫂溺援之以手者，權也。」(*Mengzi*, 4A17; *Mengzi zhengyi*, 15.520–22).

22. If one gives credit to some of the anecdotes recorded in the ancient literature about Mengzi, he might be seen as a stickler for scrupulous application of ritual conventions. Hence, for instance, according to a story included in, among other sources, the *Han shi wai zhuan*, Mengzi wished to disown his legitimate wife because, when unexpectedly entering their married quarters one day he found her semi-naked. Although he entered the chamber suddenly, so his wife was not sufficiently forewarned to dress herself appropriately, Mengzi interpreted her state of undress as a kind of insult to his status as her husband (*Han shi wai zhuan jinzhu jinshi*, 9.328–29). It is not improbable that Chunyu Kun's criticism aimed at the figure of Mengzi in the passage I have just cited was intended to reproach him for his excessive observance of ritual norms.

23. See Vankeerberghen, "Choosing Balance"; Csikszentmihalyi, *Material Virtue*, 118–24.

24. See, for instance, Ogien, *Human Kindness*, 11–15; Greene, *Moral Tribes*, 258–59.

25. 所以謂人皆有不忍人之心者，今人乍見孺子將入於井，皆有怵惕惻隱之心。非所以內交於孺子之父母也，非所以要譽於鄉黨朋友也，非惡其聲而然也。由是觀之，無惻隱之心，非人也 (*Mengzi*, 2A6.1–6.3; *Mengzi zhengyi*, 7.232–33).

26. 子路拯溺者，其人拜之以牛，子路受之。孔子曰：「魯人必拯溺者矣。」孔子見之以細，觀化遠也。(*Lüshi chunqiu xin jiao shi*, 16.6.1013).

27. See, for instance, the above-quoted passage from the *Lüshi chunqiu* as well as *Kongzi jiayu shu zheng*, 5.125, and *Liji jijie*, 4.2.292. For a study on the relationship between moral excellence and perceptual acuity in ancient Chinese philosophical texts, see Csikszentmihalyi, *Material Virtue*, 169–70, as well as Brown and Bergeton, "Seeing Like a Sage."

28. *Liji jijie*, 5.2.359. For a detailed discussion on unbound hair as a characteristic feature of "uncivilised" people in ancient literature, see Brindley, *Ancient China and the Yue*, 143–48.

29. *Liji jijie*, 1.2.41. In another passage from the *Yanzi chunqiu*, the guardian at the gates of the city of Qi severely censures the behaviour of his lord, Lord Jing of Qi (who ruled from 547 to 490), because he dared to appear in broad daylight riding in a chariot with his hair flowing loose (*Yanzi chunqiu ji shi*, 5.315).

30. Letting one's hair loose was a sign frequently associated with possession by spirits in the ancient literature. See, in this regard, the article by Schwermann, "Feigned Madness."

31. *Shuihudi Qin mu zhu jian*, 217. On this issue, see also Harper, "Spellbinding," 250.

32. For a detailed discussion on the role of *shen* in the *Zhuangzi* and other philosophical texts from the late Warring States period, see, for instance, Puett, *To Become a God*, 122–44.

33. According to various passages from the *Analects* and the *Zuozhuan*, Confucius condemned idle wandering as harmful; see, for instance, *Lunyu huijiao jishi*, 16.1477; *Chunqiu Zuozhuan zhu* (Zhao gong, year 12), 1335. More specifically, a passage in the manuscript purchased by the Shanghai Museum, titled *Junzi wei li* (君子為禮), and transcribed and edited by Zhang Guangyu (張光裕) offers a description, not exempt of normative aims, of the ideal corporal demeanour of the nobleman in which it censures the distracted, erratic gaze: "Eyes should not wander but remain fixed on the object pursued" (*Shanghai bowuguan*, 257). There is, then, a clear contrast between the scrutinising gaze of Confucius at the beginning of the story and the erratic, carefree (*you*) gestures of the swimmer, both in and out of the water.

34. In the ancient literature, the expression "大丈夫" refers to a superior man who stands out for his great wisdom (see, for instance, *Han Feizi xin jiao zhu*, 21.385), in contrast to the common man (丈夫), and this is precisely the expression used by the author or authors of the apologue to refer to the swimmer.

35. See Nivison, "The Paradox of Virtue."

36. It would not seem unreasonable to think that the author or authors of the anecdote might have this problem in mind since the swimmer, perhaps suspecting the selfish nature of Confucius's interest, denies that he is in possession of such a technique or method.

37. Slingerland has demonstrated with convincing arguments that the paradox of virtue as formulated by Nivison structures a good part of the debates on morality in ancient China, including among them some of the classical texts ascribed to the Confucian school (*Mengzi, Xunzi*) as well as manuscript material exhumed in Guodian in 1993. See his article "The Problem of Moral Spontaneity."

38. See Graziani, "Optimal States."

39. "Natural condition emerges by itself from the mandate, and the mandate is sent down from Heaven" (*Guodian chujian jiaoshi*, 88).

40. "The way begins with basic emotions, and basic emotions are born of natural condition. Its beginning is close to the basic emotions, while its end is close to propriety" (*Guodian chujian jiaoshi*, 88).

41. On this issue, see, for instance, Perkins, "Recontextualizing Xing."

42. *Guodian chujian jiaoshi*, 89. For a detailed study of the different ways of conceiving of the term *gu* in pre-imperial philosophical literature, see the article by Qiu Xigui, "You Guodian jian Xing zi ming chu."

43. As far as I know, one of the few works which has set out to rescue the importance of this verb and analyze its sense in the *Zhuangzi* from a standpoint which is different from the one I offer here is the article by Ai Yuan, "On Acceptance."

44. *Zhuangzi jishi*, 13.478.

45. For a comprehensive and detailed study of the scope and meaning of the idea of "adaptation," both in the *Zhuangzi* and in other philosophical works of early China, see Valmisa, "Changing Along with the World."

46. See, for instance, *Lüshi chunqiu xin jiao shi*, 20.3.1355.
47. On autotelic behaviour, see Csikszentmihalyi, *Beyond Boredom and Anxiety.*
48. For a comprehensive analysis of the relationship between bodily action, the dissolution of the self, and the experience of pleasure, see Montero, *Thought in Action*, esp. 178–88.

REFERENCES

PRIMARY SOURCES

Chunqiu Zuozhuan zhu 春秋左傳注. Annotated by Yang Bojun 楊伯君. Beijing: Zhonghua shuju, 1995.

Guodian chujian jiaoshi 郭店楚簡校釋. Annotated by Liu Zhao 劉釗. Fuzhou: Fujian renmin chubanshe, 2003.

Han Feizi xin jiaozhu 韓非子新校注. Annotated by Chen Qiyou 陳奇猷. Shanghai: Shanghai guji chubanshe, 2000.

Han shi wai zhuan jinzhu jinshi 韓詩外傳今註今釋. Annotated by Lu Yuanjun 盧元駿. Taibei: Taiwan shangwu, 1994.

Hou Hanshu 後漢書. Annotated by Fan Ye 范曄. Beijing: Zhonghua shuju, 1965.

Huainanzi jiaoshi 淮南子校譯. Annotated by Zhang Shuangdi 張雙棣. Beijing: Beijing Daxue chubanshe, 1997.

Huangdi sijing jinzhu jinyi 黃帝四經今註今譯. Edited by Chen Guying 陳鼓應. Taibei: Taiwan shangwu, 1995.

Kongzi jiayu shu zheng 孔子家語疏証. Annotated by Chen Shike 陳士珂. Shanghai: Shanghai shudian, 1980.

Liezi jishi 列子集釋. Annotated by Yang Bojun 楊伯君. Taibei: Zhong zheng shuju, 1976.

Liji jijie 禮記集解. Annotated by Sun Xidan 孫希旦. Beijing: Zhonghua shuju, 1996.

Lunyu huijiao jishi 論語彙校集釋. Annotated by Huang Huaixin 黃懷信. Shanghai: Shanghai guji chubanshe, 2008.

Lüshi chunqiu xin jiaoshi 呂氏春秋新校釋. Annotated by Chen Qiyou 陳奇猷. Shanghai: Shanghai guji chubanshe, 2002.

Mengzi zhengyi 孟子正義. Annotated by Jiao Xun 焦循. Beijing: Zhonghua shuju, 1987.

Shanghai bowuguan cang zhanguo Chu zhu shu 上海博物館藏戰國楚竹書. Vol. 5. Edited by Ma Chengyuan 馬承源. Shanghai: Shanghai guji chubanshe, 2009.

Shuihudi Qinmu zhujian zhengli xiaozu 睡虎地秦墓竹簡整理小組. *Shuihudi Qinmu zhujian* 睡虎地秦墓竹簡. Beijing: Wenwu chubanshe, 1990.

Shuo yuan jiaozheng 說苑校証. Annotated by Xiang Zonglu 向宗魯. Beijing: Zhonghua shuju, 1989.

Shuowen jiezi zhu 說文解字注. Annotated by Duan Yucai 段玉裁. Shanghai: Shanghai guji chubanshe, 1996.

Xin xu jinzhu jinshi 新序今註今釋. Annotated by Lu Yuanjun 盧元駿. Beijing: Tianjin guji, 1987.

Xunzi jijie 荀子集解. Annotated by Wang Xianqian 王先謙. Beijing: Zhonghua shuju, 1988.

Yanzi chunqiu ji shi 晏子春秋集釋. Annotated by Wu Zeyu 吳則虞. Beijing: Zhonghua shuju, 1987.

Zhuangzi jishi 莊子集釋. Annotated by Guo Qingfan 郭慶藩. Beijing: Zhonghua shuju, 1989.

SECONDARY SOURCES

Ai Yuan 艾袁. "On Acceptance: A Zhuangzian Perspective." *Dongwu zhexue xuebao* 東吳哲學學報 33, no. 2 (2016): 97–121.

Allan, Sarah. *The Way of Water and Sprouts of Virtue*. Albany, NY: SUNY Press, 1997.

Billeter, Jean-François. *Leçons sur Tchouang-tseu*. Paris: Allia, 2002.

————. *Un paradigme*. Paris: Allia, 2012.

Brindley, Erica. *Ancient China and the Yue: Perceptions and Identities on the Southern Frontier, c. 400 BCE–50 CE*. Cambridge: Cambridge University Press, 2015.

Brown, Miranda, and Uffe Bergeton. "Seeing Like a Sage: Three Takes on Identity and Perception in Early China." *Journal of Chinese Philosophy* 35, no. 4 (2008): 641–62.

Bruya, Brian. "Action without Agency and Natural Human Action: Resolving a Double Paradox." In *The Philosophical Challenge from China*, edited by Brian Bruya, 339–65. Cambridge, MA: MIT Press, 2015.

Cervantes, Miguel de. *Don Quijote de la Mancha*. Madrid: Cátedra, 1991.

Csikszentmihalyi, Mark. *Material Virtue: Ethics and the Body in Early China*. Leiden: Brill, 2004.

Csikszentmihalyi, Mihalyi. *Beyond Boredom and Anxiety. Experiencing Flow in Work and Play*. San Francisco: Jossey-Bass, 2000.

Elster, Jon. *Sour Grapes: Studies in the Subversion of Rationality*. Cambridge: Cambridge University Press, 1983.

Goldin, Paul R. "Xunzi in the Light of the Guodian Manuscripts." *Early China* 25 (2000): 113–46.

Graziani, Romain. *Le corps dans le taoïsme ancien*. Paris: Les Belles Lettres, 2014.

————. "Optimal States and Self-Defeating Plans: The Problem of Intentionality in Early Chinese Self-Cultivation." *Philosophy East and West* 59, no. 4 (2009): 440–66.

Greene, Joshua. *Moral Tribes. Emotion, Reason, and the Gap between Us and Them*. New York: The Penguin Press, 2013.

Harper, Donald. "Spellbinding." In *Religions of China in Practice*, edited by Donald S. Lopez, 241–50. Princeton: Princeton University Press, 1996.

Hutton, Eric L. *Xunzi: The Complete Text*. Princeton, NJ: Princeton University Press, 2014.

Levi, Jean. *Le Petit Monde du Tchouang-tseu*. Paris: Philippe Picquier, 2010.

Montero, Barbara G. *Thought in Action: Expertise and the Conscious Mind*. Oxford: Oxford University Press, 2016.

Nivison, David S. "The Paradox of Virtue." In *The Ways of Confucianism: Investigations in Chinese Philosophy*, 31–44. Chicago: Open Court, 1996.

————. "Philosophical Voluntarism in Fourth-Century China." In *The Ways of Confucianism: Investigations in Chinese Philosophy*, 130–32. Chicago: Open Court, 1996.

Ogien, Ruwen. *Human Kindness and the Smell of Warm Croissants: An Introduction to Ethics*. New York: Columbia University Press, 2015.

Perkins, Franklin. "Recontextualizing Xing: Self-Cultivation and Human Nature in the Guodian Texts." *Journal of Chinese Philosophy* 37 (2010): 16–32.

Puett, Michael J. *To Become a God: Cosmology, Sacrifice, and Self-Divinization in Early China*. Cambridge, MA: Harvard University Press, 2002.

Qiu Xigui 裘錫圭. "You Guodian jian Xing zi ming chu de shi xing zhe gu ye shuoduo Mengzi de tianxia zhi yan xing ye zhang 由郭店簡《性自命出》的「室性者故也」說到《孟子》的「天下之言性也」章." In *Zhongguo chutu guwenxian shi jiang* 中國出土古文獻十講, 260–76. Shanghai: Fudan daxue chubanshe, 2004.

Schwermann, Christian. "Feigned Madness, Self-Preservation, and Covert Censure in Early China." In *Zurück zur Freude. Studien zur chinesischen Literatur und Lebenswelt und ihrer Rezeption in Ost und West*, edited by M. Hermann, C. Schwermann, et al., 531–72. Sankt Augustin: Monumenta Serica, 2007.

Shun, Kwong-loi. *Mencius and Early Chinese Thought*. Stanford, CA: Stanford University Press, 1997.

Slingerland, Edward L. "The Problem of Moral Spontaneity in the Guodian Corpus." *Dao: A Journal of Comparative Philosophy* 7, no. 3 (2008): 237–56.

Trauzettel, Rolf. "Stellenwert und Funktion des Beispiels in antik-chinesischen philosophischen Texten." In *Form und Gehalt in Texten der griechischen und chinesischen Philosophie*, edited by Heinz Pohl and Georg Wöhrle, 77–89. Stuttgart: Franz Steiner Verlag, 2011.

Valmisa, Mercedes. "Changing Along with the World: Adaptive Agency in Early China." PhD diss., Princeton University, 2017.

Van Els, Paul, and Sarah A. Queen, eds. *Between History and Philosophy: Anecdotes in Early China*. Albany, NY: SUNY Press, 2017.

Vankeerberghen, Griet. "Choosing Balance: Weighing as a Metaphor for Action in Early Chinese Texts." *Early China* 30 (2005–2006): 47–89.

Vávra, Dušan. "Skillful Practice in the *Zhuangzi*: Putting the Narratives in Context." *Asian Studies* 5, no. 1 (2017): 195–219.

Wu, Zhongwei 吳忠偉. "Lun guan—dui xian Qin dianji yujing zhong 'guan' gainian de kaocha 論觀—對先秦典籍語境中觀概念的考察." *Kong Meng yuekan* 孔孟月刊 38, no. 1 (1999): 22–27.

Chapter Fourteen

Woodworker Qing

Matching Heaven with Heaven

Kim-chong Chong

Zi Qing (梓慶) carved wood to make a bell stand. When the bell stand was completed, those who saw it were astonished, taking it to be the work of spirits (*guishen* 鬼神). The marquis of Lu asked, "What art (*shu* 術) enabled you to make this?" Zi Qing replied, "I am a workman—what art would I have? Nevertheless, there is one thing. When I am about to make a bell stand, I take care not to squander my *qi* (*hao qi* 耗氣) and must fast so as to still my heart-mind (*jing xin* 靜心). After fasting for three days, I do not harbour thoughts of congratulations, rewards, titles, and stipends. After five days, I neither think of censure and acclaim, nor assessments of skill or lack of it. And after seven days of fasting, I forget (*wang* 忘) that I have four limbs and a body. At that time, the court no longer exists for me. My skill is concentrated, while external distractions have faded away. It is then that I enter the mountain forest and observe the heavenly nature (*guan tian xing* 觀天性) of the trees. Only when one with an excellent form presents itself as a bell stand do I set to work with my hands. Otherwise, I would not do anything. Thus, matching heaven with heaven (*yi tian he tian* 以天合天), perhaps this is why it is thought that the instrument I have made is the work of spirits!"[1]

This story of Zi Qing, or Woodworker Qing, has been read in conjunction with other stories, such as that of Cook Ding, as expressing the power and value of spontaneity. Much has also been written about the psychological processes underlying spontaneity. These processes are sometimes equated with a sense of mysticism. In this chapter, however, I shall discuss the story within two contexts which have been somewhat neglected. The first context is the *Zhuangzi*'s parody of prevalent shamanic practices. Against such practices, we find in Zi Qing a notion of self-cultivation bringing about a non-shamanic *shen* or spirit which can be characterised as both physical and mental. There is no mind and body dualism in the *Zhuangzi*. In the discussion below, when the terms "body" and "spirit" are mentioned, readers should not assume such a distinction. This is especially true since *qi*, a material substance, will also come into the discussion. At the same time, this self-cultivation is in accordance with heaven or nature, and this is the second context, namely, the relation between heaven and the human. There is sometimes a tension in the text between the admonition to act in accordance with heaven on the one hand, and human action on the other. I shall show how the story of Zi Qing helps to resolve this tension. In the end, the two contexts are related through understanding that "heaven" should not be taken to refer to a realm of spiritual beings that confer magical abilities through the ritual auspices of shamans. Instead, it refers to the potential in human beings to cultivate a vitality in accordance with nature. As illustrated by Zi Qing and other figures in the *Zhuangzi*, this can have aesthetically powerful results.

1. SHAMANS AND SPIRITS

There existed both before and during Zhuangzi's time groups of people variously referred to as *wu, shenwu*, or *wuzhu* (巫, 神巫, 巫祝)—the equivalent of shamans—believed to possess the art (*shu*) of communicating with spirits through special rituals to attain magical powers (Yü, *Lun tian ren zhi ji*, passim). In the *Zhuangzi*, we find parodies of the *wu*. For example, in chapter 7, "*Yingdiwang*" (應帝王), Ji Xian (季咸) is said to be able to foretell the auspicious and inauspicious, and even the day of a person's death.[2] In the light of these parodies, it is not a coincidence that the above story about Zi Qing takes the following form:

1. observers attribute the result of his work to spirits,
2. the marquis of Lu believes that he possesses some (*wu* or shamanic) art,
3. Zi Qing explains a process of self-cultivation before starting work, and
4. attributes the result to "matching heaven with heaven," which is perhaps why it is believed that his work is due to spirits.

Zi Qing in effect denies that what he does has anything to do with the spirits. We may appreciate this better by looking at another story appearing shortly before Zi Qing's. This concerns Duke Huan (桓公) of Qi. While hunting in a marsh with Guan Zhong (管仲, the legendary chief minister), Duke Huan is frightened by (what he thought to be) a spirit. He grasps Guan Zhong, asking what he had seen. But the latter denies having seen anything. Duke Huan becomes ill. An adviser, Huangzi Gaoao (皇子告敖), tells him:

Your Grace, you are doing this injury to yourself! How could a spirit have the power to injure you! If the vital breath (*qi*) that is stored up in a man becomes dispersed and does not return, then he suffers a deficiency. If it ascends and fails to descend again, it causes him to be chronically irritable. If it descends and does not ascend again, it causes him to be chronically forgetful. And if it neither ascends nor descends, but gathers in the middle of the body in the region of the heart, then he becomes ill. [3]

Duke Huan, however, remains unsettled and asks if spirits really exist. Affirming that they do, Huangzi names various spirits and the places where they reside, such as the hearth, stove, trash, water, mountains, and meadows, ending with "Weishe" (委蛇, read by Watson as "Weituo"), who lives in the marshes. This arouses Duke Huan's interest, since he had (allegedly) seen a spirit in a marsh. Huangzi obliges his request for a description of this particular spirit, concluding that "anyone who sees it will become a hegemon (*ba* 霸)." Immediately, "Duke Huan's face lit up and he said with a laugh, '*That* must have been what I saw!' Then he straightened his robe and hat and sat up on the mat with Huangzi, and before the day was over, though he didn't notice it, his illness went away."[4]

Huangzi's description of spirits and the common, everyday places where they live was evidently based on folk belief. This makes them less frightening. He adds that anyone who has seen the spirit of the marshes would become a hegemon. This seems to affirm both the existence of spirits and their power. But in fact it is a clever psychological ploy which plays upon the political ambition of Duke Huan, gladdens him, and relieves his illness. In the medical terminology of the *Zhuangzi*'s times (and even up to the present), this would be described in terms of allowing him to regain his *qi*. We shall say more about theories of *qi* below.[5]

In what follows, we ask two central questions in discussing the story of Zi Qing. First, what does self-cultivation aim at and what does it involve? Second, what is the significance of the expression "matching heaven with heaven"? The attempt to answer these questions will entail relating the story to other parts and aspects of the *Zhuangzi*.

2. SELF-CULTIVATION

Chapter 19 of the *Zhuangzi* in which Zi Qing appears is titled "Da sheng" (達 生). The term *da* means to have accomplished something at a superlative level, and the title is translated by Watson as "Mastering Life."[6] The term *sheng* nominally means "life." The remarks at the very beginning of this chapter, however, assert that the nurturing of *sheng* requires more than the provision of material things:

He who has mastered the nature of *sheng* does not go after things that are not necessary to *sheng*. He who has understood the nature of fate does not pursue what fate has, helplessly, denied. To nurture the body, it is first necessary to provide it with material things. However, there are those who possess an overabundance of things but are unable to nurture their body. The body is the precondition of *sheng*. Still, there are those who keep their body but have lost their *sheng*. The coming of life cannot be refused and its departure cannot be stopped. How sad it is! When people of the world think nurturing the body is enough to preserve *sheng* when in fact this is not the case, what is there in the world that is worth doing![7]

These remarks introduce the stories that follow and have a bearing on them. The stories, in turn, both supplement and illustrate the remarks. As mentioned, "life" is a nominal translation of *sheng* (生). But *sheng* is ambiguous. It could mean material or biological life per se, or it could mean something beyond that, connoting vitality. There are seven occurrences of *sheng* in the above passage. I have translated it as "life" in only one instance. This is in the sentence "The coming of life cannot be refused and its departure cannot be stopped." There is a central contrast in the passage between nurturing the body on the one hand, and *sheng* on the other. Life is coterminous with the body insofar as it is necessary to nurture the body with material things. The term *xing* (形), literally meaning "form," is used here to refer to the body. Thus, when the (form of the) body is said to be "the precondition of *sheng*," what is meant is the necessity of providing materials for maintaining *sheng*. But we gather that there is more to *sheng* than just life per se when it is said, "Still, there are those who keep their body but have lost their *sheng*." This is further emphasised in the lament that "people of the world think nurturing the body is enough to preserve *sheng* when in fact this is not the case" and in the indirect suggestion that something of worth is missing.

An explanation is required to see what is missing. For Zhuangzi and his followers, despite the fact that the coming and ending of life are beyond our control, humans have the capacity to maintain a vital essence (*jing* 精) in harmony with "heaven" (*tian* 天) or nature.[8] The state of harmony involves abandoning human entanglements such as the pursuit of wealth, status, and reputation so as not to wear out the body, and to "forget life" (*yi sheng* 遺生) in the sense of not being led astray by these entanglements. As the introduction to chapter 19 also says, "if you forget life, your vital essence will be unimpaired (*jing bu kui* 精不虧). With your body complete and your vital essence made whole again (*xing quan jing fu* 形全精復), you may become one with heaven (*yu tian wei yi* 與天為一)."[9]

Thus, to be "one with heaven" here means to maintain vital essence of the body, instead of merely its bodily or physical form. We learn from chapter 15, "*Keyi*" (刻意, "Carving the Mind's Intent"), that this first requires nurturing, keeping, and not losing the spirit (respectively, *yang* 養, *shou* 守, and *wu shi* 勿失or *bu kui* 不虧) (Chen, *Zhuangzi*, 416–17).

> The *dao* of purity and plainness is only to keep the spirit; keeping without losing it, becoming one with spirit; this oneness brings with it an unobstructed vital essence, matching with the heavenly order. There is a common saying, "the ordinary person prizes gain, the person of integrity prizes reputation, the worthy person honours (the integrity of his) aspirations, the sage values vital essence." Thus plainness means there is no admixture, purity means there is no loss of the spirit. He who is able to embody purity and plainness is called the true person. [10]

We shall say more about the "true person" in the conclusion. Here, the sense of "spirit" is something that belongs to the heavenly or natural order. It can be nurtured and kept in the human body in order to maintain vital essence. In fact, a few sentences before the above passage, *jing* and *shen* are joined together to give us the notion of a quintessential spirit, *jingshen* (精神), which is said to permeate heaven and earth and nourish all things. [11] As such, *shen* or spirit is a natural force that can be nurtured by the individual to maintain vital essence.

The passage on Zi Qing tells us something about what is involved in this nurturance. It mentions fasting and stilling the heart-mind and not squandering *qi*. Although not stated, an implied sense of spirit (*shen* 神) is involved in his accomplishment of making the bell stand, different from the supernatural spirits (*guishen* 鬼神) mentioned in the passage. The mention of not squandering *qi* tells us that this involves cultivating *qi* in some way.

There were different theories of *qi* during the Warring States period. As we have seen in the case of Duke Huan, some of these directly concern the maintenance of health. We find another theory in the *Mencius*, when Mencius speaks of nurturing "flood-like *qi*" (*hao ran zhi qi* 浩然之氣). He explains this as a *qi* which is

> in the highest degree, vast and unyielding. Nourish it with integrity (*zhi* 直) and place no obstacle in its path and it will fill the space between heaven and earth. It is a *qi* which unites rightness (*yi* 義) and the Way. Deprive it of these and it will starve. It is born of accumulated rightness and cannot be appropriated by anyone through a sporadic show of rightness. Whenever one acts in a way that falls below the standard set in one's heart-mind, it will starve. [12]

Here, Mencius links the nurturing of *qi* to the nurturing of rightness or *yi*, which has its beginning as a germ or sprout in the heart-mind (see *Mencius* 2A:6). As he says, the *qi* will "starve" if it is deprived of the notion of rightness and the Way. Other remarks in *Mencius* 2A:2 suggest that *qi* and rightness mutually reinforce each other. But in the *Zhuangzi*, the most famous passage regarding the cultivation of *qi* makes no mention of rightness.

This occurs in chapter 4, "*Renjianshi*" (人間世, "The Human World"), where Confucius advises his disciple Yan Hui, "Don't listen with your heart-mind, but listen with your *qi*." Here, to "listen with *qi*" is defined as a state of emptiness *xu* (虛), and the latter is in turn defined as "fasting the heart-mind" (*xin zhai* 心齋).[13] In the Zi Qing passage, we have, "I take care not to squander my *qi* (*hao qi*) and must fast so as to still my heart-mind (*jing xin*)." His fasting for several days ultimately results in "forgetting" the body. This is reminiscent of Yan Hui's statement that he can "sit down and forget everything," which is further described as "I smash up my limbs and body, drive out perception and intellect, cast off form, do away with understanding, and make myself identical with the Great Thoroughfare (*tong yu da tong* 同於大通, or identifying with the *dao*)" (Chen, *Zhuangzi*, 217; Watson, *Complete Works*, 90).

Attaining stillness, nurturing spirit, and maintaining vital essence are compatible with a healthy and long life. This is perhaps more so than pursuing wealth, status, and reputation, since we are familiar with circumstances in which the pursuit of these things would be more harmful than beneficial. However, "stillness" is also part of a general equanimity towards life and death. As stated in the introduction to chapter 19 (cited above), "The coming of life cannot be refused and its departure cannot be stopped."

This is a pervasive theme in the *Zhuangzi*. It is linked to fate in chapter 6, "*Dazongshi*" (大宗師, "The Great Ancestral Teacher"), for instance, where it is said that "death and life are fate (*ming* 命), they have the constancy of night and day, they constitute *tian* (heaven). There are matters which humans can do nothing about, and this is a fact about all things" (Chen, *Zhuangzi*, 188). Similarly, the introduction to chapter 19 states, "He who has understood the nature of fate does not pursue what fate has, helplessly, denied." This does not mean that Zhuangzi is a determinist or perhaps even a fatalist who believes that everything is determined and there is no free action, and that whatever anyone does, what is "fated" must inevitably transpire. Instead, the point is aimed at those concerned with slowing the arrival of death or extending life. This is the case with those who believe they have some power through communicating with the spirits via shamanic ritual, for instance.

We cannot say how exactly self-cultivation through "listening with *qi*," "not squandering *qi*," "fasting," "forgetting," "keeping spirit," and maintaining vital essence are supposed to work. In Zi Qing's case, at least, we understand more specifically that fasting leads to a state which enables him to be undistracted by all kinds of worldly things and to concentrate in such a way as to observe the nature of the trees. Besides the mention of not squandering *qi*, no instructions are given about any technique of *qi* and how to maintain vital essence. Nevertheless, it is a popular view that the expressions of *qi* in the *Zhuangzi* mean that it is one among other texts devoted to the promotion of a healthy body and the prolongation of life. But a note of caution is in order here, given the earlier point that there is more to *sheng* than mainte-nance of the body, and what we have said about the *Zhuangzi*'s general attitude towards life and death. To put it succinctly, equanimity and "forget-ting" are compatible with a long life. But to be consciously concerned about the body and prolongation of life is incompatible with equanimity. In other words, self-cultivation in the context of the *Zhuangzi* is focused on cultivat-ing *sheng* (*xiu sheng* 修生), as distinct from cultivating the body only.

Generally, practices involving the nurturance of *qi* and other forms of self-cultivation constitute forms of *gongfu* (功夫), which require many years both to understand and to achieve at a high level. They are usually taught by masters instead of being learned from texts. Even so, the important thing is the experience gained from immersion in a practice. This is the lesson of Wheelwright Bian, who tells Duke Huan that what he is reading "is nothing but the chaff and dregs of the men of old," and explains that his craft is a matter of practical experience with his chisel instead: "Not too gentle, not too hard—you can get it in your hand and feel it in your mind. You can't put it into words, and yet there's a knack to it somehow. I can't teach it to my son, and he can't learn it from me. So I've gone along for seventy years and at my age I'm still chiseling wheels" (Watson, *Complete Works*, 152–53). The lack of specific "bookish" instructions about how to nurture *qi* in the *Zhuangzi* is consistent with this emphasis on self-cultivation as a practice.

This view that the *Zhuangzi* mentions a certain form or forms of self-cultivation that can only be learned through rigorous practice and experience is an attractive one. Part of this attractiveness is a mystical allure, and there have been references to "mysticism" in the literature which include the sto-ries of Zi Qing and Cook Ding.[14] But we should be careful in applying this term to the *Zhuangzi*. As I have stated, it is best to think of nurturing *qi*, *jing*, and *shen* within a form or forms of self-cultivation practice. To someone like Zi Qing, there is nothing mystical in the process of what he accomplishes, since this is a process of harnessing natural forces or what the *Zhuangzi* refers to as *tian*. In his perspective, it is the supernatural art of the *wu* that would count as mystical, instead. Also, we—modern-day readers of the text—may regard Zi Qing's process of self-cultivation as "mystical" because we are ignorant of what is involved, especially in a practical sense, as Wheel-wright Bian reminds us.

Perhaps what is common to the notion of mysticism in the *Zhuangzi* is a sense of the "oneness" of all things.[15] But, again, we should be cautious, since there are different notions of "oneness" in the *Zhuangzi*. As we have seen above, the text mentions being one with spirit and being one with heaven. In the context of the above discussion, to be one with heaven means to maintain vital essence. But this is not its only meaning, and we shall have more to say about this below. Confining ourselves at the moment to the idea of the oneness of things, it should be noted that there is more than one way to understand this. At a metaphysical level, for example, there may be an under-lying argument here in terms of Zhuangzi's concept of "the transformation of things," that any single thing (including humans) may potentially be trans-formed into any other thing whatsoever. This means that there is no underly-ing essence to a "thing." Surprisingly, this is also the argument of the philos-opher of science John Dupré, who writes:

> Essentialists once hoped that genetics would offer up a master key to the differences between various organisms. However, actual genetic knowledge disappointed. The genes that vary most *between* species also tend to vary *within* related species, so genes alone could not delimit individual organisms. Evolution tells us that, if we take a wide enough perspective, there are no sharp lines between species. For a mushroom and a butterfly, or a fern and an elephant, in principle we could trace a continuous series of ancestors back to some first common ancestor, providing a complete connecting sequence with no sharp boundaries within it. If there are no sharp boundaries, then there are certainly no essences that define such boundaries. (Dupré, "Metaphysics of Metamorphosis")

The following further remarks of Dupré's are also reminiscent of the *Zhu-angzi*:

> The criterion of stasis is equally shaky. As we saw with thermodynamic dis-equilibrium,[16] stasis isn't an option for living organisms. Stillness means death. Moreover, all organisms—and cells and organs—have life cycles, and can have very different properties at different stages. A golden-haired boy becomes a grey-haired old man; a larva hatches from an egg and becomes a pupa, imago and finally an insect. If we are committed to thingness, it becomes a real quandary as to how something can undergo such profound changes to its fundamental properties without ceasing to exist. (Dupré, ibid.)

In other words, there is no "thing" as such, since every "thing" is continuous-ly transforming, as Zhuangzi says (Chong, *Zhuangzi's Critique*, chapter 3). Dupré's insight is that it would be unintelligible to talk of transformation at all, "if we are committed to 'thingness.'"

The idea of the oneness of things can be read, too, in terms of a criticism of Confucian morality. As I have argued elsewhere, "the questioning of distinct identity through the images of transformation extends to a leveling out of the hierarchical selves of Confucianism" (Chong, *Zhuangzi's Critique*, 63–64). Thus, the "oneness of things" can be read in different ways and not necessarily in terms of mysticism.

3. SPONTANEITY AND HUMAN AGENCY

Another way in which the story about Zi Qing and other similar stories in the *Zhuangzi* have been interpreted is to take them to be about the cultivation of a skill set involving spontaneous "effortless action." David Velleman, for instance, tells us:

> The performance of artisans like Butcher Ding and Woodworker Qing is guided by an inexpressible knack. . . . The way to exercise such a knack is not to keep one's eye on an ultimate goal, or to follow the precepts of a method, or even to focus on one's actions themselves. On the contrary, Woodworker Qing must forget external goals . . . forget evaluative judgment . . . and, indeed, forget himself. . . . Such forgetfulness is necessary because spontaneous action is inhibited by distinctions between good and bad, right and wrong." (Velleman, "Way of the Wanton," 184)

Velleman compares examples of spontaneous action in the *Zhuangzi* to Mihaly Csikszentmihalyi's description of "flow" experience (Csikszentmihalyi, *Flow*, 53–54, 64). This is "a category of 'optimal experiences' that occur in the course of highly challenging activities in which the subject exercises appropriate skills" (Velleman, "Way of the Wanton," 185). The characteristics of these experiences are an absorption and attentiveness to the activity at hand, the suspension of evaluative judgement, lack of reflection, spontaneity, and loss of consciousness of self.

The main context of Velleman's discussion is what it means to have human agency. For the most part, he analyses Harry Frankfurt's claim that this involves second-order desires and reflectiveness (Frankfurt, "Freedom of the Will," 5–20). Following this analysis, Velleman mentions the *Zhuangzi* and the experience of flow, as we have briefly described, before reverting to Frankfurt. He says, "Frankfurt regards reflective awareness as the distinctive characteristic of humanity. A spiritual ideal of transcending reflective awareness would thus be, in Frankfurt's terms, an ideal of transcending what makes us human. But transcending what makes us human is just what the *Zhuangzi* and Csikszentmihalyi recommend" (Velleman, "Way of the Wanton," 186). Just as the multi-legged millipede mentioned in the *Zhuangzi* need not think about how to walk, "agency is more readily attained because there is no reflectiveness that needs to be overcome." And although humans cannot avoid "exercising their reflective essence," they may transcend it.[17] This does not mean that "forgetfulness" should replace reflectiveness. Instead, non-reflectiveness, or what Frankfurt calls wantonness, "is also a consummate example of agency" (Velleman, "Way of the Wanton," 188).

Velleman's discussion is insightful in that it allows us to understand the power of spontaneous action and what is involved in such action. He argues that human agency is not necessarily or only characterised by the kind of reflectiveness that Frankfurt emphasises. But in any case, the point about Zi Qing is not just how skilful he was or how beautiful his bell stands were as a result. [18] And although it may be legitimately used to make a point about the nature of human agency, this is not the apparent concern of the *Zhuangzi*. Zhuangzi was more concerned about acting in accordance with heaven and, in this regard, the relation between heaven and the human.

In fact, Xunzi criticised Zhuangzi, saying he was "blinded by heaven and did not know the human" (Li, *Xunzi*, 478). Given Xunzi's concern with instituting social order, we should read this as saying that Zhuangzi was not interested in expounding on human institutions and how these might bring about social order. Thus, in Xunzi's view, Zhuangzi was more concerned with how to live a life which is in accord with heaven or nature. Indeed, Zhuangzi was critical of, and parodied, the ritual institutions and distinctions that the Confucians emphasised.

As mentioned before, the Zi Qing story is one of several about "mastering life," given a particular understanding about *sheng* as meaning something more than the nourishment of bodily form. Central to this are the attainment of a state of stillness, nurturing spirit, and maintaining vital essence. We might expect this to be described as "being one with heaven," as mentioned in the introduction to chapter 19. Why, then, does Zi Qing mention "matching heaven with heaven," instead?

4. MATCHING HEAVEN WITH HEAVEN

For Zhuangzi and his followers, *tian*, or "heaven," refers to nature in all its wondrous formations and transformations. The ideal course of action is "not to allow the heart-mind to harm the *dao*, and not to let the human (unnecessarily) help *tian* (不以心損道，不以人助天)" (Chen, *Zhuangzi*, 179). In other words, one should not let the purposeful ideas, artful constructions, classifications, and distinctions made by humans harm nature. One way to understand this is in the context of a criticism of the Confucian ritual and moral system. In this regard, a distinction is made between what belongs to the human and what belongs to nature. For instance, some authors of the Outer Chapters (8–22) of the *Zhuangzi* describe the true nature and capacities of animals and human beings and what it means to act and live naturally. In chapter 9, "*Mati*" (馬蹄, "Horses' Hooves"), the sages who had imposed the rites and morality are compared to craftsmen who have destroyed the material they worked on. That is, they destroyed an original human nature in the process of instituting rites and morality. Prior to this, people had exercised their natural capacities in an unspoiled state by weaving and ploughing, living in harmony with one another and with the animals, there being no distinction between the noble and ignoble, and (relatively speaking) lacking desires. But there seems to be a contradiction, or at least a tension, in the idea that instituting rites and morality is unnatural, while weaving and ploughing are natural. The latter are both crafts. They involve the use of animals, trees, and other things which, according to the craftsmen analogy, have destroyed their true nature.[19]

There are indications that Zhuangzi and some followers were aware of the problem of drawing a firm distinction between heaven and the human. This awareness aligns with the main tendency of the *Zhuangzi*, especially in the Inner Chapters (1–7), to resist such distinctions. In chapter 6, "*Dazongshi*," for instance, Zhuangzi asks, "How is it to be known that what I call *tian* is not human? That what is called human is not *tian*?" (Chen, *Zhuangzi*, 178). In other words, the distinction between *tian* and human action is not always self-evident, and it remains open whether we construe something as one or the other. Instead of a firm distinction, the stories of Cook Ding (Watson, *Complete Works*, 50–51; cf. Velleman's "Butcher Ding") and Zi Qing illustrate a harmonious relation between the two. Significantly, they are both "craftsmen"—those accused of destroying nature in the "Horses' Hooves" chapter as we have just seen. Through years of practice, Cook Ding has an intuitive feel for his object, described as being able to "connect with his spirit" (*yi shen yu* 以神遇) instead of with his eyes (Chen, *Zhuangzi*, 105). The power—or what I shall refer to as a "vital ability"—which he manifests in this connection is no longer dependent on his sense organs, such that he is able to act with remarkable ease and beauty. The notion of "spirit" here connotes the vital ability which he has to connect with the object such that the process and its result (the carving of an ox) are inadequately described as just a human action. Neither can these be attributed to heaven or nature alone. In the case of Zi Qing, as we have seen, his bell stand is thought to be the result of spirits. But he denies that what he does is through some shamanic art of tapping into a realm of spirits. Instead, we may implicitly attribute the "spirit" involved to concentrating such that he is able to match heaven with heaven. That is, he has the vital ability to intuitively perceive the natural pattern of his material and to work harmoniously with it in a marvellous way. The expression "matching heaven with heaven" reminds us that humans, too, are a part of nature and emphasises the natural process of Zi Qing's work. Of course, generally speaking, there is a difficulty about what constitutes the human and what constitutes nature. Someone might ask, for instance, whether it may not have been better to leave the trees alone instead of cutting them down to make bell stands to be used in courtly rituals and musical performances. But this assumes a strict opposition between nature and the human which the story does not assert. What gives content to the natural process in Zi Qing is the notion of a vital ability as a result of self-cultivation and which allows him to connect with nature.

5. CONCLUSION

The story of Zi Qing illustrates a sense of life (*sheng*) in terms of nurturing and guarding its spirit (*shen*) and maintaining its vital essence (*jing*). In this regard, it is important to note that the *Zhuangzi* is not providing a definition of the essence of a human being, because other animals, too, may manifest vital essence. A story in chapter 19, for example, concerns a gamecock whose virtue (in the sense of a "power") becomes complete (*de quan* 德全) such that the other cocks do not dare to engage it.[20] Instead, what is at issue is the vitality of life, whether human or non-human. Combining the two terms *jing* and *shen*, we have the concept of a quintessential essence, *jingshen* (精神), which gives rise to a vital force or energy in the body. This is achieved through not "squandering" *qi* and by fasting—which perhaps also involves meditation—so as to still the heart-mind, leading to the "forgetting" of worldly gains and even of one's own body or self. In Zi Qing's case, this allows a concentrated vital ability to craft an astonishingly beautiful bell stand.

At the same time, the story illustrates an idea that runs through the *Zhuangzi* as a whole, namely, to be "at one with heaven." We have already seen that one meaning of this is to nurture the spirit and maintain vital essence. Another meaning is the harmonious relation between heaven and the human. Unlike some parts of the *Zhuangzi*, there is no tension between heaven and the human in the story of Zi Qing. The passage from chapter 15, "*Keyi*," cited above, concludes with mentioning the "true person." Zhuangzi's true person (*zhen ren* 真人)—which Zi Qing may be said to exemplify—transcends the distinction between heaven and the human and gives content to what it is to live naturally, by harmonising the two.

Furthermore, in the "Dazongshi," Zhuangzi tells us that the true person is able to have a calm attitude towards life's contingencies (encompassed by the notion of "life and death") and has attributes such as not being concerned about being poor, not being ostentatious, not scheming, not having regrets, and not being self-contented about right and wrong. It is also mentioned that the true person "breathes deeply," "breathing through the heels, while the mass of people breathe with their throats" (Chen, *Zhuangzi*, 178–79; Watson, *Complete Works*, 77–80). Apparently, this refers to a form of *qi* cultivation. Together with nurturing the spirit and maintaining vital essence and the other attributes of the true person just mentioned, this gives content to the kind of life that some of Zhuangzi's followers have in mind when they mention "matching heaven with heaven."

Zi Qing is in fact the antithesis of the *wu* or shaman who communicates with spirits in order to attain magical powers. Through this figure, the *Zhuangzi* gives an account of the human potential to act in a way which harnesses a natural vital energy and which is at the same time both aesthetically appealing and powerful, as against (the belief in) attaining supernatural power through shamanic ritual.

ACKNOWLEDGEMENTS

I am grateful to James Sellmann for very helpful comments on an earlier draft of this chapter.

NOTES

1. Chen, *Zhuangzi*, 508. Translations are mine unless stated otherwise. Sometimes, instead of *guishen*, the text mentions *gui*. I shall translate both as "spirit" or "spirits."

2. Chen, *Zhuangzi*, 231–32. See Watson, *Complete Works*, 94–97. See Moeller and D'Ambrosio, *Genuine Pretending*, 86–94, for a description of the parody of Ji Xian. See also Michael J. Puett, "Nothing Can Overcome Heaven."

3. Watson, *Complete Works*, 203, changing Watson's translation of *gui* as "ghost" to "spirit."

4. Watson, *Complete Works*, 204, changing "dictator" to "hegemon."

5. For a "glossary" explanation of *qi*, see Ziporyn, *Zhuangzi*, 215–16: "Vital Energy, Atmospheric Conditions, Breath, Air, Life Force. A key term in Chinese cosmology. . . . It refers to air in general, but more specifically to the breath, and by extension the life force, the absence of which constitutes a living creature's death (referred to as 'cutting off the *qi*'). Cosmologically, it comes to be regarded as the substance of which all things are composed."

6. Mair, *Wandering*, 174, translates as "Understanding Life." This relies on another meaning of *da*. "Mastering Life" captures better the notion of a practice that is involved here.

7. Chen, *Zhuangzi*, 484. 達生之情者，不務生之所無以為；達命之情者，不務命之所無奈何。養形必先之以物，物有餘而形不養者有之矣；有生必先無離形，形不離而生亡者有之矣。生之來不能卻，其去不能止。悲夫！世之人以為養形足以存生而養形果不足以存生，則世奚足為哉！ The second *ming* 命 replaces the original *zhi* 知. See Chen, *Zhuangzi*, 485, n. 3, for an explanation.

8. I spell "heaven" in lowercase to signify the *Zhuangzi*'s non-normative use of *tian*. This distinguishes it from, say, the *Analects* and *Mencius* where *tian* has normative connotations and "Heaven" would be more appropriate.

9. Chen, *Zhuangzi*, 484; Watson, *Complete Works*, 197–98, changing "vitality" to "vital essence."

10. Chen, *Zhuangzi*, 417. 純素之道，唯神是守；守而勿失，與神為一；一之精通，合於天倫。野語有之曰："眾人重利，廉士重名，賢士尚志，聖人貴精。" 故素也者，謂其無所與雜也；純也者，謂其不虧其神也。能體純素，謂之真人。

11. Chen, *Zhuangzi*, 416. 精神四達並流，無所不極，上際於天，下蟠於地，化育萬物。 "*Jingshen* flows everywhere, there is no limit to its reach, above it meets heaven, and below it coils the earth, nurturing the myriad things."

12. Lau, *Mencius*, 2A:2, changing *ch'i* to *qi* and "heart" to "heart-mind."

13. Chen, *Zhuangzi*, 126. Watson, *Complete Works*, 57–58, translates *qi* as "spirit."

14. See Chong, *Zhuangzi's Critique*, 79–81; 157–58, nn. 33, 34, for some of these references.

15. Thanks to James Sellmann for pointing this out.

16. This means that organisms cannot survive in a state of isolated equilibrium, independently of their environment and also of other organisms in symbiotic relationships.

17. Velleman, "Way of the Wanton," 187. See Watson, *Complete Works*, 183, for the example of the millipede.

18. According to Li, *Xiaoyao renjian*, 121, the sounds produced by the bells seemed to emanate from the wooden stands which were carved in the form of various animals. These were therefore not ordinary stands and required intricate carving.

19. See Chong, *Zhuangzi's Critique*, chapter 4, for a detailed discussion.

20. See Watson, *Complete Works*, 204. Unlike Mencius, Zhuangzi does not propound the essence of a human being. We see this in his notion of the transformation of things as mentioned in the earlier discussion above. See also Chong, *Zhuangzi's Critique*, 94, 133–34.

REFERENCES

Chen, Gu-ying 陳鼓應, ed. *Zhuangzi jin zhu jin yi* 莊子今註今譯. Taipei: Taiwan shangwu, 1999.

Chong, Kim-chong. *Zhuangzi's Critique of the Confucians: Blinded by the Human.* Albany, NY: SUNY Press, 2016.

Csikszentmihalyi, Mihaly. *Flow: The Psychology of Optimal Experience.* New York: Harper and Row, 1990.

Dupré, John. "Metaphysics of Metamorphosis." *Aeon*, November 30, 2017. https://aeon.co/essays/science-and-metaphysics-must-work-together-to-answer-lifes-deepest-questions.

Frankfurt, Harry. "Freedom of the Will and the Concept of a Person." *Journal of Philosophy* 68, no. 1 (January 1971): 5–20. Also in *The Importance of What We Care About*, 11–25. Cambridge: Cambridge University Press, 1988.

Lau, D. C., ed. *Mencius.* Hong Kong: Chinese University Press, 2003.

Li, Disheng 李滌生, ed. *Xunzi ji shi* 荀子集釋. Taipei: Xuesheng Shuju, 1994.

Li, Lingfeng 李林峰. *Xiaoyao renjian—Zhuangzi zhuan* 逍遙人間—莊子傳. Beijing: Taihai Publishing, 2017.

Mair, Victor, ed. *Wandering on the Way: Early Taoist Tales and Parables of Chuang Tzu.* Honolulu: University of Hawai'i Press, 1994.

Moeller, Hans-Georg, and Paul J. D'Ambrosio. *Genuine Pretending: On the Philosophy of the Zhuangzi.* New York: Columbia University Press, 2017.

Puett, Michael J. "'Nothing Can Overcome Heaven': The Notion of Spirit in the *Zhuangzi*." In *Hiding the World in the World*, edited by Scott Cook, 248–62. Albany, NY: SUNY Press, 2003.

Velleman, J. David. "The Way of the Wanton." In *Practical Identity and Narrative Agency*, edited by Catriona Mackenzie and Kim Atkins, 169–92. New York: Routledge, 2008.

Watson, Burton, ed. *The Complete Works of Chuang Tzu.* New York: Columbia University Press, 1968.

Yü, Ying-shi 余英時. *Lun tian ren zhi ji* 論天人之際. Taipei: Linking Publishing, 2015.

Ziporyn, Brook, ed. *Zhuangzi: The Essential Writings, with Selections from Traditional Commentaries.* Indianapolis: Hackett, 2009.

Chapter Fifteen

The Naked Scribe

The Skill of Dissociation in Society

Hans-Georg Moeller

Lord Yuan of Song ordered a figure to be drawn, and all the scribes came. They received instructions and bowed, and then stood in line, licking their brushes and mixing their ink. Half of them had to stand outside. One scribe came late. Leisurely and in no hurry, he received the instructions and bowed. He did not stand in line, and since went to the living quarters. When the Duke sent someone to inspect him, he was seen with his clothes taken off, sitting cross-legged, naked. The ruler said: "Alright! This is a '*zhen*uine' (*zhen* 真) man of the brush."[1]

1. A SKILL STORY WITHOUT SKILL

The tale of an unnamed government scribe working naked is one of the lesser known and discussed of the many skill stories in the *Zhuangzi* (莊子). Perhaps there are good reasons for its neglect. It is comprised of just a few dozen characters—five, to be precise. Unlike other such miniatures—which are no rarity in the *Zhuangzi*, or in early Chinese philosophical and historical texts in general—it could be perceived as lacking grandeur. Compared, for instance, with emblematic short narratives like Hundun's death (*Hundun zhi si* 混沌之死) or the dream of the butterfly (*hudie meng* 蝴蝶夢), there is little drama or tragedy and not much fanciful imagination in it. Furthermore, it occurs in the middle of chapter 21 (*Tian Zifang* 田子方), the second to last of the Outer Chapters (*wai pian* 外篇), which used to be regarded as less authentic and valuable than the seven Inner Chapters (*nei pian* 內篇). Not long ago, Western scholars focusing on such a "marginal" passage of the book would have opened themselves to criticism for not dealing with the philosophical and philological core of the *Zhuangzi*.[2] Perhaps most importantly, though, this somewhat obscure skill story remains all but quiet about the practical skill of its protagonist. It says nothing about his artisanship and ends before he has even made the first brushstroke.

Given a Daoist penchant for the obscure and, what is more, for the frequent use of paradox, it may be permissible to approach the story of the naked scribe paradoxically. If so, it can be regarded as important, not despite the fact that it is a skill story that does not talk about skill but precisely because of it. Taking this liberty, I will make an effort here to emancipate this often ignored tale and try to show how it connects philosophically and stylistically with many of the much more prominent skill stories. I believe that a thorough reading of this narrative can eventually allow one to see the other skill stories and their philosophical significance from a perhaps unexpected perspective. There can be no doubt that the skill stories constitute an essential narrative genre in the *Zhuangzi*: they are instrumental in making philosophical points. The way in which a reader understands them will be indicative of his or her understanding of the *Zhuangzi* as a whole. The story of the naked scribe in section 21.7 may thus serve just as well as an inroad to the intricacies of this Daoist classic.

From a sinological perspective, the story leaves readers—at least those of a later age—wondering what kind of "figure" (*tu* 圖) the ruler had commissioned. While the seventh-century commentator Cheng Xuanying (成玄英) assumes that the word *tu* here refers to geographical maps (Guo, *Zhuangzi*, 314), it can also plausibly denote cosmological diagrams, such as the legendary "River Chart" (*Hetu* 河圖), or a portrait of the ruler or his ancestors.[3] Not really knowing what the brushwork in question precisely is, we still do know something about the craftsmen: they were scribes (*shi* 史), that is, court officials, or, in contemporary language, government employees or public servants, in charge of producing and managing official documents.

While placed at a ruler's court, and in a historical context, the story is not about any known or notable historical event. And while Lord Yuan of Song, the only named character, was a real-world figure, the episode is quite irrelevant to his biography. He does not appear here as a historical agent, but merely provides the story with a historical and political *setting*. In a similar function, he is found in a much more famous—and more obviously fantastic—narrative in *Zhuangzi* 24.6, namely that of Carpenter Shi (*Jiang Shi* 匠石), slicing off a piece of dirt from another man's nose. Unlike didactical accounts of historical events believed to be true—which abound in early Chinese texts and usually fulfil the function of proving by example a specific ethical, political, or strategic point—this story operates in the hazy realm of pseudo-historical fiction.

The question, then, is this: If this tale is neither about any specific skill nor about a historical exemplar of skilfulness, what is it about—and how can it be a skill story, and a paradigmatic one at that?

2. A READING OF THE STORY OF THE NAKED SCRIBE

The exercise of skill is clearly not a narrative focus of this skill story. If we look closely at the wording of the final sentence, the naked scribe is not even praised for his skill there. And how could he be praised for it prior to having done anything? The ruler does not commend the extraordinary talent or marvellous artistry of the scribe, unlike, for instance, the rulers commending Cook Ding (*Pao Ding* 庖丁) and Woodworker Qing (*Zi Qing* 梓慶) in the more famous skill stories in sections 3.2 and 19.11 of the *Zhuangzi*, but rather his paradoxical "genuineness" (*zhen* 真)—and precisely because we conceive of *zhen* as paradoxical (as will be explained in more detail below), Paul D'Ambrosio and I prefer to translate it not as "genuine" but as *zhen*uine (see Moeller and D'Ambrosio, *Genuine Pretending*, 126–37). The ruler's judgement that the scribe is a "*zhen*uine man of the brush" does not relate to what the scribe has produced, or how exactly he did so, but to how he goes about his job. The praise therefore, precisely speaking, does not directly address the skills of the scribe, but his professional attitude.

This fact should direct the reader's attention away from a primary concern with craftsmanship or aesthetics. Instead, the story's narrative focus is first and foremost on how to approach one's work. It is not necessary to impose an orthodox Marxist outlook on the story and to interpret it in terms of a suppressive relation between an aristocratic ruling class, represented by Lord Song of Yuan, and a class of laborers, represented by the scribes, who had to work under conditions of economic exploitation and existential alienation. It is equally inappropriate, however, to completely abstract the interpretation of the story from the concrete sociopolitical context in which it takes place and which constitutes its basic narrative framework.

In ancient China, professions were commonly inherited or closely tied to the social position one was born into. There was little social mobility, and people could not freely choose a line of work or acquire training or schooling outside their kinship group. Children of farmers would normally become farmers, just as children of craftsmen would become craftsmen. The same was true for scribes. Until at least the second century BCE, "the status of scribe was hereditary at this early stage of the empire and had probably been handed down from generation to generation for centuries" (Yates, "Soldiers, Scribes, and Women," 350). Scribes, of course, had to be literate and were therefore part of a small educated stratum. However, among this top stratum of society they were among the "lower orders" (ibid., 339), and, what is more, their social status did not provide them with any personal independence or liberty. The profession of the scribe, as an integral part of an ancient system of enforcing government regulations and control, was itself subject to tight regulations and controls (see Yates, "Soldiers, Scribes, and Women").

The story clearly depicts the profession of the scribe as a uniform group of intellectual, but nevertheless thoroughly subordinated, employees—perhaps faintly comparable to professional academics in our own times. A vivid description of their servility makes up the first part of the narrative: the ruler calls them, and they all heed the call. Obediently they receive their orders, submissively they bow down, obsequiously they lick their pencils and mix their ink, and sheepishly they queue up one after another in a long row that leaves many of them out in the open. While these adverbs are not expressively mentioned in the story, the reader is all but forced to supply them by him- or herself when envisioning the scene as it is described.

The description of the diligent and dutiful group of submissive civil servants also clearly evokes stereotypical images of the Confucian scholar. On the one hand, Confucianism (*rujia* 儒家) was associated with the culture of script (*wen* 文) and historical record keeping (*shi* 史) at the time.[4] On the other, it was just as much linked to an ethics of assiduous reverence to political authority and unwavering adherence to rules of proper comportment and attire. Specifically, the book of *Zhuangzi* contains numerous passages painting a picture of Confucian scholars, often represented by Confucius himself or by one of his disciples, as wilful servants of a corrupted state and obsessed with conformity and propriety. The long line of scribes in the narrative thus presents an image that could easily be taken to symbolise a caste of streamlined and compliant scholar-officials supporting a regime of "actually existing Confucianism" in late pre-Qin or early Han dynasty China.

The image of the long line of servile scribes sets the scene for the second part of the short narrative. Something surprising happens. A final scribe appears, but, contrary to what should be expected, he is neither ashamed nor worried about his being late and is in no haste at all. He, too, picks up the instructions and bows (*yi* 揖), but he does not line up with all the others outside the hall. Probably because he wants to avoid the inconvenience of having to stand out in the open—this is how the "since" (*yin* 因) in the text can be interpreted—he returns to his living quarters. Presumably the scribes were for practical reasons assigned such living quarters in the vicinity of the ruler's court.

The behaviour of this scribe is literally out of line with that of the other scribes. Not only does he arrive on his own well after them and without apology, but moreover he seems oblivious to the seriousness of the event. He displays neither eagerness nor dedication. Altogether, his behaviour is rather disrespectful. The oddness of the man's behaviour does not escape the ruler, and so he sends an underling to check on the strange scribe. Through this servant's eyes readers witness the climax of the tale: the scribe is sitting naked (*luo* 臝; the term does not necessarily imply complete nudity—it can also mean "half naked") and in a cross-legged position in his lodge. This posture may be interpreted as meditative or preparatory for drawing a chart or painting a portrait, but readers are not explicitly told so. Rather, one can only marvel at this revealing but not quite revelatory image of the naked scribe. The story then ends abruptly with a verdict from the lord of Song. For him, the naked scribe is *zhen*. But, again, readers are left to their own devices to figure out why this is so and what it means.

The depiction of the naked scribe's behaviour is in direct contrast to that of all the other scribes depicted at the beginning of the story. They are many and arrived on time. He is single and a latecomer. They are eager and nervous; he is nonchalant and serene. They line up properly, but he does not and returns to his personal space. They stand up; he sits down. Most strikingly, he takes off his clothes, whereas they, we can trust, are dressed in their official robes or uniforms.

Evidently, the multiple contrasts in behaviour indicate an "ideological" contrast. While the lined-up scribes connote Confucianism, the naked scribe combines a whole range of Daoist attributes: singular and alone,[5] he is calm and his mind is at ease. He shows no specific concern for ritual conventions, and, most notably, he is comfortable being (half) naked, just as, for instance, the diver at the Lüliang (呂梁) waterfall who appears in another famous skill story in the *Zhuangzi* (section 19.10). Philosophically most relevant, however, is that he is praised as being *zhen*, that is, as *zhen*uine. Thereby, he is explicitly given the status of a "*zhen* person" (*zhen ren* 真人). The *Zhuangzi* uses, and possibly even coined, this term as a Daoist title that somewhat ironically mirrors established Confucian honourific appellations of the time, such as, most importantly, *sheng ren* (聖人, sage).

It is feasible to read the lord's final verdict in a humorous key since the story entails numerous comical clues. Its major stylistic tool is its emphasis on the opposition between the "normal" government scribes depicted at the beginning of the story and the naked scribe who follows them. This opposition has clearly "carnivalesque" characteristics, to employ a concept introduced by Mikhail Bakhtin. The very profession of the scribe already represents a system of regulations and control that, quite literally, prescribed conformity throughout society. Their subservient and homogenous behaviour in the story signals the exercise of social conformity and collective obedience to codes of conduct. At the same time, the description of this behaviour has satirical overtones. The image of the scribes simultaneously licking their brushes, paired with the somewhat grotesque extension of their line far beyond the court hall, seems almost cartoon-like, at least to readers today. It can be reasonably assumed, though, that the mocking nature of this image would also not have been lost to people in ancient China.

The lampooning of representatives of sociopolitical power and a (corrupted) mainstream ethics is a core element of the carnivalesque, particularly if it is achieved by means of a direct contrast with an inverted mirror image—which, in our story, is presented in the form of the naked scribe. Nudity, along with its associations of a non-conformist "naturalism" and connotations of sexuality liberty, is a prime carnivalesque tool. Symbolically it reveals the nakedness of a governing morality and the emptiness of its power while at the same time conveying feelings of liberation. The debunking of sociopolitical authority through satirical critique and carnivalesque humour provides comic relief and has, in Bakhtin's terms, the cathartic effect of providing a relaxation of the "moral fear" (Bakhtin, *Literatur und Karneval*, 35) produced by the experience of relentless social constraints in everyday life and constantly looming sanctions for moral transgressions.

Once the carnivalesque features of the story and, in particular, of the character of the naked scribe are noticed, the verdict of the lord of Song must appear in an ironical light. It becomes the final pun of a comical tale. The ruler, himself a representative of social control, paradoxically turns into a spokesperson for the subversion of Confucian discipline by conferring an (ironic) honourific title on the naked scribe. The naked scribe becomes the Daoist anti–*sheng ren*, or anti-sage, namely the *zhen ren*. This is an act of carnival—just as when in medieval European carnival the plebs would assume, for a short period of time, the mantles of the high clergy and aristocracy.

It is important to note that if the story is read in such a carnivalesque way, the character of the naked scribe cannot be regarded as a straightforward role model. If the story is fundamentally humouristic, then the naked scribe, too, is a humouristic figure. As a carnivalesque anti-sage, he is not merely a "better" sage than the Confucian ones. More radically, the naked scribe mocks not only the representatives of a Confucian discipline, but also the very mode of establishing moral and political idols. The Daoist *zhen ren* does not seek to replace the Confucian idols but to subvert them by means of a carnivalesque critique.

This being said, it must also be emphasised that there is more to the naked scribe than just satire and subversion. While he is by no means a moral and cultural hero and straightforward role model calling for emulation, he does embody some paradoxical Daoist "virtues." As a satirical and comically exaggerated character, he should be immune to idolisation, but he still conveys a certain Daoist teaching. This teaching is medicinal and therapeutic in nature. It is not about achieving extraordinary sage status but about learning to endure a regular, common life. By means of humour, and other means, the character of the naked scribe allows an insight into the art of survival and of achieving some sort of contentment amidst the discontent and discomfort brought about by "civilisation."

In early China the occupation of scribe, as must be noted again, could not be freely chosen but was allotted by birth—just as most other occupations at the time. The vast majority of people had to live and work strictly according to the roles prescribed to them by society. There was no meaningful "agency" or "privacy" in the modern sense for the common person, neither within the kinship group nor within one's profession. A mainstream Confucian role ethics, and role model ethics, fulfilled the function of glamourising such socially prescribed roles as being a perfect embellishment of human nature; it encouraged people to identify and fully commit to them. A Daoist negative ethics, however, did not accept these assumptions about the inherent goodness of social roles and rather looked for ways to effectively cope with or alleviate the pressures and frustrations produced by the sociopolitical conditions of the time, including those produced by a role and role model ethics. The story of the naked scribe, I believe, fits into this basic trajectory of Daoist philosophy—and so do the skill stories in the *Zhuangzi* in general.

If seen in its actual historical context, our story can hardly be understood as embellishing the art of the scribe. To become a scribe did not mean, in a modern sense, to follow an inner "calling" or "vocation." A calling, as the Anglicised form of vocation, in its originally religious (Christian) sense, meant being called by God to devote one's life to Him, and thus to join the clergy or to serve Him in any other full-time social role. The term was eventually secularised and could refer to any profession. Reflecting the modern "age of authenticity" (Taylor, *A Secular Age*, 473–503), it came to imply that any person has some unique talents or gifts that can be expressed in one's job. Accordingly, artists and artisans were regarded as following an inner calling and as manifesting their individuality in their work. Such a connection between authenticity and art deeply influenced the image of the artist in modern Europe, particularly in Romanticism. As a side effect, it also thoroughly informed a modern understanding of the skill stories in the *Zhuangzi*.

However, as we saw, the understanding of a profession or a craft as a calling does not correspond to the social reality of early China. One should be very careful not to impose it on the skill stories of the *Zhuangzi*, which are typically about artisans and other employed professionals—such as the naked scribe—of (relatively) low social rank. A profession or craft in ancient China had very little to do with notions of authenticity, but a lot with notions of an inevitable fate, or, more precisely, *ming* (命), to use a term that appears frequently throughout the *Zhuangzi*. *Ming* were the circumstances one found oneself placed or born into. They could be natural circumstances, but also of a social and political kind. They were not seen as indicative of or corresponding to the unique characteristics of an individual. *Ming* was the often rather difficult situation a person happened to have to cope with. Therefore, it is prudent *not* to conceive of artisanship and the skilful exercise of a craft in the

Zhuangzi in terms of the modern authenticity paradigm as represented by the notion of a calling. Instead, artisanship has to be understood in the context of hereditary professions and the notion of *ming*. Accordingly, we must assume that the naked scribe did not regard his job as his individual vocation, but rather as an inescapable social assignment that he was forced to comply with. And this he did.

Despite its subversive and carnivalesque characteristics, the story is not one of rebellion against social conventions or against *ming*. To the contrary, it illustrates how someone complies with his *ming*—though, admittedly, in a quite unusual way. As their subservient behaviour shows, the normal scribes in the story all committed themselves meekly to their role. They seem to have completely internalised their roles and "become" them (see Ames, *Confucian Role Ethics*). They have personally integrated themselves into the government system that they were born to serve. To the contrary, the strange—and in carnivalesque fashion comically exaggerated—behaviour of the naked scribe demonstrates a *dissociation* from his social role. He does not line up with and dress like all the others. At the same time, he still complies with his task and sets out to do his job. There is an obvious *incongruity* between his actual performance and the common expectations of the job. In other words, his actual performance (*shi* 實 or *xing* 形) and job or title (*ming* 名) do not fully match. The naked scribe scribes bizarrely and unlike all other scribes. In response to Confucius's famous maxim of having to "father fatherly" (*fu fu* 父父, see *Analects* 12.11), one might say that this scribe does not scribe "scribely."

The normal scribes who all scribe scribely are mocked as contrived and suppressed. Different from them, the incongruent scribe, who has dissociated himself from his profession to some extent, is depicted as being at ease and calm. This existential state of ease as expressed in his nakedness and posture—and not his actual brushwork, which the story says nothing about— makes the lord of Song call him a *zhen* scribe. We must conclude, then, that *zhen* here neither indicates an authentic commitment to an art nor a genuine devotion to a profession. Instead, it indicates the naked scribe's capacity to dissociate himself from the pressures of his profession and to maintain a state of ease while exercising it. The naked scribe thus emerges as a metaphorical, carnivalesque, and ironic illustration of the unlikely skill of achieving contentment in one's allotted fate, or, in Chinese, of achieving *an ming* (安命), to once more make use of terminology used elsewhere in the text. The naked scribe's *zhen*uineness consists in his paradoxical ability to maintain sanity in his socially prescribed role by not fully committing to or over-identifying with it. Somewhat paradoxically, this very skill of dissociation will allow him, as we may presume along with the lord of Song, to perform his task well and to be a skilful scribe. The point of such a reading, then, is that "skill" in being a scribe does not primarily consist in being able to draw excellent figures for an authority, but in being able to exercise one's allotted task in society with as much grace and as little damage to others and oneself as may be possible, given the respective situation.

As a carnivalesque illustration of the capacity to achieve contentment in contingent, inevitable, and potentially harmful and oppressive circumstances, the naked scribe corresponds to another more famous protagonist in the *Zhuangzi*: the superhuman diver at the Lüliang waterfall in section 19.10 mentioned briefly above. Both stories contrast formal and somewhat stiff Confucian behaviour with Daoist ease; and both stories operate with fictional exaggeration and caricaturist elements. Moreover, the Daoist protagonists in both stories evoke images of nudity; although the diver is not explicitly described as nude, readers will not fail to imagine him so when he is depicted emerging from the water. Importantly, upon being questioned by Confucius about his *dao* (道, way), the diver denies having one. Instead, he explains that he was born on land and was content (*an* 安) there, that he grew up with the water and was content there as well, and that thus he was capable of complying with a contingent fate (*ming*). If read in conjunction, both stories can be understood as humouristic tales of living well and being at ease within an environment that cannot be chosen and that is difficult to navigate—one natural and the other one social.

3. THE STORY OF THE NAKED SCRIBE IN THE CONTEXT OF THE *TIAN ZIFANG*[6] CHAPTER

The principles underlying the composition or editing of chapters in the *Zhuangzi* are unclear, or, to put it more bluntly, there does not seem to exist a general rule according to which they were put together. Nevertheless, individual chapters commonly contain passages and anecdotes revolving around similar literary motifs and philosophical themes, such as, to give just one example, the intriguing chapter on the "Markers of Full Virtuosity" (*De Chong Fu*, 德充符), which collects stories of cripples and mutilated criminals paradoxically supposed to illustrate the Daoist notion of *de* (德, vitality, power, or health).

The main literary motif connecting most, if not all, of the eleven episodes of the *Tian Zifang* chapter is a, usually contrastive, pairing of a Daoist (or Daoist-leaning) with a Confucian (or Confucian-leaning) protagonist, teaching, or attitude. In section 21.4, for instance, Confucius (Kongzi 孔子) is instructed by Lao Dan (老聃), that is, Laozi himself. Section 21.3 consists of a conversation between Confucius and his disciple Yan Yuan (顏淵). Here, Confucius, as is common in the *Zhuangzi*, ironically becomes a spokesperson for Daoist views. Other sections, such as 21.1 and 21.2, present fictional Daoist masters with funny "master names" (one almost wants to compare them with today's rap names), such as "Master-Lot Field" and "Snow-Master Warmuncle" (Wenbo Xuezi 溫伯雪子) in discussion with a feudal lord, and, respectively, a man from Confucius's home state, Lu (Lu ren 魯人). The latter characters are associated with Confucianism, either by their social rank or place of residence.

Two pronouncements summarise the various criticisms brought forth against Confucianism in this chapter quite well. In section 21.2, Snow-Master Warmuncle declares that the *junzi* (君子) of the Central States, or the Confucian "gentlemen," are "enlightened about ritual and righteousness, but ignorant about the knowledge of the human heart" (*ming hu li yi er lou yu zhi ren xin* 明乎禮義而陋於知人心). In section 21.5, Zhuangzi appears in person to tell the (presumably Confucian) Duke Ai of Lu (Lu Ai Gong 魯哀公) that "just because someone is wearing a certain kind of clothing does not yet mean that he necessarily knows something about the way" (*wei qi fu zhe, wei bi zhi qi dao ye* 為其服者，未必知其道也). Both statements clearly mock Confucian pedantry and hypocrisy and decry its lack of understanding of the human condition.

However, the criticisms of Confucianism are not the main focus of chapter 21. Just as in the story of the naked scribe, their function is to provide a background for illustrations of Daoist teachings. One major Daoist philosophical theme permeates explicitly or implicitly the whole chapter: an affirmation of change and the ability to go along with it with equanimity. In typical Daoist fashion, this core topic, which has a strong presence already in the *Laozi*, extends to a philosophy of nature as well as to a sociopolitical philosophy. Both philosophical dimensions are approached from what can be called an existential perspective. In short, the point of Daoist equanimity is to be capable of accepting and living well with the "transformation of things" (*wu hua* 物化) in nature—and thus to accept one's mortality—as well as to be able to achieve contentment in the social world despite inevitable ups and downs and the emotional stress they produce. The following passage from section 21.4 is taken from Lao Dan's speech to Confucius and represents the integration of these two aspects into one well-known philosophical teaching:

> Beasts which eat grass are not irked by a change of pastures, nor creatures born in water by a change of waters, for in passing through a small alteration great permanence is not lost. Neither pleasure and anger, nor sadness and joy, enter a halting place in the breast. The world is that in which the ten thousand things are of one. If you grasp the oneness and unite with it, the four limbs and hundred members become dust and grime; death and life, end and start, become a daytime and a nighttime, and nothing can disturb you, least of all distinctions drawn by gain and loss, and between good and ill fortune. [7]

Daoists, it is suggested, are good at allowing for changes to occur, and they do not get upset by them. Their underlying strategy is to be capable of "dissociating oneself from one's ego," to freely translate the famous expression *wu sang wo* (吾喪我) occurring in section 2.1 of the *Zhuangzi*. Daoists do not take things personally, neither their own death nor what occurs to them in a society where one's role is assigned by coincidence of birth and where larger sociopolitical circumstances are beyond the control of the individual.

Equanimity towards death and the capacity to accept low social rank, and thereby to develop skill in one's assigned task, are the intertwined themes of a little-known skill story directly preceding the tale of the naked scribe (section 21.6):

> Considerations of rank and reward did not enter the mind of Baili Xi. So he fed the cattle, and the cattle fattened. This made Duke Mu of Qin forget the lowness of Baili's position, and he entrusted him with the government. Considerations of life and death did not enter the mind of the lord of Yu, and therefore he was fit to move others.[8]

Indifference to one's mortality and to what from the perspective of mainstream culture at the time was regarded as a non-reputable profession, it must be implied, both result from the capacity to mentally and emotionally free oneself from an over-identification with one's fate. This dissociation, though, it must be emphasised, should not be understood as a realisation of the inauthenticity of one's role compared with a supposed real self, but, quite to the contrary, as the realisation that social personhood, as well as life, are contingent and transitory states which should not give rise to an all too rigid and inflexible ego construction. A Daoist can withstand the temptation to invest his or her intellectual and emotional efforts into establishing notions of an unchangeable identity based on the present circumstances of one's life. This very skill allows a Daoist, as the story signals, to be a good cattle feeder as much as a good ruler. A cattle feeder who is not frustrated with his role can feed the cattle with equanimity and therefore is enabled to do it well; and someone with a small ego who is not obsessed with his power and success will probably be able to be a good and well-liked politician.

The same Daoist teaching, with its emphasis on the mundane sociopolitical aspects of an existential equanimity and on the skill of dissociating oneself from the esteem or dis-esteem stemming from one's social roles is expressed in a longer narrative towards the end of the *Tian Zifang* chapter in section 21.10:

> Jian Wu asked Sunshu Ao: "You became three times chief minister, and did not put on any airs; you were three times dismissed from this position, and did not express any disappointment. At first I found you suspicious, but now I see that you breathe regularly and relaxed. How do you operate your mind?" Sunshu Ao replied: "How should I be better than others? When the position

came, I thought it could not be rejected; when it went away, it thought it could not be kept. I took it that getting or losing it had nothing to do with me, and so I did not express any disappointment—that was all. How should I be better than others? And, also, I did not know if the esteem was due to the position or to me. If it was due to the position, it had nothing to do with me; if it was due to me, it had nothing to do with the position. While wandering around and looking in all directions, what time do I have to care about others regarding me as of high or low status?"

Confucius heard of this and said, "The *zhen ren* of old could not be talked into anything by a wise guy, nor be seduced by a beauty, nor be conned by a thief. Neither Fuxi nor Huang Di could buddy up with them. Death and life are surely great, but they made no difference to them; how much less could rank and reward do so? In this way, their spirits could cross the Tai mountain and find no obstacle there; they could enter the deepest springs and not get wet; they could have the lowest and meanest positions and feel no frustration. They were all over heaven and earth; the more they let others have, the more they had for themselves."[9]

As formulated in Jian Wu's[10] question, the story—which also contains humorous elements, particularly in the irreverent and hyperbolic comment put in Confucius's mouth—is about how Daoists "operate their heart-minds" (*yong xin* 用心), that is, about their mindset. Sunshu Ao's answer to this quite fundamental existential question is, fortunately for a modern-day reader, relatively clear cut. He simply does not think in a judgemental way about good and bad luck—just like the "old man at the fort" in the popular Daoist tale found in *Huainanzi* (淮南子) 18.9 (*sai weng shi ma* 塞翁失马). Most importantly, he does not relate twists of fate, and the acclaim or rejection that results from them, to himself. It is clear that the dissociation from his role, along with the attached value judgements projected onto him, is not grounded in the idea that the role does not reflect his true calling. The point is that no social role whatsoever should be constructed as a calling and personalised in this way. Identity, it is implied, never precedes roles but is an effect of erroneously personalising social roles. From a Daoist perspective, personal vanities, anxieties, and discontents result from such false personalisations of social roles and social status. Social roles and social status are unavoidable; they come and go with life in society. Sunshu Ao's performative skill consists in being able to not internalise them—and to thus perform his tasks free from skill-diminishing factors such as the just mentioned personal vanities, anxieties, and discontents.

The stories of Sunshu Ao and the naked scribe both use physiological imagery to illustrate the existential ease resulting from operating one's mind in dissociation from social functions and ascriptions. The naked scribe walks without haste and completely "chills out" before scribing, as indicated by his posture and nudity. Sunshu Ao breathes calmly. In the *Zhuangzi*, nudity and relaxed breathing (which is also referred to in the famous opening passage

2.1 of the *Qi Wu Lun* (齊物論) chapter depicting Nanguo Ziqi (南郭子綦) losing his ego) are prime bodily indicators of a state of tranquillity and heightened vitality. They signal the kind of immunity to existential afflictions—such as the fear of death, sexual and ideological obsessions, or overwhelming ambitions—that a Daoist Confucius extols in provocative and at times grotesquely inflated imagery at the end of the tale of Sunshu Ao.

Confucius equates Sunshu Ao with the "*zhen ren* of old" (*gu zhi zhen ren* 古之真人). The naked scribe, too, was praised as *zhen* by the lord of Song. Read in conjunction, the stories of the two men make it obvious that *zhen ren* are neither great moral exemplars, such as the Confucian *sheng ren*, nor fairytale-like superhumans such as the *xian ren* (仙人, immortals) venerated in religious Daoism (*dao jiao* 道教). Unlike these Confucian or Daoist role models, they are neither awe-inspiring political or spiritual leaders nor wondrous beings outside of or at the fringes of society. Instead, they are common people with regular jobs and subject to being hired and fired. They live in the midst of society and are in this sense "real people"—as the expression *zhen ren* could also be translated. With Sunshu Ao one could ask: How should they be better than others? Or, speaking with the diver at the Lüliang waterfall, one can say: They have no special way (*dao*). Their skill does not consist in any unique artistic or otherwise spectacular talent but relates to the way in which they operate their minds so that they can stay sane and do their jobs well—or cope well with losing them.

A good definition of *zhen* is given by Tian Zifang in the first section of chapter 21. Explaining why his teacher Donggu Shunzi (東郭順子, Eastside Go-with-the-Flow-Master) is *zhen*, he says: "He is a person by demeanour, but naturally he is empty. Going along with circumstances *zhen* is maintained" (*ren mao er tian xu, yuan er bao zhen* 人貌而天虛，緣而葆真). Decisively distinct from the modern authentic individual, the *zhen ren* has no identity. He assumes social personhood merely provisionally through behavioural performance. This performance is contingent upon extra-personal circumstances and does not lead to false ego constructions. In this paradoxical way, genuineness is maintained. This Daoist genuineness consists in not falsely identifying with social roles. *Zhen ren* assume no consistent selfhood. Therefore their social performances can never be in bad faith or in violation of their true nature. To say that someone acts fake or insincere implies that a social role performance can, and ought to, correspond to a true self. If no assumption of such a true self is made to begin with, there can be no fakeness or insincerity. Paul D'Ambrosio and I use the expression "genuine pretending" to convey this basic Daoist existential idea.[11] We translate *zhen* as *zhen*uine to indicate a paradoxical kind of genuineness that conceives of the social persona as genuine not when it reflects a true self, but when it does not lead to the construction of identity. In this way, *zhen* is maintained.

4. CONCLUSION: *ZHEN*UINE SKILL

When read as a skill story, the story of the naked scribe is not primarily about the skill of scribing—it says nothing about this skill. It is explicitly about the skill of being a *zhen*uine scribe. A *zhen*uine scribe, however, is a scribe who is capable of dissociating himself from the profession of a scribe. It is a scribe who, like Eastside Go-with-the-Flow-Master, maintains *zhen* by going along with circumstances. This skill of dissociation from social roles and performances allows common people to not construct false ideas of personal identity, and thereby it allows them to avoid frustration in the case of social failure and to avoid conceit in the case of social success. The skill of operating one's mind in such a way in turn gives rise to a state of ease and relaxation that supplies a person with immunity from mental torment and obsessive afflictions in everyday life. Humour, thanks to its inbuilt incongruity, is a mental, and literary, skill that helps subvert over-identifications with social roles, and thanks to its relaxing and relieving effects, it contributes to remaining sane. It also helps one to distance oneself from larger-than-life role models manifesting illusionary and potentially harmful moral, spiritual, or political ideals.

The skills of dissociation from roles and role models, of maintaining *zhen*, of achieving ease and being humorous, and of staying sane are basic Daoist existential and social knacks. They are entirely mundane and free from mystical, metaphysical, or religious speculation. If one can cultivate these skills, he or she may be expected, like the naked scribe, to perform his or her job—that is, the role society has ascribed to one—without too much stress and anxiety, and therefore to be reasonably good at it. Daoist skill is about such things as being a good carpenter, or a good scribe, or, for that matter, about being good at falling off carts when drunk (*Zhuangzi* 19.2). It is about doing alright in a society where one has little control and power. To achieve some degree of vitality in a society experienced as a system of control, regulation, discipline, and as contingent fate, is, as the story of the naked scribe paradigmatically illustrates, the prime concern of the skill stories in the *Zhuangzi*.

NOTES

1. 宋元君將畫圖。眾史皆至，受揖而立；舐筆和墨，在外者半。有一史後至者，儃儃然不趨，受揖不立，因之舍。公使人視之，則解衣般礴，臝。君曰：「可矣，是真畫者也。 In this essay, all quotations from the *Zhuangzi* are taken from the *Chinese Text Project* database. The indication of section numbers from this and other Chinese texts follows this database. Translations from the *Zhuangzi* are mine if not indicated otherwise. The English translation of the *Zhuangzi* by James Legge as provided by the *Chinese Text Project* has been consulted as well as the English translations by A. C. Graham and Victor Mair.

2. Among others, Esther Klein has presented a convincing argument against a general privileging of the "Inner Chapters" over other parts of the *Zhuangzi*; see Klein, "Inner Chapters."

3. The *Chinese Text Project* lists only one other passage in pre-Qin (秦) and Han (漢) literature including the expression *hua tu* (畫圖), namely section 60.4 of the first-century text *Lun Heng* (論衡, Critical Essays). There it means "painting a portrait" (of a high government official or ruler).

4. It might be more appropriate to speak here of "Ruism" rather than "Confucianism" when referring to the bureaucratic culture and not to the philosophy associated with Confucius, both of which can be designated as *rujia* in Chinese. However, the term "Ruism" is less commonly used in English and, in my personal view, sounds odd. Therefore I prefer using "Confucianism."

5. Aloneness (*du* 獨) is a quality of quite some importance in Daoist philosophy as early as in the *Laozi* (老子).

6. The name Tian Zifang can be translated as "Master-Lot Field" (see below).

7. 草食之獸不疾易藪，水生之蟲不疾易水，行小變而不失其大常也，喜怒哀樂不入於胸次。夫天下也者，萬物之所一也。得其所一而同焉，則四支百體將為塵垢，而死生終始將為晝夜而莫之能滑，而況得喪禍福之所介乎！ (See Graham, *Chuang-Tzu*, 131. Translation modified.)

8. 百里奚爵祿不入於心，故飯牛而牛肥，使秦穆公忘其賤，與之政也。有虞氏死生不入於心，故足以動人。

9. 肩吾問於孫叔敖曰：「子三為令尹而不榮華，三去之而無憂色。吾始也疑子，今視子之鼻間栩栩然，子之用心獨奈何？」孫叔敖曰：「吾何以過人哉！吾以其來不可卻也，其去不可止也，吾以為得失之非我也，而無憂色而已矣。我何以過人哉！且不知其在彼乎，其在我乎？其在彼邪，亡乎我；在我邪，亡乎彼。方將躊躇，方將四顧，何暇至乎人貴人賤哉！」

仲尼聞之曰：「古之真人，知者不得說，美人不得濫，盜人不得劫，伏戲、黃帝不得友。死生亦大矣，而無變乎己，況爵祿乎！若然者，其神經乎大山而無介，入乎淵泉而不濡，處卑細而不憊，充滿天地，既以與人，己愈有。」

10. The character of Jian Wu appears three times in the Inner Chapters of the *Zhuangzi* and, according to A. C. Graham, is "said to be a mountain god" who in section 7.2 appears as "a friend of Jieyu (接輿), the madman of Chu (*Chu kuang* 楚狂)" (Graham, *Chuang-Tzu*, 289).

11. See Moeller and D'Ambrosio, *Genuine Pretending*.

REFERENCES

Ames, Roger T. *Confucian Role Ethics: A Vocabulary*. Hong Kong: Chinese University Press, 2011.

Bakhtin, Mikhail [Michail M. Bachtin]. *Literatur und Karneval: Zur Romantheorie und Lachkultur* [Literature and carnival: On the theory of the novel and the culture of laughter]. Frankfurt am Main: Fischer, 1990.

Chinese Text Project. Accessed March 12, 2018. https://Ctext.org.

Graham, A. C. *Chuang-Tzu: The Inner Chapters*. Indianapolis: Hackett, 2001.

Guo, Qingfan 郭慶藩. *Collected Annotations on the Zhuangzi* (*Zhuang Zi Ji Shi* 莊子集釋). In *Collected Works of Masters* (*Zhu Zi Ji Cheng* 諸子集成). Beijing: Zhong Hua Shu Ju, 1954.

Klein, Esther. "Were There 'Inner Chapters' in the Warring States? A New Examination of Evidence about the Zhuangzi." *T'oung Pao* 96 (2010): 299–369.

Mair, Victor. *Wandering on the Way: Early Taoist Tales and Parables of Chuang Tzu*. Honolulu: University of Hawai'i Press, 1998.

Moeller, Hans-Georg, and Paul D'Ambrosio. *Genuine Pretending: On the Philosophy of the Zhuangzi*. New York: Columbia University Press, 2017.

Taylor, Charles. *A Secular Age*. Cambridge, MA: Harvard University Press, 2007.

Yates, Robin D. S. "Soldiers, Scribes, and Women: Literacy among the Lower Orders in Early China." In *Writing and Literacy in Early China: Studies from the Columbia Early China*

Seminar, edited by Feng Li and David Prager Branner, 339–69. Seattle: University of Washington Press, 2011.

Chapter Sixteen

The Forger

The Use of Things

Wai Wai Chiu

The Grand Marshal's forger of buckles was eighty years old, but [the buckles he made] did not deviate by even a hair [from the standard].

"Are you just skilful", asked the Grand Marshal, "or do you have your way?"

"I have that which I hold on to. When I was twenty I became interested in forging buckles. I did not look at other things and did not examine anything but buckles. Therefore, that something is put to use relies on something's not being put to use, so the use can be sustained for a long time. How much more one may get if he leaves nothing unused! Is there anything that is not supported by that?" (60/22/68–70)[1]

1. INTRODUCTION

Although most stories of skill (skill stories) in the *Zhuangzi* are recorded in chapter 19, "*Da sheng*" (達生, "Fathoming Life"), an often-overlooked story on the same topic is found in chapter 22, "*Zhi bei you*" (知北遊, "Knowledge Roaming North"). It is about a forger working under the grand marshal.[2]

Chapter 12 of the *Huainanzi* records a slightly different version of the story, but we focus on their similarities here. Zhuangzi[3] uses the story to illustrate the process of skill cultivation and its relationship with things (*wu* 物). Of all the skill stories in the text, this is the only one to discuss the relationship between use (*yong* 用) and non-use (*bu yong* 不用). Whilst it is generally agreed that the value of uselessness (*wu yong* 無用) is a recurring theme in the *Zhuangzi*, the forger emphasises that he "leaves nothing unused" (*wu bu yong* 無不用),[4] leading one to wonder how these two ideas can be reconciled when thinking about skill. Against this backdrop, this chapter offers a detailed interpretation of the forger's words. I argue that they contain at least three messages. First, every improvement to skill is accompanied by concentration, leading to proficiency but possibly also blind spots. Second, ordinary skill improvement is "surpassed" if one can achieve the state of "leaving nothing unused". Third, attaining this extraordinary state enables one to support all things, and perhaps to be simultaneously supported by them. After explaining these messages in detail, I articulate a possible socio-political implication of the story, namely that emptiness and flexibility are regarded as key to the art of governance.

2. TEACHERS AND CULTIVATION

Like most characters in skill stories, the forger in the above story did not start practising his skill until he reached adulthood.[5] Interestingly, in ancient China, the year twenty was widely regarded as the age at which young men reached maturity, having undergone a coming-of-age ceremony (i.e., the capping ceremony).[6] Forging was certainly not a noble profession at that time, but the forger finally settled into it. His self-review at eighty reminds readers of Confucius's review of his own learning progress, starting from fifteen and ending at seventy (Lau, *Analects*, 10–11). Given Zhuangzi's familiarity with Confucianism, it is reasonable to say that he is hinting at an alternative model of self-cultivation by this alluded association with a renowned elder, a kind of "weighted saying" (*zhong yan* 重言). Both Confucius and the forger are devoted to their professions. At seventy, Confucius's heart-mind (*xin* 心) is in full accordance with rituals and music; at eighty, the forger is so skilful that his products show no deviation. Whilst both cases clearly indicate that arduous cultivation is necessary for accomplishment, they show at least two considerable differences. First, the forger does not mention any master or teacher (*shi* 師). This is consistent with many other famous skill stories, such as that of Cook Ding and the cicada catcher. This does not entail that literally no one teaches the forger,[7] but it distances the forger a bit from cultural elites and political figures, who are supposed to follow and transmit the heritage of ancient kings, and who are presumably the audience of Confucius and his disciples. Unlike Confucian texts, in which the term "teacher" denotes either a good role model or a way of following such a model, the *Zhuangzi* often uses the term negatively to show how one can easily follow partial or misleading instructions.[8] Even when the term "teacher" is used in positive examples, the one who teaches is typically not a Confucian gentleman, or even human.[9] Thus personal development is less constrained by sociopolitical and historical-customary norms in the *Zhuangzi* than in Confucian texts.

We can better analyze these different attitudes towards masters and teachers by reflecting on their functions. The following observation is made in the *Xunzi*.

> Ritual is that by which to correct your person. The teacher is that by which to correct your practice of ritual. If you are without ritual, then how will you correct your person? If you are without a teacher, how will you know that your practice of ritual is right? (Hutton, *Xunzi*, 14)

For Xunzi and Confucian thought in general, using models to inculcate social norms is an effective method, if not the most reliable, for training people in the correct behaviour. This focus on model emulation may seem authoritarian, but it does capture an important aspect of human psychology. Human beings, compared with other creatures, depend more heavily on social organisation and coordination to survive and thrive. One cannot think and act independently prior to being socialised, for one simply cannot develop the ability to think or act without being first immersed in a social environment of interaction. Accordingly, one's sociability should be regarded as more fundamental than one's rationality (i.e., capacity for independent thinking). This differs from the emphasis in certain ethical traditions on rationality detached from a person's character and context. However, norms and models can be enlightening as well as obstructive, and the attitude towards this duality reflects the difference between Zhuangzi and two leading schools, Confucianism and Mohism.[10] As a person cannot think and act maturely without socialisation, Zhuangzi notices that when one first develops a mature pattern of thinking and acting—that is, one's *dao*—some conventions must be taken for granted. One's perceptions and conceptions are limited by certain habits, frames, and even prejudices (Chong, "Zhuangzi's *Cheng Xin*," 439). This is why it is so difficult to avoid the formation of a completed heart-mind (*cheng xin* 成心), a heart that fixes a particular scheme for distinguishing right and wrong (*shi fei* 是非) and asserts itself as the ultimate authority (Chiu, "Zhuangzi's Idea of 'Spirit'," 40). In this context, Zhuangzi laments that it is too easy to take one's completed heart-mind as master (4/2/21–22). Following the completed heart-mind, one insists that some ways of doing things are right, good, or noble; this insistence develops into an obsession (Wong, "Obsession," 91), which in turn impedes self-cultivation. One prejudice instilled by the completed heart-mind is that some skills are not worth cultivating, or that some skills deserve to have a low social status. Confucius discourages a disciple from learning husbandry (Lau, *Analects*, 122–23), and Mencius worries that arrow making may lead to deviation from the practice of benevolence (Lau, *Mencius*, 74–75). In rebutting a disciple of Xu Xing, who thinks that kings should undertake agricultural work just like farmers, Mencius points out that gentlemen are supposed to use their heart-mind in governing people, and it is a confusion of roles if one asks them to undertake physical labour (Lau, *Mencius*, 112–13). Given this view of division of labour, we can say that buckle forging is hardly considered as a skill worth serious attention in the eyes of Confucians. It would be demeaning for a man to choose buckle forging after his coming-of-age ceremony. Even in the *Zhuangzi*, buckles sometimes symbolise trivial things (24/10/9). [11] Therefore, the absence of teachers in Zhuangzi's skill stories and the portrayal of unconventional masters and disciples in other stories [12] already suggest a critique of conventional education, implied by the completed heart-mind: skill practitioners do not need to follow orthodox instructions to acquire knowledge or pursue personal cultivation. They do not seek to glorify the names of their teachers, they do not attract students, they do not form groups with colleagues, and they do not hold on to any official curriculum. Their value is often not recognised by society. In this respect, they are "alone" (*du* 獨), a term used to describe Zhuangzi's independent wandering through heaven and earth (93/33/65–66). The forger is alone and distanced from convention and thus less influenced by the completed heart-mind.

3. *QI* AND THINGS

Deriving from the first difference, the second point of divergence between the forger's process of cultivation and that of Confucius is that the forger relies more on *qi* (氣, energy). Admittedly, the forger's story does not mention *qi*. Instead, it mentions "things" and hints that examining buckles is a process of becoming acquainted with things. However, there are several passages in the *Zhuangzi* that reveal the relationship between *qi* and things. In the famous dialogue on fasting the heart-mind between fictional Confucius and Yan Hui, Zhuangzi suggests that one listens not with one's (completed) heart-mind but with *qi* (9/4/27). This contrasts with Confucius in the *Analects*, whose cultivation involves following what one's heart-mind desires without overstepping the mark (Lau, *Analects*, 10–11). Listening with *qi* involves perceiving and responding to the circulation of energy in and around one's person, which often requires minimal deliberation or forethought (Graham, *Disputers of the Tao*, 197–98; Fraser, "Psychological Emptiness in the Zhuāngzǐ," 131), exceptional fluency, and a carefree attitude towards conventions. The story further notes that "*qi* is empty and awaits things" (9/4/27–28), which can be interpreted in two ways. First, it may suggest that a person listening with *qi* always fine-tunes her actions to suit their context. That is, her *qi* has no predetermined way of moving but moves spontaneously when it is actually in contact with things. Second, it may indicate that *qi*, understood as the flow of the world, always has the potential to form things (58/22/11–12). [13] One who grasps this flow is enabled to interact with things spontaneously. Regardless of which interpretation we choose, the point is that being guided by *qi* is more flexible and fitting (*shi* 適).[14] In another story, the engraver Qing says that fasting the heart-mind enables him not to waste his *qi* (50/19/56) and that he can observe the nature of trees in a way that he sees the kind of bell stands they can be turned into.[15] Listening with *qi*, therefore, is a prerequisite for someone to attend to things and bring out their potential as the situation affords. It is not far-fetched to suggest that the forger's becoming acquainted with buckles is similar to Qing's becoming acquainted with trees.

The difference between this focus on *qi* and the Confucian focus on the heart-mind can then be articulated in two respects. First, the focus on *qi* rather than the heart-mind implies that one is more responsive to things' shifting appearances, properties, and subtleties. This facilitates the exercise of human agency, which for Zhuangzi is manifest in a rich plurality of possibilities in one's interactions with things. Focusing on *qi* helps one to tap into the vast potential of the world, unconstrained by human conceptions or conventions, so that one can wander freely in the world (18/6/68) and go with the natural course of things efficaciously (20/7/11). That interacting with things is an aspect of agency is barely discussed in early Confucian texts. In the *Analects*, only one passage mentions "things" (Lau, *Analects*, 176–77), and this passage refers to heaven rather than human action. In the *Mencius*, things are identified as obstacles to self-cultivation because they disrupt one's behaviour (Lau, *Mencius*, 258–59). In both the *Mencius* and the *Xunzi*, things are supposed to be controlled or used by gentlemen or sage kings,[16] which means that they serve some social function. These texts do not advocate the appreciation of things out of curiosity or imagination, let alone self-cultivation. Consequently, their conception of human agency places greater emphasis on managing human affairs, such as developing ties with other people or negotiating one's position in society. The openness and flexibility of *qi* should be controlled by one's heart-mind, for as Mencius puts it, "where the will [of the unmoving heart-mind] arrives there the *qi* halts" (Lau, *Mencius*, 60–61). Granted, the forger is working under the grand marshal, and to this extent he is also engaging in human affairs.[17] His buckles are probably made to fulfil some social functions. However, he does not need to identify with the conventional pursuits of personal growth and satisfaction. That his perfectly forged buckles meet the official standard should be regarded as a natural result of his cultivation, not his conscious goal.[18]

The second point is that focusing on *qi* not only detaches things from their social function but also detaches one's body (*shen* 身) from its social functions and reflections. As Sommer points out, the *Analects* uses the term "stooped body" (*gong* 躬) frequently and positively, referring to a ritualised body.[19] Zhuangzi prefers the term "shape" (*xing* 形), which refers to the corporeality of the body uncircumscribed by social identity (Sommer, "Concepts of the Body in the *Zhuangzi*," 218). As a result, many skill stories describe the marvellous movements of skill practitioners' bodies without fitting them into social roles. As these movements are guided by *qi*, we might say that skill stories implicitly acknowledge the significance of subconscious activities that are not circumscribed by social norms, during which our bodies appear to move automatically yet appropriately. These activities are often not brought out by reflective thinking or deliberation (*si* 思). In Confucian texts, the term *si* refers to the main function of the heart-mind and describes a mindful attitude and introspection according to certain norms. [20] This attitude and introspection are crucial for one's negotiation of social involvement. However, *si* is not a critical term, nor even prominent, in the *Zhuangzi*. The forger's examination of things cannot involve too much thinking. Granted, he needs to prepare psychologically in various ways, such as developing the inclination to make buckles and gaining knowledge of the relevant tools. However, it is more important to concentrate on the task itself and let the concentrating body move spontaneously. Deliberation and forethought are not totally absent, but they are set aside to the periphery of consciousness and reappear at the centre only in a complementary way (Wong, "Obsession," 105). Ideally, as Rur-bin Yang says, "there is no distinction between the conscious and the unconscious" (Yang, "Wandering in Unitary Qi," 91). For if conscious thinking does not assert itself as the overseer of every practice, it can be incorporated into the process by which all organs and faculties jointly and spontaneously respond to a situation. [21] The forger makes buckles smoothly not because he thinks to do so, but precisely because he does not think to do so.

4. USE AND NON-USE

That the forger needs to concentrate deeply to be efficacious, often ignoring things other than what is at hand, reveals some features of skill development relating to the theme of usefulness. One is the partiality of skills. The forger has a thorough understanding of buckles, but presumably he cannot use his skill directly to make other things. After all, he reports that he "did not look at other things". So the usefulness of his skill is constrained. Like the cicada catcher, who "knows only the cicadas' wings" (48/19/20), the forger discriminates buckles from other things, leaving blind spots in his knowledge. Zhuangzi seems to notice this feature when he says that "Qi-Ji and Hua-liu horses gallop a thousand miles in a day, but for catching rats they are not worth a wild cat or a weasel, which is to say that their skill is different" (43/17/36–37). The last chapter of the *Zhuangzi* also notes that "the wholeness and comprehensiveness of the ancient way and technique is broken into pieces, just as the various skills of a hundred schools all have their strengths

but are ...). Bearing these
passages ... hing is put to use
relies or ...)oth reflecting on
how use ... to the forger and
his skill ... ng distance from
other pr ... orger's eyes and
hands, a ... to buckles, but if
he were ... ner, for instance,
Cook D ... of excellence. In
chapter ... ge king Yao that
"even if ... rson in charge of
making ... d pans to replace
him" (2/ ... ctly to the nature
of skill, ... occupies only a
humble ... 'ern well without
knowing ... the hermit could
become ... ing as better than
his own ... .ermit. Extending
this point, skill in any particular field inevitably comes at a cost, and no fixed
standard is available to judge the superiority of any particular skill. Different
skills generate heterogeneous values (Fraser, "Skepticism and Value," 449).
This further supports Zhuangzi's criticism of the prejudice that some skills
are simply inferior to others. Experts who want people to admire and learn
their "superior" skills end up creating confusion and blocking mutual understanding (5/2/44–45), because they do not accept that different people have
different ways of realising skilfulness. To regard one's own achievement as
full and complete is to be obsessed with the part rather than the whole; hence
the term "petty achievement" (4/2/25). The only way to avoid petty achievement is to recognise it as such, to accept that the ultimate *dao* is ever changing and cannot be wholly expressed in a single art.

Probably due to their knowledge of their positions, Zhuangzi's skill masters do not engage in the common practice of seeking recognition and support from feudal lords, and they speak only in response to a question or
request, or when compelled to do so. They remain humble and do not claim
that their skilfulness is extraordinary. Indeed, the extraordinary performance
of most skill practitioners is based on ordinary activities, which are "useful
only when the time comes". Therefore, they stand in contrast with two other
kinds of role model in the text. The first are mystical figures such as the
dragon-riding daemonic person living on Gu Ye Mountain (2/1/28–29), who
does not engage in craftsmanship or ordinary skill training but instead displays supernatural powers. The second are people who are looked down on
as useless by conventional standards but in fact have attained a high level of
cultivation. An example is Shu Shan the Toeless, who admits that he does not

attend to his body wisely and is criticised by Confucius for having been deprived of his feet as a punishment (13/5/24–29). Again, Toeless does not engage in ordinary skill training, but later he seems to attain ultimate spiritual enlightenment. The contrast between the daemonic person and skill practitioners leads to the question of whether it is possible to become an ideal person in ordinary life. One may read stories about mystical figures as requiring one to live a life that transcends the physiological and psychological limits of normal human beings. From this perspective, all human affairs—including, of course, forging buckles and making bell stands—are trivial. As Yearley comments on the radical vision of Zhuangzi, "religious views are often characterised by the grandeur of their affirmations, by how different their ideas are from normal ideas" (Yearley, "The Perfected Person," 135). The contrast between Toeless and skill practitioners leads to the question of whether skill training is necessary for one to become an ideal person.[23] Sometimes it is better to be useful, like a cackling goose (51/20/3); sometimes it is better to be as useless as a defective tree (51/20/1–2). So, although skill practitioners are regarded as embodiments of spontaneity, operating counter to conventional values, we are not told unequivocally that their lives are the only kind we should emulate. Not only is a trade-off between skills required, but the whole process of becoming skilful also puts one in a position different from those who are unskilful. The skilful do not have an absolute advantage in navigating their way in life.

The second way of interpreting the statement "that something is put to use relies on something's not being put to use" concerns buckles: their functioning relies on other things' functioning in different ways. In other words, the use of buckles requires other things not to be used as buckles. Anvils and hammers are used to make buckles, which are then used to fasten belts and dresses. That buckles and professional forgers are needed also presupposes certain customs and social practices. Putting all these factors together, one can construct a web of relations with buckles in the centre, surrounded by non-buckles. An interesting feature of this web is that in principle it can be extended to include anything, even things that seem useless and irrelevant. To appreciate this, consider one of the stories in chapter 26. Here, Huizi criticises Zhuangzi's words as "useless", and the latter responds that although one requires only a tiny portion of earth under one's feet to stand, that portion of earth will be useless if the surrounding ground is dug away (74/26/32–33). Zhuangzi's response can be interpreted in two ways. One is that ground not currently in use is potentially useful. As one moves, one's standing point shifts, so new ground is needed. The further one wishes to move, the more idle space one needs (69/24/105). Second is that it serves as a contrast to identify and evaluate one's current standpoint. If one cannot compare where one stands with other places, one will fail to understand one's current situation and will be unable to decide whether to stay or leave.[24] This is an application of the statement in chapter 2 that "'that' comes from 'this' and 'this' depends on 'that'" (4/2/27–28). Identification implies discrimination. Returning to the story of forging buckles, the usefulness of buckles may depend on seemingly useless things because the latter may help to make or use buckles, and they can serve as a contrast when one needs to identify and evaluate buckles. The same rationale can be extended to anything. A thing's usefulness can be associated with any other thing, not just things directly involved in its production and consumption. This shows that the usefulness of things simultaneously involves heterogeneity and interdependence. Combined with the idea that things are continuously transforming into each other (7/2/96) and replacing each other without beginning or end (75/27/10), we may say that for Zhuangzi, a thing is always embedded in the world's greater transformation processes, whereby nothing, not even human beings, stand in isolation. Viewed in this way, one comes to see things as equal; no fixed hierarchy of value exists. As Xu Fuguan says, "A thing's existence is manifest in its functioning. . . . Zhuangzi only views things from their functioning . . . thus everything has its own function . . . and all things return to equality".[25] Note that the statement that 'everything has its own function' does not mean that things can be used solely to achieve human goals. The giant but useless tree seen by Nan Bo Zi Qi illustrates this point (11/4/75–12/4/81).

Even if we do not possess a refined skill like the forger's, the above view of things may still change our treatment of them. It prevents us from attaching too much value to any one thing. As all things are useful only contextually, it is unwise to insist on pursuing something at any cost.[26] Cost is not bad per se; indeed, it is inevitably incurred when something new comes into existence, from a buckle to a civilisation. However, one's strong desires sometimes blind one to possible costs and become self-defeating: one may end up giving up things that are necessary to produce or enjoy the desired good as expected. Realising the interdependence of things helps one to attend to the relationships between them, avoiding biases such as "seeing oneself as noble and others as base" (43/17/29). Note that the avoidance of bias and strong desires does not necessarily involve moral principles. The point is not whether having biases or strong desires is morally wrong, or whether things deserve to be treated as equal. Rather, when one, like the forger, concentrates on interacting with things for a long time without judging them by conventional standards, one may naturally come to appreciate how they work and develop a holistic view of them. This is also a step towards ideal personhood, to which we now turn.

5. SUPPORTER OF ALL THINGS

Like Cook Ding, who says that he is fond of *dao*, which advances skill, the forger describes a level higher than possessing ordinary skill, namely "leaving nothing unused". This may seem puzzling, given the previous section's discussion of the partiality of skills and usefulness. The value of any skill or thing varies with context. How, then, can one leave nothing unused, that is, use everything? I suppose an answer can be found by considering that *dao* prepares for all and accommodates all (36/13/61), and those who attain it can bring anything to destruction or completion (17/6/42). In other words, only *dao*, which advances skill, leaves nothing unused. However, to use everything rather than being limited to only one profession, *dao* cannot be just one way of doing things. It must be the way towards ideal personhood, matching the "grand corpus of the ancients" (91/33/15), which embodies wholeness and comprehensiveness, rather than the fragmentary skills of a hundred schools. When elaborating on this ideal way, Zhuangzi does not refer to skill masters[27] but uses other metaphors and abstract descriptions. One is the saying that the ideal person is empty (*xu* 虛), meaning that she can listen with the shapeless *qi* and await things, as stated in section 3. Precisely because she is empty, she can become "great" (30/12/40) and wander in the world without being harmed (52/20/24).[28] An empty person focuses on things' potentiality rather than their actuality. Consequently, one can see oneself and things as possibly becoming any other thing, always open to change. This open-mindedness enables one to become useful in different ways to fit different situations; accordingly, we may say that usefulness depends on emptiness, although emptiness is not a particular use. This is a further elaboration of the idea that usefulness depends on uselessness.

Recall that human agency is manifested in changes of ways of interacting with things. Expressions like "walking two roads (*liang xing* 兩行)", "wandering (*you* 遊)", or "going through (*tong* 通)" describe the process of exercising agency to its fullest extent; an ideal person changes her way to fit every new context she encounters. Zhuangzi remarks on this as follows:

> Shoes best fit us when we forget our feet, a belt best fits us when we forget our waist, our heart-mind best fits us when we know how to forget right and wrong and engaging with our circumstances is easiest when we neither vary inwardly nor yield to external pressure. To fit from the start and never fail to fit is to suit in forgetfulness of what it is that fits. (50/19/62–64)

Of course, these ideas are also relevant to skill training[29] and remain significant throughout life. If we are able to minimise friction when we use a thing, the thing will fit us and become like a part of us. The same goes for our fit with the environment. However, as the environment is always changing, one must reorient oneself constantly. The ability to reorient oneself is accompanied by the understanding that all things have infinite potential and are interdependent and equal, as discussed in section 4. This equality does not imply that one should treat all things in the same way. On the contrary, when the text says that one *qi* goes through the world and the sage values "one" (58/22/13), this "oneness" is not to be conceived as antagonistic to plurality. Only when a person comes to realise that "all things indeed have certain affirmable qualities" (4/2/34) and sees precisely which qualities (including human psychological traits) can be affirmed in which contexts can the person fully understand *how* things are equal.[30] One who attains this understanding goes through different contexts by shifting one's evaluations and acting accordingly. Indeed, "understanding" and "going through" are translations of the same Chinese character, 通. Understanding something is seen as passing through it or finding a way for it. This also keeps one from unnecessary conflict and ensures that one fits the thing in question. In traditional Chinese medicine, the same character also refers to one's vital *qi* flowing fluently without obstacles, and thus without damage or pain.

The brief analysis above should help us to understand why an ideal person can leave nothing unused. This need not mean that she can directly access and control everything simultaneously. Instead, her flexibility, that is, knowing how to reorient herself to fit every new context, already involves knowing how to make things fit their contexts. This is hinted at in a story in which Zhuangzi proposes an unconventional use of big gourds (3/1/41–42). The injunction to think unconventionally may seem at odds with the saying that those who attain great understanding "lodge in the ordinary" (4/2/36). However, "ordinary" does not necessarily mean "conventional". In the context of "use",[31] "ordinary" does not suggest that one should use something according to its role in daily life, which is often determined by social categorisation or personal bias. Otherwise, one will be as stubborn as Huizi in the big gourds story. Rather, the point is to temporarily forget the stereotypes associated with a thing and in this sense treat it as ordinary. This aids an appreciation of things' subtleties, as discussed in section 3.

According to the forger, those leaving nothing unused are supporters of all things. The original Chinese sentence may also mean that all things support those leaving nothing unused. Both readings are possible, and indeed they refer to the same state: fitting the interdependence of all things. Elsewhere in the *Zhuangzi*, we are told that authentic persons' emotions can "go through the four seasons and do what fits in with things" (15/6/10), and that their virtue (*de* 德) can "circulate through the making of things" (48/19/12). Whilst one can associate these descriptions with mystical powers like that of the daemonic person on Gu Ye Mountain, one can also offer a down-to-earth interpretation by taking them as the perfected form of one's flexibility and adaptiveness, which even normal people can cultivate to a certain extent.

After all, the big gourd story shows that using things flexibly does not depend on mystical powers. More specifically, the relationship between flexibility and "supporting things" has two sides, one passive and the other active. The passive side involves fitting every context by causing minimum damage and waste either to oneself or to other things. It is "passive" because it focuses on *not* interfering with things. I say "minimum" because it is impossible not to cause damage in one's life when very strict criteria are applied. The continuous search for and depletion of resources for one's survival almost inevitably involves damage and waste. Even skill masters may not be able to fully avoid such interference; some even cause more than minimum damage to things. Cook Ding's ox carving still has room for improvement, or the whole practice simply reflects life's inevitable conflict and sacrifice.[32] Still, it is said that nothing can injure a sage because her spirit[33] remains intact (48/19/15), and that she does not injure things when situated with them (60/22/80). This should not be understood as doing literally nothing to prevent contact with things, but instead as the constant process of reorientation mentioned above. To further illustrate, imagine that one's life is like being in a boat on a rushing river with many other boats heading in different directions. One cannot avoid crashing into rocks or other boats simply by doing nothing. Instead, one must concentrate on the situation and continuously adjust one's direction and momentum.[34] It is "one moment going up and one moment going down, taking harmony as the only measure" (51/20/6–7).[35]

The active side of supporting things through flexibility focuses on bringing out things' potential and enhancing their harmony. For Zhuangzi, as anything may function in an infinite number of ways during the grand transformation process, the potential of a thing can be as unlimited as the whole world. What is fetid and rotten can become wonderful and marvellous, and vice versa (58/22/12–13). The more flexible one is, the deeper one can delve into things' potential, and the more chance one has of fine-tuning them to fit each other. The big gourds story depicts Zhuangzi's ingenuity, as he not only prevents Huizi's waste but also finds a new way for Huizi and the gourds to fit together. The monkey keeper story, which illustrates the sage's "walking two roads", shows how the very same nuts can trigger anger or joy depending on how one uses them. Having more resources is not always better, and how one does something matters as much as what one does. Indeed, it is hard to firmly distinguish between the question of what and the question of how, because if things' existence cannot be separated from their transformation, then saying that one uses something differently is not fundamentally different from saying that one uses a different thing. One not only supports things by recreating them, but also recreates oneself during the process. This should also remind readers that interacting with things is a creative art rather than simply the avoidance of harm. It is just that this art evades rigid rules.

We have now interpreted all three parts of the forger's statement. As discussed in section 4, it is unclear whether the forger's excellence at forging implies that he himself has reached the level of ultimate person. Nonetheless, his words reflect that however humble one's social background, one can gain a sense of comfort and reduce life's conflict through cultivation. With this lesson in hand, we now ponder the story's sociopolitical implications.

6. RULING OF EMPTINESS

Whilst the forger's words do not seem to be political, the story's setting that some advice comes from a person working under an officer in the imperial court may itself generate sociopolitical implications.[36] In the *Huainanzi* version, the narrator of the story relates it to the *Daodejing*, a text focusing on how a sage governs a state. Whilst not claiming that the author of the forger story intends to persuade readers to accept a particular political view, I think that the claims that all things are interdependent and that being empty can bring one into harmony with the environment can be translated into an account of ideal society and ideal government, assuming that "the way of inner sagehood and outer kingship" (91/33/14) is a whole. After all, if one must always orient oneself *in context*, one cannot make sense of one's self-cultivation without seeing that it also changes one's view and position in a society, the general context of most human practices.

The sociopolitical implications of the forger story have three dimensions. The first relates to the qualities of an ideal ruler, or an ideal person in a political context. The second concerns the relationship between the ruler and the ruled. The third relates to the art of governing and handling social conflict, which draws on the idea of being a supporter of all things.

As discussed in section 5, an ideal person minimises the friction between herself and things. She does not injure things when situated with them. It is said that those who do not injure things will not be injured, and that only those who are free from injury can lead or welcome people (60/22/80–81). This shows that one who overcomes resistance from things can also overcome resistance from people. The more resistance from people one overcomes, the more powerful one becomes in society. However, this power comes not from violence, wealth, or moral charisma, through which hierarchies arise. It comes from one's emptiness and flexibility. The image of water, which is common in the *Daodejing* and *Zhuangzi*, is helpful here. No one can bend water, not because it is strong, but because it dissolves the incoming force. So the world's biggest natural reservoir of water, the sea, often symbolises the character of an ideal ruler. Just as the sea encompasses all streams (42/17/7), the sage encompasses all things and is thus able to carry and measure them (58/22/34–59/22/36). In previous sections we have seen that an ideal person does not attach too much value to one thing. In a political context, such a person lacks a strong will to power and remains humble even if her merit covers the whole world (20/7/14–15), and her emptiness can also dissolve other people's will to power. The lack of a will to power constitutes part of the ideal ruler's power, as such a will to power pushes one to manipulate and seek dominance and easily compromises one's ability to reduce friction. Therefore, it is not surprising that Zhuangzi says, on the one hand, that only the ideal ruler can best lead and welcome people and, on the other, that she neither leads nor welcomes (21/7/32–33). If one applies the rationale that usefulness depends on uselessness, then Zhuangzi is saying that one's way of leading or welcoming in a particular context is unsuitable in other contexts, so the ideal ruler does not need to seek a universally right way of leading or welcoming. Instead, she simply fits each context without insisting on classifying "this" as leading or "that" as welcoming.

As the power of an ideal ruler need not be manifest in a social hierarchy, she does not need to look down on people, and people do not need to look up to her. The *Zhuangzi* is full of stories in which conventional rulers or officials look for advice from people working under them or even outside government, such as the forger. Similarly, the Nameless says that governing the world requires impartiality (20/7/8–11), and a boy shepherd teaches the Yellow Emperor to "get rid of whatever would harm the horses" when governing the world (65/24/25). Zhuangzi implicitly suggests that the functioning of a government depends on the functioning of people outside the government, because only when the government does not regard itself as over and above people and people do not regard themselves as under and below the government can good governing occur. This is again a variant of the idea that the useful depends on the useless, and a unique view of government among pre-Qin thinkers.[37]

How is the idea of being a supporter of all things related to the art of governing? As mentioned in section 5, the relationship between flexibility and supporting things has a passive and an active side. The passive side focuses on non-interference. In a political context, this can be translated into a cautious attitude towards using regulations, especially moral codes and standards of right and wrong, as these can injure people's capacity to wander (17/6/83–84). Passages that stress the importance of protecting human nature[38] sometimes express the radical view that the whole idea of "governing" should be discarded (25/11/1–2) and that the art of governing need not be considered. Even the less radical view still warns readers that the act of promoting moral codes, rituals, and decorative arts may arouse people's desire for fame and power (23/9/6–14). They all emphasise the importance of reducing control, manipulation, and agitation. In addition, a story (47/18/33–39) is told by the fictional Confucius about the marquis of Lu, who seeks to welcome and entertain a bird with an extravagant banquet and music but kills it unintentionally. Confucius remarks that one should "nourish a bird according to the bird, not according to one's self". Nourishing birds normally involves letting them live in the wild, not imposing on them what they cannot bear. This is compared to the governance of a sage, who "neither unifies people's talents nor makes their tasks alike, but limits names by reality and set rightness according to what is fit". The first half of the saying is about retaining people's plurality and hence vitality, and the second half is more active, admitting that in some cases, names (the basic unit for categorising and guiding action) and standards of right and wrong need to be set, but these are expedient measures that fit only certain situations.

As in the monkey keeper story, the active side of the art of governance can be further illustrated by cases in which the ruler brings out things' potential to allow different parties to live together harmoniously. One such story concerns the fictional King Wen (56/21/47–55), who is retrospectively honoured by Confucians as the founder of the Zhou dynasty and Chinese culture. When King Wen discovers a wise old man near a river and seeks to hand over government affairs to him, the king faces a dilemma: either the rulership of a stranger will cause unease and distrust among ministers, or the people will lose the chance to be governed well. He then tells his ministers about dreaming of his father to rationalise his appointment of the old man. The dilemma is solved by alluding to the power of ancestor worship, a common practice in China. Certainly, ordinary people would not foresee this use of the practice, just as Huizi does not foresee that a big gourd can function as a boat. One must go beyond conventional thinking to seize the chance to change the use of something and better satisfy both parties' needs. The nature of the thing is not determined by its conventional use, but by what it fits. Whilst King Wen's actions might not be the perfect solution (and indeed Yan Hui complains that it may be insincere and not fully reflective of the king's virtue (56/21/55–56)), Confucius explains that he does his best by "following the moment" (*xun si xu* 循斯須). What he does is timely, but not necessarily "correct". A better solution may exist, but it still can be found only when one concentrates on the total situation. Thus, whilst it does not provide a formula for success, "following the moment" involves a combination of tranquillity, creativity, and responsiveness that makes a ruler a supporter of all things.[39] Although we are not sure whether the forger possesses all of these capacities, the setting of the forger story already hints at them: for Zhuangzi, the totality of the world's changes can be metaphorically expressed by images of casting and forging (17/6/58–59). Those who understand this remain at ease with whatever they encounter and bring ease to their surroundings.

7. CONCLUSION

Starting with a humble profession, the forger story casts light on Zhuangzi's view of the world, things in the world, and skill as a response to the world. It reminds one of the spontaneous relationship between humans and things that arises when humans interact with things without the urge to dominate or exploit. It also reconciles the tension between valuing uselessness and valuing the principle of "leaving nothing unused" by hinting at the interdependence of uselessness and usefulness, and ultimately the interdependence of all things. Understanding this interdependence entails not only noting an abstract principle but also cultivating corresponding capacities: those of emptiness and flexibility. The result is practical knowledge of how to deal with conflicts and bring out things' potential in a timely manner. Those with this knowledge will eventually become supporters of all things. For Zhuangzi, this is the highest level of fitting, as "in stillness, they share the same virtue as *yin* and in movement they share the same current as *yang*" (34/13/14).

NOTES

1. All references to the Chinese text of the *Zhuangzi* are from Hong, *Zhuangzi Yinde*. All translations in this chapter are my own, although I rely on the following commentaries and translations: Guo, *Zhuang Zi Ji Shi*; Graham, *Chuang-Tzu*; Mair, *Wandering on the Way*; and Chen, *Zhuang Zi Jin Zhu Jin Yi*. The order of the chapters and sentences is given as explained in Chen's book.

2. Although the story in the *Zhuangzi* uses only two characters, *Da Ma* 大馬, to refer to the forger's superior, the majority of commentators agree that the person in question should be referred to as *Da Si Ma* 大司馬, denoting the highest rank of military official. The story in the *Huainanzi* also uses *Da Si Ma* 大司馬. In the *Zhouli*, the term *Si Ma* 司馬 refers to an official responsible for leading the army and delineating the boundary of states, among other duties (4.0/53/7–8). References to the Chinese text of the *Zhouli* are from Lau and Chen, *A Concordance to the Zhouli*. Although the historical accuracy of the *Zhouli* is contested, we see in the *Zuo Zhuan* that the term *Si Ma* appears quite frequently and refers to someone holding a high military rank.

3. The term "Zhuangzi" refers only to the author(s) of the text *Zhuangzi*; it does not imply an association with any historical figure, such as Zhuang Zhou (莊周). The same approach is taken to other classical texts bearing the names of pre-Qin thinkers.

4. One can therefore read this story along with the famous "useless tree" story in chapter 4, "*Ren jian shi*" (人間世, "Realm of Living World"), and the goose-cooking story at the opening of chapter 20, "*Shan mu*" (山木, "Mountain Tree"), in which Zhuangzi thinks that neither being talented nor being non-talented can free one from entanglement (*lei* 累).

5. An exception may be the swimmer, as he seems to hint that part of his talent is inborn.

6. In chapter 44 of the *Liji*, we see a detailed description of this ceremony. In the ceremony, one is expected to fully take up the responsibilities of a son, a younger brother, a subject, and a junior (44/167/6). It is regarded as "the beginning of rites" (44/167/11). References to the Chinese text of the *Liji* are from Lau and Chen, *A Concordance to the Liji*. Undergoing the capping ceremony marks that one is completed (*cheng* 成), that is, one becomes a person who is able to fulfil the requirements in moral, social, and political realms. See also Confucius's discussion of completion in Lau, *Analects*, 134–35.

7. Among all skill masters in the *Zhuangzi*, some of them may possess a skill that is relatively easy to learn without a trainer, such as swimming. Other skills may be more difficult,

like making bell stands. However, all of them show no intention of placing themselves in an honorific cultural heritage (like the series of sages in Confucianism).

8. For example, in "*Ren jian shi*," Confucius says that Yan Hui's plan will not work if he continues to regard his heart-mind as his teacher (9/4/24).

9. For example, in "*Da zong shi*" (大宗師, "Great Ancestral Teacher"), Xuyou hints that the teacher he exalts is actually that which "covers heaven, supports earth and carves a multitude of shapes" (17/6/89).

10. This does not mean that Zhuangzi rejects the teacher-student or master-disciple relationship altogether. It does mean, however, that Zhuangzi doubts whether these two relationships are essential for transmitting *dao*, and whether they must be connected to the core of political power and social fame. For a detailed analysis of Zhuangzi's model of pedagogy, please refer to Romain Graziani's discussion in chapter 5 of this volume.

11. As in the famous saying, "He who steals a buckle is executed, he who steals a state becomes a feudal lord" (Mair, *Wandering on the Way*, 86).

12. It should be noted that, not only do those masters and disciples (e.g., 3/2/1, 16/6/36) show little affinity to Confucian and Mohist values, but the relationship between teacher and student, especially in a political context, is also less hierarchical. In the *Zhuangzi*, Duke Ai of Lu refers to Confucius as "friend of virtue" (14/5/49), while the *Mencius* hints that a king should serve a Confucian gentleman instead of regarding him as a friend (Lau, *Mencius*, 234–35).

13. Under this interpretation, the term *wu* 物 is taken as a verb.

14. "Fitting" is discussed further in section 5.

15. For a detailed discussion of how Qing's work involves listening with *qi*, please refer to Kim-chong Chong's discussion in chapter 14 of this volume.

16. See, for example, Lau, *Mencius*, 292–93, 306–9; Hutton, *Xunzi*, 12, 180–81.

17. Of all the skill practitioners discussed in this anthology, some work within or are aligned with a social organisation, whereas others distance themselves from human society. However, this difference does not seem to impact their cultivation. Those who distance themselves do not thereby gain special insight. This suggests that at least in the context of skill development, Zhuangzi does not advocate total detachment from society. Indeed, given that the dialogue on fasting the heart-mind is situated in a diplomatic scenario, Zhuangzi seems to allow that one's skill may be developed in response to social issues.

18. This does not exclude the possibility that the forger's choosing a career and becoming skilful are his conscious goals. This echoes the dialogue on fasting the heart-mind, in which we are told that Yan Hui unifies his intention (*zhi* 志) while listening with *qi*. He need not give up his original goal to persuade a tyrant.

19. Sommer, "Concepts of the Body in the *Zhuangzi*," 214. The same is true of the *Liji*.

20. See, for example, Lau, *Analects*, 164–67; Lau, *Mencius*, 258–59; Hutton, *Xunzi*, 251. Arguably, Confucius himself also seeks to have cultivated persons acting automatically yet appropriately (see, for example, Lau, *Analects*, 10–11, 148–49). However, he also expects them not to transgress social norms (see, for example, Lau, *Analects*, 140–41), and he never holds that a gentleman should stop *si*.

21. Yang also hints that the sentence "He who puts something to use relies on something that is not put to use" refers to the state of one who uses vital energy to guide her behaviour without consciously relying on the discriminating function of heart-mind and senses (Yang, "Wandering in Unitary Qi," 108). Yang's own translation of the sentence is "using the method of deliberately not using other things." This is not a common translation, and the term "deliberately" is not present or implied in the original text. Therefore, I take only Yang's theoretical point that the heart-mind and senses can merge together functionally, as effected by skill practitioners in the *Zhuangzi*; I do not take this to be a faithful reading of the above sentence in the forger story.

22. Whether people's positions are fixed or equal is another issue.

23. For a critique of taking skill as a core theme in the Inner Chapters, please refer to Eric Schwitzgebel's discussion in chapter 7 of this volume.

24. Analogously, although Zhuangzi's words are sometimes indeterminate and do not provide concrete guidance on engaging in worldly affairs, this indeterminacy offers a contrast that helps one to understand the functions and limitations of ordinary language.

25. Xu, *Zhong Guo Ren Xin Lun Shi*, 402. Note that both "functioning" and "usefulness" are translations of the same Chinese character, 用.

26. Even the act of pursuing may become problematic if it is accompanied by strong desires and self-aggrandisement. It may strengthen one's completed heart-mind and become an obstacle to spontaneity. One then loses the chance to fully appreciate a thing and all of the possibilities associated with it.

27. In descending order of frequency, the terms most frequently used in the *Zhuangzi* to denote an ideal personhood are "ultimate person" (*zhi ren* 至人), "authentic person" (*zhen ren* 真人), and "daemonic person" (*shen ren* 神人). These terms do not appear in the skill stories. The term "sage" (*sheng ren* 聖人) is sometimes used ironically or pejoratively and thus does not necessarily refer to ideal personhood. It does not appear in the skill stories either.

28. A state of emptiness can be exalted for its instrumental or intrinsic value. For a detailed discussion, see Fraser, "Psychological Emptiness."

29. For example, a buckle forger may need to meet the demands of different buckles.

30. This understanding does not simply entail the general belief that all things are equal, which is one reason why attaining ideal personhood is difficult.

31. Some versions of the text contain the following characters in chapter 2: "庸也者用也用也者通也通也者得也適得而幾矣" (4/2/36–5/2/37), which can be roughly translated as "the ordinary is the use, the use is the going through, the going through is the attaining. Attaining is to be closet to there." These characters are absent from Chen, *Zhuang Zi Jin Zhu Jin Yi*. Like Chen, I treat them here as a later interpolation.

32. Huang suggests that knack stories tell us only how to perform an action effortlessly, not whether such actions are right (Huang, "Respecting Different Ways of Life," 1056). This is quite plausible. Cook Ding's story does not presuppose that carving an ox is right. Huang also claims that for Zhuangzi, rightness consists in following or respecting things' natural disposition (1055). I leave open whether this claim is plausible.

33. One's spirit is the purest *qi* or the mechanism by which a person acts spontaneously. We need not regard it as a mystic force or a "ghost" residing in one's body. See Billeter, *Zhuang Zi Si Jiang*, 7.

34. Avoiding crashing is the default goal, but not the absolute goal. Other goals may exist, such as enjoying scenery or passing through certain checkpoints. These goals cannot be ranked a priori.

35. I take harmony to be a meta-level fitting: it arises when two or more sets of fitting things fit each other. Obviously, like flexibility, harmony admits gradation.

36. Note that the Chinese character meaning "buckle" is 鉤, which can also denote "sword." If one takes the forger to be a swordsmith, his advice more obviously addresses the issue of power.

37. Even the *Daodejing*, which, like the *Zhuangzi*, entertains the concepts of emptiness and uselessness, usually speaks from the perspective of a ruler, rather than people outside government.

38. Controversy has arisen over whether the absence of the term *xing* 性 (nature) from the Inner Chapters is compatible with the character's presence in passages from the Outer and Miscellaneous Chapters. I pass over this controversy here, as I am not articulating a systematic and comprehensive Zhuangzist political philosophy.

39. Even when conflict is inevitable, one must still act to cause the least damage to all parties. The image of water in the *Art of War* and the text's emphasis on avoiding physical combat, even in war, are applications of this point and could well be lessons designed specifically for the grand marshal in the forger story.

REFERENCES

Billeter, Jean-François. *Zhuang Zi Si Jiang* 莊子四講 [*Leçons sur Tchouang-tseu*]. Translated by Song Gang 宋剛. Taipei: Linking Publishing, 2011.

Chen, Guying 陳鼓應. *Zhuang Zi Jin Zhu Jin Yi* 莊子今注今譯 [Contemporary Notes and Translations of the *Zhuangzi*]. Hong Kong: Zhonghua Shuju, 2001.

Chiu, Wai Wai. "Zhuangzi's Idea of 'Spirit': Acting and 'Thinging Things' without Self-Assertion." *Asian Philosophy* 26, no. 1 (January 2016): 38–51.

Chong, Kim-chong. "Zhuangzi's *Cheng Xin* and Its Implications for Virtue and Perspectives." *Dao: A Journal of Comparative Philosophy* 10, no. 4 (November 2011): 427–43.

Fraser, Chris. "Psychological Emptiness in the Zhuāngzǐ." *Asian Philosophy* 18, no. 2 (August 2008): 123–47.

———. "Skepticism and Value in the Zhuāngzǐ." *International Philosophical Quarterly* 49, no. 4 (December 2009): 439–57.

Graham, A. C. *Chuang-Tzu: The Seven Inner Chapters and Other Writings from the Book Chuang-tzu*. London: Allen and Unwin, 1981.

———. *Disputers of the Tao*. La Salle, IL: Open Court, 1989.

Guo, Qingfan 郭慶藩. *Zhuang Zi Ji Shi* 莊子集釋 [Collective Commentaries on the *Zhuangzi*]. Beijing: Zhonghua Shuju, 1961.

Hong, Ye 洪業, ed. *Zhuangzi Yinde* 莊子引得 [A Concordance to the *Zhuangzi*]. Shanghai: Shanghai Classics Publishing House, 1986.

Huang, Yong. "Respecting Different Ways of Life: A Daoist Ethics of Virtue in the *Zhuangzi*." *Journal of Asian Studies* 69, no. 4 (November 2010): 1049–69.

Hutton, Eric. *Xunzi: The Complete Text*. Princeton, NJ: Princeton University Press, 2014.

Lau, D. C. *Confucius: The Analects*. Hong Kong: Chinese University Press, 1992.

———. *Mencius*. Hong Kong: Chinese University Press, 2003.

Lau, D. C., and Chen Fong Ching, ed. *A Concordance to the Liji*. Hong Kong: Commercial Press, 1992.

———. *A Concordance to the Zhouli*. Taipei: Commercial Press, 1994.

Mair, Victor H. *Wandering on the Way: Early Taoist Tales and Parables of Chuang Tzu*. New York: Bantam, 1994.

Sommer, Deborah. "Concepts of the Body in the *Zhuangzi*." In *Experimental Essays on Zhuangzi*, edited by Victor H. Mair, 212–27. Dunedin, FL: Three Pines Press, 2010.

Wong, David. "Zhuangzi and the Obsession with Being Right." *History of Philosophy Quarterly* 22, no. 2 (April 2005): 91–107.

Xu, Fuguan 徐復觀. *Zhong Guo Ren Xin Lun Shi Xian Qin Pian* 中國人性論史先秦篇 [The History of Chinese Theories of Human Nature: Pre-Qin Period]. Taipei: Commercial Press, 1969.

Yang, Rur-bin. "From 'Merging the Body with the Mind' to 'Wandering in Unitary Qi 氣': A Discussion of Zhuangzi's Realm of the True Man and Its Corporeal Basis." In *Hiding the World in the World: Uneven Discourses on the Zhuangzi*, edited by Scoot Cook, 88–127. Albany, NY: SUNY Press, 2003.

Yearley, Lee. "The Perfected Person in the Radical Zhuangzi." In *Experimental Essays on Zhuangzi*, edited by Victor H. Mair, 122–36. Dunedin, FL: Three Pines Press, 2010.

Index

Embodied Cognition Theory (ECT), 144, 151–156

emotion, 6, 9, 13n7, 33, 39–40, 42, 42n5, 42n7, 43n14, 164, 170, 172, 176; disruptive, 33, 35, 36–37, 38, 42; markers, 186, 188, 190, 198n7; positive (or supportive), 33, 37–38, 43n13

empty space, 92

engagement, with the world, 143

engraver. *See* Woodworker Qing

Eno, Robert, 194

environment, 150, 152, 152–154, 155; dynamic, 155

epistemic tool, 156

equality, 266, 268

equanimity, 252, 253

ethics, 196. *See also* moral; values

ferryman [person], 5, 26, 27, 28, 63, 86, 87, 88, 90, 92, 163, 165, 172, 192, 193

ferryman [story], 88, 98n5, 145, 163–164, 166, 167, 168, 170, 171, 174, 175, 177, 178, 192, 193

fighting, 184, 193, 194

final vocabulary, 45, 47–48, 49, 53, 57–58

fisherman, 63

fluency, 89

flexibility, 269–270, 271, 272, 274, 276n35

flourishing, 157

flow, 50, 112, 113, 113–114, 115, 116, 117, 118–119, 120, 122–123, 124, 237

focus, 188, 189

forger, 37, 259, 260, 261, 262–263, 264, 266–267, 268, 269, 271, 272, 273, 274, 274n2, 275n18, 276n29, 276n36

forget, forgetting, 22, 23, 27, 28, 89, 94, 166, 167, 168–169, 170–172, 174–176, 178, 179n7, 180n22, 192; water, 163, 165–166, 166–168, 168, 170, 179n4

Frankfurt, Harry, 237

Fraser, Chris, 39, 42n6, 179n6, 180n16, 180n19, 180n20

good life, Zhuangist view of, 163–164, 170, 172, 177, 178

government, 243, 244, 245, 247, 250, 253, 257n3, 271, 272, 273, 276n37

Graham, Angus Charles, 101, 115, 138, 147–148

gu 故 [conditions, origin, purposive action], 87, 202, 217–218

guan 觀 [scrutinise, observe, attentive gaze], 203–204, 205, 207–208, 212, 213

guiju 規矩 [compass and square], 133, 134, 135, 136, 137, 139

Guo Xiang 郭象, 24

habit, 3, 4, 5–6, 10, 13n3, 154, 261

Hanfeizi [text], 8, 214, 224n34

Hansen, Chad, 101

Han shi wai zhuan, 206, 223n12, 223n22

haowu 好惡 [likings and dislikings], 36

harm, 184, 194, 195–197. *See also* conflict

harmony, 269–270, 271, 276n35

heaven. See *tian* 天 [heaven, nature]

heredity, 245, 249

Huainanzi [text], 18–19, 29, 30n10, 209, 224n26, 224n27, 254, 259, 271, 274n2

Huang, Yong, 196

Hui Shi 惠施. *See* Huizi 惠子

Huizi 惠子, 9, 102–103, 134, 266, 269, 270, 273

humour, 247–248, 251, 254, 256

hunchback. *See* cicada catcher

Hundun 渾沌, 243

ideal personhood, 13n14, 267, 268, 276n27, 276n30

identity, 249, 250, 253, 254–255, 256

ideology, 247

impact, 183–184, 187, 190, 194, 197, 198n7–198n8; definition of, 188; impact reduction, 188–189; and presence, 189–190, 193; and skill, 188–189, 191; in archery fragment, 189; in ferryman story, 192; in Wang Tai story, 192–193

impact reduction. *See* impact

incongruity, 250, 256

Inner Chapters [*Nei pian*], 101–104, 107n2, 244

innovation, debates about, 137, 139

intellectuals, 246

intelligent, 150

interaction, 184, 187, 190, 194, 197

About the Contributors

Wai Wai Chiu is assistant professor at Lingnan University. His interests include pre-Qin Daoist and Mohist philosophy, especially epistemology and ethics. He has published articles on Zhuangzi's conception of knowledge, language, and efficacious action, as well as Mozi's conception of benefit.

Kim-chong Chong is professor emeritus, Division of Humanities, Hong Kong University of Science and Technology. He was also previously a member of the Department of Philosophy at the National University of Singapore. He is the author of *Early Confucian Ethics: Concepts and Arguments* (2007) and *Zhuangzi's Critique of the Confucians: Blinded by the Human* (2016).

Tim Connolly is professor of philosophy at East Stroudsburg University, located in northeastern Pennsylvania. His research focuses on early Confucian ethics and Zhuangzi's perspectivism. He is the author of two books: *Doing Philosophy Comparatively* (2015) and *Foundations of Confucian Ethics: Virtues, Roles, and Exemplars* (2019).

Steven Coutinho is professor and chair of the Department of Philosophy at Muhlenberg College. He is author of *Zhuangzi and Early Chinese Philosophy: Vagueness, Transformation and Paradox* (2018) and *An Introduction to Daoist Philosophies* (2014), and he is co-translator, with Kurtis Hagen, of the anthology *Philosophers of the Warring States* (2018).

Wim De Reu is assistant professor at the Department of Philosophy, National Taiwan University. His interests include early Chinese views on language and human interaction, the theory and practice of argumentation, and cognitive linguistics. He has published articles on early Chinese paradoxes, the role of metaphors in the construction of early Chinese philosophy, the relation between coexistence and writing in the *Zhuangzi*, and the structure and argumentation of later *Zhuangzi* chapters.

Chris Fraser is associate professor and chair in the Department of Philosophy at the University of Hong Kong. He is the author of *The Philosophy of the Mozi* (2016), *The Essential Mozi* (2019), and *Late Classical Chinese Thought* (forthcoming). He has published more than a dozen research articles on *Zhuangzi* and many others on early Chinese ethics, epistemology, philosophy of language and logic, and philosophy of mind and action. His work can be accessed at cjfraser.net.

Albert Galvany is assistant professor in the Department of Philosophy at the University of the Basque Country UPV/EHU. His research and publications are in the areas of early Chinese intellectual history and classical Chinese philosophy.

Romain Graziani is professor in Chinese studies at the Ecole Normale Supérieure de Lyons and senior lecturer at the University of Geneva's Department of East-Asian Studies. His primary research interests are in early Chinese intellectual and social history. In his work, he has explored such themes as the nascent traditions of self-cultivation in pre-imperial China, the figure of the father in Chinese culture, military strategy in Chinese history, discourses on rulership, political rhetoric, ruler-minister and master-disciple relationships, visions and uses of the human body, the ritual exploitation of animals, the shaping of subjectivity through epistolary practice in the late Han and early medieval period (third century CE), and the economic and fiscal debates centred on the creation of material wealth and the distribution of labour in the states of Qin and Qi.

Karyn Lai is associate professor of philosophy in the School of Humanities and Languages at the University of New South Wales, Sydney. She specialises in comparative Chinese-Western philosophical research, drawing insights from Chinese philosophies to engage in debates in areas including moral philosophy, environmental ethics, reasoning and argumentation, and epistemology. Her books include *Introduction to Chinese Philosophy*, second edition (2017), and *Cultivating a Good Life in Early Chinese and Ancient Greek Philosophy: Perspectives and Reverberations* (edited by Karyn Lai, Rick Benitez, and Hyun Jin Kim, 2019).

David Machek is a research fellow at the Department of Philosophy, University of Berne, Switzerland. He works in ancient philosophy, both Greek and Chinese, with a special focus on moral psychology.

Hans-Georg Moeller is professor of philosophy at the University of Macau. His research focuses on Chinese and comparative philosophy and on social and political thought. He is the author of *Genuine Pretending: On the Philosophy of the Zhuangzi* (with Paul D'Ambrosio), *The Radical Luhmann*, *The Philosophy of the Daodejing*, and *The Moral Fool: A Case for Amorality*, and he contributes to the YouTube podcast "The Issue Is Not the Issue" with Dan Sarafinas.

Franklin Perkins is professor of philosophy at the University of Hawai'i at Mānoa and editor of the journal *Philosophy East and West*. Perkins is the author of *Heaven and Earth Are Not Humane: The Problem of Evil in Classical Chinese Philosophy* (2014), *Leibniz: A Guide for the Perplexed* (2007), and *Leibniz and China: A Commerce of Light* (2004), and he is co-editor of *Chinese Metaphysics and Its Problems* (2015).

Lisa Raphals (瑞麗) is professor of Chinese, classics, and comparative literature at the University of California, Riverside, and chair of the Program in Classical Studies and the Program in Comparative Ancient Civilizations. Her books include *Knowing Words: Wisdom and Cunning in the Classical Traditions of China and Greece* (1992), *Sharing the Light: Representations of Women and Virtue in Early China* (1998), and *Divination and Prediction in Early China and Ancient Greece* (2013), and she is co-editor of *Old Society, New Belief: Religious Transformation of China and Rome, ca. 1st–6th Centuries* (2017).

Eric Schwitzgebel is professor of philosophy at the University of California, Riverside. In addition to Chinese philosophy, he works on moral psychology (especially the moral behaviour of ethics professors), the nature of attitudes (more about walking the walk than talking the talk), people's poor self-knowledge, and the shortcomings of philosophical method. He blogs on these topics and many others at *The Splintered Mind*. His most recent book is *A Theory of Jerks and Other Philosophical Misadventures*.

James D. Sellmann earned BA degrees in psychology and philosophy from the University of Nevada and MA degrees in Asian religions and comparative philosophy and a PhD in Chinese philosophy from the University of Hawai'i. He has published over one hundred articles in various peer-reviewed books and journals, such as *Philosophy East and West*. He is also the author of *Timing and Rulership in Master Lü's Annals* (2002). He is the dean of the College of Liberal Arts and Social Sciences and professor of philosophy at the University of Guam.